The Perfect

CAKE

The Perfect
CAKE

Susan G. Purdy

ILLUSTRATED BY

Susan Breck Smith

BROADWAY BOOKS
NEW YORK

Broadway Books titles may be purchased for business or promotional use or for special sales. For information, please write to: Special Markets Department, Random House, Inc., 1540 Broadway, New York, NY 10036.

BROADWAY BOOKS and its logo, a letter B bisected on the diagonal, are trademarks of Broadway Books, a division of Random House, Inc.

Portions of this work were previously published by Collier Books, a division of Macmillan Publishing Company, under the title *A Piece of Cake* by Susan G. Purdy, Copyright © 1993 by Susan G. Purdy.

Visit our website at www.broadwaybooks.com

Library of Congress Cataloging-in-Publication Data
Purdy, Susan Gold
The perfect cake/Susan G. Purdy.—1st ed.
p.   cm.
Includes index.
1. Cake.   2. Baking.   I. Title.
TX771.P87 2002
641.8'653—dc21   00-069896

FIRST EDITION

Book design by Judith Stagnitto Abbate / Abbate Design

Illustrations copyright © 1989, 2002 by Susan Breck Smith

PRINTED IN THE UNITED STATES OF AMERICA

ISBN 0-7679-0537-7

1   3   5   7   9   10   8   6   4   2

For my father,
Harold A. Gold,
with love

CONTENTS

ACKNOWLEDGMENTS

A CEREMONIAL PIECE of cake is offered with love to the memory of Bruce Whitney Bacon (1940–1984), friend, artist, connoisseur of food and wine.

And thanks to . . . nearly everyone involved in my life, from family to friends, neighbors, teachers, and professional colleagues. A project as big and diverse as this one necessarily involves a great number of people. To all who visited our home and shared cakes, recipes, and reminiscences, to all the new friends we made traveling in search of cakes and recipes, to anyone inadvertently omitted from the following list, I say a grateful thank you. It is only by tasting, talking, and testing many times over that recipes and techniques become refined enough for publication.

For their encouragement, support, and helpful critiques of hundreds of cakes as well as for their enthusiasm and culinary judgment during extensive research and traveling, I thank my husband, Geoffrey, and our daughter, Cassandra. For family recipes, I thank my parents, Frances and Harold Gold; my sister, Nancy G. Lieberman; my aunts, Phoebe Vernon and Beatrice Joslin. For suggesting literary quotations, I thank Lucille Purdy, and Alexandra and Sesyle Hine. For endless hours in the kitchen working with patience, good humor, and skill, I thank my baking assistant on this project, Barbara Went

Cover. For research during travel to Venice and Vienna, I thank Marylois Purdy Vega, Jesse Birnbaum, Traudel Lessing, and Molly and Walter Bareiss.

For sharing recipes, techniques, research, and ideas, as well as for tasting and testing, I thank the baking students in all my classes at cooking schools in this country and in France, as well as Charley Kanas, and Katia Kanas-Roberts, Chef Lynn Pageau; Chef Michael La Croix; Fran and Wally Sheper of Franni's Café-Pâtisserie, Montreal; Chef Vicky Zeph, Pâtissier Robert Dause of Azay-le-Rideau, France; Pastry Chef Fredrich Pflieger of the Hotel Sacher, Vienna; Sandra Calder Davidson; Jo Trogdon Sweatt; Marie Swanson; Norma Went; Nancy German; Pat and Terry Glaves; Michele Peasley; Shirley Johansen; Elizabeth MacDonald; Joan Moore; and Leslie Sutten.

For technical consultation on the introductory chapters, I am indebted to Chef Albert Kumin. For recipe ideas as well as for organizing a remarkable visit with his family in France, I thank Chef Jacques Pépin, and his mother, Jeannette Pépin. For kindness and encouragement throughout the original concept and first edition of this book, I thank agent Susan Lescher; for the development of this book in its present edition, I thank my agent, Olivia Blumer. For editorial skill and creative support, I thank editors Pam Hoenig, Harriet Bell, and Jennifer Josephy, as well as designer Judy Abbate, and production editor Chava Boylan. Special gratitude goes to my friend Susan Breck Smith, whose skillful drawings enhance these pages.

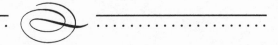

Introduction

THE IDEA FOR this book evolved from the classes I teach in pastry-making. It has become more and more apparent to me that while many people are interested in learning one or two particularly showy cakes for a grand finale dessert, they are less inclined to add cake-baking to their general cooking repertoire. Coffee cakes, which can take less time to prepare at home than a salad, are automatically bought boxed at the supermarket. For birthday cakes, people head for a bakery or reach for a cake mix rather than consider the healthier and more delicious alternative of baking from scratch. Even many restaurant chefs who are expert entrée cooks are intimidated by serious baking. Usually, they rely on a pastry chef or buy cakes from an outside pastry shop or private baker. A restaurant chef may have too many things on his plate to worry about baking, but for the home cook, cakes are completely within the realm of possibility, even pleasurable probability.

Everyone can bake cakes. There is no magic to it, although there seems to be when you watch a simple mixture of eggs, butter, flour, and sugar mount into thick waves of luxuriously silken batter, then bake into delicate flavorful crumbs that literally melt in the mouth.

While there is no magic, there is chemistry, and there is technique. Both can be explained, taught, and learned. Unlike baking pies, which can require getting your hands into the dough and relying on some manual dexterity, making cakes allows preparation of batters entirely with an electric mixer. If you stop short of making fancy decorations, you can be a complete klutz and still turn out a respectable cake. My premise is that everyone can and should bake. We should all treat our souls, our palates, and our families to the delectable tastes, textures, and aromas of home-baked cakes.

As a matter of fact, so-called environmental scents, or room potpourri, which are such popular gift items, are nothing more than the marketing of what I call baking perfume—herbs and spices one simmers in water on the stove top or applies as an essence of oil to a lightbulb to impart "the scent of home baking"—in flavors such as gingerbread cake or cinnamon-apple crisp. Why do they exist? Because everyone loves a home to smell as if there were a cake in the oven, but no one wants to put it there. We are either too busy or too intimidated by the science of baking. Science plays a part, to be sure, but baking is also an art, a craft, and fun.

To gather background material, my husband, daughter, and I set ourselves the somewhat less than arduous task of tasting cakes and collecting recipes in several famous pastry-making regions of Europe: Paris, Lyons, northern Italy, Venice, Vienna, and Munich. We lingered for hours in Viennese coffee houses, tasting yet another torte and having yet another dollop of *Schlag* long after the late-afternoon regulars had gone. We breakfasted in our hotel rooms on cake slices gleaned the evening before from Konditorei and restaurants; we snacked midmorning on astonishing cakes plucked from the lavish jewel-box windows of every bakery we passed. We sat by Venetian canals sampling cream-filled, rum-soaked, marzipan-topped sponge cakes, and we shared the crumbs of our all-cake picnic lunches with sparrows in the gardens of Munich's Nymphenburg Palace. I took hundreds of snapshots of cake slices and filled notebook after notebook with sketches and detailed descriptions of ingredients, layers, and fillings. I have refined these recipes, testing them myself before passing them on to other home bakers for independent scrutiny; for inclusion in the book, they had to be consistently reliable and, of course, they had to taste good, very good.

The recipes in this book range from the quick and easy to make to the complex and time-consuming. Recognizing the time pressures facing today's baker, I have included tips and hints for advance preparation, as well as storage and freezing of ingredients and complete cakes. If you are a beginner, I advise you to read the introductory material for each category of cakes as well as the opening chapters on ingredients so that you will understand the reason for each procedure. It will help you, for example, to read "What Happens When a Cake Bakes" in order to comprehend the reaction between ingredients and oven heat. After this, the importance of folding egg whites gently into batter will make more sense. If you are already a confident baker, you may pick up a few ideas from reading the problem-solving hints and tips that follow each introductory chapter. A skilled baker can work from the Index, going straight to specific information.

While some techniques require no special skills, others demand more precision and care. If a recipe appears lengthy, it does not necessarily mean it is complex; length is directly related to the degree of detail required to clearly explain a specific procedure. Instead of leaving you alone at a critical moment, I prefer to have you feel you are at a cooking class with a teacher by your side.

The cakes are generally divided into categories, depending upon the type of or lack of fat used: shortening and/or butter cakes versus non-shortening cakes. If you are looking for a particular type of cake, chocolate, for example, use the Index to see a listing of all the chocolate cakes, regardless of category. In addition, you will find sections on elegant and special cakes, fillings, icings, and cake decoration.

This book is not intended to be the ultimate, complete international cake collection. Rather, it is a group of personal favorites, student-tested recipes, and selected classics, presented with the hope that you will try a few and discover that it's a piece of cake to bake.

ℬAKING ℰQUIPMENT

IN THIS AGE of ubiquitous food processors and electronic gadgets, it is important to remember that not too long ago arm power was the home baker's primary tool. Cake batters were beaten with wooden spoons in wooden or earthenware bowls and egg whites were whipped with a fork or a bundle of twigs. The wooden spoon blended ingredients perfectly well (and still does); the fork- or twig-whipped whites foamed well, given enough time and effort. However, if you really want to "feel" the transformation of raw ingredients into a cake batter, you can do so only by beating them by hand. For today's home baker, it is usually more practical to beat batters and egg whites with an electric mixer to save time, and use a spoon or rubber spatula for folding.

While hands are still a basic tool, there are certain pieces of equipment that are essential to today's baker. These are described in this chapter. Be aware that baking is a creative art, and part of that creativity may involve improvisation with equipment. Feel free to substitute what you find in your cupboard before you run out to buy something new. Put a saucepan into a frying pan to make a double boiler. Use a wine bottle for a rolling pin. Consult the Pan Volume and Serving Table (pages 61–63) to substitute baking pan sizes based on cake batter quantities given in the recipes.

Note: I assume that since you are reading this book, your kitchen has the basic cooking essentials: liquid and dry measuring cups, measuring spoons, mixing bowls, whisks, a rubber spatula, a wire rack for cooling pans, potholders, and a hand-held or stand-type electric mixer. Each cake recipe carries a list of "special equipment" needed. This refers only to items *beyond* the above-mentioned basics, such as extra bowls or pots, a double boiler, grater, decorating tubes and tips, sifter, wax paper, etc.

CAKE PANS

. . . .

THE FIRST THING to note when selecting cake pans is the size. Every manufacturer measures by a different system. In this book, all pans are measured across the top inner edge and volume is measured in cups of water needed to fill the pan to the brim. The Pan Volume and Serving Table (pages 61–63) compares different pan sizes and volumes. Many cakes can be baked in a variety of shapes and sizes, and for these cakes, the recipes note the number of cups of batter the recipes yield. Select alternate pan sizes from the chart by comparing volumes. Note that pans should be filled about ⅔ full so there is room left for the batter to rise; for this reason, the table notes maximum batter amounts for each size, as well as the number of cups of water needed to fill the pan to the brim.

You can calculate the comparative pan sizes by square inches: An 8 × 8 square has 64 square inches, while an 11 × 7 pan has 77. Deeper pans hold more batter even if dimensions are otherwise the same. Remember that a round 9-inch diameter pan equals ¾ the area of a 9-inch square pan because the corners add more area.

To modify the size of a large pan, line it with foil, fold the foil into a lip at the cut-off point, and fill the excess area with dry beans.

The wrong size pan may result in baking failure. Batter must be at least 1 inch deep in the pan, preferably deeper, for the cake to rise properly. Batter that is too thin bakes into a cake that is too flat. On the other hand, if the pan is too small and the batter too near the top, it may overflow while the cake is rising, causing the cake to sink after baking and the overflow to burn onto your oven floor.

Buy layer-cake pans in pairs or threes. For cake baking basics, you will need two 8- × 1½-inch rounds, two 9- × 1½-inch rounds, one 8-inch-square 2 inches deep, one jelly-roll pan 10½ × 15½ × ½ to 1 inch deep, one 9-inch tube pan (6-cup capacity), one 10-inch tube or Bundt pan (12-cup capacity), one 8- or 9-inch diameter springform pan with a flat bottom, and one loaf pan 9 × 5 × 3 inches.

As a general rule, I prefer to bake cakes in aluminum or heavy, tin-plated steel. Look for well-sealed seams and good construction. You do not need nonstick cake pans if you grease your pans properly. Black steel or iron is fine for some types of baking, but not for cakes. The blackness causes a dark, heavy crust that is undesirable in delicate cakes.

Springform pans are two-piece pans that have either a flat or tubed center panel surrounded by a hoop fastened with a spring latch; these are used for delicate tortes and cheesecakes that might be damaged by inverting from a solid-bottom pan.

Removable-bottom layer-cake pans make unmolding easy. These are simply round pans containing a central flat disk that is a removable bottom. The cake is inverted onto a wire rack, the side piece lifted off, then the bottom disk removed. Avoid this type of pan for very liquid batters, as they may leak from beneath the bottom while in the oven.

Tube pans vary amazingly in manufacture, size, and shape. Plain tubes, ring molds, Bundt pans, and kugelhopf molds are all variations on the same theme, and can be used interchangeably as long as the size is correct; check volume in cups of water needed to fill to capacity. The tube shape is designed to conduct heat to the center of the batter, allowing the dough to rise and bake evenly. For this reason, the tube is excellent for heavy or dense batters like pound cakes and their relatives. The kugelhopf and other yeast doughs are baked in a tube because it gives the rising yeast dough more surface to cling to, thus helping the rise. Angel-food cakes are also baked in tube pans because the added surface area gives the fragile batter structure something to cling to as it rises. The best angel-food pans have removable bottoms as well as small feet sticking up on the rim so the baked cake may be inverted and suspended as it cools. If your pan has no feet, invert your baked angel cake onto a funnel or tall bottle until thoroughly cool (see page 75). As a general rule when selecting tube pans, the heavier the metal, the more evenly the cake will bake.

Square, oblong, or rectangular pans 1½ to 2½ inches deep are used for sheet cakes. They come in a wide variety of dimensions; in the home, one can use a lasagna pan or turkey roasting pan.

Jelly-roll pans have many uses. Select a sturdy, nonwarping pan with a firm lip all around, ½ to 1 inch deep. A nonstick surface is not essential, though it works well. I use the jelly-roll pan for roulades, for fairly thin sheet cakes from which to make *petits fours,* and I have also been known to invert the pan and use it as a cookie sheet. In addition, I like to use the jelly-roll pan beneath the springform when baking cheesecakes, for ease in handling and to catch any leaks or drips of batter.

DOUBLE BOILERS

COMMERCIAL DOUBLE BOILERS have a bowl or basin with a lip that sits inside a saucepan; usually there is a pot lid as well. Hot or boiling water goes in the lower pot; the item to be melted or cooked sits in the raised top container. The purpose is to provide gentle, indirect heat for cooking. You can improvise your own double boiler by setting one pan with the ingredients to be cooked inside a slightly larger pot or frying pan holding water.

ELECTRIC MIXERS

ALL CAKES CAN be mixed by hand with a spoon and a bowl. Some, like Swedish Butter Cake (pages 102–103), are even best made that way. However, I have written the recipes in this book assuming the availability of an electric mixer because it gives good results and saves time.

There is a wide variety of electric mixers available. I like to use a heavy-duty KitchenAid with its wire whisk or flat paddle-type beater for all general-purpose cake baking. I use a KitchenAid Model K45SS, with the head that tips back to raise the beater; I find this model practical because the design makes it easy to add ingredients or scrape down the sides of the bowl. Models with fixed heads are larger but make these tasks awkward; a detachable collar is available to facilitate adding ingredients to them.

For whipping cream, I prefer to use a hand-held beater and a small, deep stainless-steel bowl that has been well chilled. (I finish whipping cream, however, with a hand whisk, so I can control the degree of stiffness.) The hand-held beater is excellent for beating yolks or sauces in a double boiler, as for zabaglione, but a whisk or egg beater will work well, too.

MIXING BOWLS

I PREFER TO use heavy pottery or stainless-steel bowls, with wide, flat bottoms. Avoid metal bowls with rounded bottoms, as they can tip over if you leave a spatula or whisk inside. It is good to have a variety of sizes, and a small, deep metal bowl is handy for whipping small amounts of cream. I also like my heavy Pyrex glass bowl that is microwave safe, has a handle and pouring spout, and is marked with graduations up to 2 quarts. It is great for whipping cream, for blending batters by hand, or for whipping eggs. Avoid plastic bowls for general use because the plastic surface retains grease, damaging beaten egg whites for instance, and occasionally plastic bowls retain odors that may be passed on to your cakes.

SIFTERS/STRAINERS

FLOUR SETTLES IN packing and shipping, and even brands labeled "pre-sifted" are not, for our purposes. For most cake baking, it is important to sift flour before measuring by the scoop and sweep method (see page 51) and again with the other dry ingredients. This second sifting blends the dry ingredients together, distributing them evenly throughout the batter. For most cakes, I find this method sifts sufficiently; I rarely use a triple-tier sifter, though I own one; I do use it occasionally for a génoise, an especially fine sponge cake. My regular sifter is actually a sieve, or strainer, with a very fine mesh.

DRY AND LIQUID MEASURING CUPS

DRY MEASURING CUPS are designed so you can fill them to the brim and level the top by passing a straight edge over it. These cups are available in graduated sizes, with a separate cup for each unit from ⅛ or ¼ cup up to 2 cups; usually they nest together for storage. By contrast, liquid measuring cups are usually Pyrex (select this type) or plastic, with a handle and pouring spout. They are commonly available in 1-, 2-, and 4-cup sizes. To use a liquid measure, you simply fill the cup to the desired mark and read it at eye level. Another feature of liquid measuring cups is the space left just above the topmost measuring mark. If you fill the cup with liquid to the highest mark, there will still be a space above this mark so that the liquid will not spill while being moved. If you were to fill this cup with dry ingredients and level it off, you would have much too much. If you filled it to a measurement below the brim, you would have no way to level it off; the cup will not work properly for dry ingredients. Be sure to use each type of cup for its designated purpose. Read How to Measure Ingredients (see page 50).

SCALES

SCALES ARE USED for accurate measuring of flour, sugar, fat, and some other ingredients in cake baking. Read About Using Scales (page 52). There are two types of scales—balance and spring. Both are accurate, but professionals use the balance system in bakeshops. The spring-type can be checked for accuracy by weighing a known quantity: a pound (454 grams) of butter, for example. After practice, you will find it much more practical to measure 100 grams of flour on a scale than to measure 1 cup; your cups may be of differing sizes, you may compact the flour by tapping the cup, in any number of ways the volume may vary, but the scale weight will not. Butter and other solid fats, of course, are easy to measure on a scale, as opposed to packing them into a measuring cup and hoping no air holes lodge in the bottom.

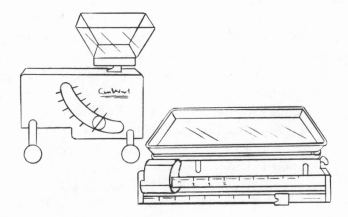

PASTRY BRUSHES

A PASTRY BRUSH is essential for applying egg washes and jelly glazes to tarts. It is also excellent for spreading soaking syrups on cake layers and fruit glazes atop finished cakes. For the most delicate tasks, I prefer an imported European goose-feather brush with a handle of braided quills. This is lovely to look at, lasts a very long time, and is inexpensive. After use, you simply wash it in warm soapy water, rinse, and air dry. Find it in gourmet cookware shops or bakeware catalogues. Ordinary bristle pastry brushes from 1 inch to 2½ inches wide are better for spreading jam glazes on sponge layers.

SPATULAS

THERE ARE TWO types of spatulas referred to in this book. Rubber spatulas are used for mixing, folding, and scraping out the inside of a bowl or mixer beater. They come in all sizes, but the most common for home kitchen use has a plastic or wood handle about 6 inches long, topped by a flexible tongue about 2 × 3½ inches. One edge of the flexible top is curved, to ride neatly against the side of a bowl.

A metal spatula is equally essential. It resembles a blunt-edged, round-ended knife with a metal blade and is useful for all spreading tasks—fillings and icings, for example. The basic icing spatula that I use is about 10 inches long overall, with a 1- × 6-inch blade that will flex but is not flimsy. For fancy decorative work with icing, I use an artist's palette knife, kept just for this purpose. For smoothing icing on the tops and sides of large layer cakes or for icing sheet cakes, I use a large metal spatula built like a fine knife, with a strong wooden handle and a 12- × 1¾-inch blade. For lifting, I use an offset, or step-down spatula with a broad long blade. The ideal tool for lifting whole cakes or cake layers is a broad rectangular *kuchenloser* (cake-lifter), with a hand grip at one end and a flexible metal (or plastic) blade about 10½ × 9½ inches (see Sources, page 477).

DOUGH SCRAPER

MY FAVORITE TOOL for working with yeast doughs is the dough scraper, or *coupe-pâte*. It is simply a rectangular metal scraper with a wooden handle on one edge. Similar tools are made of flexible plastic. Use this ingenious device for cutting, kneading, lifting, and scraping dough, as well as for cleaning off countertops. You can substitute a wide putty knife or pancake turner.

CARDBOARD CAKE DISKS

FOR BAKING CAKES, you will quickly find it hard to live without these disks of corrugated cardboard sold in dimensions that correspond to cake pan sizes—6, 8, 9, 12, 14 inches. Some manufacturers refer to them as "cardboard cake circles." They come covered with glazed white or plain brown paper or gold or silver foil and with plain or fluted edges. They are available in restaurant supply houses, party and paper goods shops, and more and more frequently in bakeware shops. If you have trouble finding them, ask at a local pizzeria; these are the same boards put under baked pizzas. If you cannot find these boards, simply cut your own out of any corrugated box and cover them with foil. They are indispensable for handling cakes, especially when spreading on icing or pressing crumbs or chopped nuts onto the iced cake sides.

COOLING RACKS

WIRE COOLING RACKS are essential in cake baking. As soon as the cake comes from the oven, the pan is set on the rack, which has short feet lifting it off the counter. The air circulating beneath the pan prevents condensation on the cake bottom and helps it cool evenly. Cakes have a fragile structure that needs to cool in the baking pan, on a wire rack, for at least 10 minutes before unmolding. After unmolding, cakes should continue cooling on a wire rack so air circulation will remove the moisture or steam given off by the hot cake. If contained inside the cake, this steam would make it soggy.

CAKE TESTERS

ONE STICKS A cake tester into a baking cake to see if the batter is completely baked. If the tester comes out clean, the baking is complete; if there is raw batter clinging to the tester, the cake must cook longer. Cake testers can be simple or elaborate. In the old days, the most common tester was a clean broom straw. My favorite is a thin bamboo skewer, also called a cocktail or saté skewer (available in gourmet or Oriental shops). A toothpick may be used, but for some cakes it is not long enough to penetrate to the center of the batter. Metal cake testers are sold in hardware or baking shops. These are simply metal needles with a handle, but I prefer wood to the metal, for metal gets hot fast and may cause batter to cling to it even when the cake is completely baked.

CAKE STANDS

A REVOLVING CAKE stand is a lazy Susan made for the baker. The fact that the stand is raised above table height makes it easy to see decorations at eye level. One hand can rotate it while the other applies the decoration, making efficient and regular patterns more easily than on a flat and stationary surface. Select a stand of heavy-duty aluminum, with a platform about 12 inches in diameter that turns very easily.

THERMOMETERS

SPECIALIZED THERMOMETERS ARE important for accuracy in different stages of pastry and confectionery work. For making candy, sugar syrups, and pastry creams, I use a "candy-jelly-deep-fry" thermometer with a mercury-filled glass tube fastened to a stainless-steel casing. Buy the best quality you can find. Do not settle for inferior thermometers; there is no point in having them. Take care of your thermometers; never put a cold one directly into boiling syrup, but rather warm it in hot water first. Thermal shock can crack the glass tubes if you are not careful. Always read your thermometer at eye level; when it is fastened to your saucepan, bend down in order to see the reading correctly.

For instant read-out temperatures for sauces or baked goods, I like to use a stainless-steel long-stemmed thermometer with a large dial. These are made with digital read-out displays or are instant bi-therm thermometers with a round face at the end; most have shorter temperature ranges than regular thermometers and are meant to be placed in food periodically for just a few seconds, then removed. Instant thermometers are available at hardware and cookware shops, or by mail order (see Sources, page 477).

OVENS AND OVEN THERMOMETERS

EVEN HEAT IS vital in a baking oven, whether gas or electric. My own ovens are both gas and electric, and they have distinct and rather obstinate personalities. Fortunately, we are old friends, and I know how to cajole them into behaving. I have learned to rely on auxiliary thermometers that I place inside the ovens. I use two thermometers, front and back, and I replace them every few months to be sure I have reliable instruments. One should never rely on the built-in oven thermometer alone. Instead, buy a small thermometer, mounted on a metal stand, and put it in your oven. These gadgets are available at modest cost in hardware stores. Once it is in place, adjust your outer oven thermostat so the internal oven temperature is correct at all times. And remember not to blame a cookbook until you are sure the fault for a failed cake does not lie within your own oven.

Always preheat your oven 15 to 20 minutes before starting to bake. If a batter is set into a cool oven, the ingredients will react entirely differently from when set into the correct temperature; results will be disastrous. Glance at your auxiliary oven thermometer inside the baking chamber to check that the heat is correct before putting in the cake. Learn to know your oven, but never trust it. Constantly monitor its hot spots. Sometimes a back corner may suddenly bake more quickly than the front and your cake will overbrown in one spot only, or sink on one side. If you have this problem, rotate cakes from one shelf to another, or front to back, *after* half of the baking time is past, but only do this if you must. Never have cake pans on the shelf touching each other or the oven walls. Allow at least an inch or more between pans and the oven wall for good heat circulation. If you are baking several layers at one time, stagger them on two shelves so one is not directly above the other and heat can circulate freely.

Positioning Oven Shelves

Recipes in this book specify the position of the oven shelf upon which the cake is to be baked. The point is to locate the direction of the heat source in the oven, and figure out where the hottest and coolest areas will be. For example, the floor of my large gas oven contains a border of holes that release heat from the gas jets below up into the oven chamber. As the heat comes from these holes, the oven sides deflect it right up to the top of the chamber. Therefore, the topmost shelf will be hotter than the middle, and the floor will be the hottest of all. Usually, the center of the cake should be in the center of the oven. Single-layer cakes can be baked in the lower third of the oven because there the heat is moderately hot. Single layers can bake fairly quickly, drying all the way through before either the top or bottom crust overbakes. Thicker cakes, with more than 2 inches of batter, or cakes with delicate structure, should be baked in the center of the oven where the heat is more moderate. For these cakes it is important to heat the batter evenly throughout, without forming an overcooked crust before the center dries out.

Convection Ovens

Convection ovens contain an interior fan that blows the heat around. This constant circulation causes the ovens to cook about 25 percent faster than regular ovens. For most baked goods, this produces a nicely browned crust and fine interior crumb. Follow your manufacturer's directions, but as a guide, most convection ovens are about 20 degrees warmer than regular ovens. When converting ordinary recipes designed for regular ovens to use in a convection oven, most books recommend lowering baking temperatures 25 to 50 degrees and reducing baking time about 25 percent. For delicate cakes, I prefer *not* to use a convection oven.

Microwave Ovens

I use a microwave oven primarily to melt or soften butter and to melt chocolate. I love the microwave for defrosting cake layers, coffee cakes, muffins, or scones. Remember to remove any foil or freezer wrapping, then envelop the frozen baked goods in a piece of paper toweling and heat at medium power for 40 to 60 seconds. Test to see if the product is defrosted and is warm; if necessary repeat in 5- to 10-second bursts. Do not overheat or the texture will be unalterably turned to concrete.

BAKING PARCHMENT AND NO-STICK BAKING SHEETS

THIS SPECIALLY FORMULATED paper is made for lining baking pans to prevent baked goods from sticking. Some parchments are treated with silicone, some with paraffin, but whatever the material, it works. The paper is easily marked with a pencil, unlike wax paper, and can be cut to fit into any shape pan. If using it as a pan liner, you need to grease only the sides of the pan. Wax paper is a satisfactory substitute but not as durable, and it should be greased. Parchment paper is also ideal for making paper decorating cones; it is slightly stronger and less fragile than wax paper for this purpose.

Precut parchment rounds may be purchased to fit various cake pan sizes; large sheets of parchment are sold in bulk, as well as in small, home-size dispenser rolls. They are available in some gourmet shops and in baker's and restaurant supply houses.

Newer no-stick baking pan liners are flexible sheets that can be reused over and over and simply rinsed off between baking chores. Some brands can also be cut with scissors to fit your pans; check manufacturer's directions. No-stick liners are sold in bakeware shops or by mail order (see Sources, page 477).

$\mathcal{U}$NDERSTANDING $\mathcal{I}$NGREDIENTS

WHILE IT IS true that anyone who can read can, more or less, follow a cake recipe, you know from experience that the same recipe can produce different results with different cooks. This is the reason baking competitions often are based upon one distributed recipe, with entrants' results compared. Some cooks, of course, have a natural "feel" for baking, but more than anything else, success in the kitchen depends upon understanding the properties of each ingredient, why they are used, and how they are best blended together.

Although the proportions of ingredients in bread or even pie doughs can be rather flexible, cake batters must be precise. Good cakes are the product of good recipes—carefully balanced chemical compositions that blend protein foams with flour, fat, liquid, leavening, and flavoring. Each ingredient has a specific function and causes a specific reaction.

FLOUR

WHEAT FLOUR CONTAINS gluten, the stretchy elastic cell walls that develop when two of wheat's unique proteins are mixed with liquid and worked together. Gluten is actually made up of two of the several proteins present: gliadin (located in the endosperm, or core of the wheat kernel) and glutenin (located in the outer layer of the kernel). Gliadin provides elasticity and glutenin provides strength; both are needed to give flour the characteristics required for baking. The proportions of these two elements in flour are affected by the method of milling as well as by the type of wheat (hard or soft) and where it was grown. Some flours are more elastic, others more delicate and tender, and each has a specific purpose.

For a tender, flaky, or short piecrust, low gluten flour is most desirable. On the other hand, the rich development of a large quantity of gluten is essential for kneaded yeast doughs, which require a strong elastic structure to support the gases given off by the expanding yeast. For a cake, you need very little gluten, but some is required to support the carbon dioxide given off as a leavening agent by the baking powder and/or baking soda. The ability of flour to absorb and retain moisture from the batter stage through the final baking depends upon the amount and quality of the protein in the flour; it is critical to a good cake to select the best flour.

Bread flour is milled from hard wheat and has a high gluten content, 12 to 15 percent. All-purpose flour is milled from a blend of hard and soft wheats and contains roughly 10 to 13 percent gluten; pastry flour is milled from soft wheats only and has a lower gluten content, 8 to 12 percent. Cake flour, also milled from soft wheat, has somewhat less gluten, 6½ to 10 percent, and is specifically designed to produce a tender grain in cakes. Self-rising cake flour is another item altogether and should not be substituted for regular cake or pastry flour; it contains added calcium acid phosphate or monocalcium phosphate, bicarbonate of soda, and salt. I prefer not to use self-rising cake flour for two reasons. First, I like to control the amount of salt and leavening in my recipes. Second, and most important, baking powder loses its strength after about three months; if the self-rising flour has been stored too long (and the consumer never knows for sure), your cakes may not rise properly.

Many commercially available brands of all-purpose flour are actually prepared blends of all-purpose flour (80 percent) and cake flour (20 percent). These are excellent for many cakes, and are specified in many recipes in this book. When the texture of the cake is particularly light and delicate, the finest and lightest flour, cake flour, is called for instead.

You can make your own cake flour from all-purpose flour by substituting 2 tablespoons cornstarch for 2 tablespoons flour in every cup. To substitute cake flour for all-purpose flour, use 1 cup plus 2 tablespoons cake flour for every cup of all-purpose flour.

If you are not sure of the protein content of your flour, read the flour package label, or write to the flour company if the label is not helpful. Under "Nutritional Information," many brand labels note that per 1 cup flour there are a specific number of grams of protein. For example, Pillsbury's Best All Purpose Enriched contains 11 grams per 1 cup (4 ounces) flour; Gold Medal All Purpose and Hecker's Unbleached All Purpose are the same. King Arthur Unbleached All-Purpose has 12 grams protein per 4 ounces flour, and Softasilk *Cake* Flour contains 8 grams protein per 4 ounces flour.

Though it varies depending upon the type of wheat, most flour that is newly milled contains quite a high moisture content and is yellowish in color because of the xanthophyll and other natural carotenoid pigments in the wheat. If left in storage at controlled temperatures, it will age after a period of many weeks, and oxygen will bleach it white while it oxidizes the proteins. The aging process strengthens the stretching and bonding characteristics of gluten, thus developing better baking qualities than are found in freshly milled flour. This process can be speeded up and made more efficient with chemicals. Thus most flour is bleached with chlorine dioxide or a similar gas; this ages the flour and removes the yellowish color naturally present in the wheat while also removing many vitamins. These are returned artificially in a later process.

Unbleached flour is said to be more nutritious because some of the wheat bran is retained during the milling and refining process. In fact, however, most commercially milled American flours, both bleached and unbleached, are actually bleached and highly refined. Some are chemically bleached with either potassium bromate or iodate, others are bleached by aging in the air. Unbleached flours are usually a little heavier than bleached flours, and thus less desirable for use in very delicate cakes.

Instant-blending flour is processed to be granular so that it will mix with water without lumping. It is fine for making gravy, but not suitable for baking cakes. Do not use it as a substitute for all-purpose or cake flour.

Flour should be stored in a cool, dry place, raised off the floor, and well ventilated. It will absorb odors if stored next to a strongly scented product or kept in a damp location. Flour stored for any length of time in a warm location or in warm weather can develop insects even when chemically bleached. The best solution is to store all flour in the freezer or refrigerator. At 0°F, flour keeps for about a year.

Sifting Flour

Sifting flour has two purposes: it removes lumps and foreign objects and aerates the flour. Good aeration ensures proper moistening of the flour during mixing of the batter. Flour is also sifted with other dry ingredients (baking powder, salt, sugar) to blend these ingredients evenly. Ignore flour labels that say "presifted"; store handling and shipment have effectively settled and compacted that flour if it ever was aerated. Cake flour is finer than all-purpose flour and tends to lump or settle even more; it must always be sifted.

Before sifting flour, read How to Measure Dry Ingredients (page 51), Sifters/Strainers (page 10), and Dry and Liquid Measuring Cups (page 10).

It is important in cake baking to remember that too much flour makes a heavy and/or tough cake. You should use the precise amount of flour called for. Note that 1 cup of cake flour weighs more (4½ ounces; 120 grams) when measured before sifting than after (3½ ounces; 100 grams). In recipes where sifting is not critical to the texture of the cake, unsifted flour is specified.

LIQUIDS

THE LIQUID CATEGORY in cake batters includes eggs, honey, molasses, oil, melted butter, and coffee, as well as water, milk, cream, sour cream or yogurt, and fruit juices. Liquids are added to a batter to dissolve the salt and sugar, and to create steam that pushes apart the cells of the batter, giving the cake a good rise and fine texture.

In addition, liquids moisten the leavening agent, whether baking soda, baking powder, or both, to begin production of carbon dioxide gas, which will cause the cake to rise. Liquid should be used carefully: too much will activate the gluten in the flour, causing extra elasticity and toughness, qualities undesirable in a cake. Acid liquids such as citrus juices, vinegar, and sour milk products cut the development of gluten and help produce short or flaky baked goods and tender cakes. Honey, molasses, sour cream and yogurt also add acidity to a cake batter and change its Ph balance. Read about Leavening Agents (page 35). Milk products add moisture, color, and richness to cakes and help prolong their freshness. Some bakers like to add a little milk as part of the liquid in any cake, just to improve these qualities. Liquid quantities must be adjusted when baking at high altitudes.

Milk

Homogenized milk is used in this book whenever plain milk is called for in a recipe. Homogenized milk is treated so the fat and milk are blended and will not separate. Skim milk is regular milk minus the cream content. Low-fat milk is skim milk that still contains a small portion of its cream. When a recipe requires buttermilk, it is so specified. Buttermilk is the liquid by-product created when milk or cream is churned into butter. Cultured buttermilk is pasteurized skim milk treated with a lactic-acid bacteria culture. Cultured buttermilk powder, a dried mix reconstituted by blending with water, is sold in supermarkets and is handy to keep in your pantry.

Cream

There are many types of cream on the market and all have specific uses in baking. The butterfat content of the cream is what determines the way it can be used, although package labeling information is often lacking. Heavy cream, also called heavy whipping cream (not the same as whipping cream), has between 36 and 40 percent butterfat. This is sufficient to whip and hold its form. Use a chilled bowl and chilled beater for maximum volume. Note that cream doubles in volume when whipped (1 cup heavy cream makes about 2 cups whipped cream).

Whipping cream has only 30 percent butterfat; it will whip, but not very well; it will never hold its foam for very long, and will droop maddeningly if you use it for decoration on pastry.

Light cream has a butterfat content of between 18 and 20 percent, while half-and-half has 10½ to 12 percent; both are used primarily for beverages; neither will whip.

EGGS

EGGS ARE ONE of the most important ingredients in cakes. They aid in leavening, contribute to the structure, texture, color, and flavor, and add richness and nutritive value.

Eggs add an important liquid to the cake batter and help bind it together. The proteins in eggs work with the proteins in flour to support the structure of the risen cake. When eggs are beaten, they incorporate air, which expands in the heat of the oven to leaven the cake.

Yolks contain all of the fat of the egg and more protein than the white. Eggs add tenderness to a cake because of the high fat content of the yolk. Yolks also contain natural lecithin, an emulsifying agent, which helps yolks whip to a stabilized foam that will stand longer than egg-white foam before breaking down.

The food value of eggs is substantial. They add fat, protein, vitamins, and minerals to any product. There is no difference to the baker between brown and white eggs, but eggs do vary in freshness, size, and whipping qualities. For whipping to greatest volume, eggs should be at least 2 days old. The size of your eggs is vital to the success of your cakes. The recipes in this book are based upon large eggs, weighing 2 ounces in the shell. Sixteen of these large eggs equal 1 quart; 4 to 4½ eggs equal 1 cup. By United States law, one dozen large eggs must weigh 24 ounces; however, the individual eggs within that dozen may have varying weights. For this reason, keep an eye on your eggs; if they look small, weigh them to be sure. Or use whatever weight of egg you prefer, but calculate the quantity to be sure it is equivalent to the number of 2-ounce, "large" eggs given in the recipe. If you need to add a little more egg to increase the weight, simply beat an egg and pour in the needed additional amount. The white of 1 large egg equals about 2 tablespoons, or 1 ounce; the yolk equals 1 tablespoon, or about ½ ounce.

Eggs separate most easily when cold, but whites beat to their fullest volume when at room temperature. Eggs should be at room temperature for use in cake batters. If your eggs are cold from the refrigerator, simply set them, whole in the shell, in a bowl of very warm water for 10 to 15 minutes. If eggs must be separated, do this as soon as they come from the refrigerator, then let them sit a while; or set the bowls of whites and/or yolks inside other bowls of warm water to warm them quickly.

Separated egg whites can be stored, refrigerated, in a partially covered bowl or jar for up to 1 month.

Eggs can be frozen for storage. Whites and yolks can be frozen separately or lightly beaten whole eggs can be mixed with a few grains of salt or sugar and frozen in ice-cube trays (1 cube equals 1 egg). Theoretically, frozen egg whites should be thawed overnight in the refrigerator before bringing them to room temperature for whipping. However, I often forget to thaw my frozen whites long enough in advance, and have to set them in a bowl of warm (not hot) water to thaw. These thawed whites will make a fine angel-food cake, so you can collect whites in the freezer as you go along, and bake a cake once enough whites are stockpiled. Never refreeze thawed eggs.

How to Separate Eggs

There are several techniques for separating eggs. Whichever you select, be sure to scrape out and use the white that tends to cling inside the shell; about 15 percent of the white can be lost in the separation process if this is not done.

The first method is to break the egg into halves, then hold the half-shell containing the yolk upright in one hand while you pour the egg white from the other half-shell into a cup. Then tip the yolk out into the empty half-shell while the white that surrounds it falls into the cup below. Place the yolk in another cup. The next method is fun and infallible if you don't mind getting your hands dirty. Crack the egg by tapping it sharply against the side of the bowl. Holding the egg over a bowl, pull the halves of the shell apart, simultaneously turning one half-shell upright so it will contain the entire egg. Holding this full half-shell upright with one hand, discard the empty half-shell. Then turn your empty hand palm up, and dump the whole egg into it. Spread your fingers slightly to let the white slip through them into a bowl below. The yolk will remain in your palm and can be turned into another container. Instead, you can use a gadget known as an egg separator. This is a disk with a ring-shaped slot cut out just inside the edge. When the egg is broken onto the disk, the yolk is retained in the center and the white slides through the slot into a cup below.

Egg Safety

Egg safety and the possible health hazards of eating uncooked eggs and meringues are significant issues for cooks. Some incidents of bacterial contamination, from the bacterial organism *Salmonella enteritidis,* have been attributed to raw, improperly cooked, or undercooked eggs. Until the hazard is eliminated, it is prudent to be cautious in baking, although the likelihood of a problem is slim. According to the American Egg Board, studies have indicated that the chances of a home cook finding an infected egg are about 0.005 percent. *Here are a few simple guidelines:*

When shopping, buy only from a store that has well-refrigerated egg cases. Open the carton and look at the eggs; avoid eggs that are cracked or unclean. At home, refrigerate eggs promptly, storing them inside the refrigerator, where it is colder, rather than on the door. Wash any container, utensil, or food preparation surface that has come in contact with raw eggs before reusing it. Avoid eating raw eggs.

Refrigerate all baked goods containing custards or meringues. Refrigerate cheesecakes. Keep cold foods cold (at or below 40°F/5°C) and hot foods hot (above 140°F/60°C) to prevent growth of salmonella bacteria.

While the bacteria causing the common food poisoning salmonellosis is sometimes present in egg whites or yolks, it has also been found on the skins of fruit grown in contaminated soil. Washing produce carefully helps, and there is no question that the bacteria cannot survive high temperatures. Commercial food handlers and many restaurants avoid the possibility of this problem by routinely cooking with pasteurized liquid eggs instead of fresh eggs.

For the baker, egg white caution means following instructions carefully when preparing meringues or other preparations such as mousses. While it is highly unlikely that eating a small amount of egg glaze or uncooked meringue will make you sick, at least you should be informed. According to the American Egg Board, to destroy the bacteria, egg whites must be held at a temperature of 140°F (60°C) for 3½ minutes or at some point reach 160°F (71°C).

How to Cook Raw Yolks for Use in Uncooked Recipes

If a recipe for an unbaked soufflé, sauce, or pudding calls for raw egg yolks, they can be prepared as follows to remove any danger of bacteria: blend the yolks with at least 2 tablespoons of water or other liquid per yolk in a heavy saucepan and cook over very low heat, stirring constantly, until the mixture coats a metal spoon or reaches 160°F (71°C). Cool quickly (over an ice water bath if desired), and proceed with the recipe.

Powdered Egg Whites and Meringue Powder

To avoid any danger of salmonella contamination in raw egg whites, home bakers can substitute pasteurized pure powdered whites (such as Just Whites made by Deb El Foods) or meringue powder (such as Wilton's Meringue Powder, which contains some sugar). There are several products on the market, available in some supermarkets and most gourmet or bakers' supply shops or by mail order (see Sources, page 477). To use, follow manufacturer's directions; as a general rule, use 2 teaspoons of powder plus 2 tablespoons warm water to make the equivalent of 1 large egg white. Stir or whisk for 2 or 3 minutes until the whites are thoroughly dissolved before adding sugar or other ingredients as indicated in your recipe.

FATS

FAT IS THE generic term for butter, margarine, lard, oil, or vegetable shortening. The richness and tenderness of a baked product depend upon the type of fat used and the manner in which it is blended with the other ingredients in the batter. Fats also provide for aeration to help the leavening of a batter, contribute flavor, impart desirable grain and texture, act as emulsifiers for holding liquids in the batter, and, in the case of yeast doughs, lubricate the gluten in the flour.

As a general rule, the colder and harder the fat, the less it is absorbed by the starch in the flour. The more separate the fat remains, the more it layers with the flour. This creates desirable flakiness in pie crust but is wrong for cake batters. Here the fat must be at room temperature, roughly 70°F (about 21°C), to be soft and pliable enough to stretch around air bubbles as they are creamed or whipped into the batter. If the fat is too cold, the cell walls will be brittle and will break and let out the air, causing the cake to lose volume or fall completely. If the fat is warm enough to melt, it will not mold itself around air cells at all; however, good cakes can be made with melted butter or oil if their particular characteristics are taken into account in the blending method. As fats are not soluble in liquid, they must be well blended so that their particles are evenly distributed throughout the batter. Only in this way will they produce a tender cake.

Butter has the best flavor of all the fats used in baking. Unsalted butter is the preferred type for cake baking. Check freshness dating on the packages. I prefer unsalted butter not only for its freshness and its taste but also because I like to be the one to control the amount of salt in my recipe. Salted butter has between .5 and .6 percent salt added to enhance flavor and extend shelf life. Butter is made from pasteurized sweet cream, with a butterfat content of 80 to 86 percent. It has a melting point slightly lower than body temperature; for this reason butter melts in the mouth. Liquid content of butter varies, and in cake-baking you should select butter with the least liquid. Compare liquid content of various butters by melting an equal amount of each type, then chilling them and observing the quantity of liquid that settles out.

Margarine was invented by a French chemist during the late nineteenth century when Napoleon III needed a long-lasting and inexpensive fat for his army. A wide variety of oils and solid fats is used in making margarine. Blends of both are heated; water, milk, emulsifying agents, and flavorings are added; and the mixture is cooled. Excess liquid is extracted; preservatives, coloring, and vitamins are added; and the product is packaged to resemble the "real thing." It does, in some ways: both have roughly the same water and salt content and margarine is 85 to 100 percent fat. However, margarine has a higher melting point (110°F; 43°C) than butter, and because it is created from oils, it remains softer and more oily. Since margarine is not an animal fat, it contains less (or in some cases nonexistent amounts of) cholesterol. To satisfy Kosher dietary laws, one can select a brand of margarine made without either milk solids or animal fats. The taste of margarine is not as sweet as butter and in most cakes this makes a difference. Do not use soft tub-type margarine for cake baking; it is too soft and contains water and other additives. Use only solid stick margarine. In the cake recipes in this book, use butter or margarine where each is indicated. Margarine can be substituted for butter where dietary considerations are a factor or where spices, chocolate, or other strong flavors will mask the flavor of the fat, as in certain coffee or spice cakes.

Solid shortenings are created by forcing pressurized hydrogen gas through oils made from vegetable or animal fats. These artificially created hydrogenated fats contain 100 percent fat and are good for creaming and whipping; they are soft and flexible and will envelop a multitude of air bubbles, thus aiding the leavening of cakes. Crisco is one widely used brand of hydrogenated shortening, available both flavorless and butter-flavored. I use flavorless. Solid shortening can be used in place of margarine in cakes with strong flavors such as spice or chocolate. This type of fat gives cakes a soft crumb and fine grain but, unlike butter, adds no flavor.

Vegetable oils are used as the fat in chiffon cakes. When oil is called for in a recipe, select one with a neutral flavor such as safflower, canola, sunflower, peanut, or corn.

Oil or melted fat added to cake batter coats the starch particles and reduces the strength of the protein, weakening the gluten's elasticity and contributing to the tenderness of a cake. Store oils for short periods at room temperature. Refrigerated oil remains fresh longer but clouds when cold; it clarifies on reaching room temperature. Note that vegetable oils contain no cholesterol. Certain brands of vegetable oil contain silicates, which inhibit foaming, a quality essential to most cake batters. Check the label and select only silicate-free oil for cakes.

Cocoa butter is a by-product of processing cocoa beans to make chocolate (see page 46). This fat is primarily used in icings and confections. It is added to chocolates or chocolate products to increase the tenderness and gloss, and to help carry or hold the chocolate flavor.

SUGARS

Sugar

Sugar is used in cakes to provide sweetness, to aid the creaming and whipping of air into the batter, and to contribute to grain and texture. It also helps cakes to stay fresh longer, aids in yeast fermentation, and provides good color, especially to cake crusts.

It is sugar's ability to attract and absorb moisture that helps to keep a cake fresh. Sugar also slows down the development of gluten in wheat flour, causing the cell walls to stretch slowly so that the cake can rise to the maximum before the structure is set by the oven heat. Sugar also raises the point at which the proteins in the batter will coagulate and set. High-ratio cakes are those having more than 1 cup of sugar per cup of flour; these cakes have an especially fine texture because of the slowness with which their cell walls have stretched.

Granulated sugar needs to be sifted only if it has been in storage for a long time and looks lumpy. Confectioners' sugar should always be sifted before use.

There are many forms of sugar; the one most commonly used in baking is sucrose, a natural sugar found in plants. It is obtained from sugar beets and sugar cane, processed and refined to 99.9 percent purity. Sucrose is a complex sugar, or disaccharide, composed of 1 fructose and 1 glucose molecule joined to form a simple carbohydrate; it can be rapidly absorbed by the body to provide quick energy.

There are many types of sucrose available to the baker: white, dark or light brown sugar, and molasses. Each type comes from a different stage of the refining process. When crushed sugar cane or sugar beet juice is turned into sugar, it is first dissolved in water; the resulting syrup is boiled in steam evaporators. After evaporation, the sugar remaining is crystallized in heated vacuum pans, and molasses, the liquid by-product, is separated out by a series of spinnings in a centrifuge. At this stage, the raw sugar contains many impurities. Once it is steam-washed, it is sold as turbinado sugar. For further purity and clarification, refining continues as turbinado is heated and liquefied, centrifuged, clarified, and filtered.

Granulated brown sugar is crystallized from liquid sugar drawn from the filtering process before all the molasses, caramelized sugar juices, and minerals are removed. To remove remaining traces of color, minerals, and mineral salts, the liquid sugar is then percolated and filtered through a deep bed of bone char. Some refineries also use chemicals to bleach the sugar. Finally, the colorless liquid sugar is boiled in steam-heated vacuum pans and recrystallized, forming granulated white sugar.

WHITE SUGAR • White sugar is available in a variety of crystal sizes, from regular granulated to superfine or bar sugar, and 4, 6, and 10X confectioners' sugar. The size of the crystals is directly related to the amount of air that can be incorporated into a cake batter by creaming or whipping the sugar with fat. The sharp edges of these crystals are essential to bite into the fat and open up pores that grow to become air cells. Sugar thus contributes to a cake's structure and volume. Obviously, powdered confectioners' sugar cannot incorporate as much air as granulated sugar. The size of the crystals is also a factor in how quickly the sugar will dissolve in the batter; the tiny crystals of superfine sugar dissolve much faster than the larger crystals of regular granulated sugar. Superfine is thus best for drinks or meringues. Superfine sugar can be made by grinding granulated sugar in the food processor; the resulting crystal size will be uneven, although appearing fine to the naked eye, but this does not affect its use. Superfine is also called ultrafine or bar sugar and is the finest granulated sugar produced; it is commonly sold in supermarkets only in 1-pound boxes. Extrafine sugar is slightly finer than granulated and is used primarily by professional bakers. Baker's Special sugar is slightly finer than extrafine and is used by commercial bakeries. British "castor sugar" is similar to Baker's Special; superfine sugar can be substituted. The British term "icing sugar" refers to confectioners' sugar.

CONFECTIONERS' SUGAR • This is granulated sugar that has been ground to a specified degree of fineness. For home baking use, powdery 10X is generally used and widely available. The baker should be aware that approximately 3 percent cornstarch is added to each box of confectioners' sugar to prevent lumping and crystallization. Cornstarch gives this sugar a raw taste that is best masked by cooking or adding flavorings to hide the taste of the cornstarch. Because it dissolves almost instantly, confectioners' sugar is primarily used for meringues, icings, and confections. Confectioners' sugar is occasionally added to cake batters to produce a denser and more silken texture than that created with granulated sugar.

BROWN SUGAR • Turbinado and dark and light brown sugars are less refined than white sugar. The darker the sugar, the more molasses and moisture (both by-products of refining) it contains. Turbinado sugar has a coarser grain than granulated white sugar. It is usually sold in natural-food stores, though it is available in some supermarkets. Its moisture content varies with its molasses content, and as this is unpredictable, it is not very reliable for use in cake baking.

Brown sugars are added to cakes, streusel toppings, and icings to give color, flavor, and moisture. Brown sugars tend to make products heavy and are usually to be avoided in very light cakes. In general, the darker brown the sugar, the more intense the flavor; light brown sugar has a light, honey-like taste while dark brown sugar tastes more of molasses. Both dark and light brown sugar have the same sweetening power as an equal weight of white sugar. However, white sugar is more dense; therefore, to achieve an equivalent degree of sweetness, the brown sugar must be firmly packed before measuring by volume.

To avoid lumping, store brown sugar in a covered glass jar or strong sealed plastic bag in a cool, dry location. If, in spite of your best efforts, your brown sugar hardens, put it in a plastic bag with a slice of apple for a few days. Or sprinkle a few drops of water on it and seal it in a plastic bag for a few days. Do not try to crush hardened brown sugar with the metal blade of your food processor; you may break the blade.

To make 1 cup of your own brown sugar, combine 1 cup granulated sugar with 4 tablespoons unsulfured molasses.

SUGAR SYRUPS • When solutions of sugar are boiled, they form syrup. Syrups are used for poaching fruit, blending with buttercreams or meringues, or are caramelized to form threads or candies.

When sugar is added to cold water, it dissolves and blends—up to the point where the water is saturated and can hold no more sugar; this is a saturated solution. Beyond this point, excess sugar remains in crystals and is visible in the water. Cold water can hold double its weight in sugar. When heated, it can absorb more sugar, almost twice as much as when cold. The greater the heat, the more sugar the water can absorb. Maximum saturation is achieved at boiling point. A supersaturated solution contains more sugar than will dissolve in water at room temperature.

When a sugar-water syrup boils, the water evaporates, leaving a sugar concentration of varying density; the less water, the more sugar and the harder the sugar will set when cold. The degree of evaporation can be measured with a candy thermometer, or determined by testing the consistency of the syrup when dropped into a glass of ice water, or the density of the sugar in the syrup can be measured with a saccharimeter or Baumé sugar weight scale.

Sugar in solution has a natural tendency to recrystallize whenever there is not enough moisture to maintain the solution. Controlling the crystallization of the sugar is the essential factor in controlling the texture of fudge, fondant, icing, or candy. Crystals form when the syrup is worked, but the temperature of the syrup will determine the size of the crystal. A very hot syrup forms large crystals; a cool syrup, small crystals. Premature crystallization can ruin the final product. There are several tips that will guard against this.

First, always use an absolutely clean pot, completely free of any fat or food residues. A copper pot is ideal for cooking sugar, but any heavy-bottomed nonreactive metal or ceramic pot with a smooth surface will work.

Second, combine your sugar with water, as per the recipe, and add a pinch of cream of tartar or lemon juice. This acid is added to the sugar, or sucrose, to change it during heating into its components, glucose and fructose. This chemical reaction, called inversion, will prevent recrystallization of the sugar. Corn syrup, called an invert sugar, is an acid, and will also prevent recrystallization in sugar syrup.

Let the mixture stand for a while to form a cold saturated solution; extra sugar will sink to the bottom and remain visible. When the syrup cooks, be sure all the sugar is dissolved before boiling starts. Use a wooden spoon, never a metal one, which would pull heat from the syrup and leave cool spots. It is best not to stir the cooking syrup at all; the stirring motion pushes the sugar molecules into one another and may start crystallization. Instead of stirring, swirl the pan gently to distribute the heat and speed dissolving of the sugar. To avoid crystals on the pan sides, wash down the pan sides with a pastry brush dipped into cold water; do this several times during the boiling process.

Use a candy thermometer to determine the correct temperature of the sugar syrup. Also, at the same time, I like to perform the old-fashioned ice-water test.

First test the accuracy of your candy thermometer by rinsing it in warm water (to prevent shock), then setting it in boiling water to be sure it registers 212°F (100°C). Set the thermometer on the edge of your syrup pan, with the tip resting in the syrup. Alongside the stove, set out a Pyrex measuring cup containing ice cubes and water.

Note that it takes quite a while for sugar to begin to reach the thread stage, but once there it passes quickly from one stage to the next. As the desired temperature approaches, begin to test the syrup in ice water, and watch the thermometer. Do not leave the room. After 250° or 260°F (121°C or higher), changes happen by the second, and the syrup can overcook before you realize it.

Stages of Boiled Syrup

215° to 219°F (102° to 104°C) Thin–Thread Stage: Syrup drips from the spoon edge in a thin thread. If you touch the syrup with your fingers, join your fingers, then pull them apart, a thin thread forms between them. This is used for cake soaking syrups.

230° to 234°F (110° to 112°C) Thread Stage, also called Blow or Soufflé Stage: Similar to thin-thread stage; bubbles in the boiling syrup look like snowflakes, and the thread is slightly thicker and firmer. This is used primarily for candy and syrups.

235° to 240°F (113° to 115°C) Soft–Ball Stage: When a drop of syrup is put into ice water, you can pick it up between your fingers, but it feels very soft and nearly loses its shape when worked. This is usually used for fondants, fudge, and some buttercreams.

244° to 248°F (117° to 120°C) Firm–Ball Stage: When a drop of syrup is put into ice water, you can pick it up between your fingers and it will hold a firm shape, although it is still a little flexible. This is used for caramels, toffees, nougats, etc.

250° to 266°F (121° to 130°C) Hard–Ball Stage: When a drop of syrup is put into ice water, you can pick it up between your fingers and it forms a hard ball. This is used for many candies.

270° to 290°F (132° to 143°C) Soft–Crack Stage: A drop of syrup put into ice water forms a string that cracks when broken although it is still slightly pliable. This is used for candies. The color is pale yellow.

295° to 310°F (145° to 154°C) Hard–Crack Stage: A drop of syrup put into ice water forms a string that is completely brittle and cracks when broken; it is not at all pliable. This is used for nut brittles and coated or glacéed fruit. The color is light amber.

320° to 355°F (165° to 179°C) Caramel: The color darkens from gold to medium–amber, 340°F (171°C); to brown, then quickly blackens and burns. Use for caramel coating of pans at amber stage. Beware of overcooking.

Molasses

Molasses is the liquid separated from sugar crystals during the first stages of refining. The color and strength of the molasses depend on the stage at which it comes in the separation process. When liquid molasses is separated from sugar crystals, it is put through a series of spinnings in a centrifuge. "First" molasses is drawn off in the first centrifuging and is the finest quality. "Second" molasses, from the second round, contains more impurities, and the third, known as "blackstrap" molasses (from the Dutch word *stroop,* or syrup), is the blackest, and strongest in flavor. Most molasses used in cooking is of the first type, often blended with cane syrup to standardize quality.

Some processors treat their sugar cane with sulfur dioxide to clarify and lighten the color of its juice; this produces a sulfur taste in the molasses that many find distasteful. "Unsulfured" molasses has not been so treated; it has the best flavor for cooking and is the type of molasses recommended in this book.

Honey

While not a sugar, honey is a sweetener used in baking. Beside sweetness, it adds moistness, softness, and chewiness to a cake or baked product. Honey has the same sweetening power as sugar, but it cannot replace sugar entirely because it does not work the same way during creaming or whipping of the batter. Honey caramelizes quickly at a low temperature, and causes baked products to appear dark in color. Its degree of natural acidity varies, and baking soda is used with it as a neutralizer.

Note: To substitute honey for granulated sugar, use about ⅞ the quantity called for and decrease the liquid in the recipe by 3 tablespoons per cup of sugar. One cup granulated sugar equals ⅞ cup honey.

The flavor of honey varies depending upon the area in which it is produced and the type of flowers visited by the nectar-gathering bees. For cake baking, use clear liquefied honey rather than honey in solid or comb form. If your honey solidifies or turns granular, set the opened jar on a rack in a pot of gently simmering water until the honey melts and clarifies.

Maple Syrup

Pure maple syrup comes from the sap of the sugar maple tree boiled down until evaporated and thickened. It takes about 30 gallons of maple sap to produce 1 gallon of syrup. Grade A or Fancy Grade syrup is light amber in color, delicate in flavor, and very expensive. Grade B, usually kept for family use by the syrup producer, is my favorite. It is darker brown in color, richer in maple flavor, and less expensive, though hard to find. Store opened maple syrup in the refrigerator. If you see mold forming, put the syrup in a saucepan, heat just to boiling, and skim off the mold. Bring to a boil quickly, then cool, pour into a clean container, and refrigerate for further use.

Try to avoid imitation maple syrups. They are basically corn syrups with artificial maple flavoring, butter flavors, and caramel color added.

LEAVENING AGENTS

. . . .

LEAVENING AGENTS ARE added to cake batters to make cakes rise and to produce a light and porous texture. Air, steam, and carbon dioxide gas are the principal leaveners.

Air bubbles beaten into fat or eggs constitute one type of leavening agent for cake batters. In the heat of the oven, the air in these bubbles expands, causing the cake to rise. The steam produced by heating the liquids in the batter is another rising agent. The steam expands the air cells and lifts the batter. Read What Happens When a Cake Is Baked (page 73).

Baking Powder

Baking powder is a chemical leavening agent composed of acid-reacting materials (tartaric acid or its salts, acid salts of phosphoric acid, compounds of aluminum) and the alkali bicarbonate of soda. When baking powder is mixed with the liquid in the batter it forms a solution, causing a reaction between the acid and the alkali, which then begin to release carbon dioxide gas. When the batter is placed in the heat of the oven, the reaction is completed, releasing no less than 12 percent carbon dioxide; double-acting commercial baking powder releases about 14 percent carbon dioxide.

There are three main types of baking powders. The first is single, or fast-acting, baking powder in which baking soda is combined with tartaric acid or with a combination of cream of tartar and tartaric acid. This is known as tartrate baking powder, and it releases gas quickly when mixed with liquid; a batter containing this powder must be baked promptly. The second type is slow-acting baking powder, also called phosphate baking powder. This type contains baking soda with calcium acid phosphate or sodium acid phosphate. It releases very little gas until placed in the heat of the oven, so batters can be held a long time before being baked. This slow-acting baking powder is often used in commercial bakeries. The third type is double-acting baking powder, also called SAS baking powder. It is the only one recommended in this book, and it is the type most commonly used in home kitchens today. This product is composed of cream of tartar, tartaric acid, sodium aluminum sulfate or sodium acid pyrophosphate, and the mono-calcium phosphates. Double-acting powder produces two separate reactions. When it is first mixed with the batter at room temperature, it releases a small amount of gas, which begins to form many tiny air cells. When the batter is exposed to oven heat, the second reaction occurs. At this point, the baking powder releases its full power, expanding the gas cells as the batter sets, giving a full rise to the cake.

Starch filler is included as a stabilizer in baking powder, to keep the acid salts from reacting with the bicarbonate of soda and to act as a buffer in case any moisture is absorbed in the mixture. On the average, baking powder contains from 23 to 30 percent cornstarch.

In an emergency, if you run out of baking powder, you can make your own (but do not try to store this): for every 1 cup of flour in your recipe, combine 2 teaspoons cream of tartar, 1 teaspoon baking soda, and a few grains of salt (optional).

The amount of baking powder must be adjusted when baking at high altitudes where the air pressure is lower and gas expansion in the batter is increased; read about High Altitude Baking (page 475).

Note that if too much baking powder is used in a cake, the taste may be very bitter, and the cake may rise rapidly, then collapse.

Baking powder absorbs moisture from the air and can deteriorate quickly. It has a shelf life of about 3 months. For home baking, you should buy it in small cans and replace it if it is old. To test its effectiveness, combine 1 teaspoon baking powder with ½ cup hot water; if it bubbles up vigorously, the baking powder is still usable; if no reaction occurs, toss out the can and buy more. If in doubt, throw it out. Store baking powder and baking soda in a cool, dry place away from dampness.

Baking Soda

Baking soda is another common leavening agent. Originally known as saleratus, it is now called baking or bicarbonate of soda. This alkaline product is used in cake batters when there is an acid agent present (buttermilk, sour milk, yogurt, molasses, honey, chocolate, cocoa, etc.) in order to neutralize some of the acidity as well as to provide leavening power. The alkaline soda needs the acid in order to react, releasing carbon dioxide gas. This action is similar to that of fast-acting baking powder, for the reaction takes place as soon as the batter is mixed. Batters risen entirely with soda must be baked as soon as possible, before the rising effect is dissipated.

Bicarbonate of soda has other properties as well. Because it is an alkali, it has the ability to darken the color of chocolate or cocoa in a cake. It also causes the reddening of cocoa, giving devil's food cake its name.

If you use too much baking soda without a balancing acid in the batter, you will darken or yellow a white cake and produce off-odors and a soapy flavor.

Years ago, baking soda was coarsely ground, and for that reason was mixed with boiling water before being added to batter. Many cookbooks still refer to this method. Today, however, soda is ground very fine and may be sifted into the other dry ingredients for even distribution throughout the batter.

Yeast

There are over 160 different species of the single-celled fungus known as yeast. The particular species used in baking and brewing is *Saccharomyces cerevisiae* (brewer's sugar fungus). When combined with water, sugar, and/or flour, certain proteins, and the correct degree of warmth, this yeast has the ability to divide and grow, converting most of the sugar and starch into alcohol and carbon dioxide. The carbon dioxide gas is utilized to raise the batter or dough and the alcohol evaporates in the heat of the oven.

There are many types of yeast available to the home baker: fresh compressed and active dry granulated (regular, quick-rising, instant, and bread machine). Regular dry granulated yeast is the one I have used exclusively in this book. Rapid-rising yeast requires a special mixing procedure for success in cake baking. Follow package directions. As a general rule, substitute 1 cake of fresh compressed yeast (1 packed tablespoon, ⅗ ounce, 22 g) for 1 envelope of active dry yeast (2¼ teaspoons; ¼ ounce; 7 g). The temperature of the liquid used for dissolving each type of yeast is different and critical to the success of the yeast growth; however, all types will die if exposed to excessively high temperatures. If kept at excessively cold temperatures, the yeast will hibernate or be unable to multiply. Many recipes advise keeping rising dough away from drafts because cool air slows the multiplication of yeast cells. Once yeast growth has begun, the cells will multiply best in a temperature of between 70° and 85°F (average home kitchen temperature).

Active dry granular yeast, which contains only about 8 percent moisture, is sold for home use in envelopes weighing ¼ ounce (7 grams, about 1 tablespoon) and also in jars containing 4 ounces.

Look for freshness dates on the packages and be sure your yeast is not outdated; if too old, it will probably be dead. Store unopened envelopes or jars in a cool, dark place, ideally at temperatures of 32° to 34°F (0°C), or in the refrigerator or freezer. Open envelopes must be stored in the refrigerator.

To use, sprinkle the yeast granules into water that is 105° to 115°F or 40°C (just hotter than lukewarm to the touch), and allow the mixture to sit about 5 minutes. To hasten the growth of the yeast, a little sugar can be added. After a few minutes, a healthy, active batch of yeast will "proof," or bubble up and look frothy; after 5 or 6 minutes it will expand in volume. If the mixture is still dormant, it is too old and should be discarded. Note that while some sugar (or flour that the yeast enzymes can convert to sugar) is essential for yeast growth, a high proportion of sugar in a batter or dough slows yeast multiplication. For this reason, rich sweet coffeecake dough often requires a longer rising time than plain bread.

SALT

. . . .

COMMON SALT, OR sodium chloride, is the type used in baking. It contributes many factors: it enhances flavors and improves taste, aids digestibility, and strengthens the gluten in yeast products. Keeping in mind today's concerns about salt in relation to high blood pressure and general health, I have tried to cut the salt included in the cake recipes to a minimum. Always bake with unsalted butter so that you can control the amount of salt added to the cake; different brands of butter vary in salt content.

GELATIN

. . . .

GELATIN IS A natural product derived from collagen, the protein found in bones and connective tissue. In the United States, unflavored gelatin is most commonly sold in dry granulated form, in bulk, and in prepackaged envelopes. Each envelope contains 1 very scant tablespoon (actually a generous 2 teaspoons), or ¼ ounce (7 grams), to set 2 cups of liquid or 1½ cups of solids.

To dissolve granulated gelatin, sprinkle it on top of a small amount of cold liquid (it does not have to be water) in a small saucepan, and let it sit a few minutes so the granules swell. Then, set it over moderately low heat and stir just until the granules dissolve completely; test by rubbing a drop of the mixture between your fingers—it should feel absolutely smooth. Do not let the gelatin boil or it will lose some of its setting strength. Another method is to stir the swollen granules into boiling water until dissolved. To dissolve gelatin in a microwave, sprinkle one envelope over ¼ cup cold water in a glass measuring cup. Let stand 2 minutes to soften, then microwave at full power (high) 40 seconds; stir thoroughly, let stand 2 minutes longer or until gelatin is completely dissolved. If some granules remain, repeat at 5-second intervals, stirring after each interval to test the solution.

Some fresh fruits, such as fresh figs, kiwifruit, papaya, pineapple, and prickly pears, cannot be used with gelatin because they contain protease enzymes that soften gelatin and prevent it from setting. However, if these fruits (except kiwi) are boiled for 5 minutes, their enzymes are destroyed and they can be added to gelatin without harming its jelling properties.

Vegetarian substitutes for gelatin are available in natural foods stores.

They include agar agar (a gel or crystallized product made from seaweed) and Pomona's Universal Pectin (made from natural pectins, without sugar). For use, follow package directions.

FLAVORINGS

. . . .

SPICES, EXTRACTS, CITRUS rind (zest), liqueurs, coffee, and chocolate all add flavoring to baked products, fillings, and icings. They vary widely in their properties and purity, so pay careful attention to recipe requirements.

Spices

Once a spice is ground, the aroma is volatile and fades when exposed to the air or to heat for a period of time. If you buy ground spices, they must be kept in well-sealed jars in a cool, dry cupboard. Whole seeds and spices have a longer shelf life, but should also be stored in sealed containers away from heat, air, and moisture. It is always preferable to use freshly ground spices if you possibly can; they impart a stronger and more aromatic flavor to baked goods than do the pallid powders lingering in the back of the spice rack.

Extracts

Extracts are the concentrated natural essential oils of the flavoring agent, usually dissolved in alcohol. Some flavors are made from the oils found in the rind of citrus fruits (lemons and oranges, for example); others are made from fruit pulp.

Extract bottles are labeled "pure" or "imitation." The distinction is important. Most liquid flavors are volatile and thus dissipate in the heat of baking. To have a good flavor in the finished cake, you must start with the purest and strongest flavoring. Pure extracts cost more and are worth it. Imitation flavors are produced synthetically, and often impart a chemical taste to cakes; at best, they are weaker and less aromatic than pure extracts. Some flavors are unavailable in pure extracts—coconut or pistachio, for example. You can use the fresh nuts for flavoring instead, or use the extract in moderation. Some natural flavors do need a little enhancement from extracts. I find that pure maple syrup (even grade B, which has a stronger flavor than the lighter-colored Fancy, or grade A) may not flavor a cake enough; the flavor benefits from a very tiny bit of artificial maple extract.

The purest vanilla extract is that which you make yourself. To do this, buy 4 pliable aromatic vanilla pods (in a gourmet or baking supply shop) and slit each pod lengthwise. Soak the pods in 2 cups of vodka in a covered glass jar for at least 2 weeks. After this time, you can remove the pods or leave them in, as you wish. Use this flavored vodka, strained, for your extract. Homemade vanilla extract makes an excellent holiday gift for a baker.

Liquid extracts should be stored in dark-colored, tightly closed bottles in a cool, dark cupboard. Extracts are volatile in the presence of heat and light.

Zests

Zest is simply the bright-colored part of the peel of a citrus fruit. The zest contains all the essential oils, or flavors, of the peel. Just below the zest is a bitter-tasting white pith, which should not be used. When the recipes in this book call for grated lemon, orange, or tangerine zest, for example, I mean that only the brightest-colored part of the peel should be used. When you have a bunch of lemons, oranges, or limes to squeeze for juice, grate them first, or cut off the zest in long thin strips, and freeze it for later use in baking; then extract the juice.

Grating citrus zest with a box or panel grater is difficult, because of the struggle required to free the fruit. Use a gadget called a citrus peeler, a tool with a wooden handle and a flat metal head containing 5 tiny, sharp-edged round holes. This tool is scraped across the skin of the fruit, shredding it into long very thin slivers. I love to use these slivers just as they are for decorations on a buttercream-covered orange or lemon cake. Or put the slivers on a wooden board and mince them with a sharp knife, creating a texture nearly as fine as grating, with less waste.

My favorite grater is the Microplane, originally designed as a wood rasp for carpenters. It is sharp, easy to clean, and incredibly efficient for every task from grating lemon zest to grating cheese or chocolate. Microplanes are sold in cookware shops and by mail order (see Sources, page 477) in a variety of sizes, with or without handles.

Nuts

The preparation technique for nuts is determined by their use. Toasting nuts brings out their flavor and darkens their color somewhat. For cake batters with a good strong nut flavor, it is best to toast nuts before grinding or chopping them. However, for cookies, meringue cake layers (dacquoise), or streusel toppings, where the chopped nuts will be exposed more directly to the heat source, they will effectively be toasted during baking, so it is not necessary to do so in advance. Do toast nuts to be used as a garnish on cake sides or top.

TO DRY OR TOAST AND SKIN NUTS • Some nuts, walnuts in particular, have a high oil content and tend to make a paste when ground; to avoid this and improve ease of grinding, dry the nuts in the oven before grinding them. Spread the nuts on a shallow pan and set them in a preheated 300°F (150°C) oven for 5 to 6 minutes, 8 minutes for hazelnuts. To toast nuts instead of simply drying them, increase oven heat to about 325°F (165°C). Heat the nuts for 10 to 15 minutes or until they are aromatic and show a light golden color. Toss or stir several times for even heating. Or toast the nuts until golden in a heavy-bottomed frying pan set over low to moderate heat; watch the nuts and stir them constantly.

Beneath their shells, some nuts have skins that must be removed.

To remove the brown skin from hazelnuts, toast the nuts as described. As soon as the nuts come from the oven, wrap them in a coarse-textured towel for several minutes to steam. Then rub the skins off with the towel; discard the skins and pick out the nuts to use. A few bits of skin will still cling to the nuts; ignore this.

To remove the skins of almonds or pistachios, they should be blanched. This is easily accomplished by boiling the shelled nuts (skins still on) in water for 2 or 3 minutes. Drain and cool them under cold running water. Pinch off the skins with your fingers.

TO GRIND NUTS • Some nut cakes, especially European tortes and Swedish pastries, use finely ground nuts, especially almonds, hazelnuts, and walnuts. The end product must be fine and very dry, almost like a shaved powder rather than oily chopped beads. It is easiest to accomplish this with a hand-held food or nut mill in which a presser bar pushes on the nuts, forcing them onto a rotating cutting disk. This gadget is available from specialty cookware supply houses (see Sources, page 477).

A meat grinder can be used to grind nuts, but sometimes it tends to press the oils out, and this may not be desirable. A blender can also be used, but remember to add only ½ cup of nuts at a time and pulse for about 4 seconds. Stop the blender and stir the nuts before repeating the chopping action. The food processor does an excellent job of fine-chopping nuts, but may create a paste if the nuts are oily; the best way to fine-chop nuts in the processor is to add a tablespoon or two of granulated sugar (take this sugar from the measured amount used in the recipe) before turning on the machine. The sugar keeps the nuts spinning and prevents packing, thus enabling the blades to process to a finer texture.

Poppyseeds

Many Austrian and Hungarian recipes require ground poppyseeds, which are richly flavorful, highly aromatic, and moist. Certain specialty markets sell ground poppyseeds (see Sources, page 477) but grinding is a task easily accomplished at home with an imported poppyseed, spice, or coffee grinder. The seeds can also be ground in a regular meat grinder (fitted with the finest blade) or an electric herb mincer, which I prefer. The mincer I use consists of a small cup containing a set of sharp thin blades. Seeds are placed in the cup, which is pushed down onto a base, engaging a motor on contact. Simple to use and effective, it grinds poppyseeds to perfection. A regular electric blender will also work if you grind only ½ cup of seeds at a time and stir them down once or twice. Grind them in the blender on high speed for at least 1 full minute. Note that the regular food processor will not grind poppyseeds, as they are too small to be cut by the blade.

Dried Fruits

Dried fruits are used in many types of baked products: coffee and tea cakes, for example, as well as fruitcakes. It is important to use fruits that are not too hard and dried out, for baking will not soften them. Before adding dried fruits to a batter, taste them for flavor and texture. If they are too hard, place them in a strainer over (not in) boiling water, cover, and steam them for a few minutes until you can bite into them without breaking your teeth.

Dates and prunes are available pitted as well as with pits. The pitted products are easier to work with and can easily be chopped. Avoid packaged prechopped dates as they rarely have good texture; their skins are usually encrusted with undesirable crystallized sugar.

Raisins are grapes dried either by the sun or by artificial heat. In this book, I use both dark seedless raisins and golden raisins, which are regular raisins treated with sulfur dioxide to prevent darkening. The flavor of golden raisins is lighter and sweeter than that of dark raisins.

Dried currants used in baking are actually small raisins made from dried Zante grapes. This product is sold in the supermarket next to dried raisins, and the box is labeled "Zante Currants." Store currants and raisins in a sealed box or plastic bag in a dark cupboard or in covered glass jars in the refrigerator.

Note: Dried Zante currants are not related to fresh, bush-grown currants, which are white, black, or red berries.

Dried figs come primarily from California, Greece, or Turkey. Select figs that are flexible when pressed rather than hard and dried out. Store dried figs in a covered jar in a dry cupboard.

Coconut

The coconut is the fruit of the palm *Cocos nucifera,* one of the oldest food plants known. Botanically, the coconut is not a nut at all, but a "drupe" fruit. The coconut consists of a thick fibrous husk and a hard inner shell that contains the white meat and coconut liquid, correctly termed coconut water, not milk. Instead of making fresh coconut milk, you can substitute canned *unsweetened* coconut milk sold in most supermarkets. Stir well before using.

When buying a fresh coconut, generally available as the hard, brown fiber-covered shell freed from the thick outer husk, be sure it is heavy for its size. You should hear the liquid inside when you shake the coconut, and there should be no sign of mold around the eyes or cracks in the shell, which might allow bacteria to grow inside.

The coconut can be stored at room temperature. When opened, the meat should be white; if it looks gray and smells fermented, it is spoiled and should be discarded.

TO PREPARE A COCONUT • Set the coconut on a towel so it does not roll and pierce the eyes with a screwdriver and a hammer. Drain the coconut water into a bowl and store it in the refrigerator for baking or to drink. Strain the liquid if it contains fibers. Set the drained coconut on a roasting pan and bake at 350°F (175°C) for about 30 minutes. The heat should cause the shell to crack. If it needs to be cracked more, wrap it in a towel and give it a few blows with a hammer. Use the screwdriver to pry the shell away from the meat. Use a vegetable peeler to remove the brown skin from the white meat.

Break up the prepared coconut meat into small pieces and grate it in several small batches in the blender or food processor, or by hand on a box grater. Slice chips from the edges of the coconut sections and toast these with salt in a 300°F (150°C) oven for about 25 minutes, tossing occasionally, to make a delicious snack.

To make true "coconut milk," cover the grated coconut meat with about 1¼ cups boiling water, let sit for about 10 minutes, then strain the liquid into a clean container. Or pour the boiling water through the feed tube of the food processor containing the grated coconut and process for 20 to 30 seconds; let stand for 10 minutes, then strain. This strained liquid is the milk. Repeat the process if you need more liquid, or add water or milk to the first batch of liquid.

To make "coconut cream," pour no more than 2 cups boiling water over 1 grated coconut, let it sit until cold, then drain through cheesecloth, squeezing the coconut dry. Let this liquid sit until a waxy cream rises and forms on top. Remove this and refrigerate to use in baking.

Note: Canned Coco Lopez is a heavily sweetened coconut cream sold in supermarkets for use in mixed drinks. It is fine for flavoring some cake icings, but because of the high sugar content, it cannot be substituted for coconut milk in cakes.

Chocolate

As an unabashed chocoholic, I consider chocolate an essential element, right up there with fire, air, and water. I have devoted considerable time and thought to the subject, and I find its story, from cacao tree to candy bar, both complex and fascinating.

The chocolate tree is *Theobroma cacao,* a tropical evergreen native to South and Central America, also cultivated in Africa and Southeast Asia. The Aztecs were the first to appreciate the fruit of this tree, making a cocoa beverage so venerated that it was reserved exclusively for the Emperor Montezuma and his ministers. It is said that Montezuma drank as many as 50 golden cups a day of this frothy cold drink, prepared from roasted and ground cacao beans flavored with peppers and spices. Among chocolate's many virtues, the Aztecs considered it an aphrodisiac, a fact modern science has explained by isolating phenylethylamine, a natural ingredient of chocolate that produces a euphoric sensation some say is akin to the feeling of falling in love. Our words chocolate and cocoa derive from the Nahuatl *xochuatl* or *chochuatl,* meaning "bitter juice."

The tree produces large pods, which are cut from the trunk, and opened. The inner beans and pulp are scooped out, air-dried, fermented, and cured to remove the bitter taste, impart aroma, enrich the flavor, and darken the color. As beans from different geographical areas have particular qualities, most manufacturers blend them to combine the best taste, texture, and aroma, much as coffee beans are blended.

At the factory, the beans are roasted to develop their "chocolaty" taste and flavor. Their hulls are removed, and the inner nibs, containing 50 to 54 percent cocoa butter, a natural fat, are crushed and ground, or rolled between steel disks. The heat produced in this process liquefies the cocoa butter, most of which is removed. The dark brown paste remaining is called chocolate liquor. A churning procedure called conching further refines the product and enhances its quality.

Chocolate liquor can be molded and solidified. This is then sold as unsweetened or bitter chocolate. When varying amounts of sugar and cocoa butter are combined with the chocolate liquor, the results are bittersweet, semisweet, and sweet chocolate, depending on the proportions. Bittersweet is the least sweet of these. When dry milk solids are added to sweetened chocolate, it becomes milk chocolate. Depending on your taste preference and the requirements of your recipe, the different types of chocolate can be used interchangeably in cakes and icings.

TO MELT CHOCOLATE • Chocolate is an emulsion; unless handled carefully, the fat will separate out. For this reason, it must be melted very slowly, preferably in the top pan of a double boiler set over hot (125°F; 50°C) water. Ideally, you melt only about half of the chocolate in the double boiler, then remove it from heat and stir until the remaining chocolate is melted. Dark chocolate should never be heated above 120°F (49°C) because it will turn grainy.

Beware of getting liquid into chocolate as it melts. A drop of water added by mistake, or present in a damp pan, can cause the chocolate to seize and harden. This is not always salvageable, but you can try smoothing it out by stirring in 1 teaspoon solid white shortening for each ounce of chocolate.

To avoid the moisture problem, you can melt chocolate in the microwave oven. For each ounce, heat at medium-low (7) for 2 to 3 minutes. The chocolate will not lose its shape when melted, so remove it from the microwave oven and stir until it is all evenly melted; this is especially important if melting several ounces at once. It usually melts unevenly and needs stirring plus a few more seconds in the microwave. In baking, never use chocolate that is unevenly melted; check by stirring until uniformly smooth.

TO STORE CHOCOLATE • Store chocolate in a cool, dry place at about 60°F (about 16°C). At warmer temperatures, a grayish bloom develops on the surface of the chocolate; this is the cocoa butter rising to the surface. It does not affect the flavor but may be unsightly. The color returns to normal if the chocolate is melted. Some commercial candy bars are treated to have higher melting points and prevent bloom in warm stores or warm weather; this means the chocolate will no longer melt in your mouth, as the original quality has been altered.

Chocolate stored at excessively cold temperatures may sweat when brought to room temperature. It is not a good idea to store chocolate in the refrigerator or freezer.

CHOCOLATE TYPES AND SUPPLIERS • For chocolate suppliers, see the list of mail-order sources (page 477).

For the recipes in this book, I have used only pure semisweet, bittersweet, or unsweetened chocolate available in local stores or from mail-order specialty shops. As a general rule, you can substitute chocolate morsels for block chocolate, chopped, and vice versa. As a guide, ⅛ cup regular-size chocolate morsels = 1 ounce = 2 tablespoons. Hershey's, Nestle's, Maillard Eagle, Ghirardelli, Baker's, and Baker's German Sweet are some of the most widely known brands I use. Other dark chocolates I like especially include Lindt Extra-Bittersweet and Lindt Excellence, Guittard, Tobler Tradition and Tobler Extra Bittersweet, Callebaut Semi-Sweet or Bittersweet, and Poulain Bittersweet for Baking.

COCOA • To make cocoa, chocolate liquor is pressed to remove more than half of its remaining cocoa butter. The dry cake of residue is then pulverized and sifted, making fine unsweetened cocoa powder.

Note: Instant cocoa mixes for drinks have dry milk solids and sugars added and should not be substituted for baking cocoa.

Natural processed cocoa, like chocolate, is acidic and has the fruity flavor of the cocoa bean. To neutralize some of the acid, and to darken and redden the color, some cocoas are Dutch-processed, or factory-treated with alkali. The name comes from the fact that a Dutchman, Coenraad van Houten, discovered the process. Examples of brands using this method are Droste, Van Houten, Fedora, and most other imports. The most widely available American brands of unsweetened cocoa powder, Hershey's and Baker's, are "natural," not Dutch-process, and thus have higher acidity. Both types are used in recipes calling for baking soda, which interacts with their natural acidity to balance the pH, darken and redden the color, and at the same time create a leavening agent by releasing carbon dioxide when the acid and alkali mix. However, Dutch-process cocoa requires less baking soda to neutralize its acid than does natural processed cocoa. For this reason, you should take care when substituting Dutch-process cocoa for natural cocoa. It is best to use the specific type called for in the recipe. To adjust the recipe yourself, be aware that for Dutch-process cocoa you decrease the amount of baking soda slightly and add a little baking powder; excess baking soda may result in a soapy flavor in the cake.

Note: To substitute cocoa powder for solid unsweetened chocolate, use 3 level tablespoons natural (not Dutch-process) cocoa plus 1 tablespoon solid vegetable shortening or unsalted butter for each 1 ounce unsweetened chocolate. However, the flavor and texture will be slightly different because solid chocolate contains cocoa butter, which is lacking in cocoa.

WHITE CHOCOLATE • White chocolate is not a true chocolate because it does not contain any chocolate liquor. It is actually a blend of whole milk and sugar, cooked, condensed, and solidified. In the best brands, some cocoa butter is added to enhance the flavor. Other additives include whey powder, lecithin, vanilla, and egg whites. The finest quality white chocolate contains the highest proportion of cocoa butter and thus lists that ingredient first on the label.

Take care when melting white chocolate, as it tends to solidify easily. Too much heat transforms the proteins in the milk additives and causes lumps. At temperatures over 115°F (45°C), the chocolate may start to recrystallize and become grainy. Melt chopped white chocolate in a double boiler over warm (125°F; about 50°C) water; don't allow the chocolate to heat above 100° to 110°F (about 40°C), to keep it smooth. Stir often. White chocolate can be used like dark chocolate for chocolate leaves or curls.

Brands with excellent flavor and smooth melting quality include Ghirardelli Classic White Confection and Ghirardelli Classic White Chips, Baker's Premium White Chocolate Baking Squares (all three available in supermarkets), as well as Guittard Vanilla Milk Chips, Lindt Swiss White Confectionery Bar, Callebaut White Chocolate, and Tobler Narcisse.

How to Measure Ingredients

IN THE UNITED States, we use volume measurements for both dry and liquid ingredients. Elsewhere in the world, people tend to measure dry ingredients by weight on a scale. This is a much more accurate system, and once you are used to it, it is easy to work with. A quick look at 1 cup of cake flour will explain: 1 cup of sifted cake flour spooned into a 1-cup measure and leveled off will weigh 3½ ounces or 100 grams. If I tap this cup sharply, the contents will compact so that I can then spoon in as much as 2 tablespoons more flour, for a weight of about 4 ounces, or 113 grams. As we all handle measuring tools differently, we can unwittingly use more of an ingredient than we mean to. Excess flour, for example, can toughen baked goods, so one wants to use the minimum required. Thus, it is more reliable to weigh out 100 grams of flour than to measure 1 cup by volume.

Since accuracy with flour, sugar, and fat measurements are especially critical in cake baking, I have included the weights for these ingredients in both ounces and grams alongside their volume measurements. Ideally, you will weigh these items (directions for using a scale follow) and measure the other ingredients by volume. If scales daunt you, of course use the conventional method; simply measure with care.

HOW TO MEASURE LIQUIDS

· ·

USE A LIQUID measuring cup (see page 10). Set the cup flat on the counter, fill it to the desired amount, and bend down to read the mark at eye level.

Note: Eggs are considered liquids, and are measured in a liquid measuring cup.

HOW TO MEASURE DRY
INGREDIENTS

· ·

SCOOP AND SWEEP METHOD • When the recipe does not specify sifting, use this method. Stir up flour or sugar in a canister, then simply dip your dry measuring cup (see page 10) in and scoop up a heaping amount. Then take the back of a knife or other straight edge and sweep off the excess, leveling the top.

SCOOP AND SWEEP METHOD WHEN YOU ARE IN A HURRY • One level cup of unsifted flour contains about 2 tablespoons more flour than 1 cup that is sifted; therefore, if you are in a hurry and feel you must cheat, not bothering to sift when the recipe tells you to, be aware that while you are skipping the aeration value of the sifter, you can compensate for the volume difference by scooping and sweeping a *scant* cup of flour, about 2 tablespoons less than a full cup. Do your cheating on coffee cakes and their like rather than sponge cakes or génoise, or you will have disappointing results.

TO SIFT AND MEASURE BY VOLUME • When the recipe specifies sifting, use this method. Scoop flour or confectioners' sugar or cocoa from the canister and put it into a strainer (which I prefer) or sifter set over a piece of wax paper or a bowl. Sift. Spoon the item into the appropriate size of dry measuring cup, heaping the top slightly. Take the back of a knife or other straight edge and sweep off the excess, leveling the top. Lift the edges of the piece of wax paper and pour the excess back into the canister.

Note: Unless granulated sugar looks lumpy and has been in storage too long, it is not necessary to sift it before measuring.

TO SIFT AND MEASURE BY WEIGHT • First read About Using Scales, following. Line the scale container with plastic wrap. Scoop flour or other dry ingredient from the canister into a strainer and sift it onto the scale container until the correct weight is reached. Or sift onto a piece of plastic wrap or wax paper, then spoon it onto the scale.

UNSIFTED MEASURING BY WEIGHT • First read About Using Scales, following. If no sifting is required, simply weigh the item directly on the scale platform. When weighing berries or other juicy items, first line the scale container with plastic wrap.

ABOUT USING SCALES

For INFORMATION ABOUT types of scales, see page 11. Select a type that is made for cooking, not a dieter's scale, which will only hold very small quantities. It should have a container or platform large enough to hold at least 2 cups of flour or sugar; ideally, it should measure at least 16 ounces or 500 grams. Line the container or platform with a piece of plastic wrap before measuring. The wrap helps prevent washups and also can be used to transfer the measured item to the mixing bowl.

If your scale does not have a deep container, set a plastic freezer-type container on the platform to hold the ingredients; be sure to reset the dial to zero to compensate for the weight of the container before adding the ingredients to be weighed. Reset the dial when the auxiliary container is no longer in use.

In addition to using the scale for all dry ingredients, you can also use it for measuring solid fats and eggs. The size and weight of eggs varies (see page 23) and while the recipes in this book call for large, 2-ounce eggs, you may use other sizes, if the combined weight is correct.

TO MEASURE FATS

OIL IS LIQUID fat; it is measured in a liquid measuring cup, as other liquids are. There are several methods for measuring solid fats, but the easiest is with a scale, as described.

The second choice is to use butter or margarine or Crisco sold in quarter-pound sticks. Each stick is marked on the wrapper indicating tablespoon and cup divisions. One stick = 8 tablespoons = ½ cup; ⅓ cup = 5⅓ tablespoons; ¼ cup = 4 tablespoons.

To measure solid shortening without a scale, it is best to pack it into a dry measuring cup, taking care to eliminate any air pockets that may be trapped in the bottom of the cup. Level off the cup, and use.

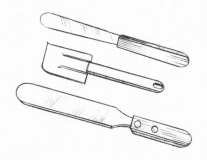

A Note About Recipe Measurements

STANDARD VOLUME MEASUREMENTS (cups and spoons) are given for all the ingredients used in the recipes in this book; in addition, weight measurements in ounces and grams are given for certain ingredients (flour, sugar, fat, and some other items) so that they may be weighed on a scale for greater accuracy. If you are using a scale, you will notice that our ounce and gram weights have been rounded off. Do not worry about discrepancies here because the amounts will all be in correct proportion to one another. See the table opposite for examples of our measurements.

Ounces	Grams (exact)	Grams (rounded off)
¼	7.0	7
½	14.17	15
1	28.35	30
1¾	49.61	50
2	56.70	60
2¾	74.85	75
3	85.05	85
3½	99.22	100
4	113.40	110
5	141.70	140
6	170.10	170
7	198.45	200
8	226.80	230
9	255.15	255
10	283.50	280
10½	297.67	300
11	311.85	310
12	340.20	340
13	368.55	370
14	396.90	400
15	424.25	425
16 (1 pound)	453.60	454

EXAMPLES OF WEIGHT EQUIVALENTS

	Unsifted ounces	grams	Sifted ounces	grams
ALL–PURPOSE FLOUR				
1 cup	5 oz;	140 g	4¼ oz;	120 g

(Note: 1 cup sifted flour = 1 cup unsifted flour minus 2 tablespoons)

	Unsifted ounces	grams	Sifted ounces	grams
CAKE FLOUR				
1 cup	4½ oz;	120 g	3½ oz;	100 g
GRANULATED SUGAR				
1 cup	7 oz;	200 g	—	
CONFECTIONERS' SUGAR				
1 cup	4½ oz;	130 g	3½ oz;	100 g
DARK BROWN SUGAR, FIRMLY PACKED				
1 cup	9 oz;	255 g	—	

Tbsp.	oz/lb	stick(s)	cup(s)	Grams (exact)	Grams (rounded off)
BUTTER					
1	½ oz	⅛	—	(14)	15
2	1 oz	¼	—	(28)	30
4	2 oz	½	¼	(57)	60
8	4 oz; ¼ lb	1	½	(113)	110
16	8 oz; ½ lb	2	1	(227)	230
32	16 oz; 1 lb	4	2	(453.6)	454

EQUIVALENTS AND SUBSTITUTIONS

Note that all measurements used in this book are level. All eggs used in the recipes are U.S. Grade A large.

Equivalents

BREAD CRUMBS

1 cup fresh bread crumbs = 2 ounces; 60 grams

1 cup dry or toasted bread = scant 4 ounces;
crumbs   110 grams

BUTTER

1 pound butter = 2 cups; 4 sticks,
    454 grams

¼ pound butter = ½ cup; 1 stick; 8 table-
    spoons; 113 grams

CHOCOLATE

1 ounce solid semisweet = 1 premeasured square
chocolate = 25 grams

1 ounce regular-size chocolate = ⅛ cup = 2 tablespoons
morsels

½ cup regular chocolate morsels = 3 ounces; 85 grams

1 cup regular chocolate morsels = 6 ounces; 170 grams

1 cup mini-chip chocolate morsels = 5½ ounces; 155 grams

COCONUT

1 average size coconut, = 3½ cups grated coconut,
    4-inch diameter   loose; 2 cups, hard
    packed

4 ounces coconut, dried and flaked = 1 scant cup
or shredded

CREAM

1 cup heavy cream (36 to 40 percent = 2 cups whipped cream
butterfat)

EGGS

1 U.S. Grade A large egg	= 2 ounces = 3 tablespoons
1 large egg yolk	= 1 generous tablespoon
1 large egg white	= 2 tablespoons = ⅛ cup
2 large eggs	= scant ½ cup = 3 medium eggs
4 to 5 large eggs	= 1 cup
6 to 7 large yolks	= ½ cup
4 large whites	= ½ cup
3 large whites, beaten stiff	= 3 cups meringue, enough to top a 9-inch cake

FLOUR

1 pound all-purpose flour	= 4 cups
5 pounds all-purpose flour	= 20 cups
1 pound cake flour or pastry flour	= 4½ cups plus 2 tablespoons

FRUITS

1 8-ounce box dried apricots	= 2 cups, packed
1 pound seedless raisins	= 3½ cups; 454 grams
1 whole lemon	= 2 to 3 tablespoons juice plus 2 to 3 teaspoons grated zest
1 whole orange	= 6 to 8 tablespoons juice plus 2 to 3 tablespoons grated zest
1 quart fresh berries	= 4 cups

GELATIN

1 envelope unflavored gelatin	= 1 scant tablespoon (¼ oz; 7 g) to hard-set 2 cups liquid

NUTS

1 pound whole almonds, shelled	= 3¼ cups; 454 grams
1 cup blanched almonds, shelled	= 5 ounces; 140 grams
1 pound walnuts, shelled	= 4 cups; 454 grams
1 cup walnuts, shelled	= 4 ounces; 110 grams
1 pound whole pecans, shelled	= 4½ cups; 454 grams
1 cup shelled pecan halves	= 4 ounces; 100 grams
1 cup shelled peanuts	= 5 ounces; 140 grams
1 pound whole hazelnuts, shelled	= 3¼ cups; 454 grams
1 cup shelled whole hazelnuts	= 5 ounces; 140 grams

SUGAR

1 pound granulated sugar	= 2¼ cups
5 pounds granulated sugar	= 11¼ cups
1 pound brown sugar	= 2¼ cups, packed
1 pound confectioners' sugar	= 4 to 4¼ cups, unsifted

Substitutions

1 ounce solid chocolate	= 3 tablespoons cocoa plus 1 tablespoon solid vegetable shortening or vegetable oil
1 cup sour milk	= 1 cup sweet milk plus 1 tablespoon vinegar, let sit for 2 to 3 minutes
1 cup whole sweet milk	= 3 to 4 tablespoons dry milk solids plus 1 cup water
1 cup buttermilk	= 1 cup plain yogurt, stirred
1 cup crème fraîche	= 1 cup heavy cream plus ½ cup sour cream (see recipe, page 417)

1 cup all-purpose flour	= ⅞ cup rice flour
2 tablespoons flour for thickening 1 cup liquid in medium-thick sauce	= 1 tablespoon cornstarch, potato starch, or arrowroot, or 3 tablespoons quick-cooking tapioca
1 cup granulated sugar	= 1 cup molasses plus ½ teaspoon baking soda and omit baking powder in recipe. Also decrease recipe liquid by ¼ cup for each cup of molasses.
1 cup granulated sugar	= ⅞ cup honey and decrease recipe liquid by 3 tablespoons
1 cup brown sugar	= 1 cup granulated white sugar plus 2 tablespoons unsulfured molasses
1 cup cinnamon sugar	= 1 cup granulated sugar plus 1 to 2 tablespoons ground cinnamon, to taste
1 teaspoon baking powder	= ¼ teaspoon baking soda sifted together with ½ teaspoon cream of tartar. Or, for each 1 cup flour in the recipe, use 1 teaspoon baking soda plus 2 teaspoons cream of tartar and a few grains of salt sifted together.

Pan Volume and Serving Table

USE THIS TABLE as a guide when substituting other pans for those called for in the recipes. The pan sizes given are those most frequently used in this book. The number of cups of batter is indicated in the notes preceding each recipe. Except where so noted in recipes, pan sizes may be changed without affecting baking results. Pans are measured across the top, from rim to rim. To find the full capacity of a pan, fill it to the brim with measured cups of water; slight variations from the table are caused by differences in the shape of the pan—pans with slightly sloping or fluted sides have a different volume from pans with straight sides. Batter is usually added to a depth of no more than half to two-thirds of the pan because room must be left to allow the cake to rise.

The number of servings indicated is for a 2- or 3-layer cake; yield depends upon the richness and the size of the pieces.

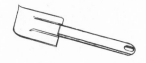

Pan shape and size	Maximum cups fluid to full pan capacity	Maximum cups batter for pan (allowing for rise)	Approximate number of servings
ROUND LAYERS			
6 × 2 inches	4	2 to 2½	6
8 × 1½ or 8 × 2	4½ to 5	2	8 to 10
9 × 1½ or 9 × 2	6 to 6½	3 to 3½	8 to 10
10 × 2	10	4½ to 6	14
12 × 2	14	7½ to 9	22
14 × 2	19½	10 to 12	36 to 40
SQUARE LAYERS			
8 × 2	8	3½ to 5	9 to 12
9 × 1½	8 to 9	4½ to 5	9 to 12
9 × 2	10	5½	9 to 12
10 × 2	12⅓	6	20
12 × 2	16	10 to 12	36
14 × 2	24	12 to 14	42
OBLONG (SHEET CAKES)			
8 × 12 (7½ × 11¾ × 1¾)	8	4 to 5	12
9 × 13 (8¾ × 13½ × 1¾)	16	8 to 9	20 to 24
11 × 17 (11⅜ × 17¼ × 2¼)	25	14 to 15	24 to 30
10½ × 15½ × ½ to 1 (jelly-roll pan)	10	4 to 5 for butter cake or 8 for genoise	35
HEART			
9 × 1½	5	3 to 3½	16
TUBE, RING, BUNDT, KUGELHOPF			
9 × 2¾ plain tube	6 to 7	4 to 4½	8 to 10
9 × 2 springform tube	9 to 10	6 to 7	10 to 12
9¼ × 3¼ fluted tube or Bundt	9 to 10	5 to 6	10 to 12
9½ × 3¾ or 10-inch plain tube or springform	12	6 to 7	12 to 14

Pan shape and size	Maximum cups fluid to full pan capacity	Maximum cups batter for pan (allowing for rise)	Approximate number of servings
9 × 4 kugelhopf	10	5 to 6	10 to 12
9¾ × 4¼ kugelhopf	12	6 to 7	12 to 14
10 × 3½ Bundt	12	6 to 7	14
10 × 4 angel cake	16	8 to 8½	12 to 14
. . . .			
LOAVES			
5½ × 3 × 2⅛ (baby)	2¼	1½ to 1¾	6 to 8
5¾ × 3½ × 2 or 6 × 3½ × 2 (baby)	2 to 2¼	1¼ to 1½	6 to 8
7½ × 3½ × 2	5 to 6	3	7 to 8
8½ × 4½ × 2¾ (average)	5¼	3½ to 3¾	7 to 8
9 × 5 × 3 (large)	8 to 9	4 to 5	9 to 10
. . . .			
SOUFFLÉ MOLDS			
6½-inch base, 3¼-inch height	6	4 to 5	8
7½-inch base, 3¾-inch height	8	6 to 7	10
. . . .			
COFFEE CANS			
4-inch diameter, 5½-inch height (1-pound size)	4	2 to 3	7 to 8
. . . .			
CUPCAKES			
1¾ × ¾ (baby)	4 teaspoons	3 teaspoons	1
2 × 1⅛ (mini)	3 tablespoons	2 tablespoons	1
2½-inch diameter	4 tablespoons	2½ tablespoons	1
2¾-inch diameter	½ cup	¼ cup	1
3 × 1¼	½ cup	5 tablespoons	1
3½-inch diameter	1 cup	generous ¾ cup	1

How to Prepare Pans for Baking

To PREVENT CAKE batters from sticking to pans during baking, most pans are specially coated or lined. From the time of the ancient Egyptians to the early nineteenth century, beeswax was commonly used for this purpose, as was oil of various types. Beeswax was preferred, because oil could turn rancid and impart off-flavors to cakes. Butter, of course, was often used, and in the 1880s vegetable shortening was introduced, providing another alternative.

Pans should be prepared before you mix your batter, so that, once made, the cake can be placed directly into the oven. If a whipped batter must stand around while you prepare the pans, volume may be lost as the batter deflates.

Pans for shortening or butter cakes are greased with shortening and flour; pans for chocolate butter cakes are greased with shortening, then dusted with sifted cocoa powder instead of flour; the cocoa powder works well and gives a browner, less gray appearance to the surface of the baked chocolate layers. I like to use solid white vegetable shortening for greasing pans as it contains no water that may cause the batter to stick. Margarine and butter do contain water. Solid shortening also has the ability to withstand high temperatures without burning, and it films on the pan with ease, holding the coating (flour or cocoa) perfectly. I prefer to spread this shortening on the pans with my fingers to achieve a more even coating than I can with a piece of wax paper or paper towel, though these will work, as will a medium-stiff pastry brush.

To apply flour or cocoa, sprinkle a tablespoon, or more if the pan is large, over the greased surface, then rotate and tap the pan to let the powder coat all the bottom; turn the pan on edge and rotate it to coat the sides with powder. If adding powder to a greased tube pan, the only way to coat the greased tube properly is to sprinkle the powder on it with a small sifter or with your fingers. Turn the pan upside down over wax paper or over the sink and tap it sharply to remove excess powder.

When I am making many cakes at one time, I follow a professional baker's tip and mix up a blend of solid shortening and flour (4 parts shortening to 1 part all-purpose flour). I store this in a covered jar in a cool cupboard or in the refrigerator and apply it to my cake pans with a medium-stiff pastry brush. As an alternative, any odorless nonstick vegetable spray or Baker's Joy, which combines flour and oil in a spray, is fine for cake and muffin pan preparation.

Pans are not greased at all for angel-food cakes or some chiffon cakes. This is so the egg-white batter can cling to the sides of the pan as it rises; it would slide and fall if the pan were greased. Sponge cakes usually have a paper liner on the bottom for easy removal of the cake, but sometimes the sides are left ungreased, again so that the fragile egg-white batter can cling as it rises.

Pans with decorative shapes such as the Bundt, kugelhopf, and Turk's-head molds must be generously buttered and floured to prevent the batter from sticking in their patterned depressions. Spray vegetable coating is especially helpful for these decorative pans. Paper liners are often added on pan bottoms and sometimes also the sides, to prevent cakes from sticking. To hold

the liners in place, dab a little shortening on the pan sides before adding the paper.

To cut liners to fit your pans, see the diagrams that follow. For round and ring liners, hold a parchment paper sheet on top of the inverted cake pan with one hand while the other hand wields a sharp long-bladed knife held at roughly a 45-degree angle. Make long clean downward strokes against the bottom edge of the pan to trim the paper to an exact fit as you slowly rotate the pan (diagram a). A simpler way is to set the pan down on the paper and draw around it with a pencil; then cut out the paper disk (diagram b). If you will be baking many layers, cut out several disks at one time. My shortcut method is to set the pan and lining paper on protective stiff cardboard, then "draw" around the pan bottom with an X-Acto knife, cutting the shape in one step. Don't do this directly on a tabletop or you will mar the surface.

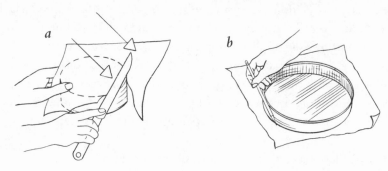

Pans for baking fruitcakes are often completely lined. The easiest way to line a rectangular loaf pan on the bottom and sides is to cut 2 long paper strips, a narrow strip to fit over the bottom and short ends and a wide strip to cover the sides and again cover the bottom. Overlap these strips in the greased pan (diagram a). Another method is to place the pan in the center of a piece of parchment or wax paper. Draw around the pan bottom (b), then tip the pan on its side and mark the side depth. Then tip the pan on its end and mark the end depth. Repeat for the other side and end. You now have two rectangles. Cut wedges out of each corner as shown (arrows, c), and fit the liner into the pan (d).

To line a tube pan, there are several choices, all easy. First, you can set the pan on a piece of parchment or wax paper and draw around the pan bottom. If possible, stick the pencil inside the tube and draw around its base; if you can't reach, hold the pan upside down and press the paper onto its base

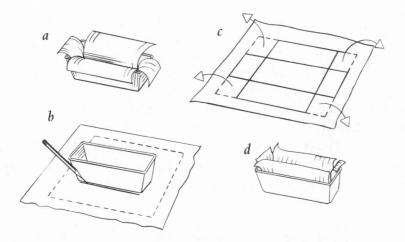

with your fingers to mark the outer and inner edges of the bottom surface (diagram e). Cut out this paper ring. Then measure the height of the pan side and the tube side and cut 2 paper strips, each slightly longer than the circumference of the pan or tube. Spread a little shortening on the inside surface of the pan. Fit both the side papers in place, overlapping them at the ends.

Note: If your tube pan has very sloping sides, cut a 1-inch-wide fringe in the side and tube strips. First position these strips with fringe facing the bottom, and overlap the fringe flaps as much as necessary to make the paper fit the slope (diagram f). Finally, add the bottom paper ring. If you must grease the paper liners, it is easiest to do so before putting them into the pan; stick them to the pan with a little grease. Dust with flour and tap very gently to remove the excess without loosening the papers.

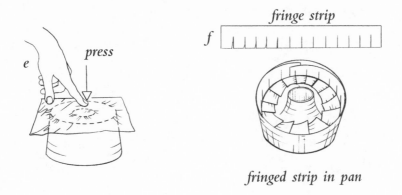

fringed strip in pan

To line jelly-roll pans, cut paper to fit, then anchor it to the pan with a few dabs of shortening. For ease in removing the cake, you can also cut the paper about 2 inches wider than the width of the pan and let 2 inches overhang at each short end. Grab these ends to lift the cake out of the pan. Peel off the paper after the baked cake is inverted.

Baking parchment does not have to be greased; wax paper should be greased and floured.

Cupcakes are baked in muffin tins. To prepare them for baking, line them with store-bought paper or foil muffin tin liners, coat them with solid shortening, or spray with nonstick vegetable coating.

BEFORE YOU BEGIN TO BAKE...

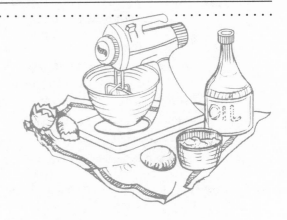

1. First, read the recipe all the way through to the end before starting. This helps you organize your ingredients, equipment, and time.

2. Before starting to bake, set out all the ingredients on the counter to see that you have everything. Bring ingredients to room temperature, approximately 68° to 70°F (about 21°C).

3. Put an auxiliary oven thermometer inside the oven baking chamber to monitor the heat. Preheat the oven at least 15 minutes before using it; never set cake batter into a cold oven; be sure the interior temperature is correct.

4. If you are planning to use whipped cream, place a bowl and beater into the freezer or refrigerator in advance so they will be well chilled when you need them.

5. Prepare (grease and flour) your baking pans before mixing the batter.

6. Set out cooling racks while the cake is baking so they are in place when needed.

7. Note that all measurements in this book are level.

8. All eggs are U.S. Grade A Large (2 ounces) and should be at room temperature before being blended into cake batter.

9. All butter used in this book is unsalted unless otherwise noted in the recipe.

10. The grated zest of an orange or lemon refers to the brightly colored part of the peel; except when making candied citrus peel, it is best to avoid the white pith beneath the zest because it can have a bitter flavor.

11. For reliable results, use the type of flour specified in the recipe (cake or all-purpose). Sift flour where specified. When unsifted flour is called for, measure it by the "scoop and sweep" method (page 51). When the recipe reads "1 cup sifted flour," it is sifted before measuring; if it reads "1 cup flour, sifted," it is sifted after measuring.

Granulated sugar is sifted only if lumpy. Confectioners' sugar is always sifted unless otherwise specified.

12. In most recipes, nuts are ground or chopped before measuring. Hence, ½ cup chopped walnuts (2 ounces; 60 g) means chopping, then measuring ½ cup nuts. When nuts are chopped *after* measuring, the recipe reads "½ cup nuts, chopped."

BASIC CAKE TYPES, TECHNIQUES, AND TERMS

. . . .

I HAVE DIVIDED the cakes in this book into two basic categories: shortening or butter cakes and non-shortening (sponge or foam) cakes. This determination is based upon the leavening, or rising method used; understanding the techniques involved in each will help you control the results.

Shortening or butter cakes • are the largest category of American cakes. These use either baking soda or baking powder for the primary leavening, with air as a secondary source. Of course, they contain a large amount of shortening (butter, margarine, oil, etc.) in proportion to the number of eggs used.

Cakes in this family include layer cakes, loaf and tea cakes, coffee cakes, pound cakes, fruitcakes, etc. There are specific methods for combining ingredients when making a butter cake (see pages 80–82).

CREAMING • is the basic technique common to cakes in this category. For butter cakes, one usually creams the butter or shortening and sugar together first. To do this by hand, use a wooden spoon and smooth the ingredients back and forth against the sides of the bowl, blending them together. Eventually the mixture will lighten in color, as air bubbles begin to mix into the fat and soften, smoothing out into a creamy, slightly fluffy paste. Some recipes ask you to "cream butter and sugar until light and fluffy"; however, they never really get fluffy, so do not feel you are missing something. Just look for a smooth, even blend. The mixture will be granular, because the sugar does not dissolve at this stage. If you are using an electric mixer, beat on medium-low speed so that many small bubbles will be created, with the fat opening up as the sugar crystals beat against it. Beating is slow at first to protect the fragile air cells; increase the speed gradually. Even though chemical leavening is added, the air cell structure must be protected as the batter is mixed. See Creaming Method, page 80.

BLENDING • is stirring or mixing ingredients until uniformly combined.

BEATING • is mixing rapidly to blend the ingredients. You can use a wooden spoon in a round-bottomed bowl, or an electric mixer, or an egg beater. Generally, in beating the purpose is not necessarily to increase the volume of air, as in whipping.

FOLDING • is a specific mixing method used for several jobs: adding whipped egg whites to a batter, adding whipped cream to a batter, or combining melted chocolate with whipped egg whites, for example. To fold, you must understand the first principle: be slow and gentle and protect every air bubble; do not deflate the volume of the whipped mixture while blending in the second ingredient. Use a large bowl and a rubber spatula. Begin by adding a small amount of the whipped ingredient to the heavier mass and stir very lightly until they are of similar texture. In several additions, add remaining ingredients, holding the bowl with one hand and the spatula with the other. Cut the spatula down through the center of the mixture, turn it, and draw it up along the side of the bowl. Give the bowl a quarter turn. Again cut down through the center of the mixture, right down to the bottom, then up and over the top, turning the spatula upside down as it comes over the top. Repeat. Never stir, never push the spatula from side to side. Simply turn it over and over in a light up-down motion, cutting through the mass to blend it gently.

KNEADING • is a technique reserved for yeast doughs. In this book, it is used for yeast-risen coffee cakes. Kneading means working the mass of dough in a specific pattern in order to develop the gluten in the flour and enable it to stretch and contain the carbon dioxide gas given off by the yeast as the bread rises.

To knead, set the dough out on a lightly floured work surface. Flour your hands. Fold the mass of dough in half toward you, then push it away while leaning on it with the heels of your hands. Give the dough a quarter turn and repeat the folding and pushing. Soon the flour will work itself into the dough as the mass turns inside out. Add a little more flour as necessary. Continue to fold and push the dough for 5 to 10 minutes, until it looks smooth and has a stretched, satiny skin that no longer feels sticky to the touch.

Non-shortening cakes • are leavened primarily with air whipped into the eggs, hence the name "foam cakes." This family includes sponge cakes, angel cakes, roulades, meringues, and flourless tortes. While many foam cakes contain no shortening, some sponge cakes and tortes do.

WHIPPING • is the primary technique for this type of cake. Whether whipping whole or separated eggs, or even cream, the important thing is to use a balloon whisk or beater. If whipping by hand, use a whisk in a large, deep bowl. Use generous arm motions, lifting the mass and carrying it up and down, incorporating as much air as possible into the mixture. Do not stir or mix from side to side, or you will deflate the air bubbles. With an electric mixer, use the whip-type beaters; begin on low speed to create a lot of tiny air cells; gradually increase the speed to whip as much air into the mass as possible. Beware, with cream, however, for overwhipping makes butter. Use a chilled bowl and beater to whip cream quickly. Whipping egg whites requires an immaculately clean bowl and beaters.

· ·

IN THE HEAT of the oven chemical reactions take place that transform the thick liquid batter into a cake with a light-textured crumb. It looks like magic, and partly it is, but the basics are understandable.

Oven heat causes flour and other starches to absorb moisture from the batter and begin to swell. Proteins in the flour, starch, eggs, and milk coagulate and set; starch gelatinizes. Heat causes the liquids in the batter to boil and make steam, which expands. The air bubbles beaten into the fats and coated with sugar and eggs also expand from the heat, as does air in egg foams or stiffly beaten egg whites. This expansion pushes up the batter, causing the cake to rise. Also, the moisture and heat cause chemical leaveners such as baking soda and baking powder to release carbon dioxide gas, which expands and rises, further pushing up the batter.

Finally, the risen batter sets into a firm shape while the sugars continue to cook and darken the color of the cake's surface.

Metal pans absorb heat quickly and retain it; therefore, the batter touching the pan walls will heat and set before the inner areas; hot spots in the oven can overbake or even burn some sections of the cake before others are heated through. Occasionally, cake pans must be turned during the baking process to ensure even heating. If it is hard to control your oven temperature, you may want to put a cookie sheet beneath the cake pan to deflect the heat, or wrap a heat insulating pad (sold in specialty stores for this purpose) around the sides of your cake pan.

Most cakes are baked at a temperature between 325° and 375°F (165° to 190°C). The most common temperature is 350°F (175°C). These temperatures are sufficiently high to cause steam and gas in the batter to expand and rise quickly and the batter texture to set, holding the rise. The cake bakes through evenly without drying out.

At a cooler temperature, the heating of the batter takes place too slowly, the rise is incomplete, and the cake dries out too much because it takes so long to bake through. In a very hot oven, the batter agitates excessively, the gases rise too quickly, and the cake may rise unevenly. Also the top and bottom of the cake will overbake before the inside has had time to cook through.

TO COOL BUTTER CAKES

As a general rule, baked cakes are left in their pans, set on a wire rack, for 5 to 10 minutes after coming from the oven. At this point, you can take a paring knife, or a long thin-bladed knife if the cake is deep, and run it between the side of the cake and the pan, to loosen the cake and to free any sticking crumbs. Top the cake with a wire rack or flat platter, and invert. Lift off the cake pan. If it sticks, tap it gently and try again. If you have used paper to line the pan bottom, peel it off the cake now, while the cake is warm. At this point, the cake is bottom up on the wire rack. It can be left this way to cool completely, or you may prefer to invert it once more so it cools top up (see diagram). The wire rack is used for cooling because it permits air to circulate beneath the cake, preventing condensation of moisture on the hot surface.

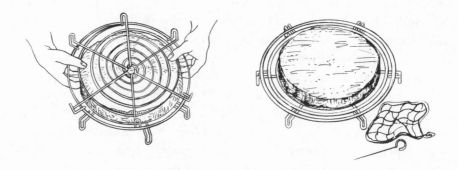

If you are planning to frost the cake with a thin icing in which the cake's own surface may show, you may prefer not to cool the cake on a wire rack because it sometimes leaves indentations in the cake. Instead, you can sprinkle granulated sugar onto baking parchment, wax paper, or foil set on the counter and invert your cake layer directly onto that. The sugar will prevent the cake from sticking to the paper while it also absorbs any moisture from condensation. The cake will remain perfectly flat as it cools.

TO COOL SPONGE, ANGEL-FOOD, AND CHIFFON CAKES

ANGEL-FOOD, CHIFFON, and most sponge cakes are leavened primarily with air. Lacking chemical leaveners or fats to support their delicate structures, they would shrink or collapse if left right side up to cool. To prevent this, they should be inverted immediately after coming from the oven and hung upside down until completely cooled. The easiest way to do this is to bake the cake in a tube pan that has "feet" on the rim that will raise the inverted cake above the countertop. If your pan has no feet, invert the pan over a funnel or tall bottle for several hours, until the cake is thoroughly cold. Then slide a sharp long-bladed knife between the cake and the pan side to free any sticking crumbs. Work the knife gently between the cake and the tube as well. Top the cake with a platter and invert it. Lift off the pan sides, then the removable pan bottom. See About Angel-Food Cakes (page 242) and About Chiffon Cakes (page 252).

Butter and/or Shortening
CAKES

ABOUT BUTTER AND/OR SHORTENING CAKES

CAKES MADE WITH butter or shortening are the most popular and widely known American cakes. They are our classics, the cakes familiar since our childhood birthday parties, beloved for their moist sweet crumb and high-stacking layers filled and frosted with buttercreams.

A well-prepared butter cake is moist and fine-grained with an even texture. Sometimes it is dense (pound cake), other times light (layer cake), but it always has tiny, evenly distributed air holes and a delicate crumb.

Some butter cakes are so moist they defy icing and require only the faintest sifting of confectioners' sugar for presentation. Compared to sponge cakes, butter cakes have a fairly firm texture and hold their shape well; they can be baked into any shape in any type pan from a Bundt to a bunny mold. Cakes in this category include basic 2-, 3-, and 4-egg cakes; the nineteenth-century 1-2-3-4 Cake; a vast array of layer and sheet cakes, including traditional white, yellow, and chocolate as well as many less common varieties; Bundt and tube cakes; coffee cakes and kuchens; tea cakes and loaf cakes; pound cakes, fruitcakes, and upside-down cakes.

Butter or shortening cakes are distinguished from other types of cake by the fact that they contain a large amount of fat in relation to the number of eggs used. Success with these cakes depends upon understanding how to incorporate ingredients correctly to achieve a perfectly creamy batter with good aeration. Butter cakes are leavened by whipping air into the batter and by adding baking powder or baking soda; only true pound cakes use no baking powder.

Because fat is the essential ingredient here, it is critical to select the best one for your purposes. Read about Fats (page 26). For the best creaming properties plus the best flavor, you can combine butter and solid shortening, up to half of each, in in preference to only shortening.

The basic rule for these cakes is to select the correct mixing method to suit the fat used (creamed method for butter, combination or blending method for softer fats). Always grease and flour cake pans. Bake cakes in the preheated oven as soon as the batter is set into the pans. Layer or sheet cakes are baked in the lower third of the oven; taller cakes with thicker quantities of batter (pound cakes, fruitcakes, and tube cakes) need less direct heat and a slower, more even temperature. They are baked in the center of the oven.

There are three traditional methods of mixing butter or shortening cakes: creaming, combination, or blending. In all methods it is essential for all ingredients to be at room temperature, approximately 70°F (21°C), in order to blend properly.

CREAMING METHOD • Butter, margarine, or shortening is creamed together with the sugar until light and smooth. During this process, sugar crystals cut into the fat, opening holes that are enlarged and multiplied as beating continues, creating small air bubbles surrounded by fat and sugar. The fat must be warm and pliable enough to wrap around the air bubbles; if the fat is too cold, the bubble walls will be brittle and will burst; if too warm, the fat may melt. In both cases air, and therefore volume, is lost.

Beating is begun on medium-low speed to prevent excessive friction damaging the fragile air bubbles as they are formed. As more ingredients are added and the cell walls strengthen, the speed can be increased. Work up to medium speed, but avoid the highest speed, as it may break down the air cells. Anything that breaks down the number and buildup of air cells results in loss of volume and a less leavened, somewhat heavier cake.

The curdling of batter, which sometimes results when eggs are added to creamed butter and sugar, also causes loss of air and volume. However, this is not exactly fatal, so don't panic if it occurs. In fact, curdling is unavoidable in some batters, and is so noted in those recipes. To prevent it, eggs are always added slowly to the creamed butter-sugar mixture. Ideally, whole eggs are lightly beaten first, then very slowly dripped into the creamed mixture while the beater runs on low speed. Or unbeaten whole eggs, or just yolks, can be added one at a time, with beating after each addition. This is done because the yolk contains all the fat of the egg; during beating this fat clings to the surface of the air cells, allowing them to expand and hold the cake's liquids. The category of liquids includes egg whites as well as milk or juice. When eggs are added too fast, or liquid is added all at once, the batter curdles because more liquid has been added than the batter emulsion can absorb at once. When eggs are beaten in a little at a time, as in a mayonnaise, the fat in the yolk is slowly incorporated into the emulsion and it does not break down or curdle. If you do see the batter begin to curdle, hold back the eggs and beat the mixture faster to smooth it out before adding more eggs.

After incorporating the eggs, the sifted dry ingredients are usually added alternately with the room temperature liquid. You begin and end with the flour mixture, the better to bind the batter together. Adding these ingredients alternately helps prevent curdling and keeps the batter light and creamy.

While the creaming can be accomplished with an electric mixer, many bakers swear by the old-fashioned method of hand beating. They willingly forgo the speed and ease of electricity in order to have complete control over the texture of the batter. I appreciate the theory and vote for electricity.

COMBINATION METHOD • This is used when the creamed ingredients are to be combined with others that are whipped (for example, when whipped egg whites are added to a butter-sugar-egg-yolk batter). In this case, the whites are whipped in a separate bowl, then a small amount of the whites is stirred into the heavier and stiffer creamed batter to lighten it. Finally, remaining whites are gently folded into the batter. Combination method cakes sometimes use baking powder to supplement the leavening action of the air whipped into the egg whites.

BLENDING OR ONE-BOWL METHOD • This is the quickest and easiest method: All the ingredients are simply combined in one bowl and beaten together. The temperature of the ingredients and the speed of the mixer are critical to this method, so follow the recipe guidelines carefully. The one-bowl method works best when the fat used is oil or solid vegetable shortening or butter that has been warmed (not melted) to the *pommade* stage.

Do not use cold butter; it will not blend properly with this technique. Eggs must be warm, at room temperature, for proper blending of the batter.

Baking powder or baking soda provides the principal leavening for the one-bowl technique because the fat here cannot be whipped up enough to hold sufficient air bubbles for leavening. Instead, the fat melts into the batter, marrying with all ingredients. This causes one-bowl cakes to be very moist, with a dense and close-grained texture. They are easy to make but never as light-textured as cakes made by the creaming method.

CHANGING METHODS • Many creamed or blended butter cake recipes that contain whole eggs can be changed, if you wish, to the combination method, whereby you separate the eggs and fold the stiffly whipped whites into the batter. This provides additional leavening and lightens the texture of the cake.

Troubleshooting

• *If the cake does not rise enough:* The fat was too cold or too warm, and did not incorporate a sufficient amount of air into the batter. Butter and shortening must be at approximately 70°F to be flexible enough to surround and trap air bubbles in the batter.

• *If the cake sinks or rises unevenly:* The eggs and liquid were too cold. If straight from the refrigerator, they can cause the creamed butter surrounding the air cells to chill, solidify, and crack, letting out the air. Similarly, hot liquids will melt the fat around the air bubbles and destroy the aeration. Either of these problems breaks the emulsion, causes curdled batter, and results in a loss of volume and lightness in the baked cake. Baking powder added to the batter helps prevent disasters but will not stop them entirely if all air is lost. Beating technique also affects rising of the cake. Note that especially in the early stages of mixing, creaming the butter and sugar at too high a speed on the electric mixer can break down air cells from excess friction.

• *If the cake collapses or sinks in the center:* It contains too much baking powder or baking soda or was overbeaten and became overaerated.

LAYER AND SHEET CAKES

Basic 1-2-3-4 Cake

A nineteenth-century classic that forms the basis for many of today's recipes, this is a light, moist, flavorful vanilla layer cake. It is easy to remember (1 cup butter, 2 cups sugar, 3 cups flour, 4 eggs), simple to prepare, and foolproof, so it was one of the first cakes taught to beginning bakers. According to James Beard's *American Cookery* (Little Brown and Co., 1972), the cake was originally made in a loaf and contained no liquid. Its popularity was due to the ease of remembering the measurements and the fact that, in the days before standardized measuring utensils were common, one could use the same cup for measuring all ingredients and ensure repeatable success.

You can add your own touches to personalize the cake. Our suggestions, which follow, include Basic Yellow, Coconut, Orange, Lemon, Almond, Spice, and Rocky Mountain Cake. Top the basic cake with your favorite icing.

Note: For the lightest texture, follow the recipe as written, separating the eggs and beating the whites stiff. For an even simpler method with just a slightly more compact texture, you can beat in whole eggs in place of the yolks, omitting the stiffly beaten whites.

Advance Preparation The cake can be made in advance, wrapped airtight, and frozen. Thaw before frosting.

Special Equipment Two 8- or 9-inch round cake pans or one sheet pan 13 × 9 × 1¾ inches, wax paper, extra bowl and beater for beating egg whites

Baking Time 30 to 35 minutes at 350°F (175°C) for layers, slightly longer for sheet

Quantity 5¾ cups batter with stiffly beaten whites added; 5 cups batter with whole eggs beaten in; one 2-layer 8- or 9-inch cake (serves 8) or one sheet cake 9 × 13 inches (serves 12)

Pan Preparation Spread solid shortening all over the bottom and sides of the pans, then dust evenly with flour; tap out excess flour.

3 cups sifted all-purpose flour (12¾ ounces; 360 g)
1 tablespoon baking powder
½ teaspoon salt
1 cup unsalted butter (2 sticks; 230 g), at room temperature
2 cups granulated sugar (14 ounces; 400 g)
4 large eggs, separated (see Note, page 83)
1 cup milk
1 teaspoon vanilla extract

1. Prepare pans as described. Position shelf in lower third of oven. Preheat oven to 350°F (175°C).

2. Sift together flour, baking powder, and salt. Set aside.

3. In the large bowl of an electric mixer, beat the butter until soft and smooth. Add the sugar and beat until light and smooth. Add egg yolks, one at a time, beating after each addition. Stop the mixer and scrape down the sides of the bowl and the beaters several times.

4. With the mixer on low speed, alternately add the flour mixture and milk, beginning and ending with flour. Stir in the vanilla. At this point, add any personal flavoring touches (grated lemon zest, coconut, etc.).

5. In another bowl, with a clean beater, beat the whites until stiff but not dry. Stir about ½ cup of whites into the batter to lighten it, then fold in remaining whites in several additions.

6. Divide the batter evenly between the pans. Smooth the batter level, then spread it slightly from the center toward the edges of the pan so it will rise evenly. Bake 30 to 35 minutes, or just until a cake tester comes out clean and the cake tops are lightly springy to the touch.

Cool the cakes in their pans on a wire rack for 10 minutes. Top with a wire rack and invert; lift off pans. Completely cool layers before frosting. Or you can leave a sheet cake in its pan to cool, and frost and serve it from the pan.

Basic Yellow Cake   Prepare Basic 1-2-3-4 Cake but use 5 eggs; do not separate them. Add whole eggs in step 3. Increase milk to 1¼ cups.

Coconut Cake   Prepare Basic 1-2-3-4 Cake but in step 3 stir in 1 cup shredded sweetened coconut and ¾ teaspoon coconut extract. Frost cake with Coconut Icing (see page 390).

Orange Cake   Prepare Basic 1-2-3-4 Cake but replace milk with orange juice. In step 3, stir in grated zest of 1 orange. Bake the cake in a 10-inch tube pan, greased and floured. Ice cake with Orange Wine Icing (page 395).

Lemon Cake   Prepare Basic 1-2-3-4 Cake but in step 3 stir in 1 teaspoon lemon extract and 2 teaspoons grated lemon zest. Ice cake with Lemon Buttercream (page 382).

Almond Cake   Prepare Basic 1-2-3-4 Cake but in step 3 add 1 teaspoon almond extract along with the vanilla. Ice with your favorite icing, but press toasted sliced almonds into the icing around the sides.

Spice Cake   Prepare Basic 1-2-3-4 Cake, but add and sift with dry ingredients 1½ teaspoons ground cinnamon; ½ teaspoon each of ground nutmeg, allspice, ginger, and cloves; 1 tablespoon sifted unsweetened cocoa.

Rocky Mountain Cake   Prepare Basic 1-2-3-4 Cake but fill and frost with Rocky Mountain Icing (page 403).

Two-Egg White Cake

*his was the first cake I ever made more or less by myself, and I can still recall the pleasure and pride I felt at age seven, when I served the slightly uneven, probably overbaked layers to my parents. Flushed with success, I made it repeatedly, in endless variations including orange and nut, which were my favorites.

The cake, also called a One-Bowl Cake, is still easy enough for a child to make and very good to eat. Frost with the icing of your choice. Variations follow for Light Two-Egg Cake, Berry Cake, Easy Nut Cake, and Marble Cake.

Advance Preparation The cake can be made in advance, wrapped airtight, and frozen. Thaw before frosting.

Special Equipment Two 7- or 8-inch layer pans or one 9-inch (6-cup capacity) tube pan, wax paper

Baking Time 20 to 25 minutes at 350°F (175°C)

Quantity About 3¼ cups batter; one 2-layer small 7- or 8-inch cake (serves 8) or one 9-inch ring (serves 8)

Pan Preparation Spread solid shortening all over bottom and sides of pan(s), then dust evenly with flour; tap out excess flour.

1¾ cups sifted cake flour (6 ounces; 170 g)
2 teaspoons baking powder
½ teaspoon salt
⅓ cup unsalted butter (5⅓ tablespoons; 80 g), at room temperature
1 cup granulated sugar (7 ounces; 200 g)
2 large eggs, lightly beaten, at room temperature
½ cup milk
2 teaspoons vanilla extract

1. Prepare pan(s) as described. Position shelf in lower third of oven. Preheat oven to 350°F (175°C).

2. Sift onto wax paper the flour, baking powder, and salt. Set aside.

3. In the large bowl of an electric mixer, cream together butter and sugar until well blended. Stop mixer and scrape down sides of bowl and beater several times. Add beaten eggs, a little at a time, mixing well after each addition.

4. Stirring by hand or with mixer on low speed, alternately add flour mixture and milk to batter, beginning and ending with flour. Stir in vanilla.

5. Turn batter into prepared pan(s). Smooth batter level, then spread it slightly from the center toward the edges of the pan so it will rise evenly. Bake for 25 to 30 minutes, or until a cake tester inserted in the center comes

out clean and the cake top is golden brown and springy to the touch.

Cool the cake in its pan(s) on a wire rack for 10 minutes. Top each layer with a rack and invert; lift off pan. Cool cake completely on the rack. Frost when cold.

· ·

Light Two-Egg Cake   Prepare Two-Egg White Cake, but separate the eggs and beat the whites until stiff but not dry. Beat the yolks into the creamed butter and sugar. After combining dry ingredients, milk, and vanilla, fold in the beaten whites. Bake as directed.

Berry Cake   Prepare Two-Egg White Cake, with the following changes: prepare a sheet pan 11¾ × 7½ × 1¾ inches (8½-cup volume). Pick over, wash, and hull a generous ½ cup fresh berries (raspberries, huckleberries, or blueberries, for example). Toss berries lightly with ¼ cup of the measured flour. Prepare batter as directed, and fold the berries in at the end. Top the baked cake with a sifted-on layer of confectioners' sugar or sweetened whipped cream; garnish with whole berries.

Easy Nut Cake   Prepare Two-Egg White Cake, with the following changes: add ¾ cup chopped walnuts or almonds to the regular cake batter, folding in the nuts at the end. If using almonds, add ½ teaspoon almond extract to the batter along with the vanilla. Frost the cake with your favorite icing and garnish with halved or chopped nuts.

Marble Cake   Prepare Two-Egg White Cake, with the following changes: in the top pan of a double boiler set over hot, not boiling, water, melt 1½ ounces semisweet chocolate. Remove from heat, stir until smooth, and set aside to cool. After preparing the batter as directed, pour half of the batter into a second bowl. Stir the chocolate into one half, blending well. Put the batter into the prepared pan by alternating spoons of vanilla and chocolate batter. With a table knife, gently draw swirls through the batter to marbleize it slightly (don't touch pan bottom or sides with knife). Bake as directed. Frost with any rich chocolate icing.

Orange Velvet Cake

*M*y inspiration for this cake came from the 1941 edition of Fannie Merritt Farmer's *Boston Cooking-School Cook Book*. You will find this a reliable and easy-to-make recipe; the Lemon Velvet variation is equally delicious.

1½ cups sifted cake flour (5¼ ounces; 150 g)
½ cup sifted cornstarch (2¼ ounces; 65 g)
2 teaspoons baking powder
½ teaspoon salt
½ cup unsalted butter (1 stick; 110 g), at room
    temperature
1½ cups granulated sugar (10½ ounces; 300 g)
4 large eggs, separated, at room temperature
½ teaspoon orange extract
Grated zest of 1 large orange
½ cup freshly squeezed orange juice

GLAZE
½ cup freshly squeezed orange juice
2 tablespoons granulated sugar
Grated zest of 1 orange
1 tablespoon butter

ICING
Orange Wine Icing (page 395) or Orange
    Buttercream (page 382)

1. Prepare pan(s) as described. Position rack in lower third of oven. Preheat oven to 350°F (175°C).

2. Sift together dry ingredients. Set aside.

3. In the large bowl of an electric mixer, cream together the butter and sugar until light and smooth. Add the egg yolks, one at a time, beating after each addition. Beat in the orange extract and grated zest. Alternately add to batter the flour mixture and orange juice, beginning and ending with flour. Beat slowly to blend after each addition. Scrape down the sides of the bowl often.

4. In a clean bowl with a clean beater, beat the egg whites until stiff but not dry. Stir about 1 cup of whites into the batter to lighten it, then gently fold in remaining whites.

5. Turn batter into the prepared pan(s). Level the batter, then spread it slightly from the center toward the edges of the pan so it will rise evenly. Bake for 30 to 35 minutes, or until a cake tester inserted in the center comes out clean, and the top is golden and lightly springy to the touch.

6. While the cake bakes, prepare the orange glaze. Combine the ingredients in a small saucepan, bring to a boil, and stir to dissolve the sugar. Set the glaze aside, but warm it just before using.

When the cake is baked, set the pans to cool on a wire rack. With a bamboo skewer or 2-tine roasting fork, prick holes over the cake. With a pastry brush, paint the warm glaze all over the hot cake, wait a few minutes, and apply remaining glaze; if you have made 2 layers, divide glaze between them.

Cool the cake completely, top with another rack, invert, and lift off pan. Serve cake as is, or fill and frost with Orange Wine Icing made with orange juice instead of wine, or Orange Buttercream. Or, if the cake was baked in a sheet pan, leave it in the pan to cool, then frost and serve from the pan.

Advance Preparation The cake can be baked ahead, wrapped airtight, and frozen. The filled and frosted cake can also be frozen, but for no longer than a month without losing flavor.

Special Equipment Two 8- or 9-inch layer pans 1½ inches deep or one 9-inch tube pan (6½-cup capacity) or one sheet pan 11¾ × 7½ × 1¾ inches; extra bowl and beater for egg whites, grater, skewer or 2-tine fork, pastry brush

Baking Time 30 to 40 minutes at 350°F (175°C) for layers, slightly longer for tube or sheet pan

Quantity About 4½ cups batter; one 2-layer 8- or 9-inch cake, one 9-inch tube, or one sheet cake 11¾ × 7½ inches (serves 10 to 12)

Pan Preparation Spread solid shortening on bottom and sides of pan(s), then dust evenly with flour; tap out excess flour.

Lemon Velvet Cake   Prepare Orange Velvet Cake, but substitute lemon juice, grated zest of 2 lemons, and lemon extract for the orange flavoring. Use lemon juice and zest in the glaze as well. Ice with Lemon Glaze (page 408), or Orange Wine Icing made with lemon extract replacing orange.

Lane Cake

This famous Southern cake is also known as White Cake, Silver Cake, or Snow Cake because the batter is pure white. The recipe makes a 3-layer cake with a fine grain and a velvet texture. This is a fine recipe for wedding cakes or petits fours. Traditionally, Lane Cake is filled with Lane Cake Filling, a rich custardy fruit and nut mixture, and iced with Boiled Icing. This basic recipe is the foundation for several famous variations that follow, including Lady Baltimore Cake and White Mountain (Colorado) Cake. The recipe is also used for Checkerboard Cake (page 94).

Note: To make a 2-layer Lane Cake, simply halve the recipe and use 4 egg whites.

3¼ cups sifted cake flour (11½ ounces; 330 g)

3½ teaspoons baking powder

¼ teaspoon salt

8 egg whites (reserve yolks for filling), at room temperature

2 cups granulated sugar (14 ounces; 400 g)

1 cup unsalted butter (2 sticks; 230 g), at room temperature

2 teaspoons vanilla extract

1 cup milk

FILLING:
Lane Cake Filling (page 370)

ICING:
Boiled Icing (page 402)

1. Prepare pans as described. Position shelf in lower third of oven. Preheat oven to 375°F (190°C).

2. Sift together the flour, baking powder, and salt onto a sheet of wax paper. Set aside.

3. In a large mixing bowl, whip egg whites until foamy, then add 2 tablespoons of the measured sugar and whip until nearly stiff but not dry. Remove bowl from mixer and set aside. Scrape whites from beaters into bowl. Without washing beaters, return them to the mixer.

4. In another large bowl, use the mixer to beat butter until soft. Add remaining sugar, and cream with the butter until completely blended to a smooth granular paste. Beat in vanilla.

5. With mixer on low speed, or mixing by hand, alternately add flour mixture and milk to butter-sugar mixture, beginning and ending with flour.

With rubber spatula, give whipped whites several gentle folds to be sure they are amalgamated. Gradually fold whites into the batter, using a light touch.

6. Divide batter evenly among the prepared pans. Smooth batter level, then spread it slightly from the center toward the edges of the pan so it will rise evenly. Arrange pans on one shelf in a triangular pattern and bake for 20 to 25 minutes, or until a cake tester inserted in the center of each layer comes out clean and the cake is lightly springy to the touch. Cool the layers in their pans on a wire rack for 10 minutes. Top with a wire rack and invert; lift off pans. Completely cool cake on the rack.

7. Dab a little icing in the center of a cardboard cake disk, then add the first cake layer. Top with Lane Cake Filling, add second layer and more filling. Top with third layer. Use Boiled Icing to frost the cake sides and top.

Advance Preparation   The cake can be made in advance, wrapped airtight, and frozen. Thaw before frosting.

Special Equipment   Three 8-inch round pans, wax paper, 8-inch cardboard cake disk (optional)

Baking Time   20 to 25 minutes at 375°F (190°C)

Quantity   About 6 cups batter, one 3-layer 8-inch cake (serves 10 to 12)

Pan Preparation   Spread solid shortening on bottom and sides of pan, then dust evenly with flour; tap out excess flour.

Lady Baltimore Cake Prepare Lane Cake. Fill with Rocky Mountain Icing (page 403), a regular boiled icing with chopped pecans, figs, and raisins added, and frost with regular Boiled Icing (page 402). Garnish cake top with halved pecans and arrange fresh roses around the base of the platter for a gracious Southern presentation.

White Mountain Cake Also called Colorado Cake, this recipe is sometimes baked in 3 graduated pans that, when stacked, resemble a mountain. Prepare Lane Cake in 3 regular layers or 3 graduated tiers. Fill and ice with double recipe of Boiled Icing.

Lord Baltimore Cake

Lady Baltimore Cake is made with 8 egg whites, and Lord Baltimore was given his due with a cake made from the yolks. Culinary history is still unsure whether this famous pair of cakes was actually named for the third Lord Baltimore, sent from England in 1661 to govern the land that was to become Maryland. It is possible that because of his despotic and unpopular rule, the cake was named instead for the city given his name. In any event, both these cakes are now classics of the Southern baking repertoire.

This is an excellent all-purpose basic yellow cake, light in texture, with an open grain resembling that of a sponge cake. Tradition is divided about its presentation, so you can select the method you prefer. Bake the cake in 3 layers, fill it with Lord Baltimore Filling (Boiled Icing with macaroon crumbs and pecans) and frost it with Plain Boiled Icing (page 402). Or bake it in a tube pan and top it with brown sugar-flavored Seafoam Icing (page 397).

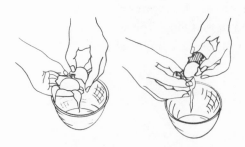

2½ cups sifted cake flour (8¾ ounces; 250 g)

1 tablespoon baking powder

½ teaspoon salt

¾ cup unsalted butter (1½ sticks; 170 g), at room temperature

1¼ cups granulated sugar (8¾ ounces; 250 g)

8 large egg yolks, at room temperature

¾ cup milk

½ teaspoon lemon extract

1 teaspoon grated lemon zest

FILLING AND ICING

Double recipe Boiled Icing, Lord Baltimore variation (page 403)

1. Prepare pan(s) as described. Position shelf in lower third of oven. Preheat oven to 350°F (175°C).

2. Sift together flour, baking powder, and salt onto a sheet of wax paper. Set aside.

3. In the large bowl of an electric mixer, beat the butter until soft. Add the sugar and cream with the butter until completely blended. In another bowl, beat the egg yolks until thick and lemon-colored. Slowly beat the yolks into the butter-sugar mixture.

4. By hand with a spoon or with electric mixer on lowest speed, alternately add flour mixture and milk to batter, beginning and ending with flour. Stir in lemon extract and lemon zest.

5. Divide batter between the prepared pans. Smooth it level, then spread it slightly from the center toward the edges of the pan so it will rise evenly. Bake in the preheated oven for 20 to 25 minutes, or until the top is lightly springy to the touch and a cake tester inserted in the center comes out clean. Cool the cake in its pan(s) on a wire rack for 10 minutes. Top with another rack and invert; lift off pans. Cool completely on the rack.

Advance Preparation The cake can be made in advance, wrapped airtight, and frozen. Thaw before filling and frosting.

Special Equipment Three 8- or two 9-inch layer pans or one 9-inch tube pan (6½-cup capacity), sifter, extra mixing bowl, wax paper, grater, 8- or 9-inch cardboard cake disk (optional)

Baking Time 20 to 25 minutes at 350°F (175°C) for layers, slightly longer for tube pan

Quantity 4½ cups batter; one 3-layer 8-inch cake or 2-layer 9-inch cake or one 9-inch tube cake (serves 10 to 12)

Pan Preparation Spread solid shortening all over the bottom and sides of the pan(s), then dust evenly with flour; tap out excess flour.

6. Fill and frost cake: Set a dab of icing in the center of a cardboard cake disk or use a serving platter with several wax paper strips between cake and plate to protect the plate edges from icing (see page 429). Spread fruited icing on the bottom layer, top with another cake layer, add more fruited icing. Top with final cake layer, align the layers neatly. Finally, coat the sides *and* top with reserved plain icing.

Checkerboard Cake

𝒯he checkerboard cake is a neat trick: 3 layers of alternating chocolate and vanilla rings that make a checkerboard pattern when stacked and sliced. Special gadgets for dividing the rings of batter are sold in cookware shops (see Sources, page 477) but they are not necessary; you can get the effect almost as neatly simply by carefully spooning or piping the batter into rings in plain round pans. Use a fairly thin layer of icing between the layers so the checkerboard pattern is not interrupted.

FILLING AND ICING
Any chocolate or vanilla buttercream (see Index)
(*not* Lane Cake Filling)

CAKE
Lane Cake (page 90), plus 3½ tablespoons
    unsweetened cocoa, preferably Dutch-process,
    and ¼ teaspoon baking soda as directed below

Prepare the cake as directed with the following changes:

1. After completing the batter in step 5, remove half of the batter to another bowl. Sift the cocoa and baking soda into the second bowl of batter and fold them together lightly to blend, making an even chocolate color.

2. Arrange the batter in the greased and floured pans as follows: In one pan, spoon a 1½-inch-wide ring of chocolate batter around the outside edge, nearly half the depth of the pan. Alongside this ring, spoon a 1½-inch-wide ring of white batter of the same depth. Fill the center with a circle of chocolate batter of the same depth (diagram a). Make a second pan in exactly the same pattern (chocolate, white, chocolate). In the third pan, spoon white batter in the outside ring, chocolate next, and white in the center (diagram b). Bake the layers as directed for 20 to 25 minutes, cool for 10 minutes, then invert onto wire racks to cool completely.

3. Prepare the icing of your choice. Dab a little icing on a cardboard cake disk and set down one of the cake layers with the outer chocolate ring. On top of this spread a fairly thin layer of icing. Add the cake layer with the

Advance Preparation Make Lane Cake batter (page 90) (preceding recipe).

Equipment Three 8- or 9-inch round pans or checkerboard cake pan set (see Sources, page 477); wax paper, scissors, 8- or 9-inch cardboard cake disk (optional)

Baking Time 20 to 25 minutes at 375°F (190°C)

Quantity About 6 cups batter; one 8- or 9-inch 3-layer cake (serves 8 to 10)

Pan Preparation See Lane Cake.

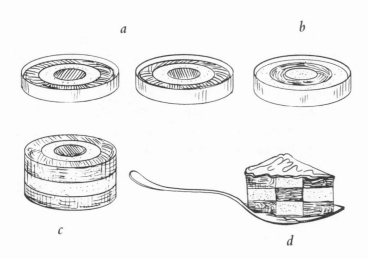

a   b

c   d

white outer ring, and top it with a fairly thin layer of icing and the second layer with the chocolate outer ring (diagram c). Finally, ice the cake sides and top with as much icing as you wish. When the cake is sliced, you will see the checkerboard pattern (diagram d).

Coconut Layer Cake

*T*his old-fashioned flavorful cake will remind you of childhood birthday parties. It is a romantic favorite for any special occasion, and looks especially pretty when the icing is topped with toasted coconut.

I used to prepare this recipe with fresh coconut but to save time now use canned coconut milk, packaged shredded coconut, and coconut extract, all available in supermarkets. Note that the cake batter includes *unsweetened* coconut milk (not Coco Lopez, a coconut cream, which contains too much sugar); the icing can, however, be made with the coconut cream. To fill the layers, you can use the icing as directed, or substitute orange marmalade, seedless raspberry preserves, or Lemon Curd (page 366) or Orange Curd (page 369).

CAKE

3 cups sifted cake flour (10½ ounces; 300 g)
1 tablespoon baking powder
½ teaspoon salt
4 large egg whites, at room temperature
2 cups granulated sugar (14 ounces; 400 g)
1 cup unsalted butter (2 sticks; 230 g), at room temperature
1 teaspoon vanilla extract
2 teaspoons coconut extract
1 cup canned *unsweetened* coconut milk
1 cup shredded sweetened coconut

FILLING AND ICING

1½ cups shredded sweetened coconut

24 ounces (three 8-ounce packages; 680 g) cream cheese (not low-fat), at room temperature

3 cups sifted confectioners' sugar (10½ ounces; 300 g)

1 tablespoon coconut extract

Pinch of salt

2 teaspoons white or dark rum (optional)

½ cup canned coconut milk (either unsweetened or sweet coconut cream, stirred well)

1. Prepare pans as described. Position racks dividing oven into thirds. Preheat oven to 350°F (175°C).

2. Sift together the flour, baking powder, and salt onto a sheet of wax paper.

3. Place the egg whites in the largest grease-free bowl of your electric mixer. With the mixer on medium speed, whip the whites until foamy, then gradually add ¼ cup of the sugar. Beat continuously, increasing speed slightly, until whites are stiff but not dry. They will look smooth and satiny, and the foam will make a peak that stands straight up on the beater tip. Remove the bowl from the mixer stand and set it aside. Scrape the beater into the bowl and return it, without washing, to the mixer stand.

4. With another bowl, use the same beater to cream together the butter, remaining 1¾ cups sugar, and both extracts. With the mixer on the lowest speed, alternately add the unsweetened coconut milk and the flour mixture just until well incorporated. Remove the bowl from the mixer stand, stir in about 1 cup of whipped whites to lighten the batter, then use a rubber spatula to fold in the remaining whites along with the well-crumbled shredded coconut.

5. Divide the batter between the prepared pans and bake for 35 to 37 minutes, or until the cake tops are a light golden color and start to pull away from the edges and a cake tester inserted in the cake center comes out clean.

Advance Preparation   Cake can be made in advance, wrapped airtight, and frozen. Thaw before frosting.

Special Equipment   Two 9-inch layer pans 1½ inches deep, serrated knife, 9-inch wax paper or baking parchment, cardboard cake disk covered in foil or flat platter

Baking Time   350°F (175°C) for 35 to 37 minutes

Quantity   6 generous cups batter; one 4-layer 9-inch cake (serves 10 to 12)

Pan Preparation   Spread shortening on bottom and sides of both pans, line bottoms with baking parchment or wax paper rounds cut to fit. Coat the papers with shortening and dust with flour; tap out excess flour.

Allow the layers to cool on a wire rack about 10 minutes, then run a knife between the cake sides and the pans, top each layer with a plate or wire rack, and invert, lifting off the pans. Allow layers to cool completely on the racks.

6. When the layers are cold, slice each one in half horizontally using a long-bladed serrated knife (see page 427). Stack the 4 layers, separated by pieces of foil or wax paper or baking parchment.

7. To make the filling and icing: First toast the coconut in a frying pan set over medium heat, stirring gently until coconut turns golden in color, about 5 minutes, then set aside to cool. With an electric mixer or food processor, blend together the cream cheese and sifted confectioners' sugar until completely smooth. Scrape down the bowl and beater. Add the extract, salt, rum if used, and coconut milk; beat smooth. Adjust sugar or liquid if needed to reach a smooth spreading consistency.

Note: Be sure the cake is completely cold before coating it with icing, or the heat will melt the cream cheese.

8. To assemble the cake: Place a dab of icing in the center of the foil-covered cardboard disk or serving plate. Set one layer, cut side up, on the disk. Spread it with about 1 cup of the icing, top with another layer, and repeat until all layers are used. Neatly align the cake sides. Spread icing over the cake sides, then the top.

Working over a piece of wax paper or a tray to catch spills, scoop up some of the toasted coconut into the palm of your hand and press it onto the cake sides; rotate the cake and repeat all the way around. Sprinkle remaining toasted coconut over the cake top. In hot weather, refrigerate the cake.

Peanut Cake

*T*his recipe—known locally as Goober Cake—was shared with me by a friend from Georgia, the leading state in peanut production. The peanut is native to South and Central America, and was eventually introduced into West Africa. During the seventeenth and eighteenth centuries, peanuts were exported from the West Coast of Africa to the American South. Africans who came to the area called the nuts *nguba,* Bantu for ground-nut, and goober became the Americanized corruption of this word. The peanut is not a true nut, but a member of the pea family, hence goober peas.

Children love the strong peanut flavor of this light-textured, fine-grained cake. It is a perfect choice for a Fall Harvest or Halloween party. Top the cake with Peanut Butter Icing and chopped peanuts.

2 cups unsifted all-purpose flour (10 ounces; 280 g)
2 teaspoons baking powder
½ teaspoon salt
Pinch of ground cinnamon
1 cup smooth peanut butter (9 ounces; 255 g),
    at room temperature
⅔ cup lightly salted butter (10⅔ tablespoons; 160 g),
    at room temperature
2 cups firmly packed dark brown sugar (18 ounces;
    510 g)
6 large eggs, at room temperature
2 teaspoons vanilla extract
¾ cup milk

ICING
Peanut Butter Icing (page 394) plus ½ cup dry-
    roasted peanuts (2½ ounces; 70 g), chopped

1. Prepare pan as described. Position shelf in lower third of oven. Preheat oven to 350°F (175°C).

2. Sift together flour, baking powder, salt, and cinnamon onto a sheet of wax paper. Set aside.

Advance Preparation   The cake can be made in advance, wrapped airtight, and frozen. Thaw before frosting.

Special Equipment   One sheet pan 9 × 13 × 2 inches, wax paper

Baking Time   40 to 45 minutes at 350°F (175°C)

Quantity   7 cups batter, one sheet cake 9 × 13 inches (serves 12)

Pan Preparation   Spread solid shortening over bottom and sides of pan, then dust evenly with flour; tap out excess flour.

3. In the large bowl of an electric mixer, cream together the peanut butter and butter. Slowly add the sugar, beating until creamy. Add the eggs, one at a time, beating after each addition. Beat in the vanilla.

4. With the mixer on lowest speed, alternately add flour mixture and milk to batter, beating after each addition, beginning and ending with flour.

5. Turn the batter into the prepared pan. Smooth the surface and spread it slightly from the center toward the edges of the pan so the cake will rise evenly. Bake in the lower third of the oven for 40 to 45 minutes, or until a cake tester inserted in the center comes out clean and the top is springy to the touch. Cool the cake completely in its pan on a wire rack. When it is cold, top with icing and sprinkle with chopped peanuts. Cut into 3-inch squares and serve from the pan.

Eggless Chocolate Cake

*T*his quick and easy-to-make egg-free chocolate cake is good for those on special diets. However, the flavor is intense and the cake delicious for anyone, anytime. Fill and frost with your favorite eggless icing (see Recipes for Special Needs, page 473). Note that the cake, though moist, tends to be fragile and slightly crumbly when freshly baked.

1⅔ cups sifted all-purpose flour (7 ounces; 200 g)

1 cup granulated sugar (7 ounces; 200 g)

¾ cup unsweetened cocoa, not Dutch-process
(2 ounces; 60 g), sifted

1 teaspoon baking soda

1 teaspoon salt

1 cup buttermilk (or sour milk made by adding
1 tablespoon white vinegar to whole milk and
letting stand for 5 minutes)

½ cup unsalted butter (1 stick; 110 g), melted and
cooled

2 teaspoons vanilla extract

1. Prepare pans as described. Position shelf in lower third of oven. Preheat oven to 375°F (190°C).

2. Place a sifter over the large bowl of the electric mixer. Add to it all the dry ingredients, and sift them into the bowl.

Mixing by hand or with an electric mixer on lowest speed, stir in the buttermilk, melted butter, and vanilla. Blend well. The batter will look like a thick brownie batter.

3. Divide batter between prepared pans. Smooth it level, then spread it slightly from the center toward the edges of the pan so it will rise evenly. Bake in the preheated oven for about 20 minutes, or until a cake tester inserted in the center comes out clean and the top of the cake is lightly springy to the touch.

Cool layers in their pans on a wire rack for 10 minutes. Top each layer with a second rack and invert; lift off pans. Cool cake on the rack. Frost when completely cool.

Advance Preparation   The cake can be made in advance, wrapped airtight, and frozen. Thaw before icing.

Special Equipment   Two 8-inch cake pans 1½ inches deep

Baking Time   20 minutes at 375°F (190°C)

Quantity   4 cups batter; one 2-layer 8-inch cake (serves 8)

Pan Preparation   Spread solid shortening over bottom and sides of pan, then dust evenly with unsweetened cocoa; tap out excess cocoa.

Anna's Swedish Butter Cake

$\mathcal{A}$nna Olson's Swedish Butter Cake has been a tradition in my family since Anna shared her recipe with my mother. Not only is it easy to make, but it is rich without being too sweet, has a fine tender crumb, and seems to taste better the longer it stands. In short, it is the perfect cake for every day, and every occasion. To serve with tea or coffee in the afternoon, we bake it in a tube pan and dust it lightly with confectioners' sugar, all the topping it really needs. For birthdays, we bake 2 heart-shaped layers and fill and frost them with buttercream. For weddings, this cake is ideal; it can be stacked in many tiers. Over the years, we have devised all sorts of variations, from chocolate to orange (see recipes following), but we always come back to Anna's original—plain almond butter cake; it is the best. My daughter proved this for us all when, at the age of eleven, she won two blue ribbons with this recipe for Best Cake at the Bridgewater, Connecticut, Firemen's Country Fair, and Best Butter Cake at the Goshen, Connecticut, 4-H Fair.

Note: As a young girl in Sweden, Anna learned to hand-mix this cake with a wooden spoon, and she steadfastly held to her preference for this method, which produces a rather dense texture. I use the electric mixer, which lightens the cake somewhat but does not detract in any way from its success.

Advance Preparation The cake can be baked in advance, wrapped airtight, and stored at room temperature for a week. It can also be frozen. One day after it is baked, the cake's flavors mellow to perfection and it is more easily sliced than when fresh from the oven.

Special Equipment One 9-inch tube pan (6½-cup capacity) or two 9-inch layer pans or one 8-inch-square pan 2 inches deep; large mixing bowl and wooden spoon, or electric mixer (preferably fitted with paddle attachment)

2 cups (8½ ounces; 240 g) plus 2 tablespoons sifted all-purpose flour

1 teaspoon baking powder

¼ teaspoon salt

1 cup lightly salted butter (not margarine) (2 sticks, 230 g), at room temperature

1½ cups granulated sugar (10½ ounces; 300 g)

2 large eggs, at room temperature

¾ cup milk

1 teaspoon almond extract (vanilla extract can be substituted)

Confectioners' sugar (optional)

1. Prepare pan(s) as described. Position rack in center of oven. Preheat oven to 350°F (175°C).

2. Sift together flour, baking powder, and salt onto a piece of wax paper. Set aside.

3. With a wooden spoon in a mixing bowl or with an electric mixer, cream together the butter and sugar until smooth and well blended. Add the eggs, one at a time, beating after each addition.

Alternately add the dry ingredients and milk, beating after each addition, beginning and ending with flour. Scrape down the sides of the bowl and the beaters. Stir in the almond or vanilla extract.

4. Spoon batter into the prepared pan(s), level the top, then spread the batter slightly toward the pan edges. Bake in the preheated oven for 55 to 60 minutes for a tube cake or 30 to 35 minutes for layers, or until the top is golden and a cake tester inserted in the center comes out clean.

Cool the cake in its pan(s) on a wire rack for about 10 minutes, then run a knife blade around the edge of the cake. Top with another rack or plate, invert, and lift off the pan(s). Cool the cake completely before sifting on confectioners' sugar or adding a frosting of your choice.

Baking Time   55 to 60 minutes at 350°F (175°C) for tube pan; 30 to 35 minutes for layers

Quantity   About 4½ cups batter, one 9-inch tube cake or one 2-layer 9-inch cake (serves 8). Recipe can be doubled or tripled.

Pan Preparation   Spread solid shortening on bottom and sides of pan(s), dust evenly with flour; tap out excess flour.

VARIATIONS

. . . .

Anna's Orange Butter Cake   Prepare Anna's Swedish Butter Cake, but add the grated zest of 1½ oranges and replace the milk with ¾ cup freshly squeezed orange juice. Use 1 teaspoon orange extract instead of almond or vanilla. Ice with Orange Buttercream (page 382) or Orange Glaze (page 408) or Orange Wine Icing (page 395).

Anna's Chocolate Butter Cake   Prepare Anna's Swedish Butter Cake, but replace ⅓ cup flour with ⅓ cup sifted unsweetened cocoa, preferably Dutch-process, and add ¼ teaspoon baking soda.

Chocolate Buttermilk Cake

*T*his is a marvelous old-fashioned chocolate fudge cake. In fact, of all the chocolate layer cakes in this book, this is my favorite, the one I invariably turn to for "Chocolate Cake Occasions," a special category in our family. The cake is moist, with a fine grain and excellent flavor. The tiny touch of nutmeg lends a barely detectable hint of spice, which enhances the chocolate. You can go even further (as I do) to create Double-Chocolate Cake by adding mini-chocolate chips to the batter.

Since it is loved equally by adults and children, this recipe is a perfect choice for family gatherings and birthday parties. It can be made equally well in cupcake tins, in a sheet pan, or in 2 layers. For a gala, you can split the 2 layers into 4, filling them with whipped cream, fresh raspberries, and shavings of semisweet chocolate. You can also use this cake as the basis for Black Forest Cherry Cake (see page 296).

Advance Preparation The cake can be made in advance, wrapped airtight, and frozen. Thaw before icing. Store iced cake in an airtight container.

Special Equipment Two 9-inch layer pans 1½ inches deep or one sheet pan 9 × 13 × 1½ inches, double boiler

Baking Time 40 to 50 minutes at 325°F (165°C) for sheet cake; 35 to 45 minutes for 2 layers

Quantity About 7 cups batter, one 2-layer 9-inch cake (serves 8); one sheet cake 9 × 13 inches (serves 12)

2 cups sifted all-purpose flour (8½ ounces; 240 g)
1½ teaspoons baking soda
¼ teaspoon salt
¼ teaspoon freshly grated nutmeg
4 ounces unsweetened chocolate (½ cup; 110 g)
1 cup unsalted butter (2 sticks; 230 g), at room temperature
1¾ cups granulated sugar (12¼ ounces; 350 g)
4 large eggs
1⅓ cups buttermilk
1 teaspoon vanilla extract

ICING

Seven-Minute Icing, Caramel Icing, or Chocolate Buttercream Icing. Or fill and frost with flavored whipped cream (page 342).

Note: If slicing cake into 4 layers, adjust icing quantities accordingly.

1. Prepare pan(s) as described. Position racks in lower third of oven. Preheat oven to 325°F (165°C).

2. Sift together the flour, baking soda, salt, and nutmeg. Set aside.

3. Melt the chocolate in the top pan of a double boiler set over hot, not boiling, water. Remove chocolate from heat, stir to make sure it is completely melted and smooth, then set aside to cool until comfortable to touch.

4. In the large bowl of an electric mixer, cream together the butter and sugar until well blended. Stop the mixer and scrape down the bowl and beaters several times. Add the eggs, one at a time, beating well after each addition.

5. With the mixer on low, add the flour mixture and buttermilk alternately to batter, beginning and ending with flour. Stir in the vanilla and cooled chocolate, blending until the color is even.

6. Turn the mixture into the prepared pan(s). Smooth it level, then spread it slightly from the center toward the edges of the pan so it will rise evenly. Bake in the lower third of the oven for 40 to 50 minutes for the sheet cake, 35 to 45 minutes for layers, or until the top is lightly springy to the touch and a cake tester inserted in the center comes out clean. Leave the cake in its pan(s) on a wire rack for 10 minutes. Top with a second rack and invert; lift off pan(s). Cool the cake completely on the rack. To split layers, use a serrated knife (see page 427). Fill and frost the layers. Or leave the sheet cake in its pan to cool, and frost and serve it from the pan, making 3-inch squares.

Pan Preparation Spread solid shortening on bottom and sides of pan(s), then dust evenly with unsweetened cocoa or flour; tap out excess cocoa or flour.

VARIATIONS

. . . .

Double-Chocolate Cake Prepare Chocolate Buttermilk Cake, but add 1 cup semisweet mini-chips (5½ ounces; 160 g), tossed together with 1 tablespoon of the flour mixture from step 2. Stir chips into batter after adding the melted chocolate.

Devil's Food Cake

I have been sorely tempted by Devil's Food Cake ever since I can remember, and for nearly that long I have wondered about its name. The very rich taste of the cake is not, as I suspected, the reason for the devilish reference; it is the color of the cake itself. The characteristically reddish color is caused by the baking soda used to neutralize the natural acidity of chocolate and at the same time leaven the cake. Baking soda has the effect of reddening and darkening certain types of cocoa.

It is important that a Devil's Food recipe specify the type of cocoa to be used, i.e., natural or Dutch-process (factory-treated with alkali; read about Chocolate, page 46). A soapy taste in the cake can be the result of an incorrect balance between the acidity of the chocolate and the quantity of baking soda.

This recipe follows the traditional method, using "natural" un-Dutched cocoa with baking soda. The result is a full-bodied, moist chocolate cake with excellent flavor.

Note: There are two different methods you can use for preparing this cake: the traditional method, as written, or the "dump and blend" quick method, which follows as a variation. They are completely opposite in technique, and produce slightly different results, but both work and taste good.

Advance Preparation   The cake can be made in advance, wrapped airtight, and frozen. Thaw before icing. Or ice with buttercream, chill, then wrap and freeze. Thaw, wrapped, in the refrigerator.

Special Equipment   Two 8-inch round pans 1½ inches deep or one sheet pan 11¾ × 7½ × 1¾ inches

Baking Time   30 to 35 minutes at 350°F (175°C)

2¼ cups sifted all-purpose flour (9½ ounces; 270 g)
1¼ teaspoons baking soda
¼ teaspoon salt
½ cup sifted regular unsweetened cocoa, not Dutch-process
½ cup unsalted butter (1 stick; 110 g), at room temperature
1½ cups granulated sugar (10½ ounces; 300 g)
2 large eggs, at room temperature
1 teaspoon vanilla extract
1½ cups buttermilk

ICING
Chocolate buttercream of your choice

1. Prepare pan(s) as described. Position rack in lower third of oven. Preheat oven to 350°F (175°C).

2. Have ingredients at room temperature. Sift together all dry ingredients and set them aside.

3. In the large bowl of an electric mixer, cream together the butter and sugar until well blended. Add eggs, one at a time, beating after each addition. Beat in vanilla. Alternately add flour mixture and buttermilk, beginning and ending with flour and beating slowly to blend after each addition.

4. Divide batter between the prepared pans. Level the top, then spread the batter slightly from the center toward the edges of the pan so it will rise evenly. Bake in the preheated oven for about 35 minutes, until a cake tester inserted in the center comes out clean and the cake feels lightly springy to the touch. Cool on a wire rack for 10 minutes. Run the tip of a knife around the edge of each layer to release it from the pan. Top with another rack and invert. Lift off pan. Cool completely before frosting.

Quantity   5 cups batter; one 2-layer 8-inch cake (serves 8)

Pan Preparation   Spread solid shortening on bottom and sides of pan(s), dust evenly with unsweetened cocoa powder or flour; tap out excess powder.

VARIATIONS

. . . .

"Dump and Blend" Quick Method: This gives a softer, more compact texture to the cake, with very tiny crumbs that melt in the mouth. The rise is the same as with the traditional method. Dump and Blend is literally that. Have all ingredients at room temperature. In the large bowl of an electric mixer, beat butter until soft, beat in sugar, dump in eggs and vanilla, sift on all dry ingredients, and pour in milk. Now, carefully beat on very low speed for 60 full seconds (KitchenAid mixer #2 speed). Scrape down inside of bowl. Beat on high speed for 3 full minutes (KitchenAid, #8), until batter is very light and fluffy. Scrape down inside of bowl. Bake as directed.

Marvelous Mud Cake

*D*ense, dark, moist, and addictive, this easy-to-prepare chocolate tube cake is my adaptation of Maida Heatter's 86-Proof Chocolate Cake (used with permission, from *Maida Heatter's Book of Great Chocolate Desserts,* Alfred A. Knopf, 1980). The original recipe uses bourbon for flavoring; rum, Amaretto, or Cognac are equally successful. This is a great dinner party cake because it is reliable to make and freeze in advance, yet it looks special and tastes heavenly with a dollop of whipped cream and a few fresh raspberries.

5 ounces unsweetened chocolate (½ cup plus
   2 tablespoons; 140 g), chopped
2 cups sifted all-purpose flour (8½ ounces; 240 g)
1 teaspoon baking soda
¼ teaspoon salt
¼ cup powdered instant coffee or instant espresso
1¼ cups hot water
½ cup bourbon, or rum, Amaretto, or Cognac
1 cup unsalted butter (2 sticks; 227 g), at room
   temperature
1 teaspoon vanilla extract
2 cups granulated sugar (14 ounces; 400 g)
3 large eggs plus 1 large extra yolk, at room
   temperature
¼ cup sour cream or buttermilk

OPTIONAL ICING:
Chocolate Water Glaze (page 414) or sifted
   unsweetened cocoa or confectioners' sugar

1. Prepare pan as directed. Position rack in center of oven. Preheat oven to 325°F (165°C).

2. Melt the chocolate in the top pan of a double boiler set over hot, not boiling, water. Remove chocolate before it is completely melted and stir until smooth. Set aside off heat.

3. Sift together flour, baking soda, and salt and set aside. In a 2-cup glass measure, dissolve the instant coffee in ¼ cup of the hot water, then stir in the remaining 1 cup water along with the bourbon or other flavoring.

4. In the large bowl of an electric mixer fitted with a paddle-type beater (if available), cream the butter with vanilla and sugar until well blended and smooth. Change to a whisk-type beater. Beat in eggs, one at a time, beating after each addition; beat in the extra yolk and sour cream or buttermilk. Scrape down the bowl and beater. Add melted and slightly cooled chocolate and beat until the batter is smooth.

5. Remove bowl from the mixer stand. By hand, using a spoon or rubber spatula, alternately stir in small amounts of the flour mixture and the coffee-bourbon liquid. Beat until batter is smooth. Don't worry if the batter looks slightly curdled or thin.

6. Pour the batter into the prepared pan. Bake in the center of the preheated oven for 65 to 70 minutes, or until the cake top is springy to the touch and slightly crackled looking, and a cake tester inserted in the center comes out clean. Do not overbake, or the cake will dry out.

7. Cool the cake on a wire rack for at least 20 minutes, then top with another rack or plate and invert. Lift off pan. Cool cake completely.

To serve, top with Chocolate Water Glaze or a light sifting of cocoa or confectioners' sugar. Or leave the cake unadorned. Serve with bourbon-flavored, slightly sweetened whipped cream (page 342) or vanilla ice cream. Or slide a cardboard cake disk underneath the baked and cooled cake, wrap airtight, and freeze.

Advance Preparation When wrapped in plastic wrap and stored in an airtight container, this cake keeps very well at room temperature for up to a week. It may also be frozen.

Special Equipment 9-inch (10-cup capacity) Bundt, kugelhopf, or tube pan; double boiler, 2-cup glass measuring cup, sifter, flat paddle for electric mixer if available

Baking Time 65 to 70 minutes at 325°F (165°C)

Quantity About 7 cups batter; one 9-inch tube cake (serves 18 to 20)

Pan Preparation Generously spread solid shortening inside pan, taking care to cover all indentations. Dust inside of pan with unsweetened cocoa or flour or fine dry unflavored bread crumbs; tap out excess.

Crazy Mixed-Up Chocolate Cake

This is the cake that beat the cake mix in our time tests, clocked at 4 minutes 35 seconds from measuring ingredients to popping the cake into the oven! Probably the oddest, quickest, and easiest cake in this book, it is known by many names: Three-Holes-In-One, Mix-In-Pan, and Crazy Cake, for example. All the names refer to the fact that the ingredients are simply dumped in the pan, stirred, and baked. The result is a surprisingly delicious, moist, eggless chocolate cake. Usually Crazy Cake is served without icing, but you can sift unsweetened cocoa on top, or confectioners' sugar, or add buttercream icing, or whipped cream and raspberries if you wish a more elegant presentation.

Advance Preparation   Cake can be baked ahead, wrapped airtight, and frozen.

Special Equipment   One sheet pan 13 × 9 × 1½ inches, mixing spoon, sifter

Baking Time   30 to 35 minutes at 350°F (175°C)

Quantity   5 cups batter; one sheet cake 13 × 9 inches (serves 20)

Pan Preparation   Although the pan is not greased, the cake pieces are easily removed when the cake is cut and served from the pan.

3 cups unsifted all-purpose flour (15 ounces; 425 g)
½ cup unsweetened cocoa, not Dutch-process
1 teaspoon salt
2 cups granulated sugar (14 ounces; 400 g)
2 teaspoons baking soda
2 tablespoons white or cider vinegar
2 teaspoons vanilla extract
⅔ cup vegetable oil
2 cups lukewarm water

TOPPING (OPTIONAL):
Confectioners' sugar or unsweetened cocoa

1. Position rack in center of oven. Preheat oven to 350°F (175°C).

2. Set the sifter in the baking pan. Into the sifter put the flour, cocoa, salt, sugar, and baking soda. Sift everything into the ungreased baking pan. (If you are really rushed, forget the sifter, just combine the ingredients and stir them together.)

Make 3 depressions in the dry mixture. Into one put the vinegar, in another the vanilla, and in the third, the oil. Pour the water over all, then stir gently with a spoon. Be sure to cover the entire pan bottom and go into the corners so no pockets of dry ingredients remain unmixed. Stir until creamy and smooth. Wipe off pan edges.

3. Place the pan in the preheated oven and bake for 30 to 35 minutes, until a cake tester inserted in the center comes out clean and the cake feels lightly springy to the touch. Cool completely in the pan set on a wire rack. Cut into squares and serve from the pan. If you wish, you can ice the top or dust it lightly with a sifting of confectioners' sugar or cocoa.

Carrot Cake

*T*his is a classic carrot cake, easy to prepare, nutritious, and everyone's favorite. It is very moist, not too sweet, and keeps well (if hidden). Serve it plain or topped with the traditional Cream Cheese Icing.

Note: This recipe may be prepared two ways, by the traditional mixing method or in the food processor. Instructions for both methods follow.

1 cup sifted all-purpose flour (4¼ ounces; 120 g)
1 teaspoon baking soda
½ teaspoon salt
2 large eggs, at room temperature
1 cup granulated sugar (7 ounces; 200 g)
¾ cup vegetable oil
1 tablespoon vanilla extract
1 teaspoon ground cinnamon
½ teaspoon ground nutmeg
4 to 5 raw carrots, peeled and grated to make
    1½ cups (6 ounces; 170 g)
¾ cup canned crushed pineapple, drained well
    (optional)
1½ tablespoons toasted wheat germ
    (optional)
½ cup walnuts (2 ounces; 60 g), chopped

ICING
Cream Cheese Frosting (page 387)

Advance Preparation The cake can be baked ahead, wrapped airtight, and frozen. It can also be iced before freezing.

Special Equipment 9-inch tube pan (6½-cup capacity) or 9-inch round or square layer pan, grater, nut chopper or food processor.

Baking Time 40 to 45 minutes at 350°F (175°C)

Quantity 4 cups batter; one 9-inch tube cake (serves 8 to 10)

Pan Preparation Spread solid shortening on bottom and sides of pan, then dust evenly with flour; tap out excess flour.

1. Prepare pan as described. Position rack in center of oven. Preheat oven to 350°F (175°C).

Note: For the traditional mixing method, follow steps 2, 3, and 4. To make the cake in the food processor, follow steps 1 and 2 below.

2. Sift together flour, baking soda, and salt. Set aside.

3. In the large bowl of an electric mixer, beat together the eggs and sugar. Add oil, vanilla, and spices and beat slowly to combine. Add flour mixture, stirring until blended. Finally, add grated carrots, pineapple (if using), wheat germ, and chopped nuts. Stir well.

4. Spoon batter into prepared pan. Level top of batter. Set pan in center of preheated 350°F (175°C) oven to bake for 40 to 45 minutes, or until a cake tester inserted in the center comes out clean. Cool cake in its pan on a wire rack for about 15 minutes. Slide a knife blade between cake and side of pan to loosen it, then invert cake onto a platter or another wire rack and cool completely before frosting.

FOOD PROCESSOR METHOD • *1.* Shred the carrots, using a medium shredding disk. Remove shredding disk and replace it with the metal blade. Leave carrots in workbowl and pulse 2 or 3 times, to cut the shreds. Turn carrots out on wax paper. Do not wash workbowl.

2. Combine in the workbowl the eggs, sugar, oil, vanilla, and spices. Process for about 3 seconds. Add walnut pieces (not previously chopped) and dry ingredients. Pulse until combined, about 6 times. Stop machine and scrape down workbowl once or twice. Stir or pulse in carrots, pineapple (if using), and wheat germ. Turn batter into pan and bake as directed in step above.

POUND CAKES

ABOUT POUND CAKE

AMERICAN POUND CAKE came from England; it is named for the fact that it traditionally contained 1 pound each of flour, butter, eggs, and sugar. In France, pound cake is known as *quatre quarts,* or four quarters, referring to the quantities of principal ingredients used: to arrive at the proportions for a classic *quatre quarts,* one weighs 3 or 4 eggs, then uses an equal weight of flour, butter, and sugar. Originally, no baking powder was used in either the classic French or English pound cake; the eggs provided both the leavening and the liquid. Sometimes the eggs were separated and the whites stiffly whipped to supplement the leavening. This is still done, though today baking powder is also added.

In spite (or because) of its density, pound cake became the cornerstone (no pun intended) for generations of bakers. Why? Because it was easy to make, reliable, delicious, and would keep practically forever. It still is, and does. Though its fine grain and weight are part of its charm, it is fairly dry. Modern tastes favor more moisture and a lighter texture. There are many up-dated recipes for pound cake that vary the proportions of ingredients so they are no longer "1 pound each."

In the nineteenth century, bakers flavored pound cake with nuts or seeds such as caraway, cardamom, or anise; today pound cakes are glamorized with everything from chocolate bits to chopped ginger.

The recipes following are a sampler of styles, including the old-fashioned classic, a lightened up-to-date version, Best Pound Cake (with nine variations), and a faintly tangy Sour-Cream Pound Cake, which is my own personal favorite.

Hints and Tips for Pound Cakes

• Bake pound cakes in loaf, tube, or Bundt pans, preferably of shiny metal rather than dark steel. Dark pans cause the outside of the cake to brown too fast, before the inside is baked through.

• For a closer-grained, more dense cake, mix the batter by hand. For a lighter texture, incorporate air by using an electric mixer to cream the butter and sugar until fluffy. If the batter is not mixed enough, the texture will be coarse. If overwhipped, however, too much air can be incorporated, causing the cake to fall, or to overflow the pan when it bakes.

• To avoid curdling the batter, add the liquid slowly, and beat after each egg or yolk is added. The flour will smooth out the batter.

• After baking, allow pound cake to cool in its pan on a rack for at least 20 minutes, and be sure it is away from drafts. Then tip the cake out of the pan, set it upright on a rack, and cool completely. If unmolded too soon or in a cool place, the freshly baked cake can sink or break apart.

Troubleshooting Pound Cakes

• *Batter overflows in pan:* Too much batter in the pan, or batter overwhipped.

• *Top crust sticky or white spots visible:* White spots are undissolved sugar in the batter. The cake may be underbaked, or too much sugar was used, or the sugar was not completely dissolved in the batter. To remedy, add about half of the sugar with the egg yolks and the other half with the whipped whites.

• *Top of cake splits:* This is normal, caused by pressure from the steam that escapes during baking.

• *Cake sinks in center:* Batter overwhipped, so it rose too quickly, then fell in the oven. Or cake underbaked, or cake unmolded from pan too soon, or excess liquid or sugar in batter.

• *Dense, heavy texture:* Underbeating, or insufficient leavening, or old baking powder used, or insufficient oven heat.

Best Pound Cake

*T*his is a contemporary pound cake, a little sweeter and lighter than the classic version. The recipe makes a marvelously flavorful, moist loaf; in our taste tests it won all the votes for flavor, texture, appearance, and general delectability. Following the recipe, you will find nine variations: Mother's Whiskey Cake, Seed Cake, New England Spice Pound, Citrus Pound, Nut Pound, Praline Pound, Chocolate Chip Pound, Marble Pound, and Rose Geranium Pound Cake.

2 cups unsifted cake flour (9 ounces; 260 g)
1 teaspoon baking powder
½ teaspoon salt
1 cup unsalted butter (2 sticks; 230 g), at room
    temperature
1⅔ cups granulated sugar (11½ ounces; 330 g)
5 large eggs, at room temperature
2 teaspoons vanilla extract

1. Prepare pan as described. Position rack in center of oven. Preheat oven to 325°F (165°C).

2. Sift together flour, baking powder, and salt.

3. In a mixing bowl with a sturdy spoon, or in the electric mixer, preferably fitted with the paddle (to avoid whipping excess air into the batter), beat the butter until soft and fluffy. Gradually add the sugar and beat until very light and creamy. Add the eggs, one at a time, beating well after each addition. Beat in the vanilla.

4. By hand or with the mixer on lowest speed, gradually stir in the flour mixture. Blend well.

5. Turn batter into the prepared pan and bake in the preheated oven for 1 hour and 15 to 20 minutes, or until cake is well risen and golden on top, and a tester inserted in the center comes out clean. Cool the cake in its pan on a wire rack for 20 minutes. Then slide a knife around the sides to loosen it. Tip the cake out of the pan, set it upright on the rack, and cool completely.

Advance Preparation The cake can be baked in advance, wrapped airtight, and stored at room temperature for a week or refrigerated for several weeks. Or the cake can be frozen.

Special Equipment One loaf pan 9 × 5 × 3 inches or one 9-inch (6½-cup capacity) tube pan, mixing bowl and wooden spoon, or electric mixer fitted with paddle attachment if available

Baking Time 1 hour and 15 minutes at 325°F (165°C) for loaf; 40 to 45 minutes for tube

Quantity 4½ cups batter; one loaf 9 × 5 inches or one 9-inch tube (serves 8 to 10)

Pan Preparation Spread solid shortening on bottom and sides of pan, dust evenly with flour; tap out excess flour.

· ·

Mother's Whiskey Cake   Prepare Best Pound Cake, but bake it in a 9-inch (6½-cup capacity) tube pan. While the cake bakes, prepare a syrup by combining in a small pan ½ cup lightly salted butter and ½ cup granulated sugar. Set over low heat and stir until the butter melts. Remove from heat and stir in ½ cup whiskey. As soon as the cake is baked, set the pan on a wire rack. Use a thin skewer or cake tester to prick holes all over the cake. Pour warm syrup over the hot cake and allow it to cool completely in the pan. When cold, top with a plate, invert, and lift off pan. Sift on confectioners' sugar.

Note: This syrup can also be poured over a larger pound cake baked in a Bundt pan; it is sufficient for a 10-inch cake.

Seed Cake   Prepare Best Pound Cake and add 2 teaspoons caraway seeds, ⅓ cup finely chopped citron, and 1 teaspoon grated lemon zest to the finished batter.

New England Spice Pound Cake   Prepare Best Pound Cake, but add 1 teaspoon ground cinnamon and 1 teaspoon ground nutmeg to the finished batter.

Citrus Pound Cake   Prepare Best Pound Cake, but add the grated zest of both 1 lemon and 1 orange to the finished batter.

Nut Pound Cake   Prepare Best Pound Cake, but add 1 cup finely chopped walnuts (4 ounces; 110 g) plus ½ teaspoon ground cinnamon and ½ teaspoon ground mace to the finished batter. Hazelnuts can be used but omit cinnamon and mace.

Praline Pound Cake   Prepare Best Pound Cake, but add ½ cup chopped toasted almonds or hazelnuts and ½ cup almond or hazelnut Praline Powder (page 450) to the finished batter.

Chocolate Chip Pound Cake   Prepare Best Pound Cake, but toss ⅔ cup semisweet miniature chocolate chips with 2 or 3 tablespoons of the sifted flour mixture and set them aside. Fold the chips into the batter at the end. You may need to increase baking time 10 to 15 minutes, baking just until a cake tester comes out clean.

Marble Pound Cake   Prepare Best Pound Cake, but place half of the batter in a second bowl. Melt 2½ ounces semisweet chocolate in the top pan of a double boiler. Stir the chocolate into half of the batter. Spoon vanilla and chocolate batters alternately into the prepared baking pan. Draw a knife blade through the batter to create a marbleized effect; do not stir.

Rose Geranium Pound Cake   Scented geraniums are available in an astonishing number of varieties including orange, lemon, apple, mint, and rose. The leaves of these plants are highly aromatic, and their oils impart a delicate flavor to foods. In the nineteenth century, when over 300 varieties were cultivated, this romantic cake was very popular.

Prepare Best Pound Cake, but line the greased and floured pan with rose geranium leaves *(Pelargonium graveolens)* that are pesticide-free, rinsed, and completely dry before adding the batter. Bake the cake as directed, remove it from the pan with the leaves in place, and dust on a light sifting of confectioners' sugar before serving.

Sour-Cream Pound Cake

*T*his cake is lighter than the classic pound cake, velvety in texture, buttery and moist, moderately sweet, with a slightly tangy flavor. The top crust is slightly crunchy, with an eggy taste. When I began to research pound cakes for this chapter, three different friends sent me this recipe from three different parts of the country, proving its popularity.

Note: Double the recipe to bake this cake in a 10-inch tube or Bundt pan.

Advance Preparation The cake can be baked in advance, wrapped airtight, and kept at room temperature for about a week, refrigerated 2 to 3 weeks, or frozen.

Special Equipment One loaf pan 8½ × 4½ × 2¾ inches or 9 × 5 × 3 inches, or one 9-inch (6½-cup capacity) tube pan, electric mixer fitted with paddle attachment if possible, extra bowl and beater for whipping egg whites

Baking Time 1 hour and 15 minutes at 325°F (165°C) for loaf; 40 to 45 minutes for tube cake

Quantity 4½ cups batter; 1 loaf (serves 8) or 9-inch tube (serves 8 to 10)

Pan Preparation Spread solid shortening on bottom and sides of pan; dust evenly with flour; tap out excess flour.

1½ cups sifted all-purpose flour
   (6¼ ounces; 180 g)
½ teaspoon baking powder
¼ teaspoon salt
⅛ teaspoon baking soda
½ cup unsalted butter (1 stick; 110 g), at room
   temperature
1½ cups granulated sugar (10½ ounces; 300 g)
3 large eggs, separated, at room temperature
½ cup sour cream
1 teaspoon vanilla extract

1. Prepare pans as described. Position rack in center of oven. Preheat oven to 325°F (165°C).

2. Sift together the flour, baking powder, salt, and baking soda and set aside.

3. In a mixing bowl with a sturdy spoon or an electric mixer, cream together the butter and ¾ cup of the sugar until very well blended and light. Add egg yolks, one at a time, beating after each addition.

4. Alternately add flour mixture and sour cream, beating slowly after each addition and beginning and ending with flour. Stir in the vanilla. The batter will be quite stiff.

5. In a clean bowl with a clean beater, whip the egg whites until fluffy. Gradually add remaining ¾ cup sugar while beating until the whites are stiff but not dry. Stir

about 1 cup of whipped whites into the batter to soften it, then gradually fold in remaining whites.

6. Turn the batter into the prepared pan and bake in the preheated oven for 1 hour and 15 minutes, or until the cake is golden brown, well risen, and a cake tester inserted in the center comes out clean.

Cool the cake in its pan on a wire rack for 20 minutes. Then slide a knife around the cake sides to loosen it. Tip the cake out of the pan, set it upright on the rack, and cool completely. Do not ice the cake.

Classic Pound Cake

*T*his is a true pound cake in which the butter, sugar, eggs, and flour each weigh 1 pound. In its classic form, this recipe does not include baking powder; it appears here as an option I generally use. The eggs are separated, and the whites are whipped to lighten the texture somewhat. The flavor is very bland unless you add sufficient brandy, rum, juice, or extract. In the nineteenth century, Seed Cake was a popular variation including a tablespoon of spices or caraway seeds. For this recipe as well as the Spice, Marble, Citrus, Nut, and Chocolate Chip Pound Cake variations, see pages 116–117.

Note: This is a large recipe, making 2 loaves. To make a single loaf, prepare half the classic recipe but use only 2 cups flour and ¾ teaspoon salt.

Advance Preparation   The cake can be prepared in advance, wrapped airtight, and kept at room temperature for a week, or refrigerated for several weeks. Or the cake can be frozen.

Special Equipment   Two loaf pans 9 × 5 × 3 inches, electric mixer fitted with paddle if available, large extra bowl and beater for egg whites

Baking Time   1 hour and 15 minutes at 325°F (165°C)

Quantity   8 cups batter, 2 loaves (serves 16 to 18)

Pan Preparation   Spread solid shortening on bottom and sides of pans, dust evenly with flour; tap out excess flour.

4½ cups sifted cake flour (15¼ ounces; 450 g)
1 teaspoon baking powder (optional)
1 teaspoon salt
2 cups lightly salted butter (4 sticks; 454 g), at room temperature
2¼ cups granulated sugar (15¾ ounces; 450 g)
8 large eggs, separated, at room temperature
2 teaspoons vanilla extract
2 tablespoons flavoring: brandy or dark rum or fruit juice, or a combination

1. Prepare pans as directed. Position rack in center of oven. Preheat oven to 325°F (165°C).

2. Sift together the flour, baking powder if using, and ½ teaspoon of the salt onto a sheet of wax paper. Set aside.

3. In a mixing bowl with a sturdy spoon, or in the electric mixer fitted with a paddle if possible (so as not to whip excess air into the batter), beat the butter until soft and fluffy, then gradually add 1½ cups of the sugar, beating until the mixture is very light and creamy. Add the egg yolks, one at a time, beating after each addition. The batter should be a pale yellow color, and very creamy. Scrape down the inside of the bowl and the beaters. Beat in the vanilla and other flavoring; some nineteenth-century cookbooks blend both rum and lemon juice, or brandy and orange juice. Be creative, but keep the total amount to 2 tablespoons.

4. By hand or with the mixer on lowest speed, gradually add the flour mixture to the batter in 5 or 6 additions. The batter will be quite stiff.

5. In a clean bowl with a clean beater, whip the egg whites with remaining ½ teaspoon salt until fluffy. Gradually beat in remaining ¾ cup sugar, whipping until the whites are stiff but not dry.

Stir about 1 cup of the whites into the batter to soften it. A little at a time, fold in remaining whites. At first this is hard going, but the batter smooths out quickly.

6. Divide batter between the prepared pans and bake in the preheated oven for about 1 hour and 15 minutes, or until the cake tops are golden brown, the centers are well risen, and a cake tester comes out clean. Cool both cakes in their pans on a wire rack for about 20 minutes. Then slide a knife around the cake sides to loosen it. Tip each cake out of its pan, set it upright on the rack, and cool completely. Do not frost the cakes. Note that the cakes mellow in flavor and also cut more easily the day after they are baked.

FRUITCAKES

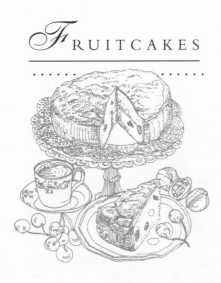

ABOUT FRUITCAKES

FRUITCAKES ARE GREAT "occasion" cakes, traditionally baked for special events and holidays. Certainly they can be baked well in advance and "aged," but that is not their only virtue. The fact that they are show-off cakes has something to do with their appeal, rather like a culinary potlatch, demonstrating wealth by using lavish quantities of rich ingredients. Most fruitcakes are virtual cornucopias of brandy-soaked fruits and nuts minimally bound by cake crumbs.

Unfortunately, many of us shy away from fruitcakes because of overexposure to sickeningly sweet supermarket glacéed fruits. A homemade fruitcake made with the best-quality ingredients bears no resemblance to the store-bought variety; if you make the cake yourself, you can use only those ingredients you prefer. Try, for example, dried peaches, mangoes, papaya, apples, pineapple, apricots, figs, pears, dates, and prunes in place of candied citron and cherries.

Hints and Tips for Fruitcakes

• Buy the best-quality dried fruits you can find, usually available at food coops and health-food stores or gourmet shops; supermarket "dried candied fruits" or "glacéed fruits" are oversweet and often of poor quality. To improve these supermarket fruits, set them in a strainer and pour boiling water over them to remove some of the sugar, then soak them in brandy before using. Don't worry about dicing all fruits to the same size; when you slice the cake, you will cut the fruit anyway; a variety of sizes makes an attractive mosaic when the cake is cut. Instead of using spirits, you can make nonalcoholic fruitcake using fruit juice, honey, molasses, maple syrup, or flavorful tea.

• Use an assortment of pans; for gifts, make small or baby loaves. Use regular loaf pans of any size, or pressed aluminum "disposable" pans. For large cakes you can use any angel-food tube pans, or springform pans with or without a tube. Fluted kugelhopf or Bundt pans can be used, but are more difficult to line with paper; I use aluminum foil to line these pans, pressing the foil into the greased flutes of the pan.

• Use shiny metal pans, avoiding black nonstick or black steel pans whose dark surface will cause the outside of fruitcakes to bake too quickly. Be sure to grease the pan lightly, then always carefully line the bottom *and* sides with wax paper, baking parchment, or brown paper cut from paper bags. Grease the paper after it is cut, fit, and neatly positioned in the pans (see page 66). Paper prevents too-quick baking of the exterior of the cake and prevents the fruit pieces from sticking to the pan. Make individual fruitcakes in muffin pans, but line the pans with fluted paper or foil liners and reduce baking time accordingly; the danger with tiny cakes is that they overbake and dry out.

• Bake fruitcake in a slow oven, 300°F to 325°F (150° to 165°C). Small cakes take between 45 and 60 minutes, while large ones can take 2½ hours or longer. To tell when a cake is done, look for a nicely browned, slightly risen top and sides that begin to pull away from the pan. Insert a cake tester in the center; it should come out moist from fruit but with no visible trace of raw batter.

• Note that freshly baked fruitcakes, especially the large ones, are rather fragile while still warm. It is best to let the cakes sit in their pans for about 20 minutes, then top them with a cardboard cake disk or flat plate or wire rack, invert, and lift off the pan. Peel off the paper while the cake is still slightly warm. Invert the cake and cool completely in an upright position. Some recipes direct you to wrap the warm cakes immediately in brandy-soaked cloth, others to wait until the cakes are cold. In any case, handle warm cakes as little as possible to prevent breakage. I prefer to let the cake sit under a tea towel for several hours until cold before storing.

• For brandy-soaking wrappers, select the best-quality cheesecloth you can find and use 3 layers; cheap cleesecloth pulls apart and covers the cakes with unsightly threads. Or use clean sheets or tea towels or muslin. Cut a piece large enough to envelop the cake, soak the cloth in the spirits, then wrap it around the cake. Cover the cake with plastic wrap, then place it inside a large heavy-duty plastic bag, well fastened, or in a plastic or metal container with a lid. Don't cover the alcohol-wrapped cake with foil unless first placed in a plastic bag, for the spirits sometimes dissolve the metallic wrap. If storing them in the basement, put the plastic-bag-wrapped cakes in a tin box or the mice will quickly arrive to feast. Occasionally check the cloth and replenish the spirits when needed to keep the cloth moist. The easiest way to add spirits is to paint them onto the cloth-wrapped cake instead of removing the wrapping. Store the cakes in a cool, dry place, but not in the refrigerator. Age them as long as you wish—for 1 week or 1 year or anything in between. A good cake full of good ingredients will taste fine even when freshly baked. Fruitcakes can also be frozen. Before serving, garnish with Apricot Glaze (page 415) or Icing Glaze (page 408), decorated with halved cherries or nuts and angelica.

Apricot-Nut Fruitcake

*T*his is the fruitcake for those who hate candied fruits. A moderately sweet cake containing chopped apricots, 3 types of nuts, 2 types of raisins, and grated fresh apples, it is wonderful to give as a gift or to serve for the holidays. It can be made with all-white flour or white flour blended with some whole-wheat flour. Read About Fruitcakes (page 122).

2 cups broken walnuts (8 ounces; 230 g)

1 cup hazelnuts or filberts (5 ounces; 140 g), toasted, skinned (see page 42), halved or coarsely chopped

1 cup Brazil nuts (6 ounces; 170 g), coarsely chopped, or halved pecans

1 cup seedless raisins (6 ounces; 170 g)

1½ cups firmly packed golden raisins (7 ounces; 210 g)

2 cups firmly packed dried apricot halves (12 ounces; 340 g), cut into quarters

¾ cup dark rum or Calvados, plus ½ cup unsweetened apple cider, or use all spirits

1½ cups unsifted all-purpose *or* whole-wheat flour (6¾ ounces; 185 g; available in health-food stores)

2 cups unsifted all-purpose flour (10 ounces; 280 g)

1½ teaspoons baking powder

¼ teaspoon baking soda

½ teaspoon salt

1 teaspoon each of ground cinnamon and nutmeg

1½ cups lightly salted butter (3 sticks; 340 g), at room temperature

1½ cups firmly packed light brown sugar (10½ ounces; 300 g)

5 large eggs, at room temperature

2 teaspoons vanilla extract

1 cup unpeeled grated apple, cooking type such as Granny Smith (6 ounces; 170 g)

1 cup applesauce, preferably unsweetened

Advance Preparation The dried fruits and the nuts are combined with the rum and soaked for 24 hours before making the batter. Plan ahead. Prepare the cake, glaze, and garnish, and wrap airtight. Store the cake in the refrigerator for about 2 weeks for the flavors to mellow, then serve or freeze. Of course, it is also fine to eat right after baking. Do not wrap this cake with alcohol-soaked cloths for storage.

Special Equipment One tube pan 10 × 4 inches, or one 9¼-inch tube pan (9-cup capacity) plus 2 baby loaf pans, each 6 × 3½ × 2 inches, or the equivalent in capacity; nut chopper or food processor, extra-large mixing bowl, electric mixer, wax paper or baking parchment, scissors

Baking Time 1½ to 1¾ hours at 325°F (165°C) for a 9- or 10-inch tube cake; about 1 hour and 15 minutes for baby loaves

Quantity About 12 cups batter; one 10-inch tube cake or one 9-inch tube plus 2 baby loaves

GLAZE
Apricot Glaze (page 415) or Icing Glaze (page 408)

GARNISH
Halved walnuts, almonds, or pecans, cut-up dried apricots

1. A day or two before baking the cake, combine all the dried fruits and nuts in a large bowl and toss well with the rum or Calvados and cider. Cover with plastic wrap and set aside in a cool place for at least 24 hours. Toss the mixture occasionally.

2. On the baking day, prepare pans as described. Position rack in center of oven for 1 large cake, or divide oven in thirds for several cakes. Preheat oven to 325°F (165°C).

3. Sift both flours, the baking powder, baking soda, salt, and spices together onto wax paper. Set aside.

To make the cake batter, use a spoon and a mixing bowl or the electric mixer to cream together the butter and sugar until well blended. Add eggs, one at a time, beating after each addition. Stir in vanilla.

Add the flour mixture in 3 or 4 additions, beating very slowly to blend after each addition. The batter will be quite stiff. Stir in the grated apple and applesauce. Stir the macerated fruit-nut-rum mixture, then add it to the batter along with all the liquid. Stir the batter with a sturdy wooden spoon until well blended; really the best way to blend is with your bare hands.

4. Spoon the batter into the prepared pan(s), filling them about ⅔ full. Bake in the preheated oven as directed until the cake top(s) are golden brown (cracking is normal as the steam escapes) and a cake tester inserted in the center shows no visible raw batter.

Cool each cake on a wire rack for 20 minutes. Run a knife blade around the cake sides to loosen, then top with a cardboard cake disk or plate and invert; remove the pan and peel off the paper. Invert again and cool the cake completely, right side up. Once cold, the cakes may be served or stored.

If you wish, wrap the cold cakes in plastic wrap, then in foil, and refrigerate them for a week or two. Before serving, brush the cake top with Apricot Glaze or Icing Glaze and set a few halved nuts and cut pieces of apricot into the soft glaze. Allow about 30 minutes for the glaze to set.

Pan Preparation Lightly grease pan(s), cut paper liners to cover both bottom and sides (see page 66), press paper in place, then grease paper.

Williamsburg Orange Wine Cake

*C*ulled from the historic papers, journals, and household books of Virginia's first settlers, versions of this recipe came to light during the development of the Colonial Williamsburg restoration. In 1938 the first recipe for the cake appeared in print in *The Williamsburg Art of Cookery Or Accomplish'd Gentlewoman's Companion,* compiled by the project's archivist, Mrs. Helen Bullock. There are still many variations, but all have a strong orange flavor and a texture flecked with nuts and currants. Traditionally, the cake is baked in a tube pan and iced with Orange Wine Icing, though it can also be formed in layers. Orange Madeira Cake is a variation on this recipe, using Madeira wine instead of sherry. Both are moist, moderately sweet cakes served in small slices.

Advance Preparation   Cake keeps well, wrapped airtight, at room temperature for at least a week. Cake can be baked ahead, wrapped airtight, and frozen.

Special Equipment   One 9-inch tube pan (8½- to 9-cup capacity) or two 9-inch layer pans, nut chopper or food processor

Baking Time   55 to 60 minutes at 350°F (175°C) for tube pan; 30 to 35 minutes for layer cake pans

Quantity   6 cups batter; one 9-inch tube cake (serves 10) or one 2-layer 9-inch cake (serves 8 to 10)

Pan Preparation   Spread solid shortening on bottom and sides of pan, then dust evenly with flour; tap out excess flour.

3½ cups sifted cake flour (12¼ ounces; 350 g)
2 teaspoons baking soda
½ teaspoon salt
1 cup shelled pecans, chopped (4 ounces; 110 g)
½ cup currants (2¼ ounces; 65 g)
½ cup unsalted butter (1 stick; 110 g), at room temperature
½ cup stick margarine (4 ounces; 110 g), at room temperature (or use all butter)
1½ cups granulated sugar (10½ ounces; 300 g)
4 large eggs, at room temperature
1¼ cups buttermilk
¼ cup dry sherry
2 teaspoons orange extract
Grated zest of 1½ large oranges, about 5 tablespoons

ICING
Orange Wine Icing (page 395)

GARNISH
Halved pecans or thin threads of orange zest

1. Prepare pan(s) as described. Position rack in center of oven. Preheat oven to 350°F (175°C).

2. Sift together the flour, baking soda, and salt. Set aside. Combine nuts and currants in a bowl and toss with ¼ cup of the flour mixture. Set aside.

3. In the large bowl of an electric mixer, cream together butter, margarine, and sugar until very well blended and fluffy. Add the eggs, one at a time, beating after each addition. The batter will look curdled; don't worry.

4. With the mixer on lowest speed, alternately add flour mixture and buttermilk to the batter, beginning and ending with flour. Beat to blend after each addition. Scrape down sides of bowl often. Beat in sherry and orange extract. Stir in grated orange zest and nut-currant mixture.

5. Spoon batter into prepared pan and smooth the top. Place in the oven to bake as directed, or until a cake tester inserted in the center comes out clean, and the top is golden and lightly springy to the touch. Cool the cake on a wire rack for 10 minutes, then top with another rack and invert. Lift off pan. Cool completely. Fill and frost a layer cake with Orange Wine Icing. For a tube cake, make the icing slightly softer than for a layer cake. Spread icing on the cake top and allow it to run down the sides. Garnish the cake top with halved pecans or fine threads of orange zest.

· ·

Orange Madeira Cake   Prepare Williamsburg Orange Wine Cake with the following changes: In the batter, replace dry sherry with Madeira wine. For icing, make Orange Wine Icing, but replace dry sherry with Madeira wine. For topping, make a syrup of ¾ cup water, ½ cup granulated sugar (3½ ounces; 100 g), and ¼ cup Madeira. Boil for 3 or 4 minutes. Peel 2 or 3 oranges and cut out the sections, taking care to remove the membrane from each piece. Poach the peeled sections in the syrup for 4 to 5 minutes. Remove the orange sections with a slotted spoon and drain on paper towels. Discard syrup. Ice the cake and top it with an arrangement of orange sections, or garnish with Candied Orange Peel (page 452).

Bourbon-Pecan Cake

*T*his cake is a Southern classic, recommended especially for bourbon lovers. The liquor flavor is strong, and the cake is moist and rich with fruit and nuts. Serve it at holiday time, with a bourbon-sugar glaze decorated with candied cherries and halved pecans. This recipe is a traditional "Groom's Cake" for weddings.

1½ cups sifted all-purpose flour (6¼ ounces; 180 g)
1 teaspoon baking powder
⅛ teaspoon salt
½ teaspoon ground cinnamon
2 teaspoons ground nutmeg
½ cup bourbon
1½ cups shelled pecans, toasted (page 42) and chopped fine (6 ounces; 180 g)
½ cup currants (2¼ ounces; 65 g)
½ cup lightly salted butter (1 stick; 110 g), at room temperature
1 cup (7 ounces; 200 g) plus 2 tablespoons granulated sugar
3 large eggs, separated, at room temperature

ICING
Bourbon-flavored Icing Glaze (page 408)

1. Prepare pan as described. Position rack in center of oven. Preheat oven to 325°F (165°C).

2. Sift together flour, baking powder, salt, and cinnamon. Set aside. In a small bowl, combine nutmeg and bourbon and set aside to soak. In another bowl, combine the chopped pecans and the currants and toss with ½ cup of the flour mixture, coating fruit and nuts well.

3. In the large bowl of electric mixer, cream butter and 1 cup of the sugar until light and smooth. Add the egg yolks, one at a time, beating after each addition. Little by little, stir in the flour mixture, beating slowly to blend after each addition.

4. Add the bourbon-nutmeg mixture, and beat well to blend. Stir in floured nuts and currants, taking care to distribute them evenly throughout the batter. Batter will be quite stiff.

5. In a separate bowl with a clean beater, beat the egg whites until foamy. Add remaining 2 tablespoons sugar and beat until stiff peaks form. Stir about 1 cup of the beaten whites into the fruit batter to lighten it. Fold in remaining whites.

6. Spoon batter into prepared pan. Bake in the preheated oven for 40 to 45 minutes, or until a cake tester inserted in the center comes out clean and the top of the cake is lightly springy to the touch. Cool cake on a wire rack for 10 minutes. Top with another rack, invert, and lift off pan. Peel off paper. Cool completely. Wrap in a bourbon-soaked tea towel and set in a plastic container or other airtight wrapping to age, if you wish. Or prepare bourbon-flavored Icing Glaze and drizzle it on the cake top. While the glaze is still soft, set halved cherries and pecans into top for decoration.

Advance Preparation The cake may be baked well ahead, wrapped in a tea towel soaked with bourbon, and set in a plastic bag, then covered with heavy-duty foil or placed in a tin and stored in a cool place for several weeks. Or it can be baked ahead and frozen. Allow cake to age at room temperature for at least 2 days to mellow flavors before serving.

Special Equipment One 9-inch tube pan (6½-cup capacity) or springform tube pan, nut chopper or food processor, wax paper or baking parchment, scissors

Baking Time 40 to 45 minutes at 325°F (165°C)

Quantity 4 cups batter; one 9-inch tube cake (serves 10)

Pan Preparation Spread a little solid shortening on bottom and sides of tube pan, then line with wax paper or baking parchment. Spread solid shortening on paper.

UPSIDE-DOWN CAKES

Old-Fashioned Pineapple Upside-Down Cake

This old-fashioned country favorite is easy to prepare and tastes as good as it looks. Originally it was baked in an iron skillet, or "spider," and to my mind this is still the best method, though enameled cast-iron skillets are fine, and any pan that can go from stove top to oven can be used. The method is simple: Butter and brown sugar are melted together in a skillet on top of the stove, fruits and nuts are arranged in this sugar glaze, cake batter is poured on top, and the cake is placed in the oven to bake. When done, the cake is inverted onto a serving platter so that the glazed fruit is on top.

This process is a great one for kindling the interest of young bakers. I always remember the fun I had as a child, making careful arrangements of fruit, covering them up with batter, then watching with eager anticipation (and a little breath-holding) for them to reappear when the cake was oh-so-carefully flipped upside down.

Note: Old-Fashioned Pineapple Upside-Down Cake is a master recipe that lends itself to the many variations that follow: Ginger-Pear, Apple-Cranberry, Cranberry-Raisin-Nut, Apricot-Prune, and Peach-Pecan. Make up other fruit combinations to create your own favorites. Serve upside-down cake by itself or topped with lightly sweetened whipped cream.

PINEAPPLE TOPPING

7 canned pineapple rings, drained, with ¼ cup juice
    reserved
7 Maraschino cherries, drained, or whole fresh or
    frozen cranberries
5 tablespoons lightly salted butter (2½ ounces; 70 g)
1 cup firmly packed dark brown sugar (9 ounces;
    255 g)
12 to 15 halved pecans or walnuts (optional)

CAKE

1½ cups sifted all-purpose flour (6¼ ounces; 180 g)
1 teaspoon baking powder
¼ teaspoon baking soda
⅛ teaspoon salt
½ teaspoon each of ground cinnamon and nutmeg
⅓ cup unsalted butter (5⅓ tablespoons; 80 g), at
    room temperature
½ cup granulated sugar (3½ ounces; 100 g)
¼ cup honey (see Note)
2 large eggs, at room temperature
½ teaspoon vanilla extract
⅓ cup milk

Note: You can substitute ¼ cup granulated sugar
for the honey; to do so, omit the baking soda and add
2 tablespoons additional milk to the batter.

SAUCE (OPTIONAL)

1 cup heavy cream, whipped with 2 tablespoons
    superfine sugar and 1 teaspoon vanilla extract

Advance Preparation
While this cake may be baked
ahead and kept for a day or
two if well covered, it is best
by far when baked fresh and
served warm.

Special Equipment　One
10-inch ovenproof heavy-
bottomed skillet, such as cast
iron or enameled iron, with
ovenproof handle, or 10-inch
round or square baking pan;
12-inch or larger flat serving
platter, paper towels for
draining fruit

Cooking Time　Butter-
sugar glaze: 3 to 4 minutes;
cake: 25 to 30 minutes in
350°F (175°C) oven

Quantity　2½ cups cake
batter; one 10-inch cake
(serves 8 to 10)

Pan Preparation　Butter-
sugar glaze (see recipe)

1. Preheat oven to 325°F (175°C).

2. Prepare topping: Drain pineapple rings, reserving ¼ cup juice and setting the fruit along with the cherries on paper towels to dry. Melt 5 tablespoons butter in a 10-inch ovenproof skillet set over moderate-low heat. Stir in the brown sugar, breaking it up with the back of a wooden spoon. Stir continually for 3 or 4 minutes, or until the mixture is creamy and begins to bubble. The sugar does not have to dissolve completely. Remove pan from heat. Stir in reserved pineapple juice. Take care here as the juice may splatter. Stir until smooth. Arrange 1 pineapple ring in the center of the pan with other rings around it. Set a cherry or cranberry in the center of each ring. Place nut halves, rounded side down, between pineapple rings. Set pan aside.

3. Prepare cake batter: Sift together flour, baking powder, baking soda, salt, and spices. Set aside. In the large bowl of an electric mixer, beat together butter and sugar until creamy. Add the honey and beat until smooth.

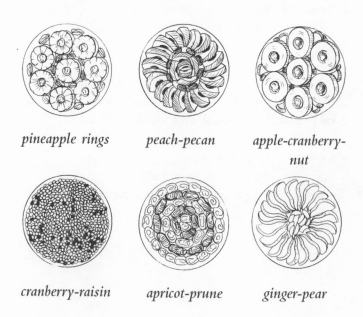

pineapple rings *peach-pecan* *apple-cranberry-nut*

cranberry-raisin *apricot-prune* *ginger-pear*

Add the eggs, one at a time, beating after each addition. Add the vanilla. Alternately add flour mixture and milk to the batter, beating slowly after each addition.

Note: This step can easily be done in a food processor, creaming butter, sugar, and honey first, then adding eggs and vanilla and pulsing briefly to blend. Add dry ingredients and milk and pulse only until smooth. Scrape down inside of workbowl several times.

4. Spoon batter over fruit in skillet. Bake in center of the preheated oven for 25 to 30 minutes, or until a cake tester inserted in the center comes out clean and the cake top is lightly springy to the touch.

5. Cool the cake on a wire rack for 3 or 4 minutes, until the glaze stops bubbling. Top the skillet with a large flat serving platter and, holding them together with potholders (the pan will be hot!), invert. Lift off skillet. Reposition on the cake any pieces of fruit that may have stuck to the pan. Serve cake while still warm so the sugar glaze will be soft and slightly runny. If you wish, prepare whipped cream with sugar and vanilla to serve alongside the cake.

VARIATIONS

. . . .

Ginger-Pear Upside-Down Cake   This is my family's favorite. The flavors are unusual and sophisticated, with maple syrup in both the topping glaze and the cake, and the bright tang of ginger to cut the sweetness.

Prepare Old-Fashioned Pineapple Upside-Down Cake with the following changes:

TOPPING
Replace pineapple topping with:

5 tablespoons lightly salted butter (2½ ounces; 70 g)
⅓ cup firmly packed light brown sugar (2¼ ounces; 70 g)
⅓ cup granulated sugar (2¼ ounces; 70 g)

¼ cup pure maple syrup

3 ripe pears, each 6 to 7 ounces (200 g), peeled, cored, each one cut in 8 lengthwise slices and sprinkled with a little lemon juice to prevent discoloration; or use canned pears, sliced and well drained

3 tablespoons finely minced crystallized candied ginger

CAKE

Prepare master recipe with the following changes:

Increase baking powder to 1½ teaspoons, increase salt to ¼ teaspoon, add 2 teaspoons ground ginger, substitute maple syrup for honey.

SAUCE

Add to master recipe for whipped cream:

½ teaspoon ground ginger and 2 tablespoons finely minced crystallized candied ginger

Prepare topping as in master recipe, melting butter in a skillet and stirring in both sugars until smooth and bubbling. Stir in maple syrup. Add pear slices and cook in glaze for about 3 minutes, turning gently with 2 forks; cook for 1 minute after turning. Remove pan from heat. Arrange pears like flower petals with thin ends toward the center. If using canned pear halves, place them cut side up. Cut 1 piece to fit in the center. Sprinkle on the minced ginger.

Apple-Cranberry-Nut Upside-Down Cake Use a tart cooking apple; cranberries contribute brightness as well as flavor.

Note: When cooked in a cast-iron skillet, the apples tend to darken in color after baking. To improve appearances, use a nonreactive skillet or sprinkle on a little nutmeg or brush warmed red currant jelly over the baked cake. Prepare Old-Fashioned Pineapple Upside-Down Cake, with the following changes:

TOPPING
Replace pineapple topping with:

5 tablespoons lightly salted butter (2½ ounces; 70 g)
1 cup firmly packed light brown sugar (7 ounces; 200 g)
½ teaspoon ground nutmeg
3 large tart cooking apples such as Granny Smith, each about 7 ounces (200 g), peeled, cored, and cut into ½-inch-thick rings
12 pecan or walnut halves
12 fresh or frozen whole cranberries, or substitute Maraschino cherries

Prepare topping as in master recipe, melting butter in the skillet, adding light brown sugar, and stirring over moderately low heat for 3 to 4 minutes, until creamy and bubbling. Add nutmeg and remove from heat. Arrange apple rings in the sugar glaze, placing 1 ring in the center and the others around it. Cut extra apples into pieces to fit between the rings. Add a cranberry or cherry in the center of each ring, and position remaining cranberries and nuts, rounded sides down, among the apples.

CAKE
Prepare as in master recipe.

SAUCE
Prepare as in master recipe.

Cranberry-Raisin Upside-Down Cake This cake makes the most colorful presentation, with the sugar-glazed cranberries glowing like rubies. Be sure to use the light brown or white sugar because dark brown sugar dims the visual effect. To retain the brightest berry color, use a nonreactive pan of stainless steel, enamel, or ovenproof glass; cast iron darkens the color of the sauce.

Prepare Old-Fashioned Pineapple Upside-Down Cake with the following changes:

TOPPING
Replace pineapple topping with:

5 tablespoons lightly salted butter (2½ ounces; 70 g)
1 cup firmly packed light brown or granulated white
    sugar (7 ounces; 200 g)
2 cups whole cranberries (8 ounces; 240 g),
    preferably frozen, picked over and stems removed
½ cup golden raisins (3 ounces; 85 g)
Grated zest of 1 orange

Prepare topping as in master recipe, melting butter in skillet, adding light brown sugar, and stirring over moderately low heat for 3 to 4 minutes, until creamy and bubbling. Toss cranberries and raisins together, then add to the butter-sugar in the pan in an even layer and sprinkle them with orange zest. Set pan aside to cool while you prepare cake.

CAKE
Prepare as in master recipe, and add grated zest of 1 orange to the finished batter. If you wish, you can replace the milk with orange juice.

SAUCE
Use Vanilla Custard Sauce or Crème Anglaise (page 418), or serve with slightly sweetened heavy cream, unwhipped.

Apricot-Prune Upside-Down Cake   The color contrast between concentric rings of sugar-glazed bright orange apricots and blue-black prunes makes a particularly attractive presentation. Prepare Old-Fashioned Pineapple Upside-Down Cake, with the following changes:

TOPPING

Replace pineapple topping with:

16 prunes, with or without pits (with pits in, use
     about 5 ounces, 140 g)
46 dried apricot halves, about 1 cup packed
     (9 ounces; 250 g)
5 tablespoons lightly salted butter (2½ ounces; 70 g)
1 cup firmly packed light brown sugar (7 ounces;
     200 g)
½ teaspoon grated lemon zest

   1. Combine prunes and apricots in a 2-quart saucepan and cover them with water. Simmer over moderate heat for about 20 minutes, until fork tender. Drain the fruit. When cool enough to touch, pit prunes if necessary. Set fruit out on paper towels to dry.

   2. Prepare topping as in master recipe, melting butter in skillet and stirring in sugar for about 3 minutes, until creamy and bubbling. Remove from heat and stir in lemon zest. Arrange apricots, cut side up and overlapping slightly, in a ring around outside edge of skillet. Arrange a ring of prunes, end to end, just inside apricots. Make another ring of apricots, then fill the center with remaining prunes.

CAKE

Prepare as in master recipe but omit cinnamon,
     nutmeg, and baking soda and in place of honey
     use granulated sugar along with 2 tablespoons
     extra milk.

SAUCE
Prepare as in master recipe.

Peach–Pecan Upside-Down Cake   A marvelous cake, especially when made with fresh ripe peaches.

Prepare Old-Fashioned Pineapple Upside-Down Cake with the following changes:

TOPPING
Replace pineapple topping with:

5 tablespoons lightly salted butter (2½ ounces; 70 g)
1 cup firmly packed light brown sugar (7 ounces;
    200 g)
½ teaspoon ground nutmeg
3 medium-size ripe peaches, each about 4 ounces
    (120 g), peeled, halved, and pitted. Cut each half
    into 5 wedge-shaped slices; or use about
    30 canned peach slices, well drained.
½ cup pecan halves (2 ounces; 60 g)

Prepare topping as in master recipe, melting butter in skillet stirring in light brown sugar for about 3 minutes, until creamy and bubbling. Add nutmeg and remove from heat. Reserve 6 peach slices, then arrange the rest side by side in a ring around the pan. In the center, arrange 4 of the reserved slices end-to-end; put the last 2 slices facing each other in the middle. Arrange nuts, curved side down, among peach slices.

CAKE
Prepare as in master recipe.

SAUCE
Prepare as in master recipe.

Basic Yeast-Risen Coffee Cake

This is a basic recipe for a moderately sweet yeast-risen coffee cake; the dough is breadlike in texture. It can be used with any type of filling and molded into any shape. You can vary the flavor by adding, for example, orange juice and grated orange zest, or almond extract; vary the sweetness of the dough by adding more or less sugar. Recipes for fillings follow. For a richer dough, see the variation for Honey-Yogurt Yeast Coffee Cake, following the basic recipe. Read about Yeast, page 37.

Advance Preparation
Using regular active dry
yeast, dough must rise twice,
for a total of 2 to 2½ hours,
so plan your time accordingly.
Dough can be prepared ahead
and kept refrigerated for a
couple of days (see step 5).
Baked cakes can be wrapped
airtight and frozen. Thaw and
serve warm for best flavor.

Special Equipment Large
heavy mixing bowl, baking
sheet, wire whisk, wooden
spoon, pastry brush, alu-
minum foil

Baking Time About 30
minutes at 350°F (175°C)

Quantity 2 loaves or cakes

Pan Preparation Spread
butter, margarine, or oil on
pan.

½ cup warm water (105° to 110°F; about 40°C)

2 packages regular active dry yeast
(each ¼ ounce; 7 g)

1 teaspoon plus ⅔ cup (4½ ounces; 130 g)
granulated sugar

1 teaspoon salt

1 cup lukewarm milk, or orange juice for orange-
flavored cake

2 large eggs, at room temperature, lightly beaten

2 teaspoons grated orange or lemon zest (optional)

1 teaspoon ground cardamom

½ cup unsalted butter (1 stick; 110 g), melted and
cooled to room temperature

4 to 6 cups all-purpose flour (20 to 30 ounces;
560 to 840 g), or more as needed

FILLING

See recipe ideas that follow; note that fillings are for
half of the dough.

EGG GLAZE

1 egg beaten with 1 tablespoon water

ICING GLAZE (OPTIONAL)

Any icing glaze (see Index)

1. In a large heavy mixing bowl, combine warm
(105° to 115°F; 40° to 45°C) water (use thermometer to
be accurate) and 1 teaspoon sugar. Sprinkle on the yeast
and let sit for about 5 minutes until the mixture looks
bubbly.

2. Use a wire whisk to blend in ⅔ cup sugar, salt,
warm milk or orange juice, beaten eggs, grated zest if using it, cardamom, and melted and cooled butter.

3. With a wooden spoon, stir in 1 cup of flour at a
time, mixing until the dough forms a soft ball. Note that
the total amount of flour used will vary with dampness of

weather, type of liquid used in recipe, etc. Add a little more flour if necessary, to make dough ball pull away from bowl sides.

4. Turn dough out onto a floured work surface and knead for about 5 minutes, adding flour, 1 tablespoon at a time, to prevent dough from sticking. When dough feels smooth and appears to be satiny, place it in a large, oiled mixing bowl. Turn dough ball once to oil all its surfaces. Top dough with a piece of oiled wax paper or plastic wrap and set aside in a draft-free location to rise for 1½ hours, until doubled in bulk. The dough has risen enough when you poke 2 fingers into the top and the depressions remain. Punch down the dough ball to deflate it.

5. Turn the dough out onto a floured work surface and divide it into halves.

Note: To hold the dough for later use, refrigerate all the dough in a bowl, covered with a plate. Check under the plate several times and punch down dough each time it rises; dough will keep overnight. Bring dough to room temperature before continuing recipe.

Select fillings. To shape and fill cakes, see pages 143–144. To bake cakes, follow steps 6 and 7.

6. Place shaped cake on a buttered baking sheet and top with oiled wax paper or plastic wrap. Set aside in a draft-free location to rise until not quite doubled in bulk; better to underrise dough now than to overdo it; it will rise more as it bakes. Preheat oven to 350°F (175°C).

7. When the dough has risen, brush the top with the egg glaze. Place the cake in the preheated oven and bake for about 30 minutes, or until the cake is golden brown on top and sounds hollow when tapped with your knuckle. If top browns too quickly, protect it with a piece of foil while continuing to bake. Use a spatula to help slide the cake off the flat baking sheet. Cool on a wire rack. If you wish, the cake can be topped with icing glaze. For holiday cakes, set blanched almonds or pecans and halved candied cherries into the glaze before it sets.

ROLLED HORSESHOE • Use half of the dough to make 1 horseshoe. After the first rising, punch down the dough, then press it out into a flat rectangle about 11 × 15 inches and ¼ inch thick. Brush the dough with melted and cooled butter (omit butter if filling with jam) to within ½ inch of edges. Spread filling mixture over butter, or spread jam filling directly on dough (a). Beginning at one long side, roll up dough like a jelly roll. Seal edges and ends with brushed-on egg glaze, pinching dough together (b). Carefully slide dough onto a buttered baking sheet, placing the seam side down. Curve the roll into a horseshoe shape. With a sharp knife or razor blade, make several slashes about ⅛ inch deep in the top of the dough (c).

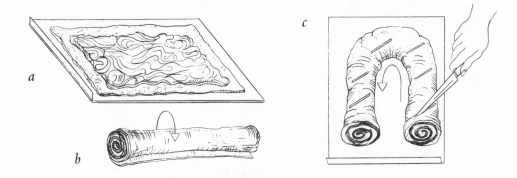

SPIRAL TWIST • Use half of the dough to make 1 twist. Prepare Rolled Horseshoe, but leave cake in a straight line. Slide the cake onto a buttered baking sheet, seam side down. The roll will now be about 14 inches long. Along one side of the roll, make 6 cuts 2 inches apart reaching ¾ of the way across the roll (a). Lift the first segment, turn it cut side up, and set it flat, with the filled spiral facing up. Lift the next segment, turn it cut side up, and pull it toward the right side of the roll; set it flat. Lift the third segment cut side up and position it to the left side, as shown (b). Repeat.

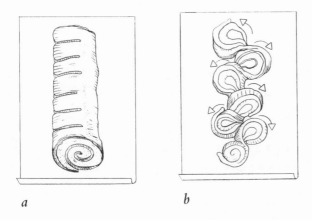

a *b*

TOP BRAID • Use half of the dough to make 1 braid. After the dough has had the first rising, press it out into a rectangle about 11 × 15 inches and ¼ inch thick on a buttered baking sheet. Marking the dough very lightly with the back of a knife, divide it lengthwise into thirds and mark 1-inch borders on each short end. Brush melted butter over the central area, then sprinkle on the filling; omit the butter if using jam (a). With a sharp knife, cut slanted parallel strips about 1 inch wide on each side of the filling (b). To make the top braid, fold the strips alternately across the filling. Overlap the strips so the end of each one hides the start of the next (c).

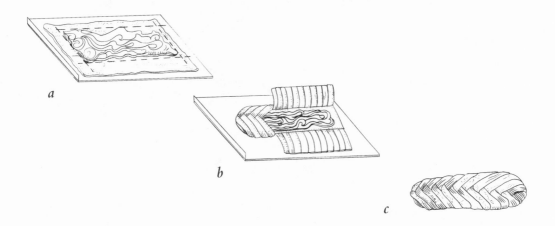

a

b

c

Honey-Yogurt Yeast Coffee Cake   This is also an all-purpose yeast-risen dough. It is a little richer and more flavorful than the Basic Yeast-Risen Coffee Cake.

½ cup warm water (105° to 110°F; about 40°C)
1 teaspoon granulated sugar
2 packages regular active dry yeast (each ¼ ounce; 7 g)
⅓ cup honey
1 teaspoon salt
1 cup plain yogurt or sour cream
2 eggs, at room temperature, lightly beaten
1 teaspoon grated lemon or orange zest
1 teaspoon ground cinnamon
½ cup unsalted butter (1 stick; 110 g), melted and
   cooled to room temperature
4 to 6 cups all-purpose flour (20 to 30 ounces;
   560 to 840 g), as needed

EGG GLAZE
1 egg beaten with 1 tablespoon water

Follow procedure for Basic Yeast-Risen Coffee Cake (pages 141–142), but in step 2, whisk into yeast mixture the honey, salt, yogurt or sour cream, beaten eggs, grated zest, cinnamon, and melted and cooled butter.

Fillings for Yeast-Risen Coffee Cakes

*E*ach recipe is enough to fill 1 cake, made from half of the total yeast dough recipe.

APPLE-NUT FILLING

1½ cups coarsely chopped peeled apples (6 ounces; 170 g)

3 tablespoons golden raisins (optional)

½ cup currants (2¼ ounces; 65 g)

½ cup granulated sugar (3½ ounces; 100 g) or firmly packed light brown sugar

1 teaspoon ground cinnamon

½ cup shelled and chopped walnuts or pecans (2 ounces; 60 g)

3 tablespoons unsalted butter, melted and cooled

Quantity   About 2¼ cups, for 1 coffee cake

In a large bowl, combine apples, raisins, currants, sugar, cinnamon, and nuts. Toss well. Shape the dough according to directions, then brush the dough with melted butter. Sprinkle on filling. Complete the shaping and baking as directed.

STREUSEL FILLING

⅓ cup firmly packed dark brown sugar (3 ounces; 85 g)

3½ tablespoons unsalted butter, at room temperature, cut up, plus 3 tablespoons, melted and cooled

5 tablespoons all-purpose flour, unsifted

¼ teaspoon salt

½ cup shelled and finely chopped walnuts (2 ounces; 60 g)

Generous ⅛ teaspoon each of ground cinnamon and nutmeg

Quantity   About 1¼ cups, enough to fill 1 coffee cake

In a mixing bowl, combine brown sugar, cut-up butter, flour, salt, nuts, and spices. With your fingertips, pinch ingredients together to make crumbs.

Shape the dough, brush melted butter over it, sprinkle on the filling, and complete shaping and baking as directed.

Quantity 1⅓ cups, for 1 coffee cake

POPPYSEED-STREUSEL FILLING

Make Streusel Filling and add ⅓ cup poppyseeds (1½ ounces; 45 g).

Quantity 1 cup, for 1 coffee cake

JAM FILLING

1 cup thick preserves or jam such as apricot, raspberry, blackberry, lingonberry

Kugelhopf

*K*ugelhopf is a delicious Eastern European coffee ring with as many variations in the spelling of its name as there are regional differences in the recipe. You may see it listed as *gugelhapf, kugelhuf, gugelhopf* or *kugelhoff.* In Alsace, it is a sweet yeast bread containing dried fruits; in Poland it is a plain yeast cake; in Germany it is a sandy-textured pound cake lightened with egg whites. In Austria, it can be either a sweet yeast cake studded with kirsch-soaked raisins or a rich raisin poundcake with plain vanilla or marbled batter.

The one thing all of these have in common is their shape, for kugelhopf is traditionally baked in a fluted ring or Turk's-head mold that is buttered and lined with sliced almonds before the batter is put in to rise. Once baked, the kugelhopf is garnished with a light dusting of confectioners' sugar.

The following Viennese recipe has a moderately sweet yeast dough that, curiously, is also lightened with stiffly beaten egg whites. Unlike many yeast recipes, this one has just one very short (25-minute) rising period, and produces a fine-grained, tender-crumbed product halfway between a bread and a cake. It is perfect for late afternoon tea or coffee, or for breakfast, toasted and covered with melting sweet butter.

15 whole blanched almonds

⅓ cup sliced blanched almonds (1 ounce; 30 g)

⅓ cup seedless raisins (2 ounces; 60 g)

⅓ cup golden raisins (1⅓ ounces; 40 g)

3 tablespoons kirsch or rum

½ cup warm milk (110°F; about 43°C)

½ cup (3½ ounces; 100 g) plus 2 tablespoons granulated sugar

2 packages regular active dry yeast (each ¼ ounce; 7 g)

4 large eggs, separated, plus 1 extra egg white, at room temperature

½ cup lightly salted butter (1 stick; 110 g), plus 2 tablespoons, melted and cooled

Grated zest of 1 lemon

½ cup milk

¼ teaspoon salt

4⅓ cups sifted all-purpose flour (18½ ounces; 525 g)

ICING

1 or 2 tablespoons confectioners' sugar (optional)

1. Prepare the kugelhopf pan as directed. Measure a couple of inches of water into the bottom of a saucepan. Set the strainer over the pan and add both types of raisins. Cover the strainer with the pan lid and set over high heat. Bring the water to a boil and steam the raisins for about 5 minutes. Remove from heat. The raisins should be soft and plump. Place them in a small bowl with the kirsch or rum, stir well, and macerate for about 30 minutes.

2. In another small bowl, combine the warm milk with 1 tablespoon of the measured sugar. Sprinkle on the yeast and let stand for about 5 minutes, until the mixture bubbles.

3. In a very large mixing bowl, combine egg yolks, remaining sugar, melted and cooled butter, grated lemon

Advance Preparation
Raisins are soaked in kirsch or rum for about 30 minutes before being added to the batter. Prepare this in advance. The cake rises for about 25 minutes before baking, so plan your time accordingly. The cake can be baked ahead, wrapped airtight, and frozen.

Special Equipment   One 8-cup kugelhopf mold 9 inches in diameter, strainer that fits into a saucepan with lid, separate bowl and beater for egg whites, small soup bowl

Rising Time   25 minutes

Baking Time   40 minutes at 400°F (204°C)

Quantity   One 9-inch kugelhopf tube cake (serves 10 to 12)

Pan Preparation   Generously spread solid shortening on inner surface of pan, taking special care in the depths of each flute. Sprinkle about ⅓ cup sliced blanched almonds in greased pan and shake to coat sides and bottom. Tap out excess. Place 1 whole blanched almond into each flute in the bottom of the pan; these will form a decorative nut ring on top of the baked cake.

zest, ½ cup milk, the salt, and the raisins with their liqueur. Stir well to combine. Stir in the yeast mixture.

4. Stir about 2 cups of flour into the mixture, stirring hard to combine. At this point, set the dough aside for a few minutes, and use the electric mixer to beat the 5 egg whites until stiff but not dry.

Stir 1 more cup flour into the dough. When well blended, gently stir in about 1 cup of the stiff whites. It looks impossible at first, but the whites will blend after a few stirs, and will soften the dough. Little by little, fold in remaining whites; have patience and a light hand, because quick stirs will flatten the whites. Finally, sprinkle on remaining 1⅓ cups flour, a little at a time, folding it into the dough.

5. Turn the dough into the prepared pan, smooth the top, and cover the pan with a piece of oiled wax paper. Set in a warm, draft-free location for about 25 minutes.

6. Preheat oven to 400°F (204°C). Place the kugelhopf on the center rack and bake for about 40 minutes, or until the top is a rich golden brown and a cake tester inserted in the center comes out clean. Cool the pan on a wire rack for about 5 minutes, then invert the cake onto the rack, lift off the pan, and cool the cake completely. Sift on a tablespoon or two of confectioners' sugar before serving.

Gingerbread

*T*he spice we call ginger *(Zingiber officinale)* is a native of tropical Asia cultivated for its pungent flavor and aroma. It was a favorite of the ancient Greeks and Romans, who made gingerbread in many variations. Gingerbread was common in sixteenth-century England and was especially enjoyed by Queen Elizabeth I. British colonists introduced ginger to America, where it quickly became an important and popular spice. Its enthusiastic reception was recorded in 1796 by Amelia Simmons, whose *American Cookery* included the first published recipe for American soft-style gingerbread. This "cake" was a creative departure from the more traditional crisp, cookie-like European gingerbreads.

Today, the popularity and versatility of gingerbread is evident in its many variations, such as the Orange Gingerbread and the Vermont Maple-Syrup Gingerbread following. Whatever recipe you select, serve the gingerbread warm, with a generous dollop of lightly sweetened whipped cream.

2½ cups sifted all-purpose flour (10½ ounces; 300 g)
½ teaspoon baking powder
1 teaspoon baking soda
½ teaspoon salt
2 teaspoons ground ginger
1 teaspoon ground cinnamon
½ cup lightly salted butter (1 stick; 110 g), at room temperature
½ cup plus 2 tablespoons granulated sugar (4¼ ounces; 125 g)
1 large egg, at room temperature
½ cup sour cream
½ cup unsulfured molasses
1 cup very hot water

Advance Preparation   Gingerbread may be prepared ahead, wrapped airtight, and frozen. Thaw and serve warm.

Special Equipment   One 8- or 9-inch-square baking pan 2 inches deep or 1 sheet pan 11¾ × 7½ × 1¾ inches; 2-cup Pyrex measure

Baking Time   35 minutes at 350°F (175°C)

Quantity   4 cups batter; one 8- or 9-inch-square (serves 9) or sheet cake 11¾ × 7½ inches (serves 12 to 15)

Pan Preparation   Spread bottom and sides of pan with solid shortening.

1. Prepare pan as described. Position rack in center of oven. Preheat oven to 350°F (175°C).

2. Sift together flour, baking powder, baking soda, salt, and spices. Set aside.

3. In the large bowl of an electric mixer, cream together butter and sugar until completely blended to a granular paste. Scrape down inside of bowl. Beat in egg and sour cream.

4. In a 2-cup Pyrex measure, combine molasses and very hot water, stirring until molasses is nearly dissolved. With the mixer on low speed, add about one quarter of the flour mixture to the batter. Alternately add remaining flour and the molasses–water, beating slowly to blend after each addition.

5. Spoon batter into prepared pan, smooth top evenly, then spread batter slightly toward pan edges. Bake in the preheated oven for about 35 minutes, or until a cake tester inserted in the center comes out clean and the top of the cake is lightly springy to the touch. Cool on a wire rack. Cut into squares and serve directly from pan, accompanied by sweetened whipped cream or vanilla ice cream.

VARIATIONS

. . . .

Orange Gingerbread   Prepare basic Gingerbread, but add 1 tablespoon grated orange zest and ⅓ cup chopped walnuts (1¼ ounces; 35 g), stirring them into the batter at the end.

Note: Hot orange juice may be substituted for the water if you wish.

Advance Preparation
Equipment, Pan Preparation, Baking Time, and Quantity are the same as for basic Gingerbread. Follow recipe and procedure that follows.

Vermont Maple-Syrup Gingerbread   This is a mildly flavored, moist gingerbread. The strength of the maple flavor depends upon the quality and grade of the syrup used. To be sure of a definite maple flavor in the cake, add a little maple extract to the batter along with the syrup. To make Maple-Nut Gingerbread, add ½ cup chopped butternuts, walnuts, black walnuts, or hickory nuts to the batter.

2⅓ cups sifted all-purpose flour (10 ounces; 280 g)
½ teaspoon baking powder
1 teaspoon baking soda
¼ teaspoon salt
1½ teaspoons ground ginger
½ teaspoon ground cinnamon
1 large egg, at room temperature
1 cup pure maple syrup
1 cup sour cream
4 tablespoons lightly salted butter (½ stick; 60 g),
    melted and cooled
1 teaspoon maple extract (optional)

1. Prepare pan as directed. Preheat oven to 350°F
(175°C). Position rack in center of oven.

2. Sift together flour, baking powder, baking soda,
and salt. Add ginger and cinnamon. Set aside.

3. In the large bowl of an electric mixer, or in a mixing bowl beating by hand, beat together egg, maple syrup,
sour cream, melted butter, and maple extract. A little at a
time, stir flour mixture into batter, blending well after
each addition.

4. Turn batter into prepared pan and bake in the preheated oven for 30 to 35 minutes, or until a cake tester inserted in the center comes out clean and the top of the
cake is lightly springy to the touch. Cool on a wire rack.
Cut into squares and serve from the pan.

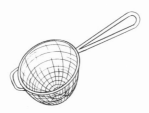

Fresh Berry Coffee Cake

*T*his quick and easy-to-prepare coffee cake is filled with plump fresh berries and topped with cinnamon-scented crumbs. It is a great cake to make in the late summer berry season, using whichever berries are ripe. My favorites are blueberries and raspberries, but you can use strawberries, blackberries, or even fresh ripe peaches, sliced thin and mixed in with the berries. For a great breakfast or brunch treat, serve this cake warm from the oven, topped with Warm Berry Sauce (page 419).

Advance Preparation The cake can be made ahead, though the flavor is best when served warm from the oven. Freezing changes the texture of the fruit and lessens its quality.

Special Equipment One 8- or 9-inch-square baking pan 2 inches deep, colander, paper towels

Baking Time 30 to 35 minutes at 350°F (175°C); add 10 minutes if berries are frozen

Quantity 2½ cups batter; one 8- or 9-inch-square cake (serves 8 or 9)

Pan Preparation Spread solid shortening on bottom and sides of pan.

1½ cups sifted all-purpose flour (6¼ ounces; 180 g)
1 teaspoon baking powder
¼ teaspoon salt
½ cup unsalted butter (1 stick; 110 g), at room temperature
¾ cup granulated sugar (5¼ ounces; 150 g)
2 large eggs, at room temperature
1 teaspoon vanilla extract
3 tablespoons sour cream or yogurt
⅓ cup milk or buttermilk
1½ cups fresh blueberries (7½ ounces; 210 g), or other berries, washed, picked over, and dried on paper towels (frozen whole berries, unthawed, ice crystals removed, may be substituted, or combine peeled and sliced peaches with the berries)

CRUMB TOPPING

3 tablespoons butter (1½ ounces; 45 g), at room temperature
⅓ cup granulated sugar (2¼ ounces; 65 g)
⅓ cup unsifted all-purpose flour (1½ ounces; 45 g)
½ teaspoon ground cinnamon

1. Prepare pan as described. Position rack in the center of oven. Preheat oven to 350°F (175°C).

2. Sift together flour, baking powder, and salt. Set aside.

3. In the large bowl of an electric mixer, cream together butter and sugar until smooth. Add eggs, one at a time, beating after each addition. Add vanilla and sour cream or yogurt and mix well. Alternately add flour mixture and milk or buttermilk to batter, beginning and ending with flour.

4. Spread half of the batter into the prepared pan and smooth the top. Spread berries on top of batter. Cover berries with remaining batter and spread the top as evenly as possible with a rubber scraper; some berries will show through and the top will look a little rough. Never mind.

5. Prepare the crumb topping. In a medium-size bowl, combine all topping ingredients and pinch them together with your fingertips to blend, making crumbs. Spread the crumbs evenly over top of cake. Place pan in the oven and bake for 30 to 35 minutes, or until a cake tester inserted in the center comes out clean and the cake top is a golden brown. Cool cake on a wire rack for a few minutes, then cut into squares and serve warm or at room temperature from the pan.

Yogurt Crumb Cake

*T*his delightfully moist orange-scented cake is made with fruit-flavored yogurt and has crunchy cinnamon-walnut crumbs for both filling and topping.

Advance Preparation This cake can be baked ahead and frozen. Thaw and serve warm.

Special Equipment Nut chopper or food processor, grater, 9-inch-square pan 1½ to 2 inches deep, small bowl

Baking Time 35 to 40 minutes at 350°F (175°C)

Quantity 2½ cups batter, 9-inch-square cake (serves 9)

Pan Preparation Spread solid shortening on bottom and sides of pan.

1½ cups sifted all-purpose flour (6¼ ounces; 180 g)
1½ teaspoons baking powder
¼ teaspoon baking soda
¼ teaspoon salt
6 tablespoons unsalted butter (3 ounces; 90 g), at room temperature
¾ cup granulated sugar (5¼ ounces; 150 g)
1 large egg, at room temperature
1 teaspoon vanilla extract
1 teaspoon orange extract
Grated zest of 1 orange, about 1 tablespoon
¾ cup orange-flavored yogurt, or lemon- or apricot-flavored yogurt, or substitute plain yogurt or sour cream

CRUMB TOPPING
3 tablespoons dark brown sugar
3 tablespoons all-purpose flour
Pinch of salt
Pinch of ground cinnamon
3 tablespoons unsalted butter (1½ ounces; 43 g), cut up, at room temperature
¼ cup chopped walnuts (1 ounce; 30 g)

1. Prepare pan as directed. Position rack in center of oven. Preheat oven to 350°F (175°C).

2. In a small bowl, combine all ingredients for Crumb Topping. Set aside.

3. Sift together flour, baking powder, baking soda, and salt. Set aside.

4. In the large bowl of an electric mixer, cream to-

gether the butter and sugar until well blended. Beat in the egg, vanilla and orange extracts, and grated orange zest.

5. Alternately add flour mixture and yogurt to the batter, beating slowly after each addition. When well blended, spoon half of the batter into the prepared pan. Sprinkle half of the crumb topping mixture over the batter, then top with remaining batter. Sprinkle on remaining crumb topping.

6. Bake in center of preheated oven for 35 to 40 minutes, or until a cake tester inserted in the center comes out clean and top is golden brown. Cool on a wire rack. Cut into 2½- or 3-inch squares and serve warm or at room temperature directly from the pan.

Buttermilk Spice Cake

*S*pice cakes are among our oldest cakes, though early versions used "ale barme," a form of yeast, to raise the dough, giving a more breadlike texture than the tender cake that follows.

This spicy down-home cake is delicious topped by either cream cheese or caramel icing. It is made with a blend of black and golden raisins; you can also add chopped walnuts to the recipe if you wish. Bake the cake in a square and serve it casually from the pan, or make layers, filled and frosted for a fancier presentation. In the summer I decorate the iced spice cake with edible nasturtium flowers.

Advance Preparation Cake can be baked in advance, wrapped airtight, and frozen.

Special Equipment One 8- or 9-inch-square pan 2 inches deep or two 8-inch round layer pans

Baking Time 40 to 45 minutes at 350°F (175°C) for 9-inch square; 35 minutes for 2 layers

Quantity 5 cups batter, one 8- or 9-inch-square, or one 2-layer 8-inch cake (serves 8 or 9)

Pan Preparation Spread solid shortening on bottom and sides of pans, dust pans with flour; tap out excess flour.

2½ cups sifted all-purpose flour (10½ ounces; 300 g)
1 teaspoon baking soda
¾ teaspoon salt
1 tablespoon ground cinnamon
1 teaspoon ground allspice
1 teaspoon ground nutmeg
½ teaspoon ground cloves
¼ teaspoon ground ginger
¾ cup unsalted butter (1½ sticks; 170 g), at room
    temperature
1 cup granulated sugar (7 ounces; 200 g)
1 large egg
½ cup unsulfured molasses
1 cup buttermilk
1 cup seedless raisins, half black and half golden
    (5¾ ounces; 160 g)
½ cup chopped walnuts (optional; 2 ounces; 60 g)

ICING
Cream Cheese Frosting (page 387) or Brown Sugar
    Caramel Icing (page 392)

1. Prepare pan(s) as described. Position rack in lower third of oven. Preheat oven to 350°F (175°C).

2. Sift together flour, baking soda, salt, and spices. Set aside.

3. In the large bowl of an electric mixer, cream together butter and sugar until well blended. Beat in the egg and molasses. Alternately add flour mixture and buttermilk, beating after each addition, beginning and ending with flour. Stir in raisins, and walnuts if using them.

4. Spread batter in prepared pan(s), and bake as directed, or until a cake tester inserted in the center comes out clean and the top is lightly springy to the touch. Cool cake on a wire rack in the baking pan(s) for 5 minutes. To serve, cut into squares and serve from pan, or invert cake layers and cool completely on a wire rack before filling and frosting.

Honey Cake

This moist, flavorful cake is traditionally served on Rosh Hashanah, the Jewish New Year, because honey symbolizes the sweetness wished for in the coming months. For a variation made with neither honey nor sugar, see Susan Richman's Sugar-Free, Honey-Free Orange Cake, following.

1½ cups honey
1 cup strong coffee, or 1½ teaspoons instant coffee
    dissolved in 1 cup boiling water
3½ cups unsifted all-purpose flour (17½ ounces;
    495 g)
2 teaspoons baking powder
1 teaspoon baking soda
Pinch of salt
4 large eggs, at room temperature
2 tablespoons vegetable oil

Advance Preparation The cake may be baked in advance and frozen.

Special Equipment Two loaf pans 9 × 5 × 3 inches, saucepan, sifter, serving platter

Baking Time 55 to 65 minutes at 325°F (165°C)

Quantity Two loaves, each 9 × 5 × 3 inches (serves 16)

Pan Preparation Spread bottom and sides of pans with margarine.

1 cup granulated sugar (7 ounces; 200 g)
1 teaspoon ground cinnamon
½ teaspoon ground nutmeg
¼ teaspoon ground cloves
⅛ teaspoon ground ginger

1. Prepare pans as described. Position rack in center of oven. Preheat oven to 325°F (165°C).

2. Measure the honey into a saucepan and set over moderate heat just until it comes to a boil. Immediately remove pan from the heat and set aside to cool. Do not let honey continue to boil. Once the honey has cooled slightly, stir in the coffee and set the mixture aside.

3. Sift together flour, baking powder, baking soda, and salt. Set aside.

4. In a large mixing bowl, combine eggs, oil, sugar, and spices and beat well. Alternately add small amounts of the flour mixture and the honey-coffee liquid, beating to blend after each addition and beginning and ending with flour.

5. Divide batter evenly between the prepared pans and set to bake in the preheated oven for 55 to 65 minutes, or until a cake tester inserted in the center comes out clean. Cool cakes in their pans on a wire rack until completely cold. To remove cakes, slide a knife blade around the edge of each loaf to release it from the pan, then invert onto a serving plate.

VARIATIONS

. . . .

Susan Richman's Sugar-Free, Honey-Free Orange Cake Omit honey and sugar in recipe above. Substitute 2⅓ cups mixed fruit concentrate (a natural sweetening syrup made from pineapples, peaches, and pears, sold in health-food stores). Instead of 1 cup of coffee, substitute ¾ cup orange juice and add 1 teaspoon orange extract and grated zest of ½ orange to finished batter.

Lemon Tea Cake I

*T*his is a light, tart cake that is spread with lemon-sugar glaze when fresh from the oven. The hot glaze penetrates the cake thoroughly and keeps it moist and flavorful.

Lemon Tea Cake is one of my favorites for holiday giving, because it can be made in advance and freezes very well. I have included 2 versions of the recipe: Lemon Tea Cake I and Lemon Tea Cake II, which is a larger batch. If you have a long Christmas list, or are cooking for a bake sale, use the larger recipe, which was developed by my friend and neighbor Marie Swanson.

1 cup shelled walnuts (4 ounces; 110 g)

1 cup granulated sugar (7 ounces; 200 g)

1½ cups sifted all-purpose flour (6¼ ounces; 180 g)

1 teaspoon baking powder

½ teaspoon salt

6 tablespoons unsalted butter (3¼ ounces; 90 g), at room temperature

2 large eggs, at room temperature

4 teaspoons grated lemon zest plus 2 tablespoons fresh juice (about 2 lemons)

6 tablespoons milk

HOT LEMON GLAZE

⅓ cup granulated sugar (2¼ ounces; 65 g)

2 to 3 teaspoons grated lemon zest (save for garnishing iced cakes) and 6 tablespoons fresh juice (save 1 tablespoon juice for icing) (about 2 lemons)

LEMON ICING

½ cup confectioners' sugar (1¾ ounces; 50 g)

1 tablespoon lemon juice (saved from Hot Lemon Glaze)

A Note About Lemons

Though lemons vary greatly in size and juiciness, an average lemon yields 2 to 3 teaspoons grated zest and 2 to 3 tablespoons juice. The first Lemon Tea Cake recipe plus its glaze and icing will require 7 teaspoons of grated zest plus 8 tablespoons of juice (a total of 4 lemons, depending upon their size and juiciness). To speed preparation you can grate the zest of 4 lemons, squeeze their juice, and set both aside before beginning to bake.

Advance Preparation

Once the cakes are glazed, iced, and completely cooled, they can be individually wrapped airtight in heavy-duty plastic bags and frozen.

Special Equipment   3 baby loaf pans 6 × 3½ × 2 inches or 1 loaf pan 9 × 5 × 3 inches, grater, wax paper, lemon squeezer, nut chopper or food processor, small bowl, pastry brush, small nonreactive saucepan

Baking Time   40 to 45 minutes at 350°F (175°C) for baby loaves; 50 to 60 minutes for large loaf

Quantity   About 4½ cups batter; 3 baby loaves or 1 standard loaf (serves 8)

Pan Preparation   Spread solid shortening on bottom and sides of pans.

1. Prepare pan(s) as described. Position rack in center of oven. Preheat oven to 350°F (175°C).

2. To chop walnuts in the food processor, combine them with 2 or 3 tablespoons of the measured sugar. Or chop them with a nut chopper, or in the blender, ¼ cup at a time. Set nuts aside.

3. Sift together flour, baking powder, and salt. Set aside.

4. In the large bowl of an electric mixer, cream together butter and remaining sugar until well blended. Add eggs, one at a time, beating after each addition. Beat in lemon zest and juice. With mixer on lowest speed, or by hand, alternately add flour mixture and milk, beginning and ending with flour. Beat well, then stir in nuts.

5. Spoon batter into prepared pan(s). Smooth the tops, and bake them in the preheated oven as directed, or until tops are golden brown and a cake tester inserted in the cake center comes out clean.

While cakes bake, prepare the glaze: Stir together glaze ingredients in a small nonreactive saucepan. Set it over moderate heat and stir until the sugar dissolves. Set pan aside. Rewarm glaze just before using it.

6. As soon as cakes come from the oven, set the pan(s) on a wire rack. Brush the cake tops with the hot lemon glaze. Wait several seconds for the glaze to penetrate, then repeat, using up all the glaze.

7. Stir together the Lemon Icing ingredients until smooth. Before cakes are completely cold, drizzle a little icing on each cake, then garnish with a sprinkling of reserved grated lemon zest or a few very thin strips of lemon zest.

When the cakes are completely cold, wrap each one in plastic wrap, then place in a heavy-duty plastic bag, label, and freeze.

LEMON TEA CAKE II

Note: This carefully proportioned enlargement of the first recipe is more or less three times as big, making 10 cups of batter for 8 or 9 baby loaves or 3 regular loaves.

This recipe, plus its glaze and icing, requires between 6 and 7 lemons, depending on size and juiciness, to make a total of 10 teaspoons grated zest and 16½ tablespoons lemon juice, 1 generous cup. To speed preparation, grate the lemons and squeeze the juice before starting to prepare the batter.

1½ cups shelled walnuts (6 ounces; 170 g)

3 cups granulated sugar (21 ounces; 600 g)

4½ cups sifted all-purpose flour (19 ounces; 540 g)

3 teaspoons baking powder

¾ teaspoon salt

1 cup stick margarine (2 sticks; 227 g), or unsalted butter

½ cup unsalted butter (1 stick; 110 g), at room temperature

6 large eggs, at room temperature

6 teaspoons grated lemon zest

9 tablespoons freshly squeezed lemon juice

1½ cups milk

HOT LEMON GLAZE

½ cup granulated sugar (3½ ounces; 100 g)

4 teaspoons grated lemon zest (save for garnishing iced cakes)

7½ to 8 tablespoons lemon juice (save 1 to 1½ tablespoons for icing)

LEMON ICING

½ cup sifted confectioners' sugar (1¾ ounces; 50 g)

1 to 1½ tablespoons lemon juice (saved from Hot Lemon Glaze)

Advance Preparation See Lemon Tea Cake I.

Equipment 9 baby loaf pans 6 × 3½ × 2 inches or 3 average-size loaf pans 8½ × 4½ × 2¾ inches; grater, wax paper, lemon squeezer, nut chopper or food processor, small bowl, pastry brush

Baking Time See Lemon Tea Cake I.

Quantity About 10 cups batter; 8 or 9 baby loaves (serves 48) or 3 regular loaves (serves 24 to 30)

Pan Preparation Spread solid shortening on bottom and sides of pans.

PROCEDURE • Follow procedure for Lemon Tea Cake I, but combine margarine with butter and sugar in step 4. Note that this recipe makes a large quantity of batter and may overfill your large mixing bowl; it is preferable to mix in flour and milk by hand rather than with an electric mixer, thereby avoiding splashes. Once it's well blended, you can beat the batter with the mixer. In step 5, divide batter evenly among the prepared pans. Use about 1¼ cups batter for each of the baby pans. For ease in handling the baby pans, set them on a flat pan before placing them in the oven. Stagger the placement of the pans so heat can circulate in the oven. Bake, glaze, and ice the cakes as directed in the first recipe.

Ukrainian Poppyseed Loaf

This old-world specialty is moist, full of flavor, and very easy to prepare. It is my idea of the perfect comfort food, just the thing to serve with a strong cup of hot tea to restore one's energy.

Because this cake keeps so well, it is good to bake in small pans for holiday gifts. Generally, the cake is topped with only a light dusting of confectioners' sugar, but for holiday giving, if you wish to add a bit of color, use the Icing Glaze (page 408) and stick on a halved candied cherry or blanched almond.

Note: To buy poppyseeds in bulk, see Sources, page 477.

1 cup ground poppyseeds (see grinding techniques, page 43) (5 ounces; 140 g)

1 cup milk

1 cup unsalted butter (2 sticks; 227 g), at room temperature

1½ cups granulated sugar (10½ ounces; 300 g)

3 large eggs, separated, at room temperature

2 teaspoons vanilla extract

2 cups sifted all-purpose flour (8½ ounces; 240 g)

½ teaspoon salt

2½ teaspoons baking powder

TOPPING

2 tablespoons confectioners' sugar (optional)

1. In a small saucepan, combine ground poppyseeds with milk and bring just to a boil over moderate-high heat. Stir once or twice. Remove from heat and allow to stand for 1 hour. Don't cheat on time because the seeds need time to absorb the milk in order to have the correct flavor and texture.

2. Prepare pan(s) as described. Position shelf in center of oven. Preheat oven to 350°F (175°C).

3. In the large bowl of an electric mixer, cream together butter and sugar until well blended. Stop mixer and scrape down inside of bowl and beater several times. Add egg yolks, one at a time, beating after each addition. With mixer on low speed, slowly beat in poppyseeds and milk, and the vanilla. Scrape down inside of bowl and beater.

4. Combine flour, salt, and baking powder. Stir this mixture into batter in several additions.

5. In a separate bowl with a clean beater, beat egg whites until stiff but not dry. Fold whites into the batter in several additions.

6. Turn batter into pan(s): divide evenly between 2 loaf pans, or put 2 cups batter into each coffee can, or

Advance Preparation The poppyseeds must soak in milk for at least 1 hour after being ground and before making the batter; plan your time accordingly. The cake can be made in advance, wrapped airtight, and kept at room temperature for at least a week. It can also be frozen.

Special Equipment 2 loaf pans 8½ × 3½ × 2¾ inches or three 1-pound coffee cans, tops removed, 5½ inches tall × 4 inches in diameter, or 4 baby loaf pans 6 × 3½ × 2 inches; small saucepan, extra bowl and beater for whipping egg whites

Baking Time 45 to 50 minutes at 350°F (175°C) for either small cylinders or baby loaves; for larger pans, increase time slightly

Quantity 5½ cups batter; 2 loaves or 3 small cylinders or 4 baby loaves

Pan Preparation Spread solid shortening on bottom and sides of pans, then dust evenly with flour; tap out excess flour.

1½ cups batter into each baby loaf. Bake all sizes for 45 to 50 minutes, or until a cake tester inserted in the center comes out clean and the cake top is lightly springy to the touch. Leave cake in its pan(s) on a wire rack for 10 minutes. Top with a wire rack and invert; lift off pan(s). Cool cake completely on the rack. Sift on sugar when cake is cold.

Cranberry Orange Loaf

*T*his easy-to-make fruit-filled loaf is a traditional Thanksgiving and Christmas treat. Because the cake freezes so well, I like to bake it in advance, making many small loaves in new baking pans. I give these as holiday gifts, wrapped in a linen napkin with the recipe attached. For an unusual variation, try the Apricot Loaf, following.

Advance Preparation   The cake can be baked in advance, wrapped airtight, and frozen.

Special Equipment   Sifter, 2 mixing bowls, pastry blender or 2 table knives or forks, nut chopper or food processor, grater, wax paper, 1 loaf pan 9 × 5 × 3 inches or 3 baby loaf pans 5¾ × 3¼ × 2 inches

Baking Time   1 hour at 350°F (175°C) for regular large loaf; 35 to 40 minutes for baby loaves

Quantity   1 regular loaf or 3 baby loaves (serves 8)

2 cups unsifted all-purpose flour (10 ounces; 280 g)
1½ teaspoons baking powder
½ teaspoon baking soda
1 teaspoon salt
1 cup granulated sugar (7 ounces; 200 g)
3 tablespoons wheat germ, toasted or plain
¼ cup unsalted butter (2 ounces; 57 g), at room temperature, cut up
Grated zest of 1 orange
¾ cup orange juice
1 large egg, at room temperature
½ cup shelled walnuts (2 ounces; 60 g)
2 cups whole fresh or frozen (unthawed) cranberries (8 ounces; 240 g), picked over and stems removed

1. Prepare pan(s) as described. Position rack in center of oven. Preheat oven to 350°F (175°C).

2. Sift together flour, baking powder, baking soda, and salt into a mixing bowl. Add sugar and wheat germ. Add the cut-up butter and work it into the dry ingredients as for a piecrust, blending the ingredients with a pastry blender or 2 cross-cutting knives until the dough forms crumbs.

3. In another bowl, combine grated orange zest, orange juice, and egg. Beat well. Set bowl aside.

With nut chopper or food processor, coarsely chop nuts and then cranberries.

4. Add orange-egg mixture to flour-butter crumbs and mix to combine. Stir in chopped nuts and cranberries. Mix well.

5. Spoon batter into prepared pans, smooth the top, then spread batter toward pan sides. Bake as directed or until the cake is golden and a cake tester inserted in the center comes out clean. Cool cake in pans on a wire rack for about 5 minutes, then tip cakes out of pans and cool completely on the rack. Note that the loaves will cut most neatly the day after they are baked.

Pan Preparation Generously coat bottom and sides of pan(s) with margarine or solid shortening.

VARIATIONS

. . . .

Apricot Loaf Prepare Cranberry Orange Loaf with the following changes: Instead of cranberries and orange juice substitute apricots and apricot juice prepared as follows:

Measure 2 cups packed dried apricots (340 g), then chop or slice them into small pieces. Add just enough water to cover the fruit in a saucepan. Cover the pan and bring water to a boil. Lower the heat and simmer for only about 2 minutes.

Save the fruit. Strain and reserve the liquid; you need ¾ cup. Pour a little more water over the apricots in the strainer if you need more liquid. Use the chopped apricots instead of the cranberries, and the liquid instead of the orange juice.

Clara Joslin's Banana Nut Cake

*T*he recipe for this moist and flavorful banana-nut cake comes from my maternal grandmother, Clara Joslin. You will also enjoy the variations, Banana Streusel and Banana Chocolate-Chip Cake, following.

Advance Preparation The cake can be made ahead, wrapped airtight, and frozen.

Special Equipment One 9-inch-square pan 2 inches deep or 1 sheet pan 11¾ × 7½ × 1¾ inches or 16 cupcake pans 2¾ inches in diameter; nut chopper or food processor

Baking Time 30 to 35 minutes at 350°F (175°C) for 9-inch-square or sheet cake 11¾ × 7½ × 1¾ inches; 20 to 25 minutes for cupcakes

Quantity 4 cups batter; 9-inch square (serves 9), larger sheet (serves 12 to 20), or 16 cupcakes

Pan Preparation Spread solid shortening on bottom and sides of pan.

2 cups sifted all-purpose flour (8½ ounces; 240 g)
1 teaspoon baking powder
½ teaspoon baking soda
⅛ teaspoon salt
½ cup unsalted butter (1 stick; 110 g), at room temperature
1 cup granulated sugar (7 ounces; 200 g)
2 large eggs, at room temperature
3 large ripe bananas, thoroughly mashed, about 1 cup (9 ounces; 260 g)
½ cup chopped walnuts (2 ounces; 60 g)
¼ cup toasted wheat germ (optional; 1 ounce; 30 g)

1. Prepare pan(s) as directed. Position rack in center of oven. Preheat oven to 350°F (175°C).

2. Sift together flour, baking powder, baking soda, and salt. Set aside.

3. In the large bowl of an electric mixer, cream together butter and sugar until well blended. Add eggs, one at a time, beating after each addition. Alternately add the dry ingredients and the mashed bananas to the batter, beating slowly after each addition. Stir in nuts, and wheat germ if used. Spoon batter into prepared pan, smooth top evenly, then spread batter slightly toward pan edges.

4. Bake in center of preheated oven as directed, or until a cake tester inserted in the center comes out clean and cake is lightly springy to the touch.

Banana Streusel Cake   Prepare Banana Nut Cake. Prepare 1 recipe Streusel Nut Topping (page 377). Before baking, sprinkle the top of a 9-inch-square cake with about 1½ cups of streusel crumbs. For a sheet cake 11¾ × 7½ inches, use 1¾ cups streusel. Extra streusel crumbs may be frozen in an airtight container for later use.

Banana Chocolate-Chip Cake   Prepare Banana Nut Cake. Add ½ cup miniature semisweet chocolate morsels to batter along with nuts.

Lauren's Peach Crumb Cake

*T*his quick and easy-to-make recipe came from my late friend Lauren Lieberman, who baked with great enthusiasm and made this versatile cake with whatever fruit was in season, including rhubarb, apples, nectarines, or any type of berries.

8 to 10 fresh ripe peaches, peeled (see step 1), sliced
    to make 4 cups, or use 4 cups other fruit
1½ cups sifted all-purpose flour (6¼ ounces; 180 g)
½ cup granulated sugar (3½ ounces; 100 g) plus
    ½ cup granulated sugar or firmly packed light
    brown sugar
Pinch of salt
½ cup unsalted butter (1 stick; 110 g), at room
    temperature, cut up
½ teaspoon ground cinnamon
2 tablespoons quick-cooking tapioca
1 tablespoon lemon juice
3 tablespoons fruit juice or water, as needed

Advance Preparation   The dough can be prepared ahead and held, covered, in the refrigerator for a day or two.

Special Equipment   One 9-inch springform pan and flat serving platter, or one 9- or 10-inch deep-dish pie plate

Baking Time   35 minutes at 425°F (220°C), or less, depending on type of fruit

Quantity   One 9-inch cake (serves 8)

Pan Preparation   None

1. To peel peaches, place them in a pot of boiling water for about 3 minutes. Remove with a slotted spoon to a bowl of cold water. Drain, then slip off peach skins.

Position rack in lower third of oven. Preheat oven to 425°F (220°C).

2. Combine flour, ½ cup sugar, and the salt in a mixing bowl. Cut in pieces of butter and combine until the mixture resembles dry rice. You can accomplish this by pinching the ingredients together with your fingertips, or cutting them together with 2 cross-cutting knives, or using a wire-loop pastry blender. Or you can pulse the ingredients in the workbowl of a food processor just until you begin to see clumps form; do not form a dough ball. You will have about 2½ cups of dough crumbs.

3. Measure ¾ cup of these crumbs and place them in a small bowl. Stir in the cinnamon; set this aside for the cake topping. Press remaining dough onto the bottom and ¾ inch up the sides of the baking pan.

4. In a large bowl, combine the sliced fruit, remaining ½ cup sugar (more or less, depending on sweetness of fruit), the tapioca, and lemon juice. If your fruit has no juice of its own (dry peaches or apples, for example), add 3 tablespoons fruit juice or water. If fruit is juicy, you can omit this extra liquid. Stir mixture well, taking care to moisten the tapioca with fruit juice. Let mixture stand for a few minutes to soften the tapioca, then arrange fruit on the dough in the pan. Sprinkle on an even layer of the reserved dough crumbs.

5. Bake in the preheated oven about 35 minutes, or until a knife tip easily pierces the fruit slices and the cake top is golden brown. Hard apples may require longer baking time than peaches or berries. Cool cake on a wire rack; release sides of springform pan and slide cake onto a flat serving platter. If cake was baked in a pie plate, serve it from the pan, omitting the serving platter. Cut the cake into wedges and serve warm with lightly sweetened whipped cream or Crème Anglaise (page 418).

Apple Crumb Cake   Prepare Peach Crumb Cake, but substitute 4 cups peeled, cored, and sliced apples. Use either cooking apples such as Granny Smith or softer varieties such as McIntosh or Delicious. This is a good recipe for apples that are too soft to hold their shape in pies. Add ½ teaspoon ground nutmeg to the crumb topping.

Applesauce Cake

*T*his is a rich, moist applesauce cake that I like to fill with a variety of chopped fruits and nuts. For Christmas, I often double the recipe and make several small loaves for gifts.

1 cup sifted all-purpose flour (4¼ ounces; 120 g)
½ cup unsifted whole-wheat pastry flour (2¼
    ounces; 65 g) (or use all white flour)
¼ cup wheat germ (1 ounce; 30 g)
½ teaspoon salt
1 teaspoon baking soda
1 teaspoon ground cinnamon
½ teaspoon each of ground cardamom and nutmeg
¼ teaspoon ground cloves
1 cup currants (4½ ounces; 130 g) or raisins
1 cup finely chopped walnuts (4 ounces; 110 g)
1 cup firmly packed light brown sugar (7 ounces;
    200 g)
½ cup unsalted butter (1 stick; 110 g), at room
    temperature
2 tablespoons honey
1 large egg, at room temperature
¼ cup apple cider or apple juice
1 cup thick applesauce

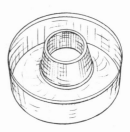

Advance Preparation   The cake can be baked in advance, wrapped airtight, and kept in a cool place for about a week. Or it can be frozen.

Special Equipment   One 9-inch tube pan (6½–cup capacity), nut chopper or food processor

Baking Time   50 to 60 minutes at 350°F (175°C)

Quantity   4 cups batter; one 9-inch tube cake (serves 10)

Pan Preparation   Spread solid shortening on bottom and sides of pan, dust pan evenly with flour; tap out excess flour.

ICING (OPTIONAL)
Icing Glaze (page 408), flavored with vanilla or bourbon

1. Prepare pan as described. Position rack in center of oven. Preheat oven to 350°F (175°C).

2. In a bowl, combine both flours and wheat germ. Sift with salt, baking soda, and spices. In another bowl, combine currants and chopped nuts. Add ¼ cup of flour mixture and toss to coat fruit and nuts well. Set both bowls aside.

3. In the large bowl of an electric mixer, cream sugar, butter, and honey until light and smooth. Add egg and cider and beat well. Little by little, stir the flour mixture into the batter, beating slowly after each addition. Stir in currant and nut mixture and applesauce.

4. Spoon batter into prepared pan and bake in the preheated oven for 50 to 60 minutes, or until a cake tester inserted in the center comes out clean though wet, and the top feels springy to the touch. Cool on a wire rack for 10 minutes. Top with another rack and invert. Remove baking pan. Cool completely. Serve the cake plain, or top with Icing Glaze.

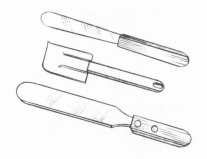

Marleni's Apple Cake

*T*his is our family's all-time favorite apple cake. We were introduced to it years ago by my Parisian goddaughter, Marleni Kanas, who used to make it when she was a little girl visiting her American grandmother, Helen Everitt, in Long Island. Perhaps it is love by association, for we spent many warm summer afternoons nibbling on this cake in Helen's flower-filled garden. The cake is easy enough for a child to make. While it is not too sweet, it is extremely moist, full of fruit, nuts, and spices. This cake was adapted from a recipe in a slim paper volume called *The Way to the Heart Cookbook* (Viet Nam Tree Memorial Committee of Huntington Township, New York, 1976).

3 cups sifted all-purpose flour (12¾ ounces; 360 g)

½ teaspoon baking powder

½ teaspoon baking soda

¼ teaspoon salt

½ teaspoon each of ground nutmeg and cinnamon

3 tablespoons wheat germ (optional)

1½ cups light vegetable oil

2 cups granulated sugar (14 ounces; 400 g)

2 teaspoons vanilla extract

3 tablespoons milk

3 large eggs, at room temperature

3 large cooking apples, about 6½ ounces each (550 g altogether), peeled, cored, and cut into ½-inch pieces to make about 3 cups

1 cup seedless raisins (5¾ ounces; 170 g)

1 cup coarsely chopped walnuts (4 ounces; 110 g)

TOPPING (OPTIONAL)

3 tablespoons confectioners' sugar

Advance Preparation   Cake can be baked ahead and frozen, though flavor is best when freshly baked.

Special Equipment   One 9- or 10-inch plain angel-food tube or springform tube pan, nut chopper or food processor

Baking Time   90 minutes at 350°F (175°C)

Quantity   8 cups batter; one 9- or 10-inch tube cake (serves 10 to 12)

Pan Preparation   Spread solid shortening on bottom and sides of pan, dust evenly with flour; tap out excess flour.

1. Prepare pan as described. Position rack in center of oven. Preheat oven to 350°F (175°C).

2. Sift together flour, baking powder, baking soda, salt, and spices. Add wheat germ if using it. Set mixture aside.

3. In the large bowl of an electric mixer, combine oil, sugar, vanilla, and milk. Beat well. Add eggs and beat again. Little by little, stir in flour mixture, beating slowly to blend. Stir in apples, raisins, and nuts. Batter will be very stiff.

4. Spoon batter into the prepared pan and smooth the top. Bake in the preheated oven for 90 minutes, or until a cake tester inserted in the center comes out clean and the cake feels lightly springy to the touch. Cool on a wire rack for 15 minutes. Slide a knife blade between cake and sides of pan to loosen it, then top cake with a plate and invert. Lift off pan. Top cake with a plate and invert again so cake is right side up. Cool completely. Sift a little confectioners' sugar on top just before serving.

Quick Chopped Apple Cake

I developed this recipe one fall when inundated with apples from a nearby orchard. There is really more fruit here than cake, and the result is very moist and flavorful. For a brunch treat, serve this warm, with a little heavy cream poured on top.

3 tablespoons unsalted butter at room temperature

⅓ cup firmly packed dark brown sugar (3 ounces; 85 g)

⅔ cup granulated sugar (4½ ounces; 130 g)

1 large egg, at room temperature

3 tablespoons toasted wheat germ

1 teaspoon vanilla extract

3 tablespoons sour cream

¾ cup (3¾ ounces; 105 g) plus 7 tablespoons unsifted all-purpose flour

¼ teaspoon salt

1 teaspoon baking powder

¾ teaspoon ground cinnamon

½ teaspoon ground nutmeg

2½ large cooking apples such as Granny Smith, each about 7 ounces (550 g altogether), peeled, cored, and chopped into ¼-inch pieces to make 3 cups

¼ cup dried currants (scant 1 ounce; 25 g), or raisins or diced dried apricots

⅓ cup chopped walnuts or pecans (1¼ ounces; 40 g)

Advance Preparation   This cake can be prepared ahead, wrapped airtight, and frozen.

Special Equipment   One 9-inch-square pan 2 inches deep or 1 sheet pan 11¾ × 7½ × 1¾ inches; nut chopper or food processor

Baking Time   50 to 55 minutes at 350°F (175°C)

Quantity   4 cups batter, one 9-inch cake (serves 9)

Pan Preparation   Spread solid shortening on bottom and sides of pan.

1. Prepare pan as described. Position rack in center of oven. Preheat oven to 350°F (175°C).

2. In the large bowl of an electric mixer, cream together butter and both sugars until completely blended. Add egg and beat well. Scrape down inside of bowl. Add wheat germ, vanilla, and sour cream and beat well.

3. In a small bowl, combine ¾ cup of the flour, the salt, baking powder, cinnamon, and nutmeg. With the mixer on very low speed, or beating by hand, add the flour mixture, a little at a time, to the butter-egg batter.

4. In a large bowl, toss the chopped apples with the currants and nuts. Stir in remaining 7 tablespoons flour, coating the apples. By hand, stir fruit-nut mixture into the batter.

5. Spoon batter into prepared pan. Bake in the preheated oven for 50 to 55 minutes, or until a cake tester inserted in the center comes out clean and the top of the cake is lightly golden. Cool cake on a wire rack. Cut into 3-inch squares and serve warm from the pan.

Jeannette Pépin's Pear Cake

Lyons, one of France's primary culinary regions, boasts an extra dimension in its tradition of *haute cuisine:* the *mères de Lyon:* women chefs who, since the late eighteenth century, have specialized in superb regional cuisine. Jeannette Pépin, mother of well-known chef Jacques Pépin, is a distinguished member of this group, having presided over two restaurants near Lyons, Le Bressan and Le Pélican. Jeannette now claims to be retired, though she continues to cook and to travel at an exhausting pace. In preparation for a magazine article I was writing, my husband, daughter, and I had the good fortune to visit with Jeannette at her home. We shopped and cooked together, and sampled many of her specialties, including this *clafoutis aux poires,* one of our favorites. The following quick and easy-to-make cake is my adaptation of the recipe she presented to us with a casual nod to conventional measurements and a flourish of her special Gallic charm and humor.

4 large ripe Bartlett pears (about 2 pounds, 900 g)

3 tablespoons granulated sugar, plus ¼ cup (1¾ ounces; 50 g)

½ cup all-purpose flour (2½ ounces; 70 g)

¼ teaspoon salt

½ teaspoon baking powder

3 large eggs, at room temperature

1 cup milk

1. Prepare pan as described. Position rack in center of oven. Preheat oven to 425°F (217°C).

2. To prepare the pears, peel them, then slice each lengthwise into halves. Remove the core with tip of a paring knife. Set each half flat side down on a cutting board and cut crosswise into ⅛-inch slices. Slip the knife blade beneath the entire pear half and lift it up, transferring it to the buttered pan; set the pear half down with the narrow stem end pointing to the center. Repeat, arranging the sliced halves like the petals of a flower in the pan. Now press gently on each pear half, fanning the slices toward the pan center. Sprinkle 2 tablespoons of the sugar over the pears; use more sugar if the pears are underripe.

3. In a mixing bowl, or in the workbowl of a food processor fitted with the metal blade, blend the flour, salt, baking powder, ¼ cup of sugar, the eggs and milk. When smooth, scrape down the inside of the bowl, blend for another second, then pour the batter on top of the pears. Sprinkle on remaining 1 tablespoon of sugar.

4. Set the cake in the preheated oven and bake for 15 minutes. Lower the heat to 350°F (175°C) and bake 30 minutes longer, or until the top has puffed, is golden brown, and a cake tester inserted in the center comes out clean. Cool pan on a wire rack for about 10 minutes before serving warm, or serve at room temperature. The cake will sink somewhat as it cools.

Advance Preparation   This quickly prepared cake is best made just before serving warm from the oven, or at least no more than 3 or 4 hours in advance.

Special Equipment   One 10-inch quiche pan, pie plate, or removable-bottom tart pan; paring knife, vegetable peeler, food processor or mixing bowl and large spoon

Baking Time   15 minutes at 425°F (220°C), then 30 minutes at 350°F (175°C)

Quantity   One 10-inch cake (serves 8)

Pan Preparation   Spread unsalted butter on bottom and sides of baking pan. Set pan aside.

Ginnie Hagan's Blueberry Cake

*G*innie Sweatt Hagan is, to my mind, the berry-picking queen of Vermont's North-east Kingdom. It is a rare summer morning that she is not off before dawn on a long-distance trek in pursuit of the perfect wild berry. Perhaps it is the magic of the mountains, or perhaps, as I suspect, Ginnie has a touch of the leprechaun about her, but uncannily she always comes home with a full berry bucket. She picks just for fun, makes jam and pies, and gives it all away to friends, among whom I gratefully count myself.

This cake is one of Ginnie's specialties, a variation on gingerbread, but the molasses and cinnamon never overpower the berries. The cake is also good made with fresh or frozen (unthawed) cranberries.

Special Equipment   One 9-inch-square baking pan 2 inches deep, 2-cup Pyrex measure

Baking Time   40 to 45 minutes at 350°F (175°C)

Quantity   3¾ cups batter; one 9-inch-square cake (serves 9)

Pan Preparation   Spread solid shortening on bottom and sides of pan.

2 cups sifted all-purpose flour (8½ ounces; 240 g)
1 teaspoon baking soda
½ teaspoon salt
1 teaspoon ground cinnamon
¼ cup unsalted butter or stick margarine (½ stick; 60 g), at room temperature
1 cup granulated sugar (7 ounces; 200 g)
1 large egg, at room temperature
½ cup unsulfured molasses
1 cup boiling water
1 to 1½ cups fresh blueberries (about 7½ ounces; 210 g), picked over, stemmed, rinsed, and thoroughly drained on paper towels; or substitute unthawed frozen berries

SAUCE (OPTIONAL)
1 cup heavy cream

1. Prepare pan as described. Position rack in center of oven. Preheat oven to 350°F (175°C).

2. Sift together flour, baking soda, salt, and cinnamon. Set aside.

3. In the large bowl of an electric mixer, cream together butter or margarine and sugar until well blended. Add the egg and beat well. In a 2-cup Pyrex measure, stir together the molasses and boiling water until the molasses is dissolved.

4. Alternately add to the batter the flour mixture and the molasses-water, beginning and ending with flour. Beat very slowly after each addition until well blended. Finally, stir in the blueberries. The batter will be quite thin.

5. Spoon batter into the prepared pan, spread the top evenly, and bake in the preheated oven for 40 to 45 minutes, 50 minutes if using frozen berries, or until a cake tester inserted in the center comes out clean and the top is lightly springy to the touch. Cool the cake on a wire rack, cut it into 3-inch squares, and serve it warm with a little heavy cream poured over each slice.

VARIATIONS

Cranberry-Blueberry Cake Prepare Ginnie Hagan's Blueberry Cake, but add ½ cup whole fresh or unthawed frozen cranberries to the recipe. Don't decrease quantity of blueberries. Or substitute cranberries (whole or chopped) for all the blueberries.

Lemon-Blueberry Pudding Cake

*P*udding cake is an old-fashioned favorite now staging a well-deserved comeback. It is quick to prepare—once the ingredients are measured and the eggs separated, it takes barely 5 minutes.

Children and beginning bakers love to make this easy recipe, and everyone admires the results. In the heat of the oven, an ordinary-looking batter is magically transformed into a rich creamy pudding studded with fruit and topped by a layer of delicate sponge cake. Served warm, it is pure heaven.

Note: To achieve the correct texture, it is essential to bake this cake in a water bath. For flavor variations, the lemon zest may be omitted and other fruit juices substituted for lemon juice. Raspberries may be substituted for blueberries.

Advance Preparation The cake can be baked ahead and served cold, but it is exceptionally good warm from the oven, and is best made fairly soon before serving.

Special Equipment One 8-inch-square baking pan 2 inches deep or 1½-quart ovenproof casserole; roasting pan large enough to hold the cake pan or casserole with at least an inch or two of space all around, for a water bath; grater; whisk or food processor fitted with steel blade; bowl and beater for whipping egg whites

Baking Time 25 to 35 minutes at 350°F (175°C)

1 cup granulated sugar (7 ounces; 200 g)
3 tablespoons unsifted all-purpose flour
⅛ teaspoon salt
Generous pinch of ground cinnamon
2 tablespoons unsalted butter, melted and cooled
Grated zest of 1 lemon
¼ cup freshly squeezed lemon juice
3 large eggs, separated, at room temperature
1 cup milk
1 cup fresh blueberries or raspberries (frozen whole berries can be used, but be sure they are drained and dry)

1. Prepare pan as directed. Position rack in center of oven. Preheat oven to 350°F (175°C).

2. In a large mixing bowl or the workbowl of a food processor, combine ¾ cup plus 2 tablespoons sugar with the flour, salt, and cinnamon. Stir or pulse for 2 or 3 seconds to mix. Add the melted butter, grated lemon zest and juice, and the egg yolks. Whisk by hand or pulse for a few seconds to blend, then blend in the milk. Do not overbeat.

3. In a clean bowl, beat the egg whites with an electric mixer until foamy. Add remaining 2 tablespoons sugar and beat until the whites are nearly stiff but not dry. Fold the whites into the lemon batter in several additions. Gently fold in the berries.

4. Turn batter into the prepared pan and set cake pan in the larger roasting pan. Carefully pour water into the larger pan until it reaches one third to one half of the way up the sides of the baking pan. Gently place the cake in its water bath in the preheated oven and bake for 25 minutes, or until the top is golden brown. Remove cake from the water bath, cool for a few minutes, and serve warm, directly from the pan.

Quantity   4 cups batter; one 8-inch cake (serves 4 or 5)

Pan Preparation   Generously coat pan with butter or margarine, not solid shortening. Set out roasting pan and pitcher of water for the water bath.

Chocolate Pudding Cake

*Q*uick, easy, and great" read my batter-stained notes for this recipe. You simply toss ingredients together, stir, and top with boiling water. Never mind the fact that it looks weird before baking. It emerges from the oven like a crisp-topped brownie rippled with dark chocolate pudding. Note that the batter is egg-free. Throw in some nuts or chopped white chocolate if you want to get creative, and serve the pudding cake warm, spooned from its baking pan and topped with heavy cream.

Advance Preparation   Cake can be baked ahead and re-warmed, but it is never quite as wonderful as when fresh. It will, however, keep fresh, covered, at room temperature for a day or two. In very hot weather, store in the refrigerator.

Special Equipment
8-inch-square baking pan 2 inches deep

Baking Time   35 minutes at 350°F (175°C)

Quantity   One 8-inch dessert (serves 4 to 6, or 1 chocoholic)

Pan Preparation   Spread butter or margarine on bottom and sides of pan.

1 cup unsifted all-purpose flour (5 ounces; 140 g)
1⅓ cups granulated sugar (9¼ ounces; 265 g)
6 tablespoons unsweetened cocoa, preferably Dutch-process
2 teaspoons baking powder
¼ teaspoon ground cinnamon
½ teaspoon instant espresso coffee powder
Generous ¼ teaspoon salt
½ cup milk
¼ cup light vegetable oil, such as canola or safflower oil
1 teaspoon vanilla extract
1 cup boiling water

1. Prepare pan as described. Position rack in center of oven. Preheat oven to 350°F (175°C).

2. In a mixing bowl, combine flour, ⅔ cup of the granulated sugar, 4 tablespoons of the cocoa, the baking powder, cinnamon, coffee powder, and salt. Stir well to blend. With a wooden spoon, stir in milk, oil, and vanilla extract. The batter will feel quite stiff.

3. Spoon batter into the prepared pan and smooth the top more or less evenly. In a small bowl, stir together remaining 2 tablespoons cocoa and ⅔ cup granulated sugar. Spread this mixture evenly over the batter in the pan. On top of this, pour the boiling water. Do not stir.

4. Carefully set the pan in the preheated oven and bake for 35 minutes, or until the top looks crisp and crackled and a cake tester inserted into a cakey area comes out clean. Cool for a few minutes. Serve directly from the pan.

Cheesecakes

ABOUT CHEESECAKE

WHO CAN RESIST the appeal of a rich, creamy, satin-smooth cheesecake? Since this is one luxury that is well within reach, and it is easy to make and freezes well, it is worth preparing for a special occasion. Read the following tips and notes on ingredients so that you will understand the reasons for each technique.

Equipment

If your mixer has a flat paddle attachment, use it in place of a regular whipping beater because it will incorporate less air; cheesecakes should be creamed, not whipped. In fact, if you happen to overbeat the batter with a whipping beater, the excess air may cause the cake to crack during baking, though there can be other reasons, explained below. If you do use regular whisk-style beaters, use them on low to low-medium speed, never high; this way, they will not whip excess air into the batter.

When setting the cake into the oven to bake, it is best to place it on a sturdy jelly-roll pan with a lip. This is especially important when using springform pans, because they can leak if not tightly fastened.

Batter

For a cheesecake to taste smooth and creamy, the batter must be smooth and creamy at every stage. To accomplish this, you must have all ingredients at room temperature (approximately 70°F; 21°C) when you begin. Beat the cream cheese until smooth and soft before adding any other ingredients to your mixing bowl. Stop the mixer several times to scrape down the inside of the bowl and beater, taking care that there are no lumps in the batter and no ingredients stuck to the bowl bottom.

Cracks

Sometimes cracks appear in the top of a cheesecake while it is baking or cooling. There are as many reasons for this as there are cures or preventive measures. Most cracks occur because the cake has released its moisture or steam too quickly, causing fissures in the delicate warm structure. This can happen when the cake is exposed to extreme changes in temperature, such as baking in too hot an oven, baking for too long a time, or being placed in a cool spot or a draft immediately after baking. Deep cavernous cracks mean the egg-white structure has partially collapsed and the cake's texture may resemble a pudding; it will be edible, but not what you expected, so top it with fruit and don't serve it to company. Shallow cracks often occur despite our best efforts, and generally can be ignored. If they show up during baking, remember that the cake will sink down as it cools and these cracks will get somewhat smaller. Also, you can cover the top with sour cream or a fruit glaze.

To help prevent cracks, professional bakeries often add steam to their ovens; some recipes call for solid-bottom (non-springform) pans to be baked in a water bath. This procedure adds both moisture and temperature control to give slow, even heat. However, in this book I have chosen the less cumbersome procedure of using the springform pan and baking in a low oven. Be sure to put an auxiliary oven thermometer (sold in hardware stores) inside your oven to moniter the heat; oven thermostats are notoriously irregular. If you can avoid it, don't open the oven door during the first half of the baking time for a cheesecake, to keep the temperature steady. Most of my recipes advise leaving the cake in the oven after baking, with the heat off, for an additional hour or so to allow the cake to cool off very slowly, away from drafts. You should follow recipe cooling procedures carefully; they make a difference. One unusual technique, described in the Tangerine Cheesecake recipe, calls for topping the cooling cake with a cardboard disk. The cardboard absorbs the moisture as the cake cools and keeps away drafts. Odd, but it works well. And remember, nothing is infallible.

Crusts

Cheesecakes are so rich that I prefer a light crust. My favorite technique is simply to butter the sides and bottom of the springform pan, then dust the butter with toasted and ground nuts or with cookie crumbs. Be sure to select nuts or crumbs with a flavor that is compatible with that of the cake. The one exception is New York Cheesecake, which has a pastry crust.

Baking

To tell if your cheesecake is done, observe the top surface carefully. For most cheesecakes, the edges of the baked cake puff up slightly and may turn just faintly golden. You do not want a deeply browned crust. The top surface should look dull, not shiny, and when the side of the pan is lightly tapped, the center should move slightly from side to side but not jiggle as if it were liquid. It is normal for the center to be softer than the edges when the cake is baked. The entire cake will rise during baking, then settle and solidify as it cools. If any cracks appear, they usually get smaller as the cake cools and sinks down.

Transferring Cakes

If you want to freeze a cheesecake but need to reuse the springform pan, you can transfer the cake to another surface. To do this, chill your cake in the refrigerator in the springform pan for at least 4 hours, or overnight, so you are sure the cake is very firm. Then cover a sturdy corrugated cardboard disk of the cake's diameter, or larger, with foil. Set out your largest longest spatula, preferably one with a blade about 1¾ inches by 12 inches. After removing the sides of the springform, very cautiously slide the spatula beneath the bottom of the cake; ease the cake off the baking pan and onto the cardboard. It helps to have a partner to hold the cardboard for you, but it works anyway if your spatula is big enough. Do not attempt this with a thin-bladed knife or a stubby pancake turner, and never try to transfer a warm cake! After transferring the cake, wrap it airtight with plastic wrap and heavy-duty foil before labeling and freezing.

Cutting Cheesecake

Cheesecake tends to stick to the serving knife, making neat slices difficult to achieve. It helps to heat the knife blade under hot running water between cuts, but this is not too convenient during a dinner party. One solution is simply to have at hand an extra knife with which to scrape the cutting knife clean after each slice. My favorite method also makes for good conversation: use dental floss or heavy button thread for cutting. Cut a length about 20 inches long, or the diameter of the cake plus enough to wrap around both hands. Then simply pull the thread taut between your hands, poise it above the cake, and press down right to the cake bottom. Release the thread in one hand and pull it out with the other hand. Repeat, making slices of desired width across the cake like the spokes of a wheel.

Ingredients

CREAM CHEESE • Cheese is what this cake is all about; while a variety of cheeses may be used, cream cheese is the basic element for these recipes.

Cream cheese contains 35 to 40 percent butterfat. Generally speaking, the higher the butterfat content, the creamier and richer will be the cheesecake. Brands of cream cheese vary in quality and flavor. Cut-rate or generic cream cheese is often less creamy, rich, and delicate of flavor than one would wish, and usually the butterfat content is the minimum permissible. Avoid using either "imitation or low-fat cream cheese" or whipped cream cheese for these recipes.

One of the most widely available national brands, and the one I prefer, is regular Kraft's Philadelphia Brand Cream Cheese, sold in 3- and 8-ounce foil-wrapped blocks that are freshness dated. Be sure to check dates.

Cream cheese must be brought to room temperature before being combined with the other ingredients in your batter. If you are in a hurry and have just removed the cream cheese from the refrigerator, unwrap the packages and put the cheese in the microwave on high speed for 2 or 3 seconds only. Test it; it should be soft to touch but not even near melting.

HOMEMADE YOGURT CHEESE • This low-calorie substitute for cream cheese is a Middle-Eastern specialty called *labna*. It is simply plain yogurt hung in a cheesecloth bag until all the water has drained out, leaving a creamy, mild, low-fat cheese.

RICOTTA CHEESE • Ricotta is a fresh, unripened cheese with a bland, slightly nutty flavor. It is moist, with a soft fine curd that gives a slightly granular texture. While ricotta in Italy is often made from the whey of sheep's milk, American ricotta is usually made from cow's-milk whey. It contains between 4 and 10 percent butterfat and has half the calories of cream cheese per ounce (about 50 as compared with 100). For cheesecakes, whole-milk ricotta is preferable to that made with skim milk.

COTTAGE CHEESE • Cottage cheese is a mild-flavored, soft-curd, unripened cheese made from either whole or skim milk. Its flavor is usually slightly sweeter or tangier than ricotta. Depending upon whether or not it has been creamed (by having whole milk or cream added to the curds), the butterfat content can vary between 4 and 15 percent; indeed, some dairies claim it to be as low as ½ to 2 percent. For cheesecake, I prefer to use creamed cottage cheese with a butterfat content of at least 3 or 4 percent.

SOUR CREAM • Sour cream, with a butterfat content of about 20 percent, contributes both smoothness and richness to cheesecake. Be sure to check the freshness date on the carton, and bring the cream to room temperature before adding it to the batter.

FLOUR • A little flour is sometimes added to cheesecake as a thickening agent. Beware, for too much can cause toughness. You can use either all-purpose or cake flour, sifted before measuring. Cornstarch and potato starch can also be used for thickening cheesecakes.

EGGS • Eggs are added to cheesecakes for several reasons. They provide body and texture because they solidify when exposed to heat, but in addition they have the ability to hold the high percentage of moisture present in the cheeses. The lecithin found in egg yolks also helps congeal the butterfat from the cheese and cream. As a general rule, the greater the amount of butterfat in a recipe, the greater the number of eggs used.

Stiffly beaten egg whites encapsulate a great deal of air between the bubbles of a fine protein web. When gently folded into a cheese batter, they add a light texture to the finished cake. Remember that eggs separate most easily when cold but whites beat to fullest volume when at room temperature. Cold whites can be warmed by setting the bowl of whites into a second bowl of warm water for a few minutes.

Frances's Light Cheesecake

*W*hen I was growing up, my mother made this delicious cheesecake for special family occasions. It has a satin-smooth texture and the addition of stiffly beaten egg whites makes it lighter than a classic cheesecake. Occasionally, we like to top the cake with a glaze of strawberries, or other berries in season, because the tang of fruit balances the cake's richness. You can use this recipe to create the Light Marble Cheesecake variation that follows. Though it is not as dense as the classic cheesecake, this version also freezes well.

CRUMB CRUST

½ cup hazelnuts (2½ ounces; 70 g), toasted
(page 42), or almonds
1 tablespoon granulated sugar (optional)

CAKE

3 tablespoons all-purpose flour
¼ teaspoon salt
1½ cups (10½ ounces; 300 g) plus 3 tablespoons
granulated sugar
18 ounces cream cheese (515 g), at room
temperature
6 large eggs, separated, at room temperature
2 cups sour cream
1 teaspoon vanilla extract

TOPPING (OPTIONAL)
Strawberry Glaze (page 406)

Advance Preparation Allow 2 to 3 hours for the baked cake to cool, then 4 hours minimum to become firm in the refrigerator before serving. In fact, this cake benefits from mellowing and firming overnight in the refrigerator. It can be made a day or two before serving, or wrapped airtight and frozen for a week or two without flavor loss. Refrigerate leftovers.

Strawberry Glaze can be prepared a day in advance and refrigerated, or the cake can be topped with glaze and refrigerated.

Special Equipment One 9½-inch springform pan, sturdy baking sheet or jelly-roll pan, blender or food processor for chopping nuts, electric mixer with paddle attachment if available, extra bowl and beater for whipping egg whites

1. Read About Cheesecake (page 185). Position rack in center of oven. Preheat oven to 300°F (150°C). Prepare pan as directed. To prepare crust, after toasting nuts, mix them with 1 tablespoon sugar and grind them in the food processor. Sprinkle ground nuts evenly over sides and bottom of prepared pan. Pat any excess nuts onto the bottom. Set pan aside; in hot weather, store pan in refrigerator.

Baking Time   1 hour and 20 minutes at 300°F (150°C), then cool in oven with heat off but door closed for 60 minutes. Prop oven door open leaving cake inside, and cool completely for at least 60 minutes longer.

Quantity   One 9½-inch cake (serves 10 to 12)

Pan Preparation   Generously spread softened butter on bottom and sides of springform pan.

2. If your mixer has a flat paddle, attach it in place of the regular beaters. Sift together flour, salt, and 1½ cups of sugar into a small bowl. In the large bowl of an electric mixer, beat cream cheese until smooth and soft. Add flour mixture and beat well. Stop mixer and scrape down beater and inside of bowl several times.

3. Lightly whisk egg yolks together in a medium-size bowl, then add them to the cheese batter and beat until very smooth and creamy. Stop mixer and scrape down inside of bowl once or twice. Add sour cream and vanilla and beat smooth.

4. In a separate mixing bowl with a clean regular whipping beater, beat egg whites until foamy. Add remaining 3 tablespoons sugar and beat until stiff but not dry. Gradually fold the whites into the cheese batter. Turn batter into the prepared pan and set on a sturdy baking sheet or jelly-roll pan for ease in handling.

5. Place cake in center of preheated oven and bake for 1 hour and 20 minutes, or until the cake edges are slightly puffed up and the top has a dull finish but is dry to the touch. When side of pan is tapped, the cake center should move slightly, but not jiggle in waves as if liquid. Turn off heat, leave cake inside, and set timer for 60 minutes. After this time, prop open oven door and leave cake inside until completely cool to the touch, at least 1 hour longer. Finally, place cake on a wire rack until cold if not already so, then cover with plastic wrap to protect flavor and refrigerate for a minimum of 4 hours, or overnight, to become firm before serving.

Strawberry Glaze can be added to cold cake before chilling in the refrigerator, or it can be added just before serving. Remove cake from refrigerator at least 30 minutes before serving. Or, after firming in the refrigerator for 4 hours, wrap unglazed cake airtight and freeze.

. . . .

Light Marble Cheesecake Prepare Frances's Light Cheesecake through the first half of step 4, when stiff whites are folded into the batter. Measure 2 cups of finished batter into a small bowl and lightly fold in 3 tablespoons sifted unsweetened cocoa. Then pour about half of the original vanilla batter into the prepared pan. Alternate half-cups full of chocolate and vanilla until the batter is used up. Pull and swirl the blade of a table knife or spatula through the batter to make a marbleized pattern. Be careful not to touch pan bottom or sides with the knife or spatula while swirling or crumb crust will be dislodged and batter may stick to pan. Bake as directed. Omit fruit topping.

Leslie's Black-and-White Cheesecake

*L*eslie Sutton, of Darien, Connecticut, won first prize with this recipe in a cheesecake contest sponsored by the Complete Kitchen cookware shop in her hometown. With over 40 entries, the competition was stiff, but once you have tried her delectable recipe you will understand why the hands-down winner was this two-tone cake with one intensely chocolate layer topping a creamy vanilla base. For a gala presentation, Leslie suggests decorating the cake top with a cluster of small Chocolate Leaves (page 454). To turn this basic cake into Marble Cheesecake, Chocolate Cheesecake, or Mocha Cheesecake, see the variations following.

Advance Preparation   Allow 2 to 3 hours for baked cake to cool, then 4 hours minimum in the refrigerator for the cake to become firm before serving. In fact, this cake benefits from mellowing and firming overnight in the refrigerator; it can be made a day or two before serving, or wrapped airtight and frozen for several weeks without flavor loss.

Special Equipment   One 9½-inch springform pan, sturdy baking sheet or jelly-roll pan, double boiler

Baking Time   40 minutes at 350°F (175°C), then 10 minutes at 450°F (230°C)

Quantity   One 9½-inch cake (serves 12 to 14)

Pan Preparation   Spread softened butter on bottom and sides of springform pan.

CRUMB CRUST

1¾ cups chocolate wafer crumbs (8½-ounce package of wafers; 240 g)

7 tablespoons unsalted butter (3½ ounces; 100 g), melted

Note: ¾ cup toasted, ground hazelnuts (3 ounces; 85 g), almonds, or walnuts can be liberally sprinkled over buttered pan sides and bottom instead of butter-wafer mixture. Or ground nuts can be combined with wafer crumbs and butter if you prefer.

CAKE

7 ounces fine-quality semisweet or bittersweet (not unsweetened) chocolate (200 g), chopped or in morsels (1 cup plus 2 tablespoons)

Three 8-ounce packages cream cheese (690 g), at room temperature

1 cup granulated sugar (7 ounces; 200 g)

⅛ teaspoon salt

3 large eggs, at room temperature

1 cup sour cream

1 teaspoon vanilla extract

TOPPING

2 cups sour cream

¼ cup granulated sugar (1¾ ounces; 50 g)

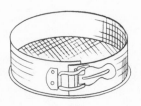

1. Read About Cheesecake (page 185). Position rack in center of oven. Preheat oven to 350°F (175°C). Prepare pan as directed. Combine chocolate wafer crumbs and melted butter; press crumbs evenly onto bottom and sides of pan. Set pan aside. If weather is hot, store pan in refrigerator.

2. Place chocolate in the top pan of a double boiler over, not in, very hot water and heat until melted. Stir until smooth. Or melt in the microwave following manufacturer's directions (power 7 for 4½ to 5 minutes is average), but be very sure all the chocolate is melted and can be stirred absolutely smooth. Remove from heat and set aside to cool.

3. If your mixer has a flat paddle, attach it in place of the regular beaters. In the large bowl of an electric mixer, beat the cream cheese until smooth and soft. Add sugar and salt and beat until mixture is very creamy and smooth. Stop the mixer and scrape down the beater and the inside of the bowl several times. Add eggs, one at a time, and beat after each addition. Add 1 cup sour cream and the vanilla and beat until well combined.

4. Pour half of this batter into the prepared springform pan. Test temperature of melted chocolate; when it is comfortable to the touch, stir well, then pour chocolate into batter remaining in the mixing bowl. Beat just to blend well, then spoon chocolate batter on top of vanilla layer in the pan.

5. Smooth cake top flat. Set filled cake pan on a sturdy baking sheet or jelly-roll pan for ease in handling. Set cake in center of preheated oven to bake for 40 minutes, or until the top has a dull finish but is dry to the touch; the surface should move slightly when you tap the side of the pan, but it should not jiggle in waves as if it were liquid. Remove cake from oven and set on a heatproof surface in a draft-free location. Increase oven heat to 450°F (230°C).

6. While oven is heating, combine 2 cups sour cream and sugar for topping. When oven heat is reached (allow at least 10 minutes), spread topping over cake and return it to the oven. Bake for 10 minutes. Remove cake from oven, set on a wire rack away from drafts, and bring to room temperature. When it is cold, cover with plastic wrap to protect flavors and refrigerate for at least 4 hours to allow cake to become firm before cutting. For best flavor, remove from refrigerator 30 minutes before serving. Release sides of springform but leave cake on pan bottom. Or, after firming in refrigerator for at least 4 hours, wrap cake airtight and freeze. Refrigerate leftovers.

VARIATIONS

Marble Cheesecake   Prepare Leslie's Black-and-White Cheesecake with the following changes: In step 4, pour half of the vanilla batter into a medium-size bowl or 4-cup liquid measure. Blend melted chocolate into batter remaining in the original mixing bowl. To create the marbleized effect, pour vanilla batter into the prepared pan until bottom is covered. Then pour about 1 cup of the chocolate batter into the pan, then 1 cup of vanilla. Continue alternating colors until all batter is used. Pull and swirl the blade of a table knife or spatula through the batter to make a marbleized pattern. Be careful not to touch pan bottom or sides with knife or spatula while swirling or crumb crust will be dislodged and batter may stick to pan. Omit sour cream topping.

Bake at 350°F (175°C) for 50 to 55 minutes. Check for doneness as in master recipe. Turn off oven heat, prop door open, and leave cake in oven until completely cool.

Chocolate Cheesecake   I prefer to bake this variation in an 8½-inch springform pan. Add ½ teaspoon ground cinnamon to the crumb crust. The crust will take slightly fewer crumbs than with the larger pan. As usual, the cake rises as it bakes, but it sinks quite a bit as it cools.

Prepare Leslie's Cheesecake through step 3. In step 4, make the following changes: Stir 1 cup of cheese batter into the melted and cooled chocolate. Stir until the color is uniform. Then turn all the chocolate mixture back into the rest of the cheese batter and beat just to blend. Pour into the prepared pan and bake as for Marble Cheesecake.

Mocha Cheesecake Prepare Chocolate Cheesecake. Dissolve 1½ teaspoons instant espresso or regular instant coffee powder in 1 teaspoon boiling water. Stir until smooth and cool. Add to batter along with vanilla. Bake as for Marble Cheesecake.

Tangerine Cheesecake

*T*his rich cheesecake sparkles with the unique tang of tangerine flavoring. Topped with tangerine-scented sour cream and garnished with tangerine zest, it is a party showstopper. You can use this as a master recipe to create lemon or lime cheesecake.

CRUMB CRUST
2 cups graham cracker or cinnamon crisp cracker
   crumbs (9 ounces; 255 g) (1 cup lightly toasted
   and ground pecans or almonds may be
   substituted for half of the crumbs. If you
   substitute a different type of crumbs, you may
   need up to ½ cup extra, as they compact
   differently.)
7 tablespoons lightly salted butter (3½ ounces;
   105 g), melted
3 tablespoons granulated sugar

Advance Preparation   Allow 2 to 3 hours for the baked cake to cool, then 5 to 6 hours minimum, refrigerated, to become firm before serving. This cake benefits from mellowing and firming overnight in the refrigerator and is best made a day or two in advance. It can be wrapped airtight and frozen for several weeks without flavor loss. Thaw in refrigerator while still wrapped. Bring to room temperature before serving.

Special Equipment   One 9½-inch or 10-inch springform pan, sturdy baking sheet or jelly-roll pan, flat paddle-type beater instead of regular whipping beater for mixer if available, 10- to 12-inch corrugated cardboard disk (use a standard cardboard cake disk or a pizza disk, or cut your own from heavy cardboard), grater

Baking Time   45 to 50 minutes at 350°F (175°C) for plain cake; 10 minutes longer after topping is added

Quantity   One 10-inch cake (serves 12)

Pan Preparation   Spread softened butter on bottom and sides of 10-inch springform pan.

CAKE

Four 8-ounce packages cream cheese (920 g), at room temperature
1¼ cups granulated sugar (8¾ ounces; 250 g)
4 tablespoons frozen tangerine-juice concentrate, thawed but undiluted
2 tablespoons tangerine or orange liqueur (Mandarine or Grand Marnier, for example)
1 teaspoon orange extract
1 tablespoon grated tangerine zest (if not available, substitute orange zest; do not use dried grated peel)
4 tablespoons all-purpose flour
⅛ teaspoon salt
4 large eggs plus 1 extra egg yolk, at room temperature

TOPPING

2 cups sour cream (16½ ounces; 470 g)
¼ cup granulated sugar (1¾ ounces; 50 g)
1 tablespoon frozen tangerine-juice concentrate, thawed, or substitute orange liqueur

GARNISH

2 teaspoons grated tangerine or orange zest

1. Read About Cheesecake (page 185). Arrange rack in center of oven. Preheat oven to 350°F (175°C). Prepare pan as directed. To prepare crust, combine crumbs, melted butter, and 3 tablespoons sugar, and toss well to blend. Press crumbs evenly onto bottom and sides of prepared pan. Set pan aside. If weather is hot, store pan in refrigerator.

2. If your mixer has a flat paddle, attach it in place of the regular beaters. In the large bowl of an electric mixer, beat the cream cheese until smooth and soft. Add 1¼ cups sugar and beat until creamy. Add remaining cake ingredi-

ents except eggs and beat until smooth. Add eggs and extra yolk, one at a time, beating for just a second after each addition. Beat to be sure batter is well blended, but don't incorporate too much air.

3. Pour batter into prepared pan and set on a sturdy baking sheet or jelly-roll pan. Place in center of preheated oven and bake for 45 to 50 minutes, or until the edges of the cake are slightly puffed up and turning light golden brown. The center surface will be firm to the touch though softer than the edges. Don't be troubled if you have slight cracks around the edges; the topping will cover them.

4. Remove cake from oven and set on a heatproof surface away from drafts while you prepare topping. In a medium-size bowl, beat together topping ingredients, stirring until smooth. Spread evenly over top of cake. With cake still on its sturdy pan, return it to the oven and bake for an additional 10 minutes.

5. Remove cake from oven, let it sit for 3 minutes, then cover with a cardboard disk. Note that the cake will be recessed about ½ inch below the pan top, so the disk will not rest atop the cake, but rather balance on the edge of the pan. Cool pan, covered with the cardboard, on a wire rack for about 60 minutes, then put the cake, still covered with cardboard, directly into the refrigerator and leave it there overnight. At this point, the cake can be served, or wrapped airtight and frozen. Take cake out of refrigerator 30 minutes before serving. Garnish with sprinkle of zest. Remove sides of springform pan but leave cake on pan bottom.

Café au Lait Cheesecake

*J*f you like coffee, you will love this mellow, richly coffee-flavored, silken cheese-cake. I developed the recipe to take advantage of a new brand of coffee liqueur I was testing and found, somewhat to my surprise, that this cake quickly became a favorite of family and friends.

CRUMB CRUST

¾ cup hazelnuts (3¾ ounces; 105 g), toasted and
    skinned (page 42)
2 tablespoons granulated sugar

CAKE

Two 8-ounce packages cream cheese (460 g), at
    room temperature
1 cup granulated sugar (7 ounces; 200 g)
3 large eggs, at room temperature
2 tablespoons best-quality coffee liqueur
2 teaspoons instant espresso powder dissolved in
    1 teaspoon boiling water, stirred smooth
7 tablespoons sifted cake flour (3¾ ounces; 105 g)
1 tablespoon sifted unsweetened cocoa powder
¼ teaspoon baking powder
⅛ teaspoon salt
1 cup sour cream
1 teaspoon undissolved instant espresso powder

1. Read About Cheesecake (page 185). Place rack in center of oven. Prepare pan as directed. Preheat oven to 325°F (165°C).

In a food processor or blender, combine nuts with 2 tablespoons sugar and grind fine. Sprinkle nut mixture on bottom and sides of prepared pan. Pat any excess nuts evenly over the bottom. Set pan aside; if weather is hot, store pan in refrigerator.

2. If your mixer has a flat paddle, attach it in place of the regular beaters. In the large bowl of an electric mixer, beat the cream cheese until smooth and soft. Add 1 cup sugar and beat until very creamy and smooth. Stop mixer and scrape down beater and inside of bowl several times. Beat in eggs, one at a time, along with coffee liqueur and dissolved coffee powder.

3. Sift together flour, cocoa, baking powder, and salt onto a sheet of wax paper. In 3 additions, add dry ingredients to cheese batter, beating to blend each time. Add sour cream and beat to combine thoroughly, but do not whip air into batter. Stir in the undissolved espresso powder. Pour batter into prepared pan. Set pan on a sturdy baking sheet for ease in handling.

4. Place cake, on baking sheet, in center of the preheated oven and bake for 45 minutes. Then turn off oven heat but leave door shut and set timer for 30 minutes. Finally, prop oven door open and allow cake to cool to room temperature, about 1 hour. Remove cake from oven, set on counter until really comfortable to touch, then cover with plastic wrap and chill in the refrigerator for at least 6 hours, or overnight.

Note: You can cover the cake with a cardboard disk instead of plastic wrap before chilling it if you are worried that it may crack further.

5. Remove cake from refrigerator 30 minutes before serving. Remove sides of springform pan but leave cake on pan bottom to serve. Serve plain or, if you wish, place a paper doily atop the cake, then sift on a light coating of unsweetened cocoa and carefully remove doily. Or garnish by placing a ring of candied coffee beans around the edge of the cake.

Advance Preparation Allow 2 to 3 hours for baked cake to cool, then 4 hours minimum, refrigerated, to become firm before serving. In fact, the cake benefits from mellowing a day or two in the refrigerator. Wrapped airtight, it may be frozen for several weeks. Thaw, wrapped, in refrigerator overnight. Bring to room temperature before serving.

Special Equipment One 8½-inch springform pan, sturdy baking sheet or jelly-roll pan, flat paddle beater for electric mixer if available

Note: You can also use a 9½-inch springform pan, but the cake will be a little less thick than with the smaller pan.

Baking Time 45 minutes at 325°F (165°C); cool in the oven with heat off and door closed for 30 minutes, then prop oven door open and cool cake to room temperature, about 60 minutes.

Quantity One 8½-inch cake (serves 12)

Pan Preparation Generously butter sides and bottom of springform pan.

Low-Calorie Yogurt Cheesecake

*W*hile not calorie-free, this is a low-fat, dieter's dream. Instead of the usual butter-rich cheeses, this is made with easily-prepared, homemade low-fat yogurt cheese. Note that this is a small cake, prepared in a pie plate.

Advance Preparation
Make the yogurt cheese a day or two before baking the cake; it takes a minimum of 12 hours for all the liquid to drip out of the yogurt. Once prepared, the cheese can be covered and refrigerated for a day or so before use. Prepare cake a day in advance, so it has time to chill for 24 hours before serving.

Special Equipment
One 8-inch pie plate or quiche pan, good-quality triple-thickness cheesecloth cut into two 14-inch squares, cotton string, hanging hook or nail, extra bowl

Baking Time
25 minutes at 325°F (165°C), plus 5 minutes after the topping is added

Quantity
One 8-inch cake (serves 8)

Pan Preparation
Line pan with crumb crust, step 3.

CRUMB CRUST
1 cup graham cracker or zweiback crumbs
    (3½ ounces; 100 g)
4 tablespoons unsalted butter or stick margarine
    (½ stick; 60 g), melted

CAKE AND TOPPING
2¼ cups homemade low-fat yogurt cheese made
    from 6 cups (48 ounces; 1362 g) low-fat, plain
    yogurt (instructions follow)
Pinch of salt
2 large eggs, lightly beaten, at room temperature
½ cup (3½ ounces; 100 g) granulated sugar plus
    1 teaspoon
2 teaspoons grated lemon zest (1 lemon yields 2 to
    3 teaspoons of zest; use 2 teaspoons here, save
    1 for garnish)
Juice of 1 lemon (about 3 tablespoons), strained
1 teaspoon vanilla extract

GARNISH
1 teaspoon grated lemon zest reserved from filling

    1. A couple of days before making the cake, prepare the yogurt cheese. To do this, cut two 14-inch-square pieces of triple-thickness cheesecloth. In a bowl, stir the 6 cups yogurt together with a pinch of salt. Spoon half of the yogurt onto the center of each double-thick cheesecloth square. Gather up the ends of each square, tie them with string, and make a hanging loop; suspend the bun-

dles from a hook or nail set over a bowl; or hang them from the faucet in the kitchen sink, for at least 12 hours, or overnight, until every drop of water stops dripping out. At this point, the cheese is done.

Note: The amount of liquid in yogurt varies among brands. Quantities here are approximate, and your yield may vary slightly. If you have any cheese left over, mix it with herbs and use as a spread on crackers.

2. Position rack in center of oven. Preheat oven to 325°F (165°C).

3. Prepare crumb crust: combine crumbs and melted butter and toss well to blend. Add a tiny bit more melted butter if crumbs will not hold their shape. Press crumbs onto bottom and sides of pie plate. Set aside. In hot weather, refrigerate crumb-lined plate.

4. Prepare cake: By hand or with an electric mixer and paddle attachment if available, beat together eggs, 1½ cups of previously prepared yogurt cheese, ½ cup sugar, grated lemon zest and juice. Avoid whipping air into the batter. When it is smooth and creamy, spoon it into the prepared crust.

5. Bake cake in preheated oven for 25 minutes. While the cake bakes, prepare topping by blending remaining ¾ cup previously made yogurt cheese, 1 teaspoon sugar, and 1 teaspoon vanilla. When the cake is baked, remove it from the oven and spread on the topping. Return cake to oven to bake for 5 minutes more. Cool on a wire rack, then refrigerate for 24 hours. Garnish with a sprinkle of grated lemon zest. Serve at room temperature.

New York Cheesecake

The biggest and the best, this is the state of the art classic, also known as Lindy's Cheesecake because it is supposed to be the cake served at that famous New York restaurant. Unlike the other cheesecakes in this section, this one has a pastry crust on the bottom and sides.

PASTRY CRUST

1 cup sifted all-purpose flour (4¼ ounces; 120 g)

¼ cup granulated sugar (1¾ ounces; 50 g)

Pinch of salt

1 teaspoon grated lemon or orange zest

½ cup unsalted butter (4 ounces; 110 g), at room temperature, cut up

1 large egg yolk, at room temperature

½ teaspoon vanilla extract

CAKE

Five 8-ounce packages cream cheese (1150 g), at room temperature

1¾ cups granulated sugar (12¼ ounces; 350 g)

¼ teaspoon salt

½ teaspoon each of grated zest of orange and lemon

½ teaspoon vanilla extract

5 large eggs plus 2 extra egg yolks, at room temperature

¼ cup heavy cream

TOPPING (OPTIONAL)

Strawberry Glaze (page 406)

1. Read About Cheesecake (page 185). Position rack in center of oven. Prepare pan as directed. Preheat oven to 400°F (200°C).

2. Prepare the pastry: In a food processor fitted with the steel blade, or in a large bowl, combine the flour, sugar, salt, and zest. Pulse or stir, then add the cut-up butter and pulse or pinch together until large crumbs form. Add the egg yolk and vanilla and pulse or pinch until the dough just begins to clump together. If using the processor, do not process long enough to form a dough ball; stop the machine as soon as the dough begins to clump. Turn the dough out onto a piece of wax paper and pat it into a ball; the warmth of your hands will soften the butter and allow the dough to be molded even if it looks powdery at first. At this stage, you can wrap the dough in wax paper and refrigerate for 30 minutes or longer. Or, if dough is not too warm and soft, use it immediately.

Take a little more than one third of the dough and pat it into a thin layer over the buttered, detached bottom of the springform pan. Cover the dough with a piece of wax paper, roll over it with a rolling pin, then trim the edges. Remove wax paper and prick dough with a fork to prevent puffing in the oven. Wrap and reserve remaining dough; refrigerate in hot weather.

Set dough-covered disk in the oven and bake for 8 minutes, or until the dough is a light golden brown color. Set the disk on a wire rack and cool completely while preparing the cake batter.

3. If your mixer has a flat paddle, attach it in place of the regular beaters. In the largest bowl of the mixer, beat the cream cheese until smooth and soft. Add sugar and beat until creamy. Add salt, zest, and vanilla and beat until smooth. Add eggs and extra yolks, one at a time, beating after each addition. Scrape down the bowl and beater(s). Finally, stir in the cream.

4. Raise oven heat to 500°F (260°C). To line the pan sides with pastry, set the springform ring on its edge. With

Advance Preparation   This cake is best made a day ahead. The pastry can be prepared in advance and chilled for 30 minutes before using, or frozen way ahead. Allow 2 to 3 hours for the baked cake to cool, then 5 to 6 hours minimum, refrigerated, to become firm before serving. The chilled cake can also be wrapped airtight, put in a box, and frozen for several weeks without flavor loss. Thaw in the refrigerator while still wrapped. Bring to room temperature before serving.

Special Equipment   One 9½-inch springform pan, wax paper, rolling pin, electric mixer fitted with flat paddle beater if available, grater, flat serving platter

Baking Time   8 to 10 minutes at 400°F (200°C) to bake bottom pastry crust. For cake: 12 to 15 minutes at 500°F (260°C), then 1 hour at 200°F (93°C)

Quantity   One 9½-inch cake (serves 12 to 14)

Pan Preparation   Remove sides from bottom disk of springform pan. Generously spread softened butter on both the bottom and sides.

your fingers, gently but firmly press remaining dough (brought to room temperature if chilled) onto the buttered inner surface in an even layer. Avoid getting dough into the track that holds the pan bottom. The dough will stick easily to the pan sides and should be about 3/16 inch thick.

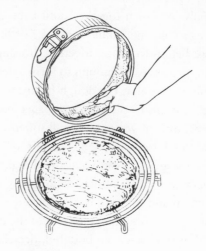

Fasten the dough-covered pan sides to the bottom disk containing the prebaked pastry and secure the spring. Set the dough-lined pan on a sturdy baking sheet or jelly-roll pan.

5. Pour the batter into the prepared pan. Place cake in the center of the preheated oven and bake for 12 to 15 minutes to cook the pastry sides. Then reduce heat to 200°F (93°C) and continue baking for 1 hour. Turn off the heat and open the oven door completely. Cool the cake in the oven for 30 minutes.

Remove cake from the oven and set in a draft-free location for several hours to cool completely. If you are baking the cake in advance, top it with plastic wrap and refrigerate it, in its pan, overnight.

Or, instead, you can run a knife around the cake edge, release the spring, and lift off the pan sides. Leave the cake sitting on the pan bottom. Spoon on the berry glaze if using it. Refrigerate cake until the glaze is set and the cake thoroughly chilled, 3 to 4 hours minimum. Remove cake from the refrigerator 30 minutes before serving so it can come to room temperature. Leave cake on the pan bottom but set it on a serving platter for presentation.

Italian Ricotta Cheesecake

*A*n Italian specialty, *torta di ricotta,* is made in a variety of ways depending upon where you are in the country. This delicately flavored cake is neither too sweet nor too fattening and has a grain particular to ricotta, unlike the silken smoothness of a cream cheese–based American-style cheesecake. Though there are several variations offered, the master recipe is lightened by stiffly beaten egg whites and the flavor is enhanced by a hint of lemon, rum-soaked golden raisins, and chopped apricots; other additions might be pine nuts, chopped candied fruit, or chopped chocolate.

Ricotta (page 189) forms the basis for many Italian cheesecakes. It has a rather bland, nutty taste, milder than cottage cheese, which it somewhat resembles in appearance. Note that sieved cottage cheese may be substituted, but will change the flavor of the cake.

You can use Italian Ricotta Cheesecake as a master recipe with which to create the variations that follow: Plain Ricotta, Holiday Ricotta, and Passover Cheesecake.

CRUMB CRUST
1 cup shelled walnuts (5 ounces; 140 g),
    or macadamia nuts
1 tablespoon dark brown sugar
2 tablespoons granulated sugar
¼ teaspoon ground cinnamon

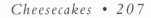

Advance Preparation   Soak raisins in rum overnight before making cake, or see step 2.

This cake can be served 2 or 3 hours after it has completely cooled from baking, still at room temperature, when the texture will be at its lightest. However, you can also bake it in advance and refrigerate it overnight to allow the flavors to blend and mellow. In this case, the texture will be slightly denser than when freshly baked. In my experience, freezing this cake changes its texture and is not recommended.

Special Equipment   One 9½-inch springform pan, sturdy baking sheet or jelly-roll pan, grater

Baking Time   45 to 50 minutes at 325°F (165°C); plus 60 minutes in oven with heat turned off

Quantity   One 9-inch cake (serves 10 to 12)

Pan Preparation   Generously butter bottom and sides of springform pan.

CAKE

⅓ cup golden raisins (1⅓ ounces; 50 g)
⅓ cup dark rum or orange juice or water
⅓ cup firmly packed dried apricot halves (2 ounces; 50 g)
3 ounces cream cheese (85 g), at room temperature
1¾ cups whole-milk ricotta (1 pound; 454 g), or creamed cottage cheese, pressed through sieve
¼ cup plain yogurt
¾ cup granulated sugar (5¼ ounces; 150 g)
3 large eggs, separated, at room temperature
1 teaspoon grated lemon zest
2 teaspoons lemon juice
4 tablespoons all-purpose flour
Pinch of salt
3 tablespoons pine nuts (optional)

1. Position rack in center of oven. Preheat oven to 325°F (165°C). Prepare pan as directed. In a blender or food processor, combine nuts, sugars, and cinnamon and process until finely ground. Press crumbs evenly onto bottom and sides of prepared pan. Pat excess crumbs onto pan bottom. Set pan aside; in hot weather, store pan in refrigerator.

2. Plump raisins either by covering them with rum to stand overnight, or more quickly, by combining them in a small saucepan and warming the rum over low heat for about 5 minutes, covered. Remove from heat and let stand, covered, for at least 30 minutes. Drain before using raisins.

Note: This rum may be used in place of lemon juice in the batter if you wish.

Cut apricots into ¼-inch dice and set them aside.

3. If your mixer has a flat paddle, attach it in place of the regular beaters. In the large bowl of an electric mixer, beat the cream cheese until smooth and soft, then beat in the ricotta and yogurt. Stop mixer and scrape down beater and inside of bowl several times. When the mixture is smooth, beat in sugar, then egg yolks, lemon zest, and lemon juice. Scrape down bowl again. Finally, with mixer on low speed, gradually add flour and salt. Last, stir in the drained raisins and chopped apricots.

4. In a clean bowl with a regular whisk beater, beat egg whites until stiff but not dry. Gently fold whites into the cheese-fruit batter. Turn batter into prepared pan, sprinkle with pine nuts if using, and set pan on a sturdy baking sheet or jelly-roll pan.

5. Place in the center of the preheated oven and bake for 45 to 50 minutes, or until the cake edges are slightly puffed up and just beginning to look golden. The center surface will be firm to the touch though softer than the edges. When you tap the side of the pan, the center of the cake should move slightly but not jiggle as though liquid. When baked, turn off oven heat but leave cake in oven, with door closed, for an additional 60 minutes. Then set cake on a wire rack in a draft-free location until completely cool. After another 2 hours at room temperature, the cake will be set enough to serve, though it can also be wrapped in plastic and refrigerated.

VARIATIONS

. . . .

Plain Ricotta Cheesecake   Prepare basic cake, but omit raisins and apricots.

Holiday Ricotta Cheesecake   Prepare Italian Ricotta Cheesecake, but replace lemon zest and juice with 1 teaspoon almond extract and replace raisins and apricots with 1 cup candied mixed fruits, chopped (7 ounces; 200 g) or ½ cup chopped semisweet chocolate (3 ounces; 30 g).

Passover Cheesecake   Prepare Italian Ricotta Cheesecake with the following changes: use an 8- or 8½-inch springform pan.

To prepare the crust, spread softened margarine on the bottom and sides of the pan. Dust the pan with a mixture of ¼ cup matzo meal (1½ ounces; 40 g), 3 table-spoons granulated sugar, and ½ teaspoon ground cinnamon. Tilt the pan to get an even coating. Pat excess crumbs onto pan bottom.

For the filling, combine the golden raisins with ⅓ cup orange juice in a small pan, cover, and warm over low heat for about 5 minutes. Remove pan from heat and let stand for at least 30 minutes. Use apricots per recipe. Instead of ricotta cheese, substitute 2 cups 4 percent milkfat cottage cheese (1 pound; 454 g), pressed through a sieve. Use sour cream instead of yogurt, and substitute 4 table-spoons potato starch for the flour. Omit pine nuts. If you wish to cover the cake with sour-cream topping, combine 2 cups sour cream with 4 tablespoons granulated sugar, spread the mixture over baked but not cooled cake, and return it to the oven, at 350°F (175°C) for 10 minutes. Remove cake from oven and set to cool in a draft-free place, topped by a folded tent of aluminum foil.

Sponge and Foam
CAKES

ABOUT SPONGE AND FOAM CAKES

SPONGE CAKES ARE light and airy, leavened primarily with eggs beaten to a foam, hence the generic name "foam cakes." Cakes in this family include sponge cakes, French sponge cakes (génoises), roulades or jelly rolls, angel-food cakes, chiffon cakes, and tortes. The dacquoise, or meringue cake, is also a foam-type cake. Sponge cakes are both lighter and drier than butter cakes. Moistened with flavored syrups and filled with buttercreams and/or Bavarian creams, or other variations on pastry creams or whipped cream, they form the foundation for many elaborate European desserts.

Whether using whole eggs, yolks, or only whites, the batter is created by whipping eggs with sugar until light in color (sometimes called "lemon-colored"), thick, and at the ribbon stage, when the mixture will form a flat ribbon falling back upon itself when the beater is lifted. At this stage, a line drawn with your finger through the batter will remain visible for at least a couple of seconds. Whisk-type or whipping beaters are always used for this process. With a KitchenAid mixer on speed 8, this can take 3 full minutes; with other mixers it can take up to 6 or 7 minutes.

The air whipped into the egg-sugar mixture during this process contributes to the rising of the sponge cake. When the cake is placed in the oven to bake, the second essential factor in the rising comes into play. In the heat of the oven, the moisture in the batter becomes steam, which rises and escapes through the foam. The heat also causes the air in these bubbles to expand, contributing to the rise.

Once the egg–sugar mixture reaches the ribboning stage, you can add flavoring and fold in sifted flour, a little at a time. Flour is never added all at once, or it sinks to the bottom of the bowl, requiring undesirable extra folding to mix it in. This breaks down the air in the foam and causes a heavy cake.

Some sponge cake recipes add richness and flavor by including melted butter, which must always be added last, after the flour; others supplement the leavening with baking powder. However, the classic foundation formula for a true sponge cake is 1 (2-ounce) egg to 1 ounce of granulated sugar and 1 ounce of sifted cake flour.

Variations in sponge cakes are nearly endless; you can be creative with flavorings and extracts, grated citrus zest, ground nuts, or cake crumbs. To make a chocolate sponge, one third of the flour can be replaced by unsweetened cocoa powder. The butter can be reduced or halved for a chocolate sponge because cocoa contains up to 22 percent butterfat; baking soda should be added to darken the color of the chocolate and make the cake a little lighter in texture. For a softer, silkier texture, sifted cornstarch can be used along with the flour.

Hints and Tips for Sponge Cakes

A well-prepared sponge cake has an even grain and a light texture, with evenly spaced air holes throughout. When the cake comes out of the oven, it should have risen well and be slightly domed in the center; the top should flatten out as it cools. There are a few basic rules to remember when baking sponge cakes:

• Use a perfectly clean, grease-free bowl and beater when whipping eggs, especially when whipping whites. Fat prevents the creation of a good foam structure.

• Sift flour and baking powder well to aerate them and remove all lumps. Sift your sugar if not perfectly lump-free. When folding in flour, add only a little at a time, and be sure to reach well down to the bottom of the bowl to incorporate the batter evenly, avoiding unmixed particles that might create hard bits in the cake. Do not overmix the batter or you will break down the foam and produce a heavy cake. Always grease and flour pans; for sponge rolls, line pans with paper and grease the paper. Handle the batter gently to retain maximum volume. Place cakes in preheated oven as soon as pans are filled.

Troubleshooting Sponge Cakes

• *If the texture is rubbery and tight, or tough and springy:* The batter was underwhipped.

• *If the cake is dense or heavy, or actually sinks as it cools:* The center has collapsed because it was overwhipped and the cell walls burst when expanding in the heat instead of retaining their structure and their air.

• *If there are lumps in the cake:* The flour and/or baking powder were not carefully sifted, or the sugar not completely dissolved. Or the folding was not done carefully, and bits of dry ingredients were not completely incorporated into the batter. Be sure to scrape down the sides of the bowl and beaters completely.

Sponge Cakes

Génoise (French Sponge Cake)

The génoise is a versatile French butter sponge cake. In addition to having a high proportion of eggs and sugar and relatively little fat, the génoise lacks baking powder; it is leavened entirely by a whole-egg foam that is enhanced by having the eggs and sugar warmed together before being whipped. This technique gives the génoise its name: warm method sponge.

The warmth causes many important reactions: It enables the sugar to dissolve in the eggs, it allows the eggs to whip to their fullest, and it softens the fat in the yolks, making it more elastic and better able to envelop the air cells as they are whipped into the foam. The texture of a génoise is light and delicate, with a fine grain. Because of the close cell structure, the cake can easily be split into thin layers by being sliced horizontally with a serrated knife. It has a tendency to be slightly dry, and is usually brushed with a flavored soaking syrup, which adds moisture and flavor. Génoise layers form a perfect base for rich fillings such as mousse or Bavarian creams.

The génoise originate in Genoa, Italy, as *pasta genovese,* a cake flavored with almonds or rum. Though one of the earliest of the Italian cakes, this is still standard in the Italian pastry repertoire. In the sixteenth century, Catherine de Médicis brought this recipe, along with her pastry chefs, with her as part of her dowry when she married Henry II and moved to France. French *pâtissiers* quickly adopted it, changing the name to *pâte à génoise,* pastry of Genoa, making it a classic of their own. In Britain, the same recipe is referred to as "gateau," and in Germany, *biscuit*.

The classic génoise requires the eggs and sugar to be warmed together before being whipped into a batter. There are several ways to achieve this: The easiest but least precise is to set the whole eggs in their shells in a bowl of warm water for about 10 minutes. Then whip the warm eggs together with the sugar in a warmed bowl. The most professional and most reliable method is to combine the eggs and sugar in a bowl set over hot water (such as a double boiler set at a simmer), add a thermometer, and stir the mixture until it reaches 110° to 120°F (43° to 49°C), when it will feel very warm to the touch and will look like a deep yellow liquid because most of the sugar will be dissolved. At this point the warm egg-sugar syrup is removed from the heat and whipped by hand or electric mixer until cooled, tripled in volume, light in color, and very thick. The batter at this stage will form a flat ribbon falling back on itself when the beater is lifted.

At this point, you gradually sift on and fold in the flour. The melted butter is incorporated with a small amount of the batter, then folded into the remaining batter. This technique blends the butter smoothly and prevents it from causing the batter to decrease in volume as it tends to do when added by itself. Immediately fill the prepared pans and put them into the preheated oven; the foam is delicate and will begin to deflate if not baked at once.

Remember that the tricks of a successful génoise are to prewarm the sugar and eggs, to use a light touch when folding in the carefully sifted dry ingredients, and to bake cakes immediately.

The génoise can be baked in many types of pans: springform, round, or rectangular layers. If you need several layers for your cake, it is best to bake 1 génoise recipe in a 2- or 3-inch-deep pan, then slice it into thin layers with a serrated knife (technique on page 427). However, many bakers are uneasy slicing 3 thin layers from 1 cake; if this seems difficult to you, simply bake ⅓ of the batter in one pan and ⅔ in another pan; slice the thicker cake into halves and you will have 3 layers with only one cut. Génoise can also be baked in muffin pans for cupcakes or in a jelly-roll pan to make a sheet cake. The sheet génoise can also be cut into sections for stacked cakes such as 7- or 8-layer cake.

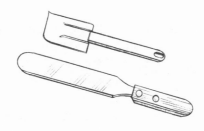

Advance Preparation   The génoise can be made in advance, wrapped airtight, and stored at room temperature for several days, for a week if wrapped and refrigerated, and for up to a month if wrapped in heavy-duty foil and frozen. Do not split the génoise into layers until shortly before filling.

Special Equipment   Two 8- or 9-inch round layer pans 1½ or 2 inches deep, or 1 jelly-roll pan, 10½ × 15½ inches, baking parchment or wax paper and scissors, large metal or other heatproof bowl for electric mixer, bottom half of double boiler (or substitute a pan with water in it), candy thermometer or instant-read spot thermometer (optional), 3-tiered or box sifter, wax paper, rubber spatula, small saucepan for melting butter, 1½-quart bowl

Baking Time   20 to 27 minutes at 375°F (190°C), depending upon thickness of batter in pan

Quantity   6-egg génoise makes 8 cups batter; two 8- or 9-inch round cakes. Each cake can be split into halves or thirds (see page 427 for slicing technique). Halve

1½ cups sifted cake flour (5¼ ounces; 150 g), plus 1 tablespoon
Pinch of salt
6 tablespoons unsalted butter (3 ounces; 85 g), cut up
6 large eggs
1 cup granulated sugar (7 ounces; 200 g)
1 teaspoon vanilla extract

SOAKING SYRUP (OPTIONAL)
Cake Soaking Syrup (page 423), with flavoring of your choice

FILLING AND ICING
Any mousse, Bavarian cream, flavored whipped cream, or buttercream

1. Position rack in center of oven. Preheat oven to 375°F (190°C). Prepare pan(s) as described. Sift flour and salt onto a piece of wax paper. Set the sifter on another piece of wax paper on a plate. Pick up the paper containing the flour mixture and gently pour it into the sifter. Just let it sit there waiting to be sifted when needed. Put the plate holding the sifter near the mixer.

Melt the butter in a small saucepan; when melted, skim off and discard any white foamy residue that rises to the surface. Set butter—and a small bowl—aside.

2. Combine eggs and sugar in the large heatproof bowl of an electric mixer. Set this over the bottom of a double boiler containing water that is hot to the touch, about 125°F (about 50°C). If water is too hot, it will cook the eggs rather than warm them. Stir the egg-sugar mixture constantly with a large whisk until it feels very warm to your finger, 110° to 120°F (43° to 49°C). It will no longer be grainy because the sugar will be dissolved. At once remove the bowl from the heat and attach it to the electric mixer. Whip the egg-sugar syrup on medium-high speed for 3 or 4 full minutes, or until it triples in volume, is very thick and light-colored, and forms a flat ribbon falling back on itself when the beater is lifted. Add the vanilla or any other flavoring and whip for 2 or 3 seconds to blend. Remove bowl from the mixer.

3. Hold the sifter over the batter bowl and sift a few tablespoons of the flour mixture onto the yolk foam. Gently fold it in with a rubber spatula or flat whisk. Repeat 5 or 6 times to use up flour, always sifting on a little flour and folding it in lightly before adding more.

4. Put about 1½ cups of the batter into the small bowl and fold the melted butter into it. Finally, fold this butter mixture into the entire bowl of batter. Do this lightly without overworking the batter.

5. Divide the batter between the prepared pans. Bake in the center of the preheated oven for 22 to 27 minutes (depending upon the depth of the batter in the pan and the pan size), or until the cake top is golden, springs back when lightly touched, and a cake tester inserted in the center comes out clean. The cake sides will begin to pull away from the pan.

Caution: Don't open the oven door wide during the first 15 minutes or the temperature change may cause the cake to fall.

Use the tip of a knife to loosen the cake sides from the pans, then top each cake with a buttered wire rack and invert. Lift off each pan, leaving the cakes on the wire rack to cool. When cold, wrap cakes airtight in plastic bags to prevent drying. Split the cakes into horizontal layers using a serrated knife (see page 427).

6. To assemble the cake, follow specific recipe instructions. The basic method is to set the split layers out flat, cut sides up, and brush on soaking syrup. Spread layers with filling, stack, then frost sides and top. If using a Bavarian cream or mousse or a mixture that must be frozen, assemble the layers and filling in a springform pan; refrigerate or freeze until filling is set, then remove pan sides. Frost top and sides if you wish.

the recipe (3 eggs; 4 cups batter) to make a single cake, which can be split into 2 or 3 layers.

Pan Preparation Spread bottom and sides of pans with solid shortening. Line bottoms of pans with baking parchment or wax paper cut to fit, then grease paper. Dust pans with flour; tap out excess flour.

Nut Génoise Prepare basic Génoise, but add ½ cup toasted and finely ground almonds, pecans, or hazelnuts, folded in just after the flour. For an almond génoise, add ½ teaspoon almond extract along with the vanilla.

Chocolate Génoise Prepare basic Génoise, but substitute ⅓ cup sifted unsweetened cocoa, preferably Dutch-process, for ⅓ cup of the flour. Add ¼ teaspoon baking soda. Sift cocoa and baking soda together with flour and salt.

Lemon or Orange Génoise Prepare basic Génoise, but add 1 teaspoon lemon or orange extract and the grated zest of 1 whole lemon or orange. Combine this flavoring with the melted butter when it is added to the batter.

Génoise Sheet Cakes When the basic 6-egg génoise is baked in a jelly-roll pan 10 × 15 inches, it makes one layer a generous ½ inch thick. This cake can be cut into bite-

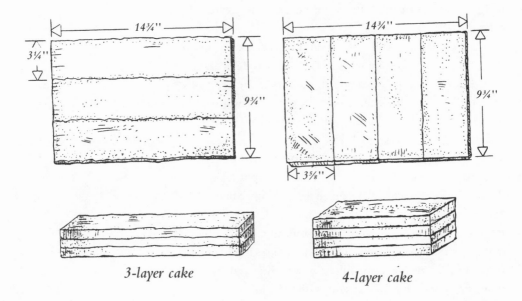

3-layer cake

4-layer cake

size pieces and sandwiched with buttercream or preserves to make petits fours, or sliced crosswise or lengthwise to make narrow layers that are sandwiched with filling (see Seven- or Eight-Layer Chocolate Cake, page 321).

Handy Measuring Guide for Génoise Sheet Cakes
When a génoise 10 × 15 inches is trimmed ⅛ inch all around, the cake measures 9¾ × 14¾ inches. This can be cut as follows:

3-layer cake (to serve 14) Cut the trimmed cake lengthwise into 3 equal strips each 3¼ × 14¾ inches. Fill and stack as directed in the recipe.

4-layer cake (to serve 8) Cut the trimmed cake crosswise into 4 equal strips each 9¾ by a generous 3⅝ inches. Fill and stack as directed in the recipe.

7- or 8-layer cake (to serve 8) Cut cake as for 4-layer cake, then use a serrated knife to split each cake strip into halves, making 8 thin layers. Stack 7 or 8 layers to make the cake.

Baking Notes for Génoise Sheet Cake When a génoise is baked in a jelly-roll pan, the procedure is the same as for a jelly roll (see Index). Prepare the baking pan with a wax paper or baking parchment lining, then butter and flour the paper.

Bake the génoise at 375°F (190°C) for about 12 minutes, or just until a cake tester comes out clean and the top feels springy; don't overbake or the cake will dry out.

Sift confectioners' sugar over the top of the cake, top with a clean tea towel, then a wire rack or cookie sheet. Invert. Lift off the pan and peel off the paper. With a serrated knife, trim off a scant ⅛ inch all around, removing the crisp edges. If making a roulade, roll the warm cake up in a sugared tea towel. For a flat sheet cake, divide the cake into sections as directed in the recipe. See notes at left for a guide.

American Sponge Cake

*T*he so-called American Sponge Cake includes baking powder, added to the egg foam to aid the leavening. The grain of this cake is open and somewhat coarse when compared with the classic French génoise sponge cake, which is leavened exclusively by whipped egg foam.

To make this cake, follow the recipe for Lemon or Orange Jelly Roll (page 234). Bake the cake in an ungreased 9-inch angel-cake tube pan at 350°F (175°C) for 45 to 50 minutes, or until a cake tester inserted in the center comes out clean.

As soon as the cake is done, invert the tube pan onto its feet, or hang it upside down over the neck of a bottle or funnel (see page 75) for several hours, or overnight, until completely cold.

To remove the cake from the pan, slide the blade of a long thin knife between the cake and the pan sides to loosen the crumbs. Repeat around the sides of the center tube. Top the cake with a plate, then invert and lift off the pan. If your pan has a removable bottom, remove the sides first, then slide the knife between the pan bottom and the cake to release it. Leave the cake upside down on the plate or invert it so it is right side up, whichever looks better. Ice the cake if you wish with any type of Boiled Icing (page 402) or Seven-Minute Icing (page 396) or Icing Glaze (page 408) or sift on a little confectioners' sugar. Cut the cake with a serrated knife.

Chocolate Sponge Cake

his is a classic chocolate sponge cake with a light and tender texture and a delicate crumb. It is based on the génoise, or French sponge method, leavened entirely by egg foam, but in this case the eggs are separated. Part of the sugar is whipped into the yolks and part into the whites, following the recipe for Chocolate Sponge Roll.

Follow the recipe for Chocolate Sponge Roll (Bûche de Noël), page 237, but bake the cake in a 9-inch (6½-cup capacity) tube pan. Grease the pan and line bottom with a ring of greased wax paper or parchment; dust with cocoa. Or make a layer cake by baking it in two 8-inch round layer pans, 1½ inches deep, greased, with pan bottoms lined with greased and cocoa-dusted wax paper or baking parchment.

Bake at 350°F (175°C), 25 minutes for 9-inch tube pan and 17 minutes for 8-inch layers, or until a cake tester comes out clean and the cake begins to pull away from the pan sides. Cool cake in its pan(s) for about 5 minutes, then invert onto a wire rack, remove pan, and peel off paper. Cool completely.

Note: It is not necessary to hang this sponge cake upside down to cool if baked in a layer or tube pan. Note that the layers may be split with a serrated knife if you wish (see page 427) to make a 4-layer cake.

Ice the cake with Boiled Icing (page 402) or Seven-Minute Icing (page 396) or coffee-flavored whipped cream (page 344). Or, for a gala, fill the 4 layers with White Chocolate Mousse (page 350).

Passover Orange Sponge Cake

A specialty of my paternal grandmother, Rebecca Gold, this flavorful lemon-orange sponge cake contains no wheat flour; it is made with potato flour (also called potato starch) and matzo meal, available in most supermarkets and health food stores. Orange Sponge Cake is delicious served with a homemade strawberry-rhubarb compote or Warm Berry Sauce (page 419) thickened with potato flour instead of cornstarch.

Advance Preparation   The cake will keep for several days at room temperature, wrapped airtight, or it can be frozen for about 1 week.

Special Equipment   9- or 10-inch angel-food tube pan, preferably with raised feet, or a tall bottle from which to suspend the cooling cake, 1 medium and 2 large mixing bowls, sifter, grater, juicer, wax paper or baking parchment, serving plate, serrated knife

Baking Time   45 to 50 minutes at 350°F (175°C)

Quantity   8½ cups batter; 9- or 10-inch tube cake (serves 10)

¾ cup matzo meal (3¼ ounces; 90 g), or ¼ cup matzo meal and ½ cup matzo cake meal
½ cup sifted potato flour (3 ounces; 85 g)
½ teaspoon salt
1 cup granulated sugar (7 ounces; 200 g)
½ cup canola or other light vegetable oil
4 large eggs, separated, plus 2 large egg whites, at room temperature
¾ cup fresh orange juice
Grated zest of 1 large orange (2 to 3 tablespoons)
3 tablespoons fresh lemon juice
Grated zest of 1 lemon (2 to 3 teaspoons)
1 teaspoon orange extract
½ teaspoon lemon extract

TOPPING
Confectioners' sugar (optional)

1. Position rack in center of oven. Preheat oven to 350°F (175°C). Do not grease tube pan.

2. In a large bowl, whisk together the matzo meal (and matzo cake meal if used), potato flour, salt, and ½ cup of the sugar. In a medium bowl, combine the oil, 4 egg yolks, orange juice and zest, lemon juice and zest, and extracts.

3. In the large bowl of an electric mixer, whip the 6 egg whites until fluffy. Gradually add the remaining ½ cup sugar, and whip the whites until stiff but not dry.

Do not overbeat. Scrape beaters onto the bowl, but do not wash them. Remove bowl of whites from mixer and set it aside. Return unwashed beaters to mixer.

4. With the mixer on low speed, beat the egg-oil mixture to blend, then slowly beat in the dry ingredients. By hand, using a rubber spatula, gradually fold in the whipped whites. Don't worry if there are some streaks of white visible in the batter.

5. Turn the batter into the ungreased pan. Bake in the preheated oven for 45 to 50 minutes, or until the top of the cake is golden brown and feels springy to the touch, and a cake tester comes out clean. As soon as the cake is done, invert the pan so it stands upside down on its own feet, or hang it upside down over the neck of a bottle. Leave the cake inverted until it is completely cool.

6. To remove the cake from the pan, slide the blade of a long thin knife between the cake and the pan sides. Also run the knife around the center tube. Then top the cake with a plate, invert, and tap the pan bottom. Lift off the pan. If pan sticks, again work the blade around to loosen crumbs. The colder the cake, the more easily it will release.

Serve the cake plain or sift on a dusting of confectioners' sugar; cut with a serrated knife.

Mocha Wheatless Sponge Cake

his light and flavorful sponge cake is made with potato flour (also called potato starch) and is suitable for Passover or wheatless diets. Rice flour may be substituted. Note that both potato and rice flours have a different texture from wheat flour, so the cake will be very slightly different from an ordinary sponge cake.

Note: Both potato flour and rice flour are available in supermarkets and many specialty, health food, or gourmet food shops.

1 cup sifted potato flour or potato starch (6 ounces; 170 g) or rice flour
2 tablespoons sifted unsweetened cocoa, preferably Dutch-process
8 large eggs, separated, at room temperature
½ teaspoon cream of tartar
Pinch of salt
1½ cups superfine or granulated sugar (10½ ounces; 300 grams)
1 teaspoon vanilla extract
4 tablespoons strong regular or espresso coffee, made from 1½ teaspoons instant coffee dissolved in 4 tablespoons boiling water
½ teaspoon ground cinnamon
1½ ounces grated semisweet chocolate (45 grams)

TOPPING
3 or 4 tablespoons sifted unsweetened cocoa

1. Read About Sponge and Foam Cakes. Position rack in center of oven. Preheat oven to 350°F (175°C). Prepare pan as described.

2. On wax paper, sift together potato starch and cocoa and set them aside.

3. In the large bowl of an electric mixer, combine egg whites with cream of tartar and salt. Whip egg whites until foamy, then gradually add ½ cup of the sugar and whip until stiff but not dry. Scrape beaters into bowl, but do not wash beaters. Remove bowl of whites from mixer and set it aside. Return unwashed beaters to electric mixer.

4. In another large bowl, beat the yolks with the electric mixer on high speed for 2 minutes, until yolks are thick and light in color. Gradually beat in remaining 1 cup sugar, the vanilla, and coffee. Stop the mixer and scrape down the sides of the bowl and the beaters. Then beat on medium-high speed for 2 full minutes.

5. With the mixer on lowest speed, or stirring by hand, gradually add half of the potato starch–cocoa mixture to the yolk batter. Fold in the cinnamon.

6. Fold the whipped whites over on themselves once or twice to amalgamate them, then fold about one third of the whites into the yolk batter. Alternately fold in remaining whites with remaining potato starch–cocoa mixture. Finally, fold in the grated chocolate.

7. Turn batter into the prepared pan and bake in the center of the preheated oven for 60 to 65 minutes, or until the top is springy to the touch and a cake tester inserted in the center comes out clean. Do not overbake or the cake will dry out.

8. As soon as the cake is done, invert it onto the feet of its pan, or hang it upside down over the neck of a bottle. Leave the cake inverted until completely cold. To remove the cake from the pan, slide the blade of a long

Advance Preparation
Wrap the cake airtight and store it at room temperature for a day or two. In fact, with potato flour, the texture improves after 24 hours at room temperature.

Special Equipment   One 10-inch angel-cake tube pan with feet, or regular tube pan and large funnel or tall bottle from which to suspend the inverted tube pan while cooling (see page 75), wax paper or baking parchment, sifter, rubber spatula or flat whisk, long thin-bladed knife, serrated knife, serving plate

Baking Time   60 to 65 minutes at 350°F (175°C)

Quantity   9 cups batter; one tube cake 10 × 4 inches (serves 12 to 14)

Pan Preparation   Line bottom of tube pan with wax paper or baking parchment cut to fit. Do not grease pan.

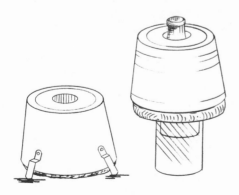

thin knife between the cake and pan sides to loosen the crumbs. Repeat around the center tube. Top the cake with a plate, invert, and lift off the pan. If the pan has a removable bottom, remove the sides first, then slide the knife between the pan bottom and the cake to release it. Peel off the paper. Leave the cake upside down if it looks good, or invert it once again so the cake is right side up on the plate. Sift on a few tablespoons of unsweetened cocoa for a topping. To serve, cut the cake with a serrated knife.

Jelly Rolls (Roulades)

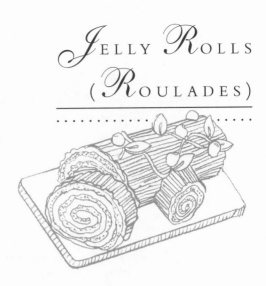

ABOUT JELLY ROLLS (ROULADES)

THE JELLY ROLL, or French *roulade,* is simply a thin sponge cake baked in a broad flat pan and rolled around a filling. Typically, fillings include jelly or preserves, custard, or mousse. When the jelly roll is filled with a buttercream and coated with chocolate icing, it is used for the Bûche de Noël (page 237), or chocolate log cake.

The texture of the rolled sponge cake is all-important: it should be light and fine-grained, but it should also be elastic and flexible enough to roll without cracking. There are several techniques for making rolled sponge cakes. The basic génoise, or French sponge cake, is made with warmed whole eggs whipped to a high foam before the dry ingredients are gently folded in. A variation on this is the Classic Jelly Roll (following recipe), in which the eggs are separated to make the sponge elastic and particularly well suited to being rolled. The so-called American sponge cake method uses separated eggs but also adds baking powder to supplement the leavening power of the whipped eggs. Angel-food cake may also be baked in a jelly-roll pan and rolled over filling.

A jelly roll is always sliced with a serrated knife, used in a sawing motion to prevent compressing the roll and squeezing out the filling.

Classic Jelly Roll

*T*his classic French roulade, or jelly roll, is made with a génoise sponge cake. Like the regular génoise, this cake is leavened only by whipped egg foam, but in this variation the eggs are separated. Separating the eggs results in an elastic, flexible cake that rolls easily without cracking. Some cornstarch is added to cut the gluten in the wheat flour and make the texture more tender. Use this for an all-purpose jelly roll; flavor it with vanilla, or use lemon or orange if you prefer. To make a Chocolate Sponge Roll, see page 237.

10 tablespoons granulated sugar (4¼ ounces; 120 g)
½ cup sifted cake flour (1¾ ounces; 50 g)
¼ cup sifted cornstarch (1⅛ ounces; 30 g)
4 large eggs, at room temperature, separated
Pinch of salt
¾ teaspoon vanilla extract, or orange or lemon
    extract (or 1 tablespoon lemon juice) plus grated
    zest of 1 lemon or orange

UNMOLDING CAKE
¼ cup confectioners' sugar, sifted

FILLING
1 generous cup of any of the following: fruit
    preserves, Lemon Curd (page 366), Zabaglione
    Cake Filling (page 365), flavored whipped cream
    or mousse or Bavarian cream

ICING
¼ cup confectioners' sugar, or Orange or Lemon
    Icing Glaze (page 408)

1. Prepare pan as described. Position rack in lower third of oven. Preheat oven to 350°F (175°C).

2. Since the sugar is divided in this recipe, it is easier to use 2 separate cups. Measure 4 tablespoons sugar and put it in 1 cup. Write the number "4" on a piece of paper and set it in the cup. Place remaining 6 tablespoons of sugar in a second cup and identify with paper marked "6." Sift together the flour and cornstarch into a medium-size bowl.

3. Put the egg yolks in a large mixing bowl and the whites in a medium-size mixing bowl.

Add the salt to the egg whites. With the electric mixer, whip the whites until they are frothy, then gradually add the 6 tablespoons sugar. Whip until the whites are stiff but not dry. They should be glossy and smooth and you should be able to invert the bowl without having the mass of whites move or slide.

Remove bowl from the mixer; scrape the beaters into the bowl. Without washing the beaters, return them to the mixer. Set the whipped whites aside.

4. With the mixer, now whip the yolks with the 4 tablespoons sugar until thick and light-colored. Stop the machine and scrape down the bowl and beaters twice. Add the vanilla extract or other flavoring and/or grated zest. Whip until the yolks form a flat ribbon falling back upon itself when the beater is lifted. This takes about 3 minutes with the KitchenAid mixer on speed #8; with other mixers it can take 6 or 7 minutes. Set this bowl aside.

5. Fold about one third of the whites into the yolks. Then sprinkle about 3 tablespoons of the flour-cornstarch blend onto the yolk batter and fold it in gently. Continue to fold in the flour-cornstarch in small additions, folding with a light touch to maintain volume. When you near the end of the flour mixture, alternate it with some of the whipped egg whites. Finally, fold in remaining whipped whites. The batter should be light, airy, and smooth.

Advance Preparation   The cake can be baked in advance, rolled up in a cloth, and left to cool for several hours or overnight. The filled jelly roll can be wrapped airtight and will stay fresh for a couple of days if refrigerated. It can be frozen, but loses its freshness in about a week. Do not freeze if filled with custard or curd fillings, which tend to soften on freezing and make the cake soggy.

Special Equipment   One jelly-roll pan 15 × 10 inches, ½ inch deep; wax paper or baking parchment, 2 cups, medium-size mixing bowl, sifter, extra bowl and beater for whipping egg whites, rubber spatula, linen or cotton tea towel somewhat larger than 15 × 10 inches, serrated knife

Baking Time   11 to 13 minutes at 350°F (175°C)

Quantity   4 cups batter; one 10-inch roll (12 to 14 servings about ¾ inch thick)

Pan Preparation   Butter bottom and sides of jelly-roll pan. Line the pan with wax paper or baking parchment, then butter the paper and dust it evenly with flour; tap out excess flour.

6. Turn the batter into the prepared pan, smoothing the top and spreading it to the edges with a rubber spatula. Place cake in the preheated oven to bake for 11 to 13 minutes, or until the top is golden and feels springy to the touch and the edges begin to draw away from the sides of the pan. Do not overbake the sponge or it will dry out too much.

7. While the cake bakes, spread the tea towel on a flat surface and sift on ¼ cup confectioners' sugar in a rectangle 15 × 10 inches.

As soon as the cake is baked, invert the pan over the sugared area of the towel. Lift off the pan and peel off the paper. With a serrated knife, slice off a scant ⅛-inch strip of crisp edging around the cake so it will roll more easily (diagram a).

Fold one short end of the towel over a short end of the cake, then roll them together (diagram b). Set the roll seam side down on a wire rack to cool.

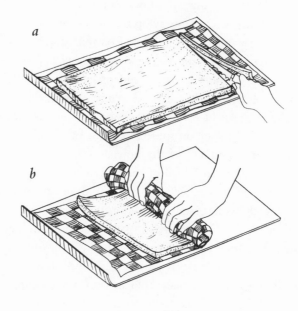

a

b

8. When the cake is cold, unroll it, spread it with the preserves or other filling (diagram c), and reroll, using the short end of the towel to lift and push the cake as it rolls up (diagram d). Set the cake seam side down and sift confectioners' sugar over the top. Or spread it with Icing Glaze. Cut the cake with a serrated knife (diagram e). If filled with Lemon Curd or other custard or with whipped cream, store the cake in the refrigerator; bring it to room temperature before serving.

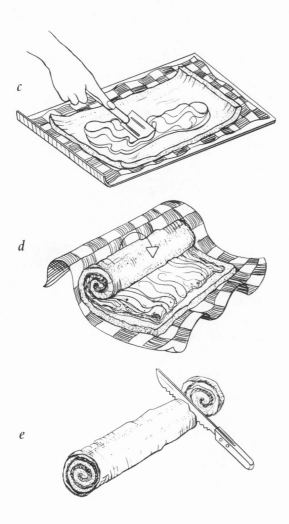

c

d

e

Lemon Jelly Roll

*T*his sponge cake is prepared by the so-called American sponge method, that is, with baking powder added to the batter for leavening. The grain of this cake is open and somewhat coarse. When rolled, it may tend to crack a bit because the texture is not as flexible as that of the Classic Jelly Roll leavened entirely by the foam of whipped separated eggs. To make an Orange Jelly Roll, see the variation following the basic recipe.

Advance Preparation The jelly roll can be baked, rolled in a cloth, refrigerated overnight, and filled on the day it is to be served. Or the cake can be filled, then wrapped airtight and refrigerated or, depending on the filling, stored at room temperature for a day or two. If the cake is filled with preserves or jelly, it can be wrapped airtight and frozen; however, custard and curd fillings tend to soften in the freezer and make the cake soggy.

Special Equipment One 15 × 10 inch jelly-roll pan, 1 inch deep, wax paper or baking parchment, medium-size mixing bowl, extra bowl and beater for whipping egg whites, small saucepan, rubber spatula, linen or cotton tea towel somewhat larger than 15 × 10 inches, sifter, grater, serrated knife

1½ cups sifted cake flour (5¼ ounces; 150 g)
1½ teaspoons baking powder
¼ teaspoon salt
3 large eggs, separated, at room temperature
1¼ cups granulated sugar (8¾ ounces; 250 g)
Grated zest of 1 lemon
¼ cup freshly squeezed orange juice
¼ cup freshly squeezed lemon juice

UNMOLDING CAKE
¼ cup confectioners' sugar

FILLING
1 cup fruit preserves such as apricot or raspberry, or
    1 cup (½ recipe) Lemon Curd (page 366)

ICING
¼ cup confectioners' sugar, or Lemon Icing Glaze
    (page 408)

1. Prepare pan as described. Position rack in lower third of oven. Preheat oven to 350°F (175°C).

2. Sift together flour, baking powder, and salt onto a piece of wax paper. Set aside.

3. Put egg yolks in the large bowl of an electric mixer. Beat until thick and lemon-colored, then gradually add 1 cup of the sugar while beating on medium speed. Stop the machine and scrape down the bowl and beaters once or twice. Beat until the mixture is thick. It will not form a ribbon.

4. Combine the grated lemon zest and both juices in a small pan. Set over high heat and bring to a boil.

Beat the yolk mixture with the electric mixer on low while pouring in the hot juice. Keep whipping as the liquid is added or the yolks will poach. Gradually increase mixer speed to medium (KitchenAid speed #5) and beat for a generous 30 seconds, until the sugar dissolves and the yolk-sugar mixture cools, thickens, and begins to increase in volume. Scrape down the inside of bowl and the beaters. Turn off the mixer.

5. In another bowl with clean beaters, whip the egg whites on medium-low speed until they look frothy. Then gradually add remaining ¼ cup of sugar, beating the whites at medium-high speed until stiff but not dry.

Use the rubber spatula to fold half of the whites into the yolk batter. Then sprinkle a little of the flour mixture onto the yolk batter and fold it in gently. Continue to fold in the flour in 6 or 7 additions, folding with a light touch to maintain volume. When you near the end of the flour, alternate it with some of the whipped egg whites. Finally, fold in remaining whipped whites. The batter should be light and airy and smooth.

6. Turn the batter into the prepared pan, smoothing the top and spreading it to the edges with a rubber spatula. Place it in the preheated oven to bake for 15 minutes, or until a cake tester comes out clean, the top of the cake feels springy to the touch, and the edges begin to look golden in color and draw away from the sides of the pan.

7. While the cake bakes, set a tea towel out on the counter, smooth it flat, and sift on ¼ cup confectioners' sugar in a rectangle 15 × 10 inches.

As soon as the cake is baked, invert the pan over the sugared area of the towel. Lift off the pan and peel off the paper. With a serrated knife, slice off a ⅛-inch-thick strip

Baking Time   13 to 15 minutes at 350°F (175°C)

Quantity   5 cups batter; one 10-inch roll (serves 8 to 10 generous slices 1 inch thick, or 12 to 14 slices about ¾ inch thick)

Pan Preparation   Spread butter or margarine on bottom and sides of jelly-roll pan. Line pan with wax paper or baking parchment, then butter the paper and dust it evenly with flour; tap out excess flour.

around all the edges, removing the cake's crisp border so that it will roll more easily (see Classic Jelly Roll diagrams, pages 232–233).

Fold one short end of the towel over a short end of the cake, then roll them together. Set the roll seam side down on a wire rack to cool.

8. When the cake is cold, unroll it, spread it with preserves or Lemon Curd, and reroll without the cloth. Sift confectioners' sugar over the top, or spread with Icing Glaze before serving. Cut with a serrated knife. If the cake is filled with Lemon Curd, store in the refrigerator, but serve at room temperature.

VARIATION

· ·

Orange Jelly Roll   Prepare Lemon Jelly Roll, but substitute orange zest and orange juice for the lemon. Orange marmalade may be used as a filling, or the Lemon Curd may be made with oranges.

Chocolate Sponge Roll or Bûche de Noël

$\mathcal{T}$his cake is a delight to make. It is easy to prepare, but more important, the results are reliable and delicious. The flavor is intensely chocolate without being sweet, the texture is light and tender, with a delicate crumb, and it rolls beautifully without cracking. The recipe is one I developed following the principles used in the Classic Jelly Roll (see Index). The génoise, or French sponge cake, is the basis for the formula, but the eggs are separated. Part of the sugar is whipped into the yolks and part into the whites. The cake is unmolded onto unsweetened cocoa, which leaves an attractive, finished coating on the filled and rolled cake. It eliminates the need for icing, though you may add any type you wish. This cake may be used for a Bûche de Noël (variation following), or it may be filled with 1½ cups of whipped cream or any mousse or Bavarian cream. To bake it as a layer or tube cake, see Chocolate Sponge Cake (page 223).

5 tablespoons sifted cake flour (1 ounce; 30 g)
2 tablespoons sifted cornstarch
⅓ cup sifted unsweetened cocoa, preferably Dutch-
    process (¾ ounce; 20 g)
⅛ teaspoon ground cinnamon
¼ teaspoon salt
½ teaspoon baking powder
¼ teaspoon baking soda
4 large eggs, separated, at room temperature
¾ cup granulated sugar (5¼ ounces; 150 g)
1 teaspoon vanilla extract

FOR UNMOLDING CAKE
⅓ cup sifted unsweetened cocoa

FILLING
¾ cup chilled heavy cream
2 tablespoons superfine sugar
½ teaspoon vanilla extract, or 2 tablespoons dark
    rum or orange or hazelnut-flavored liqueur, *or*
    substitute Viennese Custard Buttercream
    (page 359) for flavored whipped cream

Advance Preparation The cake can be baked ahead, rolled up in a cloth, and left to cool for several hours or overnight. It can be wrapped airtight and will stay fresh for a couple of days if refrigerated; it tends to dry out when frozen more than 1 week. Do not freeze if filled with custard.

Special Equipment One 15 × 10 inch jelly-roll pan, 1 inch deep, wax paper or baking parchment, medium-size bowl, sifter, extra bowl and beaters for whipping egg whites, rubber spatula, linen or cotton tea towel somewhat larger than 15 × 10 inches, serrated knife

Baking Time 15 minutes at 350°F (175°C)

Quantity 4 cups batter; one 10-inch roll (serves 10). This recipe also makes one 9-inch (6½-cup capacity) tube cake or two 8-inch layers.

Pan Preparation Spread butter or margarine on bottom and sides of jelly-roll pan. Line the pan with wax paper or baking parchment, then butter the paper and dust it evenly with unsweetened cocoa or flour; tap out excess.

TOPPING
Confectioners' sugar or unsweetened cocoa

1. Prepare pan as described. Position rack in center of oven. Preheat oven to 350°F (175°C).

2. Sift together in a bowl the flour, cornstarch, cocoa, cinnamon, salt, baking powder, and baking soda. Set bowl aside.

3. Put egg whites in the large bowl of an electric mixer and yolks in a medium bowl. Put ½ cup of the sugar in one measure and ¼ cup in another. Set the cups near the electric mixer. The ½ cup of sugar will be whipped into the whites, the ¼ cup of sugar into the yolks. Feel the whites with your finger; they should be comfortably warm, not cold to the touch. Whip the whites on medium speed until frothy, then add about 2 tablespoons of the ½ cup of sugar. Whip for about 10 seconds, then gradually add the rest of ½ cup sugar while increasing the speed of the machine to medium-high. Whip the whites until they are stiff but not dry. They should be glossy and smooth and you should be able to invert the bowl without having the mass of whites move or slide. Scrape the beaters into the bowl. Set the whites aside. Without washing the beaters, return them to the mixer.

4. Using the same beaters and a clean medium-size electric mixer bowl, whip the yolks with the vanilla until pale in color. Add the ¼ cup sugar. Whip the yolk mixture until thick and pale in color. Stop the machine and scrape down the bowl and beaters twice. Continue whipping until the yolks form a flat ribbon falling back upon itself when the beater is lifted. This takes about 3 minutes with the KitchenAid mixer on speed #8; with other mixers it can take 6 or 7 minutes. Remove bowl from mixer stand and scrape beaters into bowl.

5. By hand with a rubber spatula, fold about one third of the whites into the yolks. Then sprinkle about ¼ cup of the flour-cocoa mixture onto the yolk batter and fold it in gently. Continue to fold in the flour-cocoa mixture in 4 or 5 small additions, adding a small amount of whites occasionally. Fold with a light touch to maintain volume. When you near the end of the flour-cocoa mixture, alternate it with some more of the whipped whites. Finally, fold in remaining whipped whites. The batter should be light and airy and smooth. It should have a fairly even color, but don't worry if there are a few faint streaks of white.

6. Turn the batter into the prepared pan, smoothing the top and spreading it to the edges with a rubber spatula. Place the cake in the preheated oven to bake for 15 minutes, or until the top feels lightly springy to the touch, the sides of the cake begin to shrink away from the pan, and a cake tester inserted in the center comes out dry. Do not overbake the sponge or it will dry out too much.

7. While the cake bakes, set a tea towel on the counter, smooth it flat, and sift on ⅓ cup unsweetened cocoa powder in a rectangle 15 × 10 inches.

Note: After use, you can shake this towel outside, then wash with cold water; the dry cocoa will not stain the towel.

As soon as the cake is baked, invert the pan over the cocoa on the towel. Lift off the pan and peel off the paper. With a serrated knife, slice off a scant ⅛-inch strip around the edges of the cake to remove the crisp border so the cake will roll more easily (see Classic Jelly Roll diagrams, pages 232–233).

Fold one short end of the towel over a short end of the cake, then roll them together. Set the roll seam side down on a wire rack to cool.

8. Prepare the filling just before spreading it on the cold cake. To make the whipped cream filling, whip the cream in a chilled bowl with chilled beaters until soft peaks form. Add the sugar and vanilla or other flavoring; use a hand whisk to blend and whip for a few seconds longer. The cream should hold its shape but not be overstiff.

9. When the cake is cold, unroll it, spread it with the filling, and reroll. Set it seam side down, and sift a little confectioners' sugar or unsweetened cocoa on top. I prefer this simple topping for the cake, and like to serve it with a dollop of whipped cream on the side, or a spoonful of vanilla yogurt or vanilla ice cream. However, if you prefer, you can frost the cake with any type of icing or whipped cream. Store the cake in the refrigerator and bring it to room temperature before serving. Cut the cake with a serrated knife. For the Bûche de Noël, see the variation following.

VARIATIONS

. . . .

Bûche de Noël In France, this Yule Log Cake is a traditional part of the Christmas celebration. It is a realistic-looking log made of chocolate sponge cake filled with Hazelnut-Chocolate Buttercream or any other flavor of buttercream or mousse you prefer. The icing is Chocolate or Creamy Mocha Buttercream covered with slivers of rough chocolate bark, garnished with meringue mushrooms and green marzipan leaves. The bark, mushrooms, and marzipan can be made ahead, but the Yule Log is best made and served fresh. In a pinch you can fill and frost (but not decorate) the log, wrap it in foil, and freeze it for up to 2 weeks.

CAKE
Prepare the Chocolate Sponge Roll, roll it in a
    cocoa-covered tea towel, and set it aside to cool.

FILLING
Hazelnut-Chocolate Buttercream (page 389)

ICING
Creamy Mocha Buttercream (page 383)

Chocolate Bark (page 457)
3 ounces semisweet or bittersweet chocolate
Meringue Mushrooms (page 467)

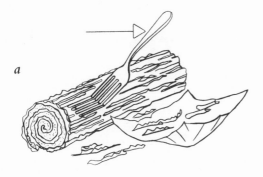

a

b

Assembly Procedure   When you are ready to assemble the Bûche de Noël, unroll the cake carefully, leaving it flat on the towel. Be sure your filling is at room temperature, well beaten and creamy. Spread the filling to within ¼ inch of the cake's edges.

Lift one end of the towel to help start the cake rolling over onto the filling. Remove the towel and set the cake, seam side down, on a cake board or rectangular platter. Cover the cake sides, but not the ends, with the icing. To emphasize the bark texture, draw the tines of a fork through the icing to make ridges (diagram a).

Prepare the chocolate bark. Press the chocolate slivers onto the frosted log cake.

Arrange 8 or 9 meringue mushrooms in groups of 2 or 3 along the log. Here and there, position sprays of green holly leaves (diagram b).

To serve, remove leaves and slice the cake with a serrated knife.

Angel-Food Cakes

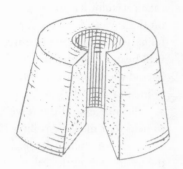

ABOUT ANGEL-FOOD CAKES

ANGEL-FOOD CAKE was created in the nineteenth century, when baking ovens with reliable heat controls became available. Its origin is disputed, but food historians often attribute the invention to thrifty bakers in the Pennsylvania Dutch community, who, it is said, developed the recipe to use up leftover egg whites.

Angel-food cake owes its success to a couple of basic tricks and an understanding of the ingredients from which it is made, primarily a large quantity of egg whites, which are whipped into a foam. This foam, and the steam that arises when it is heated, provides 100 percent of the cake's leavening. The development and handling of this foam is critical. First, you should understand how to handle egg whites. Review About Meringue (page 258) and About Sponge and Foam Cakes (page 213). Separate the eggs when they come from the refrigerator, then let the whites sit awhile, or, to speed their warming, set them in a bowl inside another bowl of warm water; stir the whites until they are comfortably warm to the touch. Frozen egg whites may be used for angel cakes; they should simply be thawed and brought to room temperature.

1 large egg white = 2 generous tablespoons = ⅛ cup; 4 large whites = ½ cup; 8 large whites = 1 cup; 10 to 12 whites = 1½ cups

The unused egg yolks may be frozen (see page 24). Whip the whites in an absolutely clean bowl, without any trace of fat or yolk, and use the biggest balloon whisk or electric beater you have. Begin whipping the whites slowly at first to develop many small air cells. Increase speed gradually, as the foam builds. As soon as the whites appear frothy, add a little cream of tartar, an acid that helps to stabilize the meringue, and a little sugar—for sweetening and stability of foam. Part of the total sugar is added in small increments as the whites are whipped, and the rest is sifted with the flour and salt and folded into the whites at the very end. The first trick is to beat the whites to the correct point, because if they are overbeaten, the air cells will enlarge too much and actually collapse when the air in them expands during baking. This can cause the cake to sink, and is the most common cause for angel cake failure. The whites should be beaten until *just before* they are "stiff." When you stop the machine and lift the beater, the whites should hold their shape but the very tip should fall over gently. The whites should be glossy and smooth, and you should be able to invert the bowl without having the mass of whites move or slide. At this stage the whites are not likely to be overbeaten, and there is still a little room for them to expand in the heat of the oven. Also, folding in the dry ingredients works the whites slightly, and if beaten "stiff," they risk being overwhipped after folding is accomplished.

Note: If your whites are overbeaten and look clumpy instead of perfectly smooth, you can save them by adding some unbeaten whites; read How to Save Overbeaten Whites (page 262).

After the whites reach the correct stage, add the vanilla or other extract and hand-whisk the batter only once or twice, just to combine ingredients.

Now you are ready for the dry ingredients. I prefer to use cake flour in angel-food cakes, as it contains less gluten and produces a more tender product than all-purpose flour. Be sure to sift the flour well, then resift it with the sugar. Some recipes call for sifting again as the flour is added to the whites; do this if you wish, to ensure lightness.

The type of sugar used can vary; the main point is to have all the sugar dissolved in the batter. Because of the large quantity of sugar, this is best achieved by using either all superfine sugar, or part superfine sugar, added early in the mixing, and part confectioners' sugar, folded in at the end, after the whites are whipped. Granulated sugar may also be used, but be sure it is completely dissolved in the whipped whites; pinch a little of the whites between your fingers; if sugar granules can still be felt, whip longer.

Using a flat whisk or rubber spatula, fold the dry ingredients into the whipped whites with a very light touch to maintain the volume. Review Folding (page 71). Never stir the batter, or the fragile air cells will deflate. It is much better to leave a few traces of flour visible in the whites than to over-work the mixture. Professional chefs often prefer to do the folding with the flat of the bare hand, to control the technique perfectly. If you are adding ground nuts or grated chocolate, fold them in at the very last minute.

The batter is gently scooped into the *ungreased* pan with a rubber spatula. The traditional angel-food pan is a tube, and is used because the central column exposes more batter to the heat and dries out the cake well. However, be aware that many different pans may successfully be used: a regular layer or springform pan, a jelly-roll pan, a loaf pan, or cupcake pan lined with fluted paper liners.

Hints and Tips for Angel-Food Cakes

• *There are four important tricks involved in the baking procedure.* First, do *not* grease the cake pan; the rising batter must cling to the pan sides and hold it-self up instead of sliding down on a slippery, greased surface.

• Second, put the cake in the preheated oven as soon as all the batter is in the pan; do not let the cake stand around or the air cells will begin to de-flate, and you need them to make the cake rise.

• Third, bake the cake at the correct heat. Egg whites are protein, and overheating them makes them toughen and tend to shrink. I find that 325°F (165°C) is the ideal baking temperature. For testing the doneness of an angel-food cake, it is handy to use a thin bamboo cocktail skewer, which is longer than a toothpick or metal cake tester and easier to have at hand than a clean broomstraw.

• Fourth, as soon as the cake is baked, turn the pan upside down and stand it on its feet or hang it upside down over the neck of a bottle or a tall funnel. Or balance the edges of the pan on inverted mugs or cups. The point is to have the cake hang inverted until it is completely cold.

• To cut angel cake, use a serrated knife with a sawing motion or a pronged angel-food cake cutter; this looks like a row of thin nails attached to a bar. Or pull the cake apart with 2 opposing forks. Do not try to cut with a regular knife, pushing down through the cake, or it will compress and flatten.

Troubleshooting Angel-Food Cakes

- *Texture of cake very shiny when cut:* Egg whites were overwhipped.
- *After removing cake from the oven, the cake sinks, collapses, looks concave on top:* Egg whites were overwhipped.
- *After removing cake from the oven, the cake appears well below the rim of the pan and the center of the cake is peaked like a mountain:* Egg whites were underwhipped, creating too little volume.
- *Cake is flat and texture is dense:* The cake was not inverted to hang unobstructed as it cooled; gravity pulled the delicate structure back onto itself as it cooled while upright in the pan.

Classic White Angel Cake

*T*his is the traditional food of the angels—heavenly, tender, not overly sweet, a perfect light dessert. The basic batter can be combined with ground nuts, or coconut, or a variety of other flavorings to create the variations that follow this recipe. To decorate the cake, you can frost it with swirls of Seven-Minute Icing (page 396) or simply dust it with confectioners' sugar and serve it with fresh berries and Zabaglione Sauce (page 362) or Lemon Curd (page 366). Or this recipe can be used as a foundation for a host of gala cakes: bake it in a jelly-roll pan and roll it up with Zabaglione Filling for a great roulade. Or bake it in the tube pan, then hollow out the cake center, fill it with ice cream or mousse, and freeze it for a festive Ice Cream Cake. You can also use this recipe to make cupcakes.

Note: The egg whites for this cake can be whipped in a copper bowl with a large whisk, in a mixing bowl with a hand-held electric beater, or in a bowl with an egg beater. The type of sugar used can vary; the main point is to have all the sugar dissolved in the batter. This is best done either with all superfine sugar or with part superfine sugar and part confectioners' sugar, as in the recipe.

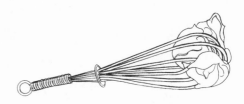

Advance Preparation Angel cake can be made in advance and wrapped airtight to
keep fresh at room temperature for several days. It can
also be wrapped airtight and
frozen, though its flavor
and texture may deteriorate
after a few weeks. Be sure to
protect the angel cake in the
freezer by placing it in a box;
the cake does not freeze
solidly and risks being
squashed by a heavier object.
Thaw the cake and bring it to
room temperature before
frosting.

Special Equipment One
10-inch tube pan, triple sifter,
wax paper, rubber spatula or
flat whisk, tall bottle or funnel large enough that the
tube pan can be hung upside
down around its neck while
the cake cools, serving plate,
serrated knife or pronged
angel-food cake cutter

Baking Time 45 to 50
minutes at 325°F (165°C)

Quantity 8 cups batter;
tube cake 10 × 4 inches
(serves 10 to 12)

Pan Preparation None.
Do not grease pan.

1 cup sifted cake flour (3½ ounces; 100 g)
½ cup sifted confectioners' sugar (1¾ ounces; 50 g)
½ teaspoon salt
¾ cup superfine sugar (5¼ ounces; 150 g); or
    substitute a total of 1¼ cups all superfine sugar
    (8¾ ounces; 250 g)
1½ cups egg whites (10 to 12 large egg whites), at
    room temperature
1 teaspoon cream of tartar
1 teaspoon vanilla extract
¾ teaspoon almond extract (optional)

ICING

**A light sifting of confectioners' sugar or any Boiled Icing
(see page 402) or Seven-Minute Icing (page 396)**

1. Position rack in center of oven. Preheat oven to
325°F (165°C). Read About Angel-Food Cakes.

2. Sift the flour through a triple sifter onto a piece of
wax paper. Then resift this flour with ½ cup sifted confectioners' sugar and ½ teaspoon salt. Set this blend of dry
ingredients aside.

3. Sift the ¾ cup superfine sugar onto another piece
of paper, then pour it into a cup and set it near the electric mixer where you will be beating the egg whites.

4. Test the temperature of the egg whites; they should
be comfortable to the touch, not cold. Warm them gently by stirring over a pan of hot water if necessary. Whip
the whites on low speed until slightly frothy.

Add the cream of tartar and whip the whites for a few
seconds, then add 2 tablespoons of the ¾ cup superfine
sugar and whip for about 10 seconds longer. Add the remaining superfine sugar gradually, whipping the whites
until they are *almost* stiff, but not dry. The whites should
be glossy and smooth, and you should be able to invert the
bowl without having the mass of whites move or slide.

5. Sprinkle on the vanilla and almond extracts and whisk the whites by hand once or twice, quickly, just to blend in the flavoring.

6. Remove the bowl of whites from the mixer. By hand, using a rubber spatula or flat whisk, fold in the flour-sugar-salt mixture, 3 tablespoons at a time. When adding flour, sprinkle it lightly over the whites or sift it on. Fold with a very light touch, cutting through the center of the whites, down to the bottom of the bowl, and bringing the spatula or whisk up again toward you while giving the bowl a quarter turn. Repeat until all dry ingredients are added and just barely incorporated. Do not stir the batter.

7. Turn the batter gently into the baking pan and smooth the top very lightly with the rubber spatula. Cut through the batter once just to be sure there are no large air pockets.

Set the pan in the center of the preheated oven and bake the cake for 45 minutes, or until it is well risen and golden brown on top, and a cake tester inserted in the center comes out clean.

8. As soon as the cake is done, invert it onto the feet of its pan or hang it upside down over the neck of a bottle or funnel; allow it to hang upside down for several hours, or overnight, until completely cold (see page 75).

To remove the cake from the pan, slide the blade of a long thin knife between the cake and the pan sides to loosen the crumbs. Repeat around the center tube.

Top the cake with a plate, then invert and lift off the pan. If your pan has a removable bottom, you may remove the sides first, then slide the knife between the pan bottom and the cake to release it. Leave the cake upside down, or top it with a plate and invert, leaving it right side up. Ice the cake as you wish; to serve, cut with a serrated knife or pronged angel-food cake cutter.

Coconut Angel Cake   Prepare Classic White Angel Cake, being sure to use the almond extract along with the vanilla.

Toss ⅓ cup shredded coconut with the flour-sugar-salt mixture and fold it into the whipped whites at the end of the recipe. Frost the cake with Coconut Seven-Minute Icing (page 397). For a stronger coconut flavor, if you wish, you can also add ¾ teaspoon of coconut extract.

Almond Angel Cake   Prepare Classic White Angel Cake, but use 1 teaspoon of almond extract along with the vanilla. In addition, add 1 tablespoon hazelnut or Amaretto liqueur along with the extracts, and ¾ cup finely ground almonds, preferably grated with a hand-held drum-type rotary nut mill (see page 42). If using a food processor, add 2 tablespoons of the pre-measured sugar to the work bowl before grinding the almonds.

Note: Hazelnuts may be substituted, but not walnuts, which contain too much oil. Combine the ground nuts with ⅓ cup of the flour-sugar-salt blend from step 2. Fold the nut-flour blend into the batter at the very end, using a light touch to maintain volume.

Orange Angel Cake   Prepare Classic White Angel Cake, but substitute 1 teaspoon of orange extract for the almond extract. Add the grated zest of 2 oranges, tossing it with a couple of tablespoons of the flour-sugar-salt mixture so it is not too wet and clumped together, before folding it into the batter at the very end. Frost the cake with Orange Icing Glaze (page 408), or orange-flavored Boiled Icing (page 404).

Double-Chocolate Angel Cake

*T*his variation on the classic angel-food cake is made with cocoa as well as grated chocolate folded in at the very end to produce flecks of chocolate throughout the baked cake. You will observe that this recipe uses the same number of egg whites as the Classic White Angel Cake, yet is baked in a smaller pan. This is because the cocoa powder contains butterfat, which weighs down the whipped egg whites somewhat, giving slightly less volume to the cake.

¾ cup sifted cake flour (2½ ounces; 70 g)
1¼ cups sifted superfine or granulated sugar
    (8¾ ounces; 250 g)
¼ cup sifted unsweetened cocoa powder, preferably
    Dutch-process (¾ ounce; 20 g)
½ teaspoon ground cinnamon
1½ cups egg whites (10 to 12 large egg whites),
    at room temperature
1 teaspoon cream of tartar
Pinch of salt
1 teaspoon vanilla extract
1½ ounces grated semisweet chocolate (45 g)

ICING
2 tablespoons sifted unsweetened cocoa powder or
    confectioners' sugar, or Boiled Icing (page 402)

Advance Preparation The cake can be made in advance and wrapped airtight to keep fresh at room temperature for several days. It can also be wrapped airtight and frozen, though its flavor and texture may deteriorate and toughen after a few weeks.

Special Equipment One 9-inch angel-cake tube pan with "feet," or regular tube pan and large funnel or tall bottle from which to suspend inverted tube pan while cooling; triple sifter, strainer, or sieve, wax paper, rubber spatula or flat whisk; long thin-bladed knife, serrated knife or pronged angel-food cake cutter, serving plate

Baking Time 55 to 60 minutes at 325°F (165°C)

Quantity 8 cups batter; one 9-inch cake (serves 8 to 10)

Pan Preparation None. Do not grease the pan.

1. Position rack in center of oven. Preheat oven to 325°F (165°C). Read About Angel-Food Cakes.

2. Sift the flour through a triple sifter onto a piece of wax paper. Then resift this flour with ½ cup of the pre-sifted sugar, the presifted cocoa, and the cinnamon. Set this blend of dry ingredients aside.

3. Pour remaining ¾ cup sugar through the triple sifter or strainer, then pour it into a cup and set it near the electric mixer where you will be beating the egg whites.

4. Test the temperature of the egg whites; they should be comfortable to the touch, not cold. Warm them over a pan of hot water if necessary. Whip the whites on low speed until slightly frothy. Add the cream of tartar and the salt and whip the whites on medium speed for about 20 seconds. Add 2 tablespoons of the reserved ¾ cup sugar and whip for about 10 seconds longer, then add 2 more tablespoons of sugar. Increase mixing speed to medium-high, then gradually add remaining sugar, a little at a time, while whipping the whites until they are *almost* stiff but not dry. Remove the bowl from the mixer.

5. Sprinkle on the vanilla extract and gently hand-whisk the whites once or twice, just to blend in the flavoring.

6. Fold the flour-sugar-cocoa blend, 3 tablespoons at a time, into the whites using a flat whisk or rubber spatula. When adding this mixture, sprinkle it lightly over the whites or sift it on. Fold with a very light touch, cutting through the center of the whites, down to the bottom of the bowl, and bringing the spatula or whisk up again toward you while giving the bowl a quarter turn. Repeat until all dry ingredients are added and just barely incorporated. Now fold in the grated chocolate, incorporating it with as few folding strokes as possible.

7. Turn the batter gently into the baking pan and smooth the top very lightly with the rubber spatula. Set the pan in the preheated oven and bake the cake for 55 to 60 minutes, or until it is well risen and lightly springy to

the touch. A cake tester inserted in the cake center should come out clean. Do not overbake, or the cake will dry out.

8. As soon as the cake is done, invert it onto the bottle or funnel and allow it to hang upside down for several hours, or overnight, until completely cold.

To remove the cake from the pan, slide the blade of a long thin knife between the cake and the pan sides and around the center tube to loosen the crumbs. Top the cake with a plate, then invert and lift off the pan. If your pan has a removable bottom, you may remove the sides first, then slide the knife between the pan bottom and the cake to release it. Leave the cake upside down, or top it with a plate and invert, leaving it right side up. Frost the cake as you wish, and serve it by cutting with a serrated knife or angel-food cake cutter or pulling the cake apart with 2 opposing forks.

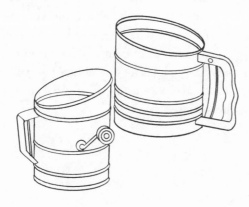

CHIFFON CAKES

ABOUT CHIFFON CAKES

THE CHIFFON CAKE is unique in cake history because its birth date is recorded. Food historians credit Californian Henry Baker with inventing the chiffon cake in 1927. He later sold the formula to General Mills, which promoted the cake as well as the vegetable oil that was its "mystery ingredient." As a result of the promotion, cakes baked with oil became very popular in the 1940s. They are having a renaissance today because we are so conscious of our cholesterol intake and vegetable oil, of course, contains none.

The chiffon cake has a marvelously light texture, and is big, tall, and only slightly richer than an angel-food cake, in whose pan it is baked. For ease in serving, cut chiffon cake with a serrated knife.

Vanilla Chiffon Cake

The basic recipe that follows contains whole eggs and makes a plain vanilla cake; to transform this into a completely cholesterol-free cake, omit the yolks and add more whites (see variation, Egg-White Chiffon, following). Follow the other easy variations to make Orange-Lemon Chiffon, Chocolate Chiffon, Mocha Chiffon, and Hazelnut Chiffon.

Note: The chiffon cake, like the angel-food cake, may be hollowed out and filled with Bavarian cream (pages 372–375) or ice cream.

6 large eggs separated, at room temperature
½ teaspoon cream of tartar
1½ cups granulated sugar (10½ ounces; 300 g)
2½ cups sifted cake flour (8¾ ounces; 250 g)
3 teaspoons baking powder
½ teaspoon salt
¾ cup water
½ cup light vegetable oil, such as canola or safflower oil
2 teaspoons vanilla extract

ICING
Any Seven-Minute Icing (page 396) or Boiled Icing (page 402) or Orange or Lemon Icing Glaze (page 408); or top with a light sifting of confectioners' sugar

Advance Preparation   The cake can be baked in advance, wrapped airtight, and frozen.

Special Equipment   One angel-food tube pan, 10 × 4 inches, preferably with a removable bottom and "feet" on the edge; if there are no feet on the pan, set out a wine bottle or tall funnel from which to hang the cake after baking; an extra large bowl, wax paper or baking parchment, scissors

Baking Time   65 to 70 minutes at 325°F (165°C)

Quantity   9 cups batter; one cake, 10 × 4 inches (serves 14 to 16)

Pan Preparation   Cut a paper or parchment liner to fit the bottom of the baking pan. Do not grease the pan.

1. Prepare pan as described. Position rack in center of oven. Preheat oven to 325°F (165°C). Read About Sponge and Foam Cakes (page 213).

2. In a large bowl, use the electric mixer to whip the egg whites with the cream of tartar until fluffy. Little by little, add ⅔ cup of the sugar, beating until the whites are very satiny and form nearly stiff peaks. Remove bowl from the mixer. Scrape the beaters into the bowl. Without washing the beaters, return them to the mixer. Set whites aside.

3. In another mixing bowl, sift together flour, remaining granulated sugar, the baking powder, and salt. Scoop a well in the center of this flour mixture. In this well add the 6 egg yolks, the water, oil, and vanilla. With a whisk or wooden spoon, or the electric mixer on medium-low speed, beat the ingredients together until well blended and smooth.

4. In 6 or 7 additions, fold the yolk batter into the whipped whites, working gently so the volume will not be lost. Pour the batter into the ungreased lined pan and bake in the preheated oven for about 65 minutes, or until the top is well risen and richly golden in color. A cake tester should come out clean.

5. As soon as cake is baked, invert it onto the feet of its pan or hang it upside down over a bottle neck or a funnel; allow it to hang upside down for several hours, or overnight, until completely cold.

To remove the cake from the pan, set the pan upright and slide a long thin knife blade between the cake and pan sides to loosen the crumbs. Repeat around the center tube. Top the cake with a plate, and invert. If the pan has a removable bottom, press on it gently. Lift off the pan. Slide the knife between the pan bottom and the cake to release it. Peel off the paper. Turn cake right side up. Frost as desired. To serve, slice with a serrated knife.

. . . .

Orange-Lemon Chiffon Cake Prepare Basic Chiffon Cake, but replace the water with orange juice, or use half orange juice and half freshly squeezed lemon juice. Add grated zest of 1 orange and 1 lemon along with 1 teaspoon of vanilla extract. Replace the second teaspoon of vanilla with 1 teaspoon of orange or lemon extract. Frost the cake with Orange or Lemon Icing Glaze (page 408) or Orange Seven-Minute Icing (page 397).

Chocolate Chiffon Cake Prepare Basic Chiffon Cake, but use only 1¾ cups sifted cake flour (6 ounces; 170 g). Add to dry ingredients ½ cup sifted unsweetened cocoa, preferably Dutch-process (1⅓ ounces; 40 g), and ¼ teaspoon ground cinnamon.

Mocha Chiffon Cake Prepare Chocolate Chiffon Cake and add 2 tablespoons instant coffee powder to the dry ingredients along with the cocoa and cinnamon.

Hazelnut Chiffon Cake Prepare Basic Chiffon Cake or Chocolate Chiffon Cake. After adding the whipped whites, fold in very lightly 1 cup finely chopped toasted hazelnuts (4 ounces; 110 g).

Egg-White Chiffon Cake Prepare Basic Chiffon Cake, but omit egg yolks. Whip a total of 8 or 9 egg whites (1 cup) until stiff. This recipe contains no cholesterol.

Lemon Chiffon Cake

Completely cholesterol-free, this light, lemony chiffon cake is slightly smaller than the Basic Chiffon Cake and the pan preparation and cooling procedures are different. The result, however, is an excellent light cake made with egg whites. Its refreshingly tart flavor and sponge texture are complemented by a simple Lemon Icing Glaze. As an alternative serve an un-iced slice with a Warm Berry Sauce (page 419), or with lemon sorbet and fresh strawberries.

6 large egg whites, at room temperature
2 tablespoons sifted confectioners' sugar
1½ cups sifted cake flour (5¼ ounces; 150 g)
1 cup granulated sugar (7 ounces; 200 g)
2 teaspoons baking powder
¼ teaspoon salt
½ cup light vegetable oil, such as canola or safflower
Grated zest of 2 lemons
½ cup freshly squeezed lemon juice

ICING (OPTIONAL)
Lemon Icing Glaze (page 408) or Orange Wine
    Icing (page 395)

1. Prepare pan as described. Position rack in center of oven. Preheat oven to 350°F (175°C). Read About Sponge and Foam Cakes (page 213).

2. In a large bowl, use an electric mixer to whip the egg whites with 2 tablespoons confectioners' sugar until stiff but not dry. Remove bowl from electric mixer; scrape beaters into bowl. Set whites aside. Without washing the beaters, return them to the mixer.

3. In another large bowl, sift together the flour, granulated sugar, baking powder, and salt. Scoop out a well in the center of the flour and add the oil, lemon zest, and juice. With a whisk or the mixer on medium-low speed, beat until well blended and smooth.

In several additions, fold the batter into the whites, working gently so the volume will not be lost.

4. Pour batter into the prepared pan and bake in the preheated oven for about 35 minutes, or until the top of the cake is golden brown and feels lightly springy to the touch. A cake tester should come out clean. Cool the cake right side up in its pan for 5 minutes, then invert onto a wire rack and lift off the pan. Leave the cake upside down on the rack to cool completely. Ice if desired.

Advance Preparation Cake can be prepared ahead and frozen.

Special Equipment One 9-inch (8-cup capacity) tube pan, extra mixing bowl, grater

Baking Time 35 to 40 minutes at 350°F (175°C) (This cake does not have to hang upside down for several hours while cooling.)

Quantity 6¾ cups batter; one 9-inch tube cake (serves 8 to 10)

Pan Preparation Spread solid shortening on bottom and sides of pan; dust pan with flour; tap out excess flour. (This cake does not have to be baked in an un-greased pan.)

MERINGUE CAKES AND DACQUOISES

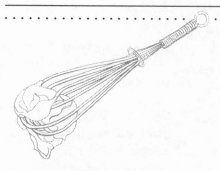

ABOUT MERINGUE

MERINGUE IS CREATED by whipping egg whites with sugar to create a foamy structure. It has innumerable uses, all of which take advantage of its uniquely light and airy quality. Meringue is used as leavening in certain cake batters, or to lighten a soufflé, mousse, Bavarian cream, or cake filling. It may be combined with softened butter to create silken buttercream icing or it may be piped from a pastry bag or spread with a spoon into many different shapes and sizes to use as cake layers. When these layers are baked until crisp in a slow oven, they can be filled and frosted with buttercream or flavored whipped cream to form meringue cakes.

Meringue may be flavored with any type of extract or citrus zest. When grated or ground nuts are added to a meringue that is shaped into layers for use in a cake or torte, it is called a dacquoise, or *japonais* or *broyage,* from the French word *broyer,* meaning to grind, referring to the nuts.

The amount of sugar combined with the egg whites determines both the final use of the meringue and the method by which it is made. The classic meringue proportions are 1 ounce of whites (the white of 1 large egg) to 2 ounces of sugar (4 tablespoons or 57 grams).

Soft meringues with a small amount of sugar, about 2 tablespoons per egg white, are easily whipped at room temperature (cold method) with a wire whisk in a bowl, preferably copper, or in an electric mixer with whisk beaters. A low-sugar meringue will remain soft inside even if baked or broiled for a short time in the oven.

Sometimes the whites and sugar are whisked together over, but not touching, hot water (warm or Swiss method) until the mixture reaches 120°F (49°C) and the sugar is dissolved. Then the meringue is whipped until stiff. This method guarantees that no undissolved sugar will bead or weep from the baked product; it makes a very stable meringue. A meringue made by either method may be added to cake or torte batters to provide leavening, or may be folded into mousses or Bavarian creams.

When a larger proportion of sugar is added (3 or 4 tablespoons of sugar per egg white), the resulting meringue may be hard or soft, depending upon how it is baked and whether it is combined with softer ingredients, as when folded into a batter. For the highest sugar-ratio meringue (typically 4 or more tablespoons sugar per white), the sugar can be cooked in water to a syrup (Italian Meringue) before being added to the whipped whites. Since Italian meringues have more sugar than any other type, they are firmer, and make a stable meringue that will not break down or bead when baked. Italian meringue may be combined with softened butter to make a luxuriously satin-textured buttercream, or it can be folded into fillings, toppings, or mousse. It can also be baked slowly at low temperature to make crisp cake layers.

Meringue Basics

Before making meringues, review the Eggs section (page 23). There are several important basics to remember when working with meringue: select a cool, dry day if possible, since humidity may soften meringue. Keep all utensils scrupulously clean; a speck of fat (such as from a broken yolk) in the egg whites prevents them from beating to full volume. Eggs separate most easily when cold, but whites beat to fullest volume when at room temperature (68° to 70°F; 21°C). For this reason, separate eggs as soon as they come from the refrigerator, then let them sit a while to warm up. To speed the process, set the bowl of whites inside another bowl of warm water and stir the whites until they no longer feel cold to the touch.

Frozen egg whites may be used for meringues, but the whites should be defrosted at room temperature. If you are in a hurry, set the container of frozen whites in a bowl of warm, not hot, water to thaw.

What Makes a Meringue?

Egg whites foam because of the peculiar properties of their albumen proteins. Albumen itself is thick and viscous, made up of large molecules that tend to cling together. As air is whipped into liquid whites, the resulting foam depends upon the combined activity of several proteins, which actually bond to each other to form a strong network protecting the foam cells and holding their water in place. When meringue is exposed to heat in a warm oven, the molecules of air in the foam cells expand as they are warmed, enlarging the cells; these might actually grow so large they could explode if not for the ability of another protein to coagulate around and strengthen each cell wall. This prevents the collapse of the wall, even when the meringue is baked and the water in it evaporates.

Other ingredients are added to egg whites to improve the quality and stability of the meringue. Acidity (usually in the form of a tiny bit of cream of tartar, vinegar, or lemon juice) lowers the pH of albumen slightly, stabilizes the meringue, and helps it resist overbeating and leaking of liquid. Add acid to the whites just before you begin to beat them. To this end, you can also wipe your bowl and beater with a paper towel dampened with white vinegar (be sure to dry them carefully), or whip the whites in a copper bowl. The copper interacts with the albumen on a molecular level to contribute to the volume and stability of the foam.

Salt is also added to whites just before beating. It is included primarily for taste, though some authorities believe it helps strengthen the albumen proteins.

Sugar is added primarily for flavor; if it is added too early in the whipping process, it can severely hinder the development of the uncooked foam. Generally, a small amount of sugar is added after the whites and acid have been whipped to the fluffy stage. After this, more sugar can be whipped in gradually as the whites approach the stiff peak stage. Once the meringue is baking, the sugar helps its stability. You can use either granulated, superfine, or confectioners' sugar; however, it is important that the sugar granules be completely dissolved in the egg white or, when baked, the meringue may "weep" as undissolved sugar granules melt and ooze out as liquid. Old-timers claim weeping can be prevented by sifting a little cornstarch into whites along with the sugar. Another preventative is to use superfine sugar, which has tiny crystals that dissolve quickly; you can make your own superfine sugar by grinding granulated sugar in a food processor fitted with the steel blade. Confectioners' sugar has cornstarch added, and in some preparations the cornstarch may actually help stabilize the meringue. Always sift confectioners' sugar, and sift superfine or granulated sugar if you suspect it may be lumpy. To be sure the sugar is completely melted in the whipped meringue, pinch some of the meringue between your thumb and forefinger. If it feels grainy, the sugar granules are still whole; if smooth, the sugar is dissolved.

Egg Whites

How to Whip Egg Whites Until Stiff But Not Dry   To hold its shape, meringue must be properly whipped. For the best results with the least effort, use an electric mixer with the largest balloon beater available and a bowl that fits it most closely. The object is to keep the entire mass of whites in constant movement. The length of the beating time will vary, depending upon your method. If you have a strong arm, try using a large balloon whisk and a copper bowl. To avoid fatigue, let your arm from the elbow down do most of the work. Hand-beating will usually result in a slightly greater volume of whites. If you prefer to beat with an electric mixer, and I confess that I do, it is best to stop the mechanical whipping before stiff peaks are reached and finish the job with a hand whisk. In this way, you control the end result perfectly.

Whip the room-temperature egg whites with a whisk or electric mixer on low speed at first, increasing to medium and finally high speed as the foam builds, begins to stiffen, and looks glossy and smooth. This point is reached just before the foam is whipped to its maximum volume. When the recipe reads "whip until stiff but not dry" it means that when the machine is turned off and the meringue-filled beater or whisk is lifted up in the air, the peak or tuft of meringue on the beater tip will stand straight up without drooping.

Ideally, you should now be able to turn the bowl of whipped whites completely upside down, and the mass in the bowl should not budge. This is the essential test I use in my baking classes.

If the meringue looks dry, or begins to clump, curdle, or lose its perfectly smooth appearance, the whites have been overbeaten, and the foam-cell structure has begun to break down. Now the mass of whites will slide in the bowl as you turn it over because water has been released from the cell structure of the overbeaten foam. A film of liquid will begin to form in the bottom of the bowl. Overbeaten whites may also become grainy.

How to Save Overbeaten Whites For every 4 overbeaten whites, you can try whipping in about ¾ of 1 egg white; stir unbeaten white in a bowl, then spoon some into the overwhipped whites and beat again, carefully, for 20 to 30 seconds.

Handy Egg White Measurements 1 large egg white = 2 generous tablespoons = ⅛ cup

4 large egg whites = 8 tablespoons = ½ cup

3 extra-large egg whites = ½ cup

4 large whites beaten stiff (with sugar as per recipe) = 4 cups meringue = two 8- or 9-inch meringue cake disks plus a few small meringue cookies.

Note: 4 large whites whipped to fullest volume will often yield three 8-inch meringue cake disks.

6 large whites beaten stiff (with sugar as per recipe) = three 8- or 9-inch meringue cake disks plus 6 or 7 small meringue cookies

All-Purpose Meringue:
Cold and Swiss Methods

*T*his is a basic recipe for an all-purpose meringue prepared by two methods: the cold method, when all ingredients are whipped at room temperature, and the Swiss method, when the egg whites and sugar are warmed together before being whipped. The Swiss or warm method is somewhat more stable and long-lived because warming dissolves the sugar completely. Either method can be used for topping cakes, for folding into mousse or Bavarian cream, or for Classic French Buttercream (page 386).

Note: Meringue may be flavored, though any flavoring should be added after the meringue is whipped so it does not affect the mounding ability of the egg whites. Suggested flavorings include extracts, grated citrus zest, or sifted unsweetened cocoa (3 tablespoons for 4 egg whites).

4 large egg whites, at room temperature
¼ teaspoon cream of tartar
Pinch of salt
½ cup superfine sugar (3½ ounces; 100 g)
1 teaspoon vanilla extract (optional)

Quantity   3½ to 4 cups

COLD METHOD • *1.* Read About Meringue (page 258). Place the egg whites in the large bowl of an electric mixer. Test the temperature of the egg whites with your finger; if they are ice cold, put them in a bowl set over another bowl of hot water and stir until the whites no longer feel cold to the touch.

2. Add to the whites the cream of tartar and salt. Beat on low to medium speed until the whites are fluffy. Add the sugar, 2 tablespoons at a time, beating after each addition while increasing mixer speed to medium-high. Beat until the whites look glossy and are nearly stiff but not dry. To be sure the sugar is completely dissolved, rub a little meringue between your fingers; you should not be able to feel the grains of sugar. Finally, fold in the vanilla or other flavoring.

SWISS MERINGUE METHOD • In step 1 above, combine the egg whites with the sugar and set the bowl over a pan of simmering water. Place a mercury candy thermometer in the bowl. Stir the mixture constantly until the sugar dissolves and the syrup reaches 120°F (49°C). Remove from heat at once, add cream of tartar and salt, and whip until stiff but not dry. Finally, fold in the vanilla or other flavoring.

Italian Meringue

*W*hen a high proportion of sugar will be added to whipped egg whites, it is best done with a cooked sugar syrup. This recipe, called Italian Meringue, produces the most stable type of meringue because the whites are actually cooked by the syrup. This meringue will not break down when baked as cake layers (dacquoise), added to Bavarian cream or mousse, or used as a topping. It can also be whipped with softened butter to make a luxurious, light Italian Meringue Buttercream (page 398). As a general rule, the sugar syrup for Italian meringue is cooked to 238°F (about 114°C) to make a meringue of average, all-purpose stiffness. If you prefer a very stiff meringue, the temperature can be higher, up to 248°F (about 120°C). With a reduction in the cooking temperature of the syrup, the same recipe is used for old-fashioned Boiled Icing (page 402). Read About Meringue (page 258).

Special Equipment   2-quart heavy-bottomed saucepan, mercury candy thermometer, pastry brush; stand-type electric mixer is helpful but not essential; metal pan of ice water large enough to hold sugar syrup pan

Quantity   About 3½ cups

¾ cup plus 2 tablespoons granulated sugar
   (6¼ ounces; 175 g)
⅓ cup water
1 tablespoon white corn syrup, or ⅛ teaspoon cream of tartar
3 large egg whites
2 tablespoons granulated sugar
1 teaspoon vanilla extract (optional)

1. Put the water in a heavy-bottomed 2-quart saucepan, then add ¾ cup plus 2 tablespoons sugar and the corn syrup or cream of tartar. Stir once or twice. Cook over moderate heat until the sugar is dissolved; swirl the pan several times.

Increase heat to medium-high. Wash down the pan sides with a pastry brush dipped into cold water to remove any sugar crystals; repeat several times. Bring the syrup to a boil, and boil *without stirring* for 7 to 8 minutes, or until the thermometer reads 238°F (about 114°C; soft-ball stage). When the thermometer reads about 228°F (about 109°C) and you near the end of the syrup-cooking time, begin to whip the egg whites.

Note: It is better to let the cooked syrup wait (standing in ice water) while the whites are being whipped than vice versa.

2. Whip the whites in the large bowl of an electric mixer until fluffy. Gradually add the remaining 2 tablespoons of sugar, and increase the mixer speed, whipping until the whites are *nearly* stiff but not dry. Do not overwhip. While whipping, keep a sharp eye on the syrup thermometer.

3. As soon as the syrup reaches 238°F (about 114°C). remove pan from the heat and set it in a pan of ice water near the mixer. The ice water stops the syrup from cooking. Check to see that the whites are stiff and satiny and completely amalgamated.

4. Turn the mixer on medium-low speed. Wipe ice water from the pan bottom. Slowly pour the hot syrup onto the egg whites in a steady stream directed between the bowl and the beater. Continue whipping until all the syrup has been added. Do not scrape the hardened syrup from the bowl.

5. The whites will increase in volume as the syrup is whipped in; they will become smooth and quite stiff. Add the vanilla if using it. Turn the mixer down to the lowest speed and whip the meringue until cool to the touch. This can take a while; you can speed the cooling by whipping over a pan of ice water. If making Italian Meringue Buttercream (see page 398), the softened butter is whipped in after the meringue is completely cool.

Meringue or Dacquoise Cake Layers

*T*his is an all-purpose recipe for crisp, light meringue cake layers. When ground nuts are folded into the meringue before baking, the resulting cake is called a dacquoise (literally "from the town of Dax"). Either way, the sweetened, whipped meringue is shaped into rounds and baked in a slow oven until dried out. The basic recipe is for a three-layer cake made with 6 egg whites, and *a two-layer* cake made with 4 whites follows.

Meringue or dacquoise layers may be filled and frosted with buttercream, Bavarian cream, mousse, flavored whipped cream, or softened ice cream. When filled with whipped cream, the layers soften on standing. To protect their crisp texture, you can brush baked layers on both sides with melted chocolate or Apricot Glaze before filling.

To make a Chocolate Dacquoise, prepare the 3-layer dacquoise below, adding 2 tablespoons sifted unsweetened cocoa (preferably Dutch-process) to the cornstarch and nut mixture. To make a Toffee Cream Dacquoise, prepare the 3-layer dacquoise below, with an additional ½ cup toasted and ground nuts set aside for a garnish. Make Toffee Cream Filling (page 371). Spread toffee cream between each layer, and frost sides and top with reserved plain whipped cream. To garnish, blend ground nuts with crushed dacquoise layer trimmings (and extra crushed toffee if you wish) and press gently onto the cake sides all around.

THREE-LAYER MERINGUE OR DACQUOISE CAKE

6 large egg whites, at room temperature
1¼ cups sifted superfine sugar (8¾ ounces; 250 g)
2 tablespoons sifted cornstarch
¼ teaspoon cream of tartar
⅛ teaspoon salt
1 teaspoon vanilla extract

For dacquoise, add:
1 cup (5 ounces; 140 g) toasted and finely ground
    hazelnuts and/or almonds
⅛ teaspoon hazelnut or almond extract

1. Read About Meringue, page 258. Prepare pans as described. Preheat oven to 300°F (150°C). Test the temperature of the egg whites with your finger; if cold, put their bowl into a larger bowl of hot water and stir until whites are no longer cold to the touch.

2. To make a 3-layer cake, set aside ½ cup of the sugar. If making a 2-layer cake, set aside ¼ cup of the sugar. For either size cake, combine remaining sugar with the cornstarch in a sifter and sift together onto wax paper. If making a dacquoise, add the ground nuts to this sugar-cornstarch mixture.

3. Put the warm whites into the large bowl of an electric mixer, add cream of tartar and salt, and beat on low to medium speed until the whites begin to look fluffy. Gradually add the reserved sugar: ½ cup (for 6 whites, 3 layers) or ¼ cup (for 4 whites, 2 layers), while beating on medium-high speed (KitchenAid #8) until whites are glossy and medium-stiff. Add vanilla if used, and the hazelnut or almond extract if making a dacquoise. Beat just a few seconds longer, until stiff but not dry.

In four or five additions, fold the cornstarch-sugar (and nuts, for a dacquoise) mixture into the whites by hand, using a flat whisk or rubber spatula. Fold gently to maintain maximum volume.

Advance Preparation
Meringue and dacquoise layers may be made up to a week in advance and stored for several days in an airtight container or frozen. If they soften in humid weather, recrisp them in a 300°F oven for a few minutes, cool completely, then fill and frost.

Special Equipment 2 or 3 large cookie sheets, large bowl for electric mixer plus another bowl slightly larger, 8- or 9-inch round template (can be pot lid or bowl or cake pan), toothpick, pencil, wax paper, baking parchment (optional); 16-inch-long pastry bag fitted with ½-inch (#6) round tip, sharp paring knife, wire rack, 8- or 9-inch cardboard cake disk, 2-cup Pyrex measure (to hold pastry bag), wide spatula, rubber spatula, icing spatula

Baking Time 40 to 50 minutes at 300°F (150°C), or until crisp

Quantity Two 8- or 9-inch layers from 4 whites or three layers from 6 whites, plus a few extra small cookies. *Note:* Whites whipped to greater volume may yield one or two extra layers.

Pan Preparation Dab a little butter on the pan as an adhesive, then add baking parchment cut to fit the pan. Spread softened butter or vegetable spray on the parchment, then dust it with flour; tap out excess flour. Or generously butter (don't use solid shortening) and flour the baking sheet directly. Use a toothpick (directly on greased sheet) or pencil on parchment to draw around a template marking two or three 8- or 9-inch rounds about 1 inch apart on the prepared pans (diagram a on this page).

4. Prepare a pastry bag by setting it, tip down, in a 4-cup measure. Fold back a 4- or 5-inch cuff, and press in the sides of the bag just above the tip, to plug the opening while the bag is being filled. Spoon in the meringue. Twist the bag closed, and pipe meringue inside the marked shapes on the prepared pans.

To do this, begin at a point in the center of the marked circle, and gently squeeze out an even column of meringue, holding the bag perpendicular to the pan and slightly above it, so that the meringue falls into place as you guide it in a spiral that completely fills the circle, ending at the drawn ring (diagram b).

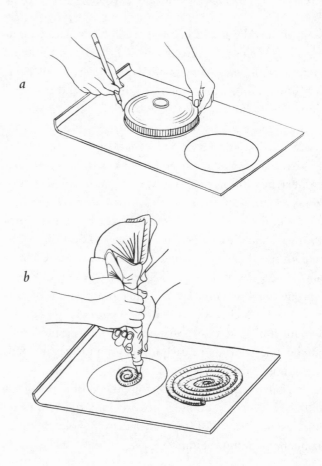

a

b

Alternatively, you may prefer to begin at the outside of the ring and spiral in toward the center. Or pipe around the outside of the ring, then simply spoon meringue into the center and flatten it very gently with an icing spatula to make a solid disk about ½ inch thick and even on top.

5. Use up any leftover meringue by piping out small cookies or spooning out small nests or cups of meringue.

Bake the meringue in the preheated oven for 40 to 50 minutes, or longer, until the meringue is thoroughly set and a very light beige color. Look in the oven after about 25 minutes; if the meringue is darkening too fast, reduce the heat to 250° or 275°F (125°C).

Note: If the oven heat is too high, the color of the meringue will darken as the sugar caramelizes; this changes the flavor of the meringue. To achieve a perfectly white meringue, you must bake the layers at 200°F (93°C) for 90 minutes, or longer, until thoroughly dried out; you can also leave the meringues in the oven, with the heat off, for a couple of hours longer (or overnight) to complete the drying if necessary. Professional bakeries often bake meringue in warming ovens, leaving them for as long as 24 hours.

6. After baking the meringue or dacquoise cake layers, set the pans on a wire rack for a few minutes. The baked shapes will be slightly pliable while warm. At this stage, use a wide spatula to lift them from the sheet and set them on the wire rack to cool completely. If you have used baking parchment, invert the sheet carefully and peel the paper off the back of the baked shapes.

After cooling the layers on the racks for 15 to 20 minutes, they should be completely crisp; test a small cookie to check texture; it should crack in half. If your shapes are still soft when completely cold, they should be set on baking parchment on a baking sheet and returned to the oven for a little while to dry out further.

7. Once cold and crisp, the layers can be trimmed so that they are all the same size and the complete cake will

have a neat appearance. Hold the template against each baked shape and trim the edge with a sharp paring knife; save trimmings to blend with nuts for the final garnish of the frosted cake. Store trimmed meringue or dacquoise layers in an airtight container with foil or wax paper between the layers, or freeze. Or fill and frost.

. . . .

Note: To prepare a 2-layer meringue or dacquoise cake, use ingredients listed here but follow steps 1 through 7 above, making changes as noted "for 2-layer cake."

TWO-LAYER MERINGUE OR DACQUOISE CAKE

4 large egg whites, at room temperature
1 cup plus 2 tablespoons sifted superfine sugar
   (8 ounces; 226 g)
2 tablespoons sifted cornstarch
¼ teaspoon cream of tartar
Pinch of salt
½ teaspoon vanilla extract

For dacquoise, add:
¾ cup (3¾ ounces; 95 g) toasted and finely ground
   hazelnuts and/or almonds
⅛ teaspoon hazelnut or almond extract

Chocolate Mousse Dacquoise

*T*oasted almonds and hazelnuts blend with meringue in the 3 crisp layers that form this very special cake. It is filled and frosted with chocolate mousse and garnished with nuts and chocolate curls. If you really want to get fancy, you can cover the entire confection with a solid chocolate skin topped with ruffled chocolate ribbons, making the Chocolate Ruffle Dacquoise, which follows.

Note: If you prefer an all-chocolate cake, add 2 tablespoons sifted Dutch-process cocoa to the dacquoise, making Chocolate Dacquoise layers (page 266).

DACQUOISE CAKE LAYERS
1 recipe Three-Layer Dacquoise (page 267) made
   with 6 egg whites and a half-and-half blend of
   almonds and hazelnuts

FILLING AND FROSTING
1 recipe Chocolate Mousse Cake Filling (page 354)

GARNISH (OPTIONAL)
1 cup toasted and ground hazelnuts and/or almonds,
   or toasted sliced almonds
Chocolate Curls (page 456)
1 tablespoon confectioners' sugar

Advance Preparation The nuts may be toasted and ground in advance. The chocolate mousse can be made in advance and chilled for at least 30 minutes to reach spreading consistency. It can also be covered and refrigerated for several hours, or overnight, before being used in the cake. Chocolate curls can be made a week or so in advance and stored in the refrigerator in an airtight container. The dacquoise cake layers may be made up to a week in advance and kept at room temperature in an airtight container, or frozen. Or you can fill and frost the cake, but omit the chocolate curls, set it in the freezer unwrapped just to set the frosting, then wrap it airtight and freeze. Unwrap while still frozen and thaw in the refrigerator for several hours. Add the chocolate curls shortly before serv-

ing. The cake cuts best after 3 or 4 hours in the refrigerator; the layers lose their crispness if left longer. If the cake must be assembled more than 3 or 4 hours in advance, keep layers crisp by coating them with melted semisweet chocolate.

Special Equipment   See recipe for Dacquoise. For the mousse, a double boiler, an electric mixer plus a second bowl and beater for whipping egg whites. For the cake base, it is helpful to have a 9-inch cardboard cake disk. To garnish the cake, a bowl for the chopped nuts and a sifter for the sugar. To cut the cake when serving, use a serrated knife.

Baking Time   For dacquoise layers, 45 minutes at 300°F (150°C)

Quantity   One 9-inch 3-layer cake (serves 12)

Pan Preparation   See recipe for Dacquoise, pages 266–270.

1. Prepare 3 (or 4 if enough meringue) dacquoise layers. While the layers are baking, prepare the chocolate mousse. Set the mousse in the refrigerator to chill until it reaches spreading consistency.

2. To prepare for assembling the cake, set out a bowl containing toasted sliced or chopped nuts and add any crumbs left from trimming the baked dacquoise layers. Also set out the previously made chocolate curls.

3. On a 9-inch cardboard cake disk or a flat plate, put a dab of chocolate mousse in the center, then set down the first dacquoise layer. Spread about 1¼ cups of mousse on the first layer, top with a second dacquoise layer, and add mousse filling as before; repeat with remaining layer(s). Align the sides of the cake neatly. Frost the sides and top of the cake generously with the chocolate mousse. You will probably have some mousse left over; it can be frozen and served at another time or piped through a pastry bag fitted with a star tip to make decorative rosettes around the edge of the cake.

4. To garnish the cake, lift it up and hold it over a piece of wax paper or a tray (to catch crumbs). Scoop the toasted and ground nuts/crumbs into the palm of your other hand and press them gently onto the lower third of the cake sides (see illustration, page 434). If you plan to freeze the cake, do so at this time (read Advance Preparation).

To complete the cake, cover the top with chocolate curls and sift on a fine dusting of confectioners' sugar. Refrigerate the cake for 3 or 4 hours for easiest slicing, or until ready to serve. Remember that because the mousse contains uncooked egg whites, leftovers should be refrigerated or frozen.

. . . .

Chocolate Ruffle Dacquoise Prepare Chocolate Mousse Dacquoise, but make only half (3½ cups) of the Chocolate Mousse Cake Filling recipe (page 354). Spread about half of the mousse between the cake layers and use the rest to thinly frost the sides and top of the cake. Refrigerate the mousse-covered cake for at least 1 hour while preparing the Plastic Chocolate Ribbons and Roses and Ruffles (pages 458 and 464). Follow those instructions for rolling out the chocolate and covering the cake. Sift on a light dusting of confectioners' sugar just before serving.

TORTES

ABOUT TORTES

ORIGINALLY, THE TERM *torte,* or *tourte,* referred to breads and sweetened cakes baked in a round form. In the cuisines of Middle and Eastern Europe, particularly in Austria, Hungary, and Germany, tortes, or *Torten,* have developed into a highly specialized art form. They are round cakes, to be sure, but they differ from butter or sponge cakes, for example, because all or part of the flour is replaced by finely ground nuts or other ingredients including poppyseeds, bread, or cake crumbs. Usually lacking chemical leaveners, tortes are lightened by egg foams and whipped egg whites folded into the batter.

Tortes are usually light and spongy, though some can be quite dense, depending upon the ingredients. They should always be somewhat moist rather than dry. Although tortes are flavorful enough to be eaten without icing, or simply dusted with confectioners' sugar, European pastry shops traditionally present them with elaborate ornamentation. Most often, the torte is sliced into 2 or 3 layers and filled with flavored whipped cream or buttercream. The outside of the cake may be coated with a thin skin of marzipan before being frosted with buttercream or glazed with dark glossy chocolate icing. Garnishes range from ground toasted nuts to buttercream rosettes and caramelized sugar cages. Austrian, Hungarian, and German pastry chefs use the torte in the same manner as the French and Italian *pâtissiers* use the génoise or sponge cake—as a base upon which to create artistic culinary fantasies.

Years of restaurant torte-tasting had convinced me that there was an enormous variety of tortes, named for more princes and politicians than one could count. However, closer analysis—a sketch pad and notebook carefully carried on a tasting expedition to Vienna and Munich—revealed that there are really endless variations on a few basic types of tortes.

There are a few points to remember about making tortes. First, be aware that nuts, which are the principal ingredient in many recipes, contain a great deal of oil. This oil is released when the nuts are crushed or improperly ground, and oily nuts clump together; they are not capable of blending properly with whipped egg whites. For light-textured tortes, dry the nuts by toasting them as directed in the recipes. Then grind them with a hand-turned drum-type rotary nut mill (see below) to produce a fine, dry, sawdust-like powder. When nuts are ground in the food processor along with a little sugar, they are fairly fine, but never as dry or fine as when ground in a mill; however, the processor is satisfactory for certain recipes, and they are so noted.

It is best to bake tortes in a standard springform pan with a hinged side and removable bottom. This pan permits minimal handling of the fragile, freshly baked torte. For easy cake removal, be sure to grease, flour, and paper-line the baking pan.

Many tortes are split into 2 or 3 layers (see page 427) by being cut horizontally with a serrated knife. If this procedure makes you nervous, you can simply divide the batter among 2 or 3 pans and bake thin layers. If you do this, reduce the baking time and watch the cakes carefully.

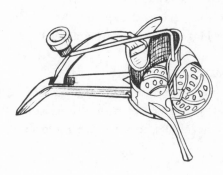

Hazelnut Torte

*T*his torte contains a small amount of flour and baking powder, which gives it a slightly drier texture than some of the other tortes in this section. It is particularly well suited to slicing into 3 layers and filling and frosting with flavored whipped cream. Hazelnut Cream is the traditional choice, but chocolate or coffee cream also blends well with the hazelnut flavor. A touch of cocoa is added to this recipe to enhance the taste without turning it into a chocolate cake. Be sure to toast the nuts to bring out their flavor, and grind them in a drum-type rotary nut mill so they are dry and powdery.

2 cups hazelnuts, toasted, skinned (see page 42), and ground to a fine powder in a drum-type rotary nut mill (6 ounces; 160 g)

⅔ cup sifted cake flour (2½ ounces; 70 g)

1 teaspoon baking powder

¼ teaspoon salt

1½ tablespoons sifted unsweetened cocoa

6 large eggs, separated, at room temperature

¾ cup granulated sugar (5¼ ounces; 150 g)

2 tablespoons dark rum or hazelnut liqueur (optional)

½ teaspoon ground cinnamon

FILLING AND ICING

Hazelnut liqueur (optional)

Double recipe (2 cups unwhipped heavy cream) Hazelnut Cream (page 343)

GARNISH

½ cup toasted and ground hazelnuts, to press onto lower third of frosted cake sides; 8 or 9 whole hazelnuts, to set in a ring around cake top

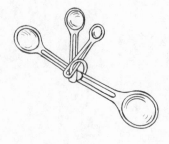

1. Prepare pan as described. Position rack in center of oven. Preheat oven to 350°F (175°C) for the cake. Read About Tortes (page 274).

2. Put ground nuts in a medium-size bowl and remove any large chunks that fell through the sides of the nut mill. Add the flour, baking powder, salt, and cocoa. Stir lightly to blend; take care not to compact the mixture.

3. In the large bowl of an electric mixer, beat together the egg yolks and ½ cup of sugar until the mixture is thick and light-colored and forms a flat ribbon falling back on itself when the beater is lifted. This takes 2 or 3 minutes with the KitchenAid mixer on speed #8; with other mixers it can take 6 or 7 minutes. Add the liqueur and cinnamon and beat to blend.

4. Using a clean bowl and beater, whip the egg whites until fluffy, gradually add remaining ¼ cup sugar, and whip until stiff but not dry. Stir about 1 cup of whipped whites into the yolk batter to lighten it. Fold in remaining whites in several additions, alternating them with the nut mixture. Fold with a light touch to maintain batter volume.

5. Turn the batter into the prepared pan and bake in center of oven for about 35 minutes, or until cake is well risen and a cake tester inserted in the center comes out clean.

Cool cake on a wire rack about 5 minutes. Release the spring and then remove pan sides. Top the cake with another rack or a plate and invert. Lift off the pan bottom; if it sticks, cut around the edge with a knife blade. Peel off the paper. Top the cake with a plate and invert again so it is right side up. Cool completely on a wire rack.

6. On the day the cake will be served, split it into 2 or 3 layers (page 427) with a serrated knife. Set one layer on a cardboard cake disk.

Top with a light sprinkling of hazelnut liqueur if you wish, then add ¾ to 1 cup whipped cream, spread evenly. Top with the middle layer and more cream, then add the cake top, cut side down. Spread cream around the cake

Advance Preparation The nuts can be toasted and ground in advance. The cake can be baked in advance and frozen. Slice, fill, and frost the cake on the day it is to be served.

Special Equipment Jelly-roll pan or roasting pan for toasting nuts, drum-type rotary nut mill; 8½- or 9½-inch springform pan, wax paper or baking parchment, scissors, medium-size bowl, extra mixing bowl and beater for whipping egg whites

Baking Time 25 to 30 minutes at 350°F (175°C)

Quantity 6 cups batter; one 2- or 3-layer 8-inch cake (serves 8 to 10)

Pan Preparation Cut a wax paper or parchment round to fit the baking pan (see page 66). Spread solid shortening on bottom and sides of pan; line pan bottom with the round of wax paper or baking parchment. Grease paper, then dust pan with flour; tap out excess flour.

sides and top. Lightly press toasted nuts around the lower third of the cake sides and garnish the top with whole nuts set in a ring around the edge. Or fill a pastry bag fitted with a star tip with whipped cream and pipe rosettes around the edge of the cake; top each rosette with a hazelnut. Refrigerate the cake until ready to serve.

Walnut Torte

This classic Austrian *Nusstorte* is light, spongy, and moderately moist, with a rich nutty flavor achieved by toasting the nuts.

In German and Austrian coffeehouses and pastry shops, nut tortes are standard, appearing in myriad guises. Often the nut torte forms the basis for the house specialty.

My favorite *Nusstorte* is a specialty of the Cafe Luitpold in Munich. In this house, known for its elegant pastries, an apricot-glazed crisp cookie dough forms the base for 3 light nut layers alternating with almond pastry cream. The top nut layer is spread with vanilla whipped cream and a slice of plain sponge cake. More whipped cream edged with toasted slivered almonds coats the sides, while the top is dusted with confectioners' sugar and crisscrossed with thin lines of dark chocolate icing studded with candied black cherries. With these inspiring thoughts in mind, be creative in combining fillings and icings.

Note: For the correct cake texture, the toasted walnuts must be ground in a rotary-type nut mill so they are light, dry, and powdery. Walnuts contain a high proportion of oil; when ground in the food processor, even with granulated sugar, they tend to be too heavy and oily to blend properly with the egg whites in this recipe.

2 cups walnuts, toasted (see page 42) and ground to a dry powder in a drum-type rotary nut mill (5¼ ounces; 150 g)

⅔ cup untoasted white bread crumbs (1¼ ounces; 35 g)

⅓ cup cornstarch, sifted (1½ ounces; 45 g)

6 large eggs, separated, at room temperature

¾ cup granulated sugar (5¼ ounces; 150 g)

¼ teaspoon salt

Pinch of ground cinnamon

¼ teaspoon almond extract, or ½ teaspoon lemon juice

½ teaspoon vanilla extract

FILLING AND ICING

Viennese Coffee Custard Buttercream (page 360), or Coffee, Chocolate, or Hazelnut Cream (pages 343–345); or ½ of recipe (3½ cups total) Chocolate Mousse Cake Filling (page 354) to fill 3 layers and frost only cake sides. Top cake with Firm Apricot Glaze (page 416) or sifted-on confectioners' sugar.

GARNISH

½ cup toasted and ground walnuts, or ½ cup halved walnuts to arrange in a ring around the top edge of the cake

1. Prepare pan as described. Position rack in center of oven. Preheat oven to 350°F (175°C). Read About Tortes (page 274).

2. Put ground nuts in a medium-size bowl and remove any large chunks that may have fallen through the nut mill. Lightly stir in the bread crumbs, and cornstarch. Set aside.

3. In the large bowl of an electric mixer, combine egg yolks and ½ cup of the sugar. Beat until the mixture is thick and light-colored and forms a flat ribbon falling back

Advance Preparation The nuts can be toasted and ground in advance. Cake can be baked ahead and frozen. Slice and fill cake on day of serving, or 1 day ahead. Refrigerate.

Special Equipment Jelly-roll pan or roasting pan for toasting nuts; drum-type rotary nut mill, medium-size mixing bowl, 9½-inch springform pan, wax paper or baking parchment, scissors, separate bowl and beater for whipping egg whites, knife with serrated blade

Baking Time 40 to 45 minutes at 350°F (175°C)

Quantity 6 cups batter; one 9-inch 2- or 3-layer cake (serves 8 to 10)

Pan Preparation Cut a wax paper or parchment round to fit baking pan (see page 66). Spread solid shortening on bottom and sides of pan; line bottom of pan with wax paper or baking parchment round. Grease paper, then dust pan with flour or bread crumbs; tap out excess flour or crumbs.

upon itself when the beater is lifted. This takes 2 or 3 minutes with a KitchenAid mixer on speed #8; with other mixers it can take 6 or 7 minutes. Add cinnamon, salt, and both extracts and beat to blend. Set bowl and beater aside.

4. Using a clean bowl and beater, whip the egg whites until fluffy; gradually add remaining ¼ cup sugar and whip until stiff but not dry.

Stir about 1 cup of the whites into the yolk batter to lighten it. Fold in remaining whites in 4 or 5 additions, alternating with the nut-crumb mixture. Fold with a light touch to maintain volume of batter.

5. Turn batter into the prepared pan and set in the preheated oven to bake for 40 to 45 minutes, or until the cake is well risen, the top feels lightly springy to the touch, and a cake tester inserted in the center comes out clean.

6. Cool cake in the pan on a wire rack for 15 minutes. Release spring and remove pan sides. Top cake with a rack, invert, and remove pan bottom; if it sticks, use a knife to cut free the edge of the pan. Peel off paper. Top cake with another rack, invert, and cool completely.

Use a serrated knife to cut the cake into 2 or 3 layers. Slide a piece of foil or a cardboard disk between the layers to lift them off without breaking them.

Place the bottom layer on a cardboard disk, spread it with about 1 cup filling, top with the middle layer, fill, and add the top layer, cut side down. Spread icing on sides. To garnish, pour some toasted nuts into the palm of your hand and gently press them onto the frosted cake sides. Then frost the top, or leave the top unfrosted and cover it with warm Firm Apricot Glaze.

Almond Torte

*T*his is an old-fashioned, moderately moist, German *Mandeltorte* with a delightfully crunchy nut texture. The almond flavor is heightened by the addition of orange juice and zest. Like most nut tortes, it is excellent served plain, topped only by a sifting of confectioners' sugar. For a more elegant presentation, it can be sliced into 2 layers and filled and frosted with an Orange Buttercream, or an Orange Whipped Cream, or Viennese Vanilla Custard Buttercream.

1 cup whole blanched almonds (5 ounces; 140 g)
1 cup granulated sugar, sifted (7 ounces; 200 g)
2 tablespoons cornstarch (optional; see step 2)
½ cup plain dried bread crumbs (2 ounces; 60 g)
6 large eggs, separated, at room temperature
Pinch of salt
Grated zest and juice of 1 orange (about 2 teaspoons
    grated zest and ⅓ cup juice)
¾ teaspoon ground cinnamon
½ teaspoon almond extract

FILLING AND FROSTING
Any Orange Buttercream, or Orange- or Almond-
    Flavored Whipped Cream, or Viennese Custard
    Buttercream flavored with 2 teaspoons grated
    orange zest or ½ teaspoon almond extract

GARNISH
½ cup toasted sliced almonds (1¾ ounces; 50 g)

Nuts may be ground in advance. The torte may be baked ahead and frozen. For ease in slicing a single cake into 2 layers, bake the torte a day in advance of slicing. Torte may be wrapped airtight and kept at room temperature for 2 or 3 days. Frosted cake may be prepared a day in advance and kept refrigerated.

Special Equipment Wax paper or baking parchment, scissors, drum-type rotary nut mill or food processor, one 9½-inch springform pan or two 9-inch layer pans, clean bowl and beater for whipping egg whites, serrated knife.

Baking Time 50 minutes at 350°F (175°C) for 1 pan; 30 minutes for 2 layers

Quantity 6 cups batter; one 1- or 2-layer 9½-inch cake (serves 8 to 10)

Pan Preparation Cut a wax paper or parchment liner to fit the baking pan (see page 66). Spread bottom and sides of pan with solid shortening. Line pan bottom with wax paper or parchment round. Grease paper. Dust pan with bread crumbs or flour; tap out excess crumbs or flour.

1. Prepare pan(s) as directed. Note that you can either use 1 pan and slice the torte into layers after baking, or divide the batter between 2 layer pans. Position rack in center of oven. Preheat oven to 350°F (175°C). Read About Tortes (page 274).

2. Grind the almonds with a drum-type rotary nut mill (page 42), or combine nuts with 2 tablespoons sugar taken from the total measured and sifted sugar and grind them together in the food processor. Note that in the processor, you must also add 2 tablespoons cornstarch to the ground nuts to compensate for the fact that they are not as dry as when milled. Put nuts in a bowl with cornstarch if used, and the bread crumbs.

3. In the large bowl of an electric mixer, beat together the egg yolks and ½ cup of the sugar until the mixture is thick and light-colored and forms a flat ribbon falling back on itself when the beater is lifted. This takes 2 or 3 minutes with the KitchenAid mixer on speed #8; with other mixers it can take 6 or 7 minutes. Add the salt, grated orange zest and juice, cinnamon, and almond extract. Stir to blend, then whip for 1 full minute.

4. Using a clean bowl and beater, whip the egg whites until fluffy; gradually add remaining ½ cup sugar, and whip until stiff but not dry. Stir about 1 cup of whipped whites into the yolk batter to lighten it. Fold in remaining whites in several additions, alternating them with the nut mixture. Fold with a light touch to maintain batter volume.

5. Turn the batter into the prepared pan(s) and bake in oven for about 50 minutes for 1 cake, 30 minutes for 2 layers, or until cake is well risen, feels springy to the touch, and a cake tester inserted in the center comes out clean.

Cool torte on a wire rack about 15 minutes. Release the spring and then remove pan sides if using a springform. Top torte with another rack or a plate, invert, and lift off pan bottom. Peel off paper. Top with another plate and invert again so torte is right side up. Cool completely.

6. If you have made one tall layer instead of two thinner ones, slice the single cold torte in half using a long-bladed serrated knife (page 427). In either case, set the bottom layer on a cardboard cake disk, add filling, then top with second layer and frost sides and top. To garnish, press toasted almonds onto cake sides (see page 434).

Italian Almond-Chocolate Torte

his is my re-creation of *torta di mandorle e cioccolata,* a wonderfully light chocolate-flecked torte I was once served in a little trattoria on a side canal in Venice. Perhaps it was the atmosphere—crumbling terracotta and ochre walls, potted red geraniums, and a nearby window of gilded and feathered carnival masks, but I have been partial to this torte ever since.

Each layer can be served alone, modestly topped with a light sifting of confectioners' sugar or cocoa, or the cake can be filled with almond-flavored pastry cream and frosted with any chocolate buttercream or Chocolate Water Glaze (page 414). Garnish cake with Chocolate Curls or press chopped toasted almonds onto the chocolate-frosted cake sides.

⅔ cup blanched, toasted (page 42), and finely ground
    almonds (2¾ ounces; 80 g), made from ½ cup
    whole almonds
½ cup vanilla wafer crumbs (1¾ ounces; 50 g)
1 teaspoon baking powder
¼ teaspoon salt
2 ounces semisweet chocolate, grated (⅔ cup; 60 g)
1 ounce unsweetened chocolate, grated (⅓ cup; 30 g)
6 large eggs, separated, at room temperature
1 cup granulated sugar (7 ounces; 200 g)
¼ teaspoon almond extract
Pinch of cream of tartar

Advance Preparation The cake may be baked in advance, wrapped airtight, and stored at room temperature for 2 or 3 days. It can also be frozen. Fill and frost with cream at least 3 hours before serving, or the night before; store cake in the refrigerator.

Special Equipment Two 9-inch cake pans 1½ inches deep, wax paper or baking parchment, box grater, extra bowl and beater for whipping egg whites, food processor or drum-type rotary nut mill, chilled bowl and beater for whipping cream for icing, sifter

Baking Time 25 minutes at 350°F (175°C)

Quantity 8 cups batter; one 2-layer 9-inch cake (serves 8 to 10)

Pan Preparation Cut wax paper or parchment rounds to fit the baking pans. Spread solid shortening on bottom and sides of pans. Line the bottom of each pan with a wax paper or parchment round. Grease paper, dust pans with flour; tap out excess flour.

CAKE FILLING

½ recipe Almond Pastry Cream (page 348), or Almond Cream (page 342) made with 1 cup chilled heavy cream

CAKE FROSTING

Any Chocolate Buttercream or Chocolate Glaze

1. Prepare pans as described. Position rack in center of oven. Preheat oven to 350°F (175°C). Read About Tortes.

Grind the toasted almonds in a drum-type rotary nut mill (page 42) or in the food processor, combined with 2 tablespoons taken from the measured sugar. Nuts should be reduced to a fine, dry powder. Put nuts in a medium-size bowl.

2. Add to the nuts the vanilla wafer crumbs, baking powder, salt, and all the grated chocolate. Toss the ingredients lightly to blend them together.

3. In the large bowl of the electric mixer, beat the yolks with ¾ cup granulated sugar until the mixture is thick and light-colored and forms a flat ribbon falling back upon itself when the beater is lifted. This takes 2 to 3 minutes with the KitchenAid on speed #8, or 6 to 7 minutes with other mixers. Beat in almond extract.

4. In another mixing bowl with a clean beater, whip egg whites and cream of tartar until fluffy. Gradually add remaining ¼ cup granulated sugar, beating until whites are satiny and stiff but not dry.

Fold the yolk mixture into the whites in 4 or 5 additions. Then sprinkle about ¼ cup of the nut-crumb mixture over the whipped batter and fold it in very gently. Repeat, adding the remaining nut-crumb mixture in 6 or 7 additions, ¼ cup at a time. Fold the dry ingredients in gently to maintain volume.

5. Divide the batter evenly between the prepared pans and bake in the preheated oven for about 25 minutes, or until a cake tester inserted in the center comes out clean. Cool cakes in their pans on a wire rack for about 10 minutes. Top each layer with a rack or plate, lift off pan, and peel off paper. Cool completely.

6. Prepare filling of your choice and spread it between the cake layers. Frost and garnish as desired. Refrigerate cake until ready to serve.

Note: Each completely cooled layer may also be sliced in half and filled to make a 4-layer torte (adjust filling quantity proportionally).

Poppyseed Torte

This classic *Mohntorte* is one of my favorites. Made with ground poppyseeds, it is easy to prepare and stays moist and fresh for at least a week, even without icing or refrigeration.

The recipe is reminiscent of one I tasted in Munich's famous Kreutzkamm Conditorei, a national institution well worth a detour when you are in Munich. My notes from one delicious visit indicate that my eighth! selection was the *Mohntorte,* and it was the favorite of the day. Moist in texture, it was studded with golden raisins and finely chopped citron, topped with a thin skin of marzipan, and glazed with bittersweet chocolate cross-hatched with mocha icing.

Mohntorte is excellent unadorned, with only a light dusting of confectioners' sugar on top. If you prefer an icing, choose Cream Cheese Frosting, or let Kreutzkamm be your guide, and use any Chocolate Glaze (see Index).

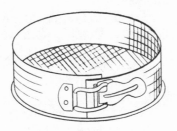

Advance Preparation   Poppyseeds can be ground in advance, or purchased already ground from a specialty store (see Sources, page 477). The cake may be baked in advance and frozen. Well wrapped or in a cake box, it will stay fresh at room temperature for at least a week.

Special Equipment   8½-inch springform or plain round cake pan, wax paper or baking parchment, scissors, blender or electric herb mincer to grind poppyseeds

Baking Time   45 to 50 minutes at 300°F (150°C)

Quantity   3 cups batter; one single-layer 8-inch cake (serves 8)

Pan Preparation   Cut a wax paper or parchment round to fit the baking pan. Spread bottom and sides of pan with solid shortening. Line bottom of pan with the wax paper or parchment round. Grease paper, then dust pan with flour; tap out excess flour.

1 cup whole poppyseeds (5 ounces; 140 g)
5 tablespoons unsalted butter (2½ ounces; 75 grams), at room temperature
¾ cup granulated sugar (5¼ ounces; 150 g)
4 large eggs, separated, at room temperature
2 tablespoons golden raisins, coarsely chopped, and/or 2 tablespoons candied citron, chopped (optional)
2 teaspoons grated lemon zest

ICING

2 tablespoons confectioners' sugar, to sift over cake top, or Cream Cheese Frosting (page 387)

1. Prepare pan as described. Position rack in center of oven. Preheat oven to 300°F (150°C). Read About Tortes (page 274).

2. To grind poppyseeds, put them in an herb mincer (see page 43) until finely ground, or grind ½ cup at a time in a regular blender on high speed for 1 full minute. Stir down the seeds in the blender once or twice. Grind them until no whole seeds remain. Set ground seeds aside.

3. If it is available, attach the flat paddle to the mixer instead of the whip-type beater.

In the large bowl of the electric mixer, cream the butter until soft, then beat in the sugar until well blended. Add egg yolks, one at a time, beating after each addition. With mixer on low speed, blend in the poppyseeds, raisins, and lemon zest.

4. With a clean bowl and regular whipping beater, whip the egg whites until stiff but not dry. Stir about ½ cup whites into the poppyseed batter to lighten it. In 4 or 5 additions, gently fold remaining whites into the batter.

5. Turn the batter into the prepared pan and lightly smooth the top. Bake the torte in the preheated oven for 45 to 50 minutes, or until a cake tester inserted in the center comes out clean. Cool in its pan on a wire rack for 10 minutes. If using a springform pan, unfasten spring and remove sides. Top torte with a rack or plate, invert, and remove pan. If bottom sticks, cut around the edge with the tip of a knife to loosen cake. Remove pan bottom and peel off paper. Top torte with another plate or rack and invert. The torte should be right side up; cool it completely on a wire rack. Sift confectioners' sugar over the cake or ice with Cream Cheese Frosting.

Note: If you wish, you can also split the torte into 2 layers with a serrated knife and spread apricot jam between the layers.

Passover Nut Torte

*T*his easy-to-make torte is suitable for Passover because it is made with matzo meal rather than cracker or dried bread crumbs, which may, however, be substituted. The recipe was shared with me by Anne Maidman, a family friend and an excellent cook. Note that this is a small, single-layer cake; the recipe can be doubled.

¾ cup walnuts, toasted (page 42, then ground in
    drum-type rotary nut mill (2 ounces; 60 g)
¾ cup matzo meal (3¼ ounces; 90 g)
4 large eggs, separated, at room temperature
½ teaspoon salt
½ cup granulated sugar (3½ ounces; 100 g)
¼ cup honey
¼ cup orange juice, preferably freshly squeezed
¼ teaspoon ground cinnamon

TOPPING
1 tablespoon confectioners' sugar

Advance Preparation   The walnuts can be toasted and ground in advance. The torte can be baked ahead and frozen.

Special Equipment   Jelly-roll pan or roasting pan for toasting nuts, drum-type rotary nut mill, 2 medium-size bowls, 8- or 9-inch-square baking pan, wax paper or baking parchment, scissors, extra bowl and beater for whipping egg whites

Baking Time   35 to 45 minutes at 350°F (175°C)

Quantity   5 cups batter; one single-layer 8- or 9-inch cake (serves 9 to 12)

Pan Preparation   Cut a piece of wax paper or parchment to fit baking pan. Spread solid shortening or margarine on bottom and sides of pan. Line pan bottom with wax paper or parchment piece. Grease paper, then dust pan with matzo meal. Tap out excess meal.

1. Prepare pan as described. Position rack in center of oven. Preheat oven to 350°F (175°C).

After grinding nuts to a fine, dry powder, place them in a bowl and add the matzo meal. Set aside.

2. Place egg whites in the large bowl of an electric mixer and add the salt. Whip whites until fluffy, then gradually add 2 tablespoons of the sugar while whipping until whites are stiff but not dry (see page 261). Scrape excess whites off beater and return unwashed beater to mixer.

3. Using the same beater but a clean bowl, beat the yolks, then add all remaining granulated sugar and beat until the mixture is thick, light-colored, and forms a ribbon falling back on itself when the beater is lifted. Add honey, orange juice, and cinnamon. Beat to blend.

4. Stir about 1 cup of whipped whites into the yolk batter to lighten it. Fold in remaining whipped whites in 6 or 7 additions, alternating with the nut-matzo meal mixture lightly sprinkled on top.

5. Turn the batter into the prepared pan and bake in the preheated oven for 25 to 30 minutes, or until a cake tester inserted in the center comes out clean. Cool cake in its pan on a wire rack for about 10 minutes. Insert a knife blade between cake and pan sides to loosen crumbs. Top cake with a rack or plate and invert. Lift off pan and peel off paper. Top with another rack and invert. Cool completely on a wire rack.

Sift 1 tablespoon confectioners' sugar over the cake top and cut cake into 2-inch squares to serve.

Sachertorte

*T*he world-famous Sachertorte is much more than a chocolate cake. It is an element of cultural history, a social and political institution, a fascinating story. In fact, it is probably more interesting to read about than to eat. Even the Viennese admit that their intensely chocolaty torte is also slightly dense, just a little dry, and definitely enhanced by a generous dollop of *Schlagobers,* or whipped cream.

3 ounces chopped semisweet chocolate (½ cup; 85 g)
3 ounces chopped unsweetened chocolate (½ cup; 85 g)
¾ cup unsalted butter (6 ounces, 170 g), at room
    temperature, cut up
¾ cup (2⅔ ounces; 75 g) plus 2 tablespoons sifted
    confectioners' sugar
6 large eggs, separated, plus 1 large egg white, at
    room temperature
¼ teaspoon salt
¾ cup sifted all-purpose flour (3¼ ounces; 90 g)
¼ cup blanched almonds, ground to a fine powder in
    a drum-type rotary nut mill (1 ounce; 30 g)

GLAZE
1½ cups Apricot Glaze (page 415), warmed before
    spreading

ICING
Chocolate Water Glaze (page 414) or Fabulous
    Chocolate Glaze (page 412). Also, 1 ounce
    semisweet chocolate, for writing the word
    "Sacher" on cake top.

GARNISH
1½ cups heavy cream whipped with 2 or
    3 tablespoons confectioners' sugar, to serve
    alongside cake

Advance Preparation   Store cake at room temperature for a day or two, or freeze. Thaw completely before slicing into 2 layers, glazing, and icing. Or, cut into layers and ice with chocolate glaze before wrapping airtight and freezing. For best results, thaw in the wrapping in the refrigerator overnight. Serve at room temperature.

Special Equipment   One 8½-inch springform pan or round 8- or 9-inch pan 2 inches deep, double boiler, wax paper or baking parchment, scissors, knife with serrated blade, small saucepan and pastry brush for glaze, paper cone or plastic bag (optional)

Baking Time   40 minutes at 350°F (175°C)

Quantity   4 cups batter; one 2-layer 8- or 9-inch cake (serves 10 to 12)

Pan Preparation   Line pan with wax paper or baking parchment round. Butter pan, add paper round, spread butter on paper. Dust inside of pan with flour; tap out excess flour.

1. Prepare pan as described. Position rack in center of oven. Preheat oven to 350°F (175°C). Read About Tortes (page 274).

2. Melt chocolate in top pan of a double boiler set over, not in, simmering water. Stir to melt chocolate completely, remove from heat, and set aside to cool until comfortable to the touch.

3. In the large bowl of an electric mixer fitted with a paddle if possible, beat the butter until soft, then add half of the sugar and cream together until well blended and smooth. Add the egg yolks, one at a time, beating well after each addition. With the mixer on low speed, beat in the melted and cooled chocolate. Scrape down inside of bowl and beaters. Beat on medium-high speed for about 30 seconds.

4. In a clean bowl with a whisk beater, combine egg whites and salt. Beat until fluffy. Gradually add remaining sugar and beat until the whites are nearly stiff but not dry.

5. Whisk about 1 cup of the egg whites into the chocolate batter to lighten it. In 1-cup additions, fold about one third of the whites into the chocolate. Fold in about half of the flour, a few tablespoons at a time. Fold in a little more of the whites, then remaining flour and the almonds, a little at a time, and finally remaining whites. The batter will be fairly stiff.

6. Gently spoon batter into the prepared pan. Place pan in center of preheated oven and bake for about 40 minutes, or until a cake tester inserted in the center comes out clean and the cake just starts to pull away from the pan sides.

Set the cake on a wire rack and allow to cool in its pan for about 5 minutes. Top cake with a wire rack, invert, lift off pan and peel off paper. Cool cake completely on wire rack.

At this point, the cake can be wrapped airtight and refrigerated or frozen.

7. On the morning of the day it is to be served, or one day in advance, slice the cake into 2 layers with a ser-

rated knife. Slide a cardboard disk or piece of wax paper between the layers and lift off the one on top. Set it aside.

8. Prepare the apricot glaze. While the glaze warms, set the bottom layer of the cake, cut side up, on a cardboard disk or a piece of foil. Set the cake on a wire rack set over a jelly-roll pan or piece of foil to catch the excess glaze.

When the glaze is warm, spread it over the cake. Place the second layer, cut side down, over the glaze. Pour warm glaze over the cake top. With an icing spatula or knife, spread glaze over cake top and down the sides. Smooth around the sides, letting excess drip down onto the rack. Leave the cake until the glaze sets and feels tacky. Refrigerate to speed this process if you are in a hurry.

9. Prepare the icing while the glaze sets. When ready to ice the cake, be sure the icing glaze is thin enough to pour. Pour icing glaze over cake top and spread it in a fairly thin layer, without going deep enough to pick up apricot glaze, working it down onto the cake sides. Finally, go around the sides, making a smooth surface. Wait until the glaze sets, about 30 minutes (or refrigerate to speed setting), then, if you wish, apply a second coat of icing glaze, for a perfectly smooth finish.

Note: Fingerprints will show on chocolate icing glaze, so lift the cake from underneath with a broad spatula.

10. In restaurants, Sachertorte has the word "Sacher" written in script across the top. To do this, prepare a small paper cone (see page 436) or a small plastic bag. Melt about 1 ounce semisweet chocolate, pour some into the cone or bag, cut a tiny hole in the tip, and test the flow on the counter. You should have a thin, neatly flowing line. Hold the cone above the cake and write the word "Sacher" with a flourish.

Elegant and Special
CAKES

I HAVE SELECTED this group of cakes because each is special in some way. Many are showstoppers, others unusual because of their ingredients or presentation. All are appropriate for a gala, a festive and important occasion. There are, of course, many other recipes in the book that would fit this definition, such as the Chocolate Ruffle Cake or the Sachertorte.

Before selecting a cake from this section, read the recipe all the way through in order to plan your time—some are made up of components from other sections (fillings, icings); some are quick and easy; others, complex and time-consuming.

Black Forest Cherry Cake

*T*his luscious 4-layer extravaganza is the classic Viennese *Schwarzwalderkirschtorte*. Kirsch, the cherry brandy used, comes from the Black Forest, hence the name in the title, although the cake was actually invented in Vienna. While it looks dramatic, the cake is easy to assemble: The Chocolate Buttermilk Cake is split into 4 layers, brushed with kirsch soaking syrup, and filled with whipped cream and kirsch-soaked tart cherries. It is iced with more whipped cream and garnished with chocolate shavings and curls, whipped cream rosettes, and Maraschino cherries. This is a dazzling party cake that really tastes as good as it looks!

Note: You will see that the liqueur in the recipe can be adjusted to your taste or omitted altogether. Bear in mind that the kirsch flavor should be subtle, not overwhelming.

CHERRY FILLING
Two 16-ounce cans tart red cherries (not Bing), drained, with 1 cup of the liquid and 4 cups of cherries reserved
¼ cup kirsch

CAKE
1 recipe Chocolate Buttermilk Cake (page 104), baked in two 9-inch round pans

CAKE SYRUP
1 cup liquid reserved from canned tart cherries
2 tablespoons kirsch, or to taste
2 tablespoons granulated sugar

WHIPPED CREAM FILLING AND ICING
3 cups heavy cream, chilled
4 tablespoons granulated or superfine sugar
3 tablespoons kirsch, or to taste

GARNISHES

Chocolate Curls (page 456) made with an 8-ounce bar of dark chocolate (226.8 g) such as Hershey's Special Dark, or other fine-quality semisweet or bittersweet chocolate

12 Maraschino cherries, well drained, with stems if possible

1. At least 2 hours before beginning to assemble this cake, drain the canned cherries, reserving 1 cup of their liquid for the cake soaking syrup. Put 4 cups of drained cherries into a bowl with ¼ cup of kirsch. Stir occasionally. This can be done the night before making the cake.

2. Prepare the chocolate cake. When layers are cold, use a serrated knife to split them horizontally (see page 427), making 4 layers. On pieces of foil or wax paper, set out the layers, cut sides up.

Set out another piece of foil or wax paper. On this, make the chocolate curls for the garnish. Note that the chocolate must be at room temperature to peel. If too cold, set it in the oven (pilot light is sufficient) for a few minutes. As you hold the chocolate bar in your hand, body heat warms it. Peel the bar on one side for a little while, then turn the bar and peel on the warmer, underneath side. Reserve the best, biggest curls for the cake top; use the broken shards to press onto the cake sides. Set the chocolate curls aside.

3. Prepare the cake soaking syrup by combining in a bowl the reserved 1 cup of cherry liquid plus 2 tablespoons kirsch and 2 tablespoons sugar. Stir to blend. Brush or sprinkle 3 or 4 tablespoons of the syrup over the cut side of each cake layer. Discard any leftover syrup; do not oversoak the layers or they will become too moist to handle.

4. In a large chilled bowl with chilled beaters, whip the cream with the 4 tablespoons sugar and 3 tablespoons kirsch until stiff peaks form. You will have about 6 cups of whipped cream.

Advance Preparation The Chocolate Buttermilk Cake can be made well in advance, wrapped airtight, and frozen. Thaw and split into 4 layers before assembling the cake. The cherries should be soaked in the kirsch for at least 2 hours before using them in the cake; this can be done the night before. The assembled and iced cake can be held in the refrigerator for several hours before serving; refrigerate leftovers.

Special Equipment Serrated knife, aluminum foil or wax paper, large flat serving dish, icing spatula, 2 medium-size bowls, strainer, pastry brush, 9-inch cardboard cake disk covered with aluminum foil, large chilled bowl and beater for whipping cream, 16-inch pastry bag fitted with #6 star tip for decorating cake, vegetable peeler for making chocolate curls

Pan Preparation and Baking Time See Chocolate Buttermilk Cake.

Quantity One 4-layer 9-inch cake (serves 10 to 12)

5. Place 1 cake layer, syrup side up, on the cake platter; use a cardboard cake disk beneath the first layer if you wish. Cut strips of wax paper and arrange them beneath the edges of the first layer to protect the platter from icing (see page 429). Spread about 1 cup of whipped cream on the layer, then sprinkle on 1⅓ cups kirsch-soaked cherries. Top this with a second cake layer, syrup side up, another 1 cup of whipped cream and 1⅓ cups cherries. Repeat with the third layer, and position the fourth layer, syrup side down, so the cake top is smooth.

6. Reserve 1 generous cup of whipped cream for garnishing, then frost the cake sides and top, using about 1⅓ cups of cream for the sides and ⅔ cup on top.

Use the palm of your hand to press about two thirds of the least perfect chocolate curls gently onto the cake sides.

Put remaining whipped cream into a pastry bag and pipe 12 rosettes around the top edge of the iced cake. Top each rosette with 1 well-drained Maraschino cherry, stem up, and pile the best remaining chocolate curls in the middle of the cake top. Remove wax paper strips protecting the plate.

Refrigerate the cake until 20 minutes before serving time; in hot weather, serve directly from the refrigerator.

Lime Mousse Cake

*R*efreshingly tart, this perfect summer dessert can be made in advance and frozen. It is simply a liqueur-soaked génoise sponge cake layered with lime mousse. To vary the flavor, substitute tangerine, lemon, or orange.

CAKE

½ recipe (3 eggs) Lemon Génoise (page 220), baked in an 8-inch round pan. Cover the cake with foil until ready to split and fill.

CAKE SOAKING SYRUP

6 tablespoons Grand Marnier Syrup (page 424) or dark rum

LIME MOUSSE CAKE FILLING (6 CUPS)

Zest and juice of 4 limes (about 8 teaspoons zest and ½ cup juice)

1 envelope unflavored gelatin (¼ ounce; 7 g)

¼ cup cold water

3 large eggs, separated, at room temperature

1 cup superfine sugar (7 ounces; 200 g)

2 teaspoons cold water

1 teaspoon cornstarch

3 tablespoons orange-flavored liqueur (optional)

Pinch of salt

2 tablespoons sifted confectioners' sugar

½ cup chilled heavy cream

GARNISH

1 teaspoon grated lime zest, reserved from filling

Advance Preparation   Cake can be made in advance and frozen. Split shortly before filling. The assembled cake can be prepared a day in advance and refrigerated, or frozen for up to a week. In any case, refrigerate for a minimum of 4 hours before serving to set the filling.

Special Equipment   One 8-inch springform pan, 8-inch cardboard cake disk covered with foil, bowl and beater for whipping egg whites, serrated knife, double boiler, rubber scraper, large mixing bowl containing ice water, whisk, extra bowl and beater for whipping cream

Chilling Time   Minimum 4 hours, to set filling

Quantity   One 3-layer 8-inch cake (serves 8)

Pan Preparation   Place foil-covered disk in pan bottom and put a dab of butter on the disk to hold in place.

1. Slice the cooled cake horizontally into 2 layers using a serrated knife (see page 427). With cut sides up, brush about 3 tablespoons cake syrup or rum onto each layer. Set one layer, cut side up, into the prepared springform pan, pressing it gently onto the butter in the center of the cake disk. This holds the cake in place.

2. Set aside 1 teaspoon grated zest for garnishing the finished cake. Put the rest in a small bowl and add the lime juice.

In the top pan of a double boiler, sprinkle the gelatin over the cold water, stir, and set aside to soften for 3 or 4 minutes. Then set the pan directly over low heat and stir constantly until the gelatin dissolves. Remove pan from heat and set aside.

3. Put the 3 egg yolks into the medium-size bowl of an electric mixer and add the superfine sugar and 2 teaspoons cold water. Beat with the electric mixer for about 2 minutes, or until the mixture is thick and pale ivory colored, and forms a flat ribbon falling back upon itself when the beater is lifted.

4. Check the gelatin; it should still be liquid. If slightly thickened from standing, stir it over low heat for a second to liquefy. Dissolve the cornstarch in the lime zest and juice, then pour the mixture into the melted gelatin. Whisk well. Place the gelatin pan over the bottom half of the double boiler set on the counter, not the stove. Whisk in the whipped egg-sugar mixture. Set the double boiler over medium heat and whisk constantly for about 12 minutes, or until the mixture thickens enough to coat a spoon. Stir in the liqueur, if using it, and cook for about 1 minute longer. Remove pan from the heat. If the mixture is not in a metal bowl or pan, transfer it to one now, to avoid the thermal shock of ice water.

5. To chill the mixture quickly, set the bowl into a larger bowl filled with ice cubes and water, plus 2 tablespoons salt to make it colder. Whisk for 12 to 15 minutes, until the mousse thickens, will mound on a spoon, and looks like soft pudding. When the mousse is nearly thick-

ened, remove it from the ice-water bath while you prepare the egg whites and cream. Do not let the mousse set
hard.

6. Whip the egg whites with a pinch of salt until
fluffy, add 1 tablespoon confectioners' sugar, and whip until nearly stiff but not dry.

With a chilled bowl and chilled beater, whip the
cream with remaining 1 tablespoon confectioners' sugar
until medium stiff. Set meringue and cream aside and return to the mousse.

7. When it has the correct consistency (if it jells too
much, stir it over a pan of hot water until soft), fold in the
whipped cream, then the meringue. Spoon about half of
the mousse on top of the cake layer in the pan. Set remaining cake layer on the mousse, then top with remaining mousse. Smooth the top gently, and sprinkle with the
reserved grated lime zest. Cover the pan with plastic wrap
and foil, then refrigerate for 4 hours, or freeze.

To unmold the cake, wrap a hot damp towel around
the pan sides for a few seconds, then unfasten the spring
and remove the pan sides.

Chestnut Mousse Cake

*R*um-laced chestnut mousse is studded with chopped candied chestnuts to make the filling for this sublime 3-layer cake. Ice the cake with Chocolate Water Glaze (page 414), or garnish the un-iced top with whole candied chestnuts, and spread whipped cream and chocolate shavings on the sides.

CAKE
½ recipe (3 eggs) vanilla-flavored Génoise (page 216), baked in an 8-inch round pan

CHESTNUTS
One 10- or 12-ounce jar of candied chestnuts in syrup, drained, with syrup reserved. Set aside several whole chestnuts for garnishing the cake, and coarsely chop the rest.

RUM-CHESTNUT CAKE SOAKING SYRUP
7 tablespoons of syrup reserved from candied chestnuts, if there is enough, or make up the difference with 1 more tablespoon of rum, or use Cake Soaking Syrup (page 423) plus 2 tablespoons dark rum and 1 teaspoon vanilla extract. Total: about 9 tablespoons syrup, blended in a bowl

RUM-CHESTNUT MOUSSE FILLING (5 CUPS)
1 can (15½ ounces) unsweetened chestnut puree
2 cups milk
½ cup (3½ ounces; 100 g) plus 2 tablespoons granulated sugar
2 envelopes unflavored gelatin (each ¼ ounce; 7 g)
1 teaspoon vanilla extract
6 large egg yolks
4 tablespoons dark rum
¾ cup heavy cream, chilled

ICING (OPTIONAL)

Chocolate Water Glaze (page 414), or ½ cup heavy
   cream, whipped, flavored with 1 tablespoon
   granulated sugar and 1 tablespoon
   dark rum

GARNISH

Chocolate Curls (page 456), or toasted almond slices
Reserved whole candied chestnuts

1. Prepare the génoise and bake in the 8-inch pan.
When cold, split it into 3 layers with a serrated knife (see
page 427). Wrap the layers in foil or plastic wrap until
ready to assemble the cake.

2. Prepare the chestnuts, reserving the liquid for the
syrup and chopping those chestnuts not reserved for garnishing the finished cake. Prepare the cake soaking
syrup.

3. Prepare the mousse filling: In a 2-quart saucepan,
mash the chestnut puree with a fork. Add the milk and sugar
and whisk until fairly smooth. Sprinkle on the gelatin right
out of the package, then set the pan over medium heat and
bring just to a boil, stirring continually with a whisk or
wooden spoon. Don't worry if there are lumps, the mixture
will be strained. When it reaches a boil, remove pan from
the heat and stir in the vanilla.

4. In a large mixing bowl, whisk the egg yolks until
frothy, then stir in about ½ cup of the hot chestnut mixture while whisking constantly. Transfer the warmed yolks
to the hot chestnut mixture in the pan, stirring constantly
so the eggs do not poach. Cook, stirring, over medium
heat until the mixture thickens slightly. Do not boil.
When thick, remove from heat and stir in the rum. Strain
through a sieve set over a bowl, then cool in the refrigerator until thickened but not quite jelled. Or, to speed the
cooling, stir the mixture over a large pan of ice water.

When the mousse is thick enough to mound on the

Advance Preparation The
cake must be refrigerated for
a minimum of 3 hours for the
filling to set before it can be
iced and decorated. It is best
to prepare this cake one day
in advance.

Special Equipment One
8-inch springform pan, pastry
brush, icing spatula, 7- or
8-inch cardboard cake disk
covered with foil (optional);
paring knife, plastic wrap, 2
small bowls, strainer or sieve,
2-quart saucepan, whisk,
wooden spoon, large mixing
bowl, pastry brush; chilled
bowl and beater for whipping
cream, plastic wrap

Baking Time for Génoise
20 to 25 minutes at 375°F
(190°C)

*Chilling Time for
Assembled Cake* Minimum
of 3 hours, or overnight, for
filling to set

Quantity One 8-inch
3-layer cake (serves 10 to 12)

spoon like a soft pudding, whip the chilled cream to soft peaks. Fold the cream into the cooled and thickened (but not fully jelled) chestnut mixture. At this point it is ready to add to the cake layers.

5. Set a foil-covered cardboard cake disk in the bottom of the springform pan and put a dab of mousse in the center of the disk to hold the cake in place. Put 1 génoise cake layer, cut side up, on the disk. Sprinkle or brush 3 tablespoons of soaking syrup evenly over the layer. Spread on about one third of the mousse. Sprinkle on half the chopped candied chestnuts, then top with another cake layer. Repeat, adding 3 tablespoons of syrup, one third of the mousse, and remaining chestnuts. Finally, top with the last cake layer, add syrup and remaining mousse, and spread smooth. Top the cake with plastic wrap and refrigerate for at least 3 hours, or overnight, for the mousse to set.

6. When ready to serve, dampen a towel with hot water, wring it out well, and wrap it around the outside of the springform pan for a few seconds. Remove the sides of the springform pan, lift the cake on its disk from the bottom of the pan, and set it on the counter. If you don't use the cardboard disk, leave the cake on the pan bottom.

7. Top the cake with Chocolate Water Glaze. Or simply whip cream with sugar and rum and spread it over the sides of the cake. Garnish the top with several whole candied chestnuts placed in the center and press chocolate curls or toasted almond slices against the sides. Refrigerate the cake in hot weather, but serve it at room temperature.

Cassis Gâteau

*T*he elegant Pâtisserie-Confiserie-Salon de Thé in the Loire Valley village of Azay-le-Rideau is filled with delectable specialties that are "handmade" upstairs in the impossibly narrow fourteenth-century building where, we are told, Joan of Arc once lived. My favorite is this cassis-soaked sponge cake layered with cassis (black currant) mousse topped with a mirror-like cassis glaze. Though time-consuming, this dessert can be made in advance for easy entertaining. *Note:* Canned cassis (black currant) puree is sold in imported food shops; with good success you can substitute fresh or frozen blackberries. Cassis liqueur (double crème de cassis) is available in any liquor shop.

CAKE
½ recipe (3 eggs) vanilla-flavored Génoise (page 216) baked in a 9-inch round pan

CASSIS CAKE SOAKING SYRUP
¼ cup double crème de cassis liqueur
¼ cup Cake Soaking Syrup (page 423)

CASSIS MOUSSE FILLING (3 CUPS)
1⅓ cups canned cassis (black currant) puree, or canned seedless blackberry puree, or 3½ to 4 cups fresh black currants, or fresh or frozen blackberries (20 ounces; 560 g) (quantity of fresh berries depends upon their size and juiciness)
¼ cup cold water
1½ envelopes (3 teaspoons) unflavored gelatin
½ cup boiling water, plain or flavored by pouring over strained berry seeds and pulp (see step 2)
1½ tablespoons freshly squeezed lemon juice
⅛ to ¼ cup granulated sugar, or to taste, depending upon sweetness of berry puree
Pinch of salt
3 tablespoons double crème de cassis liqueur
¾ cup chilled heavy cream

Advance Preparation The génoise cake can be made in advance and frozen. The filled cake must be refrigerated for a minimum of 3 hours to set the filling and topping.

Special Equipment 9-inch round layer pan, 9-inch springform pan, 9-inch cardboard cake disk covered with foil, plastic wrap, aluminum foil, chilled bowl and beater for whipping cream, serrated knife, rubber spatula, large bowl of ice water, tea towel, grater, wax paper, lemon squeezer; for topping, 3 layers of cheesecloth set in a bowl

Baking Time Génoise, about 25 minutes at 375°F (190°C)

Chilling Time Minimum 3 hours for filled cake, then 1 hour to set topping

Quantity One 9-inch cake (serves 8)

Pan Preparation Set foil-covered cardboard disk in bottom of the springform pan and put a tiny dab of soft butter in the center of the disk to hold the cake in place.

TOPPING

⅓ cup reserved berry puree from step 2
1 tablespoon granulated sugar
1 teaspoon lemon juice
½ teaspoon unflavored gelatin
1 tablespoon cold water
2 tablespoons boiling water
3 tablespoons double crème de cassis liqueur

1. Prepare the cake, bake it in a 9-inch layer pan, and when it is cold, split it into 2 layers (see pages 427–428). Cover the layers with foil or plastic wrap to prevent drying until ready to use.

2. In a small bowl, mix together the liqueur and syrup to make soaking syrup. Set the cake layers cut side up and brush each one with 4 tablespoons of syrup. Cover the cake with plastic wrap and set it aside.

3. Prepare the filling: If using canned berry puree, set aside 1 cup for the mousse, and reserve ⅓ cup for the topping. If using fresh berries (washed, drained, and patted dry) or defrosted frozen berries, put them through a food mill to make 1⅓ cups of seedless puree. Do not discard the seeds and pulp that remain in the food mill; reserve them for flavoring the gelatin liquid that follows.

Measure the cold water into a 1½ quart saucepan and sprinkle on the gelatin. Let it sit for 3 or 4 minutes to soften.

Stir in ½ cup boiling water or, if you have prepared your own berry puree, pour the water over the reserved seeds and pulp left in the food mill. Use this flavored water to add to the gelatin mixture. In either case stir the boiling water into the mixture until the gelatin is completely dissolved.

Stir in the lemon juice, sugar, salt, and 1 cup of the berry puree. Taste and add more sugar if necessary. Set the pan over low heat and stir well until the sugar is dissolved; do not boil. If the mixture is not in a metal bowl or pan, transfer it to one now to avoid the thermal shock of ice water.

4. Add 3 tablespoons of cassis liqueur to the fruit mixture. Set the bowl over ice water and stir or whisk on and off for 12 to 15 minutes, or until the mixture feels thick, mounds on the spoon, and has about the consistency of soft pudding. Remove the bowl from the ice water. Do not allow the mixture to jell hard.

The ice water speeds this process, but if you are not in a hurry, you can simply refrigerate the mixture for about 45 minutes, stirring it now and then, until it begins to thicken.

Note: If the mousse sets too hard, you can soften it by setting it over hot water and stirring for a few seconds, just to warm it up and relax the gelatin.

5. With a chilled bowl and beater, whip the cream until soft peaks form. Fold the whipped cream into the cooled and thickened berry mixture.

Set 1 cake layer, syrup side up, on the foil disk in the springform pan. Spoon 2 cups of mousse over this layer. Top with the second cake layer, then add remaining mousse, smoothing the top evenly. Cover the pan with plastic wrap and refrigerate the cake for at least 3 hours, to set the filling.

6. Prepare the topping: Put the remaining fruit puree (there should be about ⅓ cup) and 1 tablespoon sugar in a small saucepan and stir over low heat until the sugar dissolves and the puree is soft. Pour the mixture into a bowl lined with 3 layers of cheesecloth and strain, squeezing the cheesecloth to remove all liquid. Discard any solids. Stir in 1 teaspoon lemon juice. Add water if needed to make ¾ cup of mixture.

In a small saucepan, sprinkle ½ teaspoon of gelatin over 1 tablespoon of cold water and set it aside for 3 or 4 minutes. Pour 2 tablespoons boiling water over gelatin and stir. Put the pan on low heat and stir until the gelatin is completely dissolved.

Add the melted gelatin to the fruit mixture, then stir in 3 tablespoons cassis liqueur. Pour this over the cassis mousse on top of the cake and return the cake to the refrigerator for about 1 hour, to set the topping.

7. When ready to serve the cake, dampen a towel with hot water, wring it out well, and wrap it around the outside of the pan for a few seconds. Unspring the pan sides and remove. Lift the cake from the pan bottom or, if not using the cardboard cake disk, leave the cake on the pan bottom. Refrigerate leftover cake.

Génoise and Sponge Cake Creations

ℰ ndless combinations can be devised by stacking split layers of flavored génoise or sponge cake with mousse, Bavarian cream, buttercream, or flavored whipped cream. Below is a list of suggestions to get you started:

Note: If you are intimidated by the thought of dividing one cake layer into thirds, split it into halves instead and divide the filling between 2 layers. Or bake the cake batter in 2 pans, putting ⅓ in one pan and ⅔ in the other; split the thicker cake, thereby gaining 3 layers with only 1 cut.

Chocolate Marquise

CAKE

½ recipe (3 eggs) Chocolate Génoise (page 220), baked
    in an 8-inch round pan 2 inches deep and split
    into 3 layers (see page 427)

CAKE SOAKING SYRUP

3 tablespoons chocolate-mint or raspberry liqueur
    sprinkled on cut side of each cake layer. Optional
    addition: Glaze each cake layer with seedless
    raspberry jam.

FILLING

3 cups Chocolate Mousse Cake Filling (page 354).
    Alternatively, you can fill the cake with Deluxe
    French Chocolate Buttercream (page 386).

ICING

Chocolate Ganache Icing Glaze (page 409) or
    Fabulous Chocolate Glaze (page 412)

GARNISH

Chocolate Leaves (page 454) or Chocolate Curls
    (page 456) or a single Chocolate Rose (page 461)

Set a foil-covered 8-inch cardboard cake disk in an
8½-inch springform pan. Put 1 cake layer—liqueur and
jam-glazed side up—on the bottom of the pan. Add ⅓ of
the mousse. Top with another prepared cake layer. Repeat.
Top with remaining cake layer and spread on remaining
mousse. Refrigerate cake for several hours.

Release the pan sides and remove. If you don't use a
cardboard disk, leave cake on pan bottom. While cake is
cold, spread warm chocolate glaze on top and sides of cake.
Refrigerate to set glaze. Add chocolate decorations. Refrigerate cake.

Strawberry or Raspberry Mousse Cake

CAKE
1 recipe (6 eggs) vanilla Génoise (page 216), baked in two 8-inch round pans-flavored and split to make 4 layers (see page 427)

CAKE SOAKING SYRUP
3 tablespoons kirsch or framboise-flavored Cake Soaking Syrup (page 423)

GLAZE
Strawberry or seedless raspberry preserves

FILLING
1 recipe Strawberry or Raspberry Mousse (page 356)

ICING
¾ cup chilled heavy cream, whipped

GARNISHES
1 pint fresh strawberries or raspberries, rinsed, dried, and hulled just before using
Sprig of fresh mint leaves (optional)

Brush some flavored cake soaking syrup over the cut side of each cake layer, spread with preserves, and set the layers aside without stacking.

Set a foil-covered 8-inch cardboard cake disk in an 8½-inch springform pan. Put 1 cake layer, glazed side up, in the bottom. Add ¾ cup of mousse filling, and repeat 3 more times, ending with the last of the mousse, smoothed flat. Refrigerate the cake at least 3 hours, to set mousse.

Release the pan sides and remove. If you are not using a cardboard cake disk, leave cake on pan bottom. Spread whipped cream over cake sides, and put a small dollop in the center of the top. Set a few berries in the cream on top and garnish with mint if desired. Arrange berries (slice strawberries in half) around bottom edge of cake and serve extra berries alongside each slice at the table.

Lynn's Devon Lemon Cream Cake

*T*his delightfully tart cake is an often requested specialty of the North Hatley, Quebec, catering business of my good friend Lynn Pageau.

CAKE
½ recipe (3 eggs) Lemon Génoise (page 220), baked in
  an 8-inch round pan and split into 3 layers (see
  page 427)

FILLING
2 cups Lemon Curd (page 366) or Lemon Cake
  Filling (page 367)

ICING
Lemon Buttercream Ménagère (page 388)

GARNISH
Chopped candied lemon peel (page 452), or grated
  lemon zest

Set out a foil-covered 8-inch cardboard cake disk and dab a little lemon curd in the center to anchor the cake. Top with 1 cake layer and half of the lemon curd. Cover with a second cake layer and remaining lemon curd. Top with the last cake layer. Frost the cake with Lemon Buttercream Ménagère, and garnish the top with candied lemon peel or grated lemon zest. Refrigerate, but bring to room temperature to serve.

Grand Marnier Génoise

CAKE

1 full recipe (6 eggs) Orange Génoise (page 220),
baked in two 8-inch-square pans and split to
make four 8-inch square layers

CAKE SOAKING SYRUP

Sprinkle the cut side of each cake layer with
3 tablespoons Grand Marnier Syrup (page 424).

FILLING

Double recipe (4 cups) Orange Cake Filling (page 368)

ICING

Orange Buttercream Ménagère (page 388)

GARNISH

Grated orange zest or chopped candied orange peel
(page 452)

Prepare a foil-covered 8-inch-square cake cardboard. Dab some buttercream or butter in the center of the board to hold the cake in place. Set 1 cake layer, syrup-soaked side up, on the board. Add 1 cup of filling. Repeat twice, layering the flavored cake with the filling and ending with cake. Cover top and sides of cake with icing and add garnish on top. Refrigerate in hot weather.

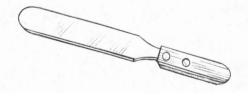

Gâteau Moka

CAKE

Chocolate Sponge Cake (page 223), baked in a jelly-
 roll pan. When cold, trim crisp ⅛-inch edges,
 then cut the cake lengthwise into 3 strips about
 3¼ × 14¾ inches.

CAKE SOAKING SYRUP

Sprinkle about 3 tablespoons coffee-flavored liqueur
 over each strip of cake.

FILLING

Viennese Coffee Custard Buttercream (page 360)

ICING

Mocha Buttercream (page 383), or Chocolate
 Ganache Icing Glaze (page 409)

GARNISH

Pipe buttercream shell borders on top and bottom
 edges of cake. Add a row of candied coffee beans
 or Chocolate Leaves (page 454) down the center
 of the cake.

Cut a cardboard strip about 3¼ × 14¾ inches and
cover it with foil. Dab some butter or buttercream on the
board to hold the cake in place. Set 1 cake strip, syrup side
up, on the board. Top with half of the filling. Repeat. Top
the second layer of filling with the last cake strip, syrup
side down. Refrigerate cake for about 2 hours to allow the
filling to become firm. When cake is cold, ice with buttercream or warm ganache glaze. Garnish, then refrigerate cake, but bring to room temperature before serving.

Orange-Chocolate Dream Cake

CAKE

Chocolate Sponge Cake (page 223), baked in two
8-inch round layers. Split each cake horizontally
to make 4 layers.

FILLING AND FROSTING

Fill and frost sides with 1 recipe (4 cups) well-chilled
White Chocolate Mousse (page 350), flavored
with 3 tablespoons orange liqueur, ½ teaspoon
orange extract or pure orange oil, and 2
teaspoons grated orange zest. Sift some
unsweetened cocoa over the unfrosted cake top.

GARNISH

Press toasted sliced almonds onto the cake sides (see
page 434). Refrigerate cake until about 30
minutes before serving; in hot weather, serve
directly from the refrigerator.

Feather-Topped Truffle Cake

*T*his marvelous recipe was shared with me by my friend Elizabeth MacDonald, a Connecticut artist, potter, and very fine cook. I have added the white chocolate topping design and adapted the procedure for the food processor to make it one of the quickest and easiest recipes I know. Once all the ingredients are set out and the pan is prepared, it takes under 5 minutes to get the cake into the oven, 7 minutes if you are doing it for the first time.

This flourless chocolate cake has a texture somewhere between a satin-smooth creamed fudge and a softly set mousse. The surprise is in the topping: a glamorous feathered pattern made with melted white chocolate and baked right onto the cake, eliminating the need for any further decoration or icing. Serve it with Champagne Sabayon Sauce (page 364) or unsweetened whipped cream and fresh raspberries.

The cake is flavored with coffee, but you could substitute 3 tablespoons of fruit- or nut-flavored liqueur such as Frangelico (hazelnut); Amaretto plus ½ teaspoon almond extract; Grand Marnier plus ½ teaspoon orange extract or orange oil; or crème de menthe plus ½ teaspoon peppermint extract.

2 ounces best-quality white chocolate such as Lindt
    Callebaut, or Tobler Narcisse, chopped (generous
    ¼ cup; 50 g)
7 ounces best-quality semisweet chocolate, chopped
    (1 cup plus 2 tablespoons; 200 g)
½ cup water
2 teaspoons instant espresso coffee powder, or other
    flavoring (see headnote)
1 cup granulated sugar (7 ounces; 200 g)
1 cup unsalted butter (2 sticks; 230 g), at room
    temperature, cut into small bits
4 large eggs, at room temperature, lightly mixed in a
    2-cup Pyrex measure or a small bowl

**GARNISH FOR CAKE
SIDES (OPTIONAL)**
⅔ cup toasted sliced almonds (2 ounces; 60 g)

Advance Preparation The cake has the best, firmest texture when made at least 1 day in advance. After being chilled in the refrigerator, it can be wrapped airtight and frozen. Thaw in the refrigerator for several hours, then bring to room temperature before serving. The cake can, however, be baked just a few hours in advance, but the texture when served will still be rather soft.

Special Equipment Paring knife, small double boiler (can be improvised from 2 pans), food processor, small (2-cup) saucepan or syrup pot (preferably with pouring spout), 2-cup Pyrex measure, two 9-inch cardboard cake disks covered with foil, small bowl, rubber spatula, one 9-inch round cake pan 1½ inches deep or one 8½- to 9-inch springform pan, ¼-inch square of heavy-duty aluminum foil (only if using springform pan), wax paper, scissors, paper decorating cone (page 436), strong plastic wrap, roasting pan big enough to hold the 9-inch pan in a water bath

1. Prepare pan as described. Position a rack in lower third of the oven. Preheat oven to 350°F (175°C).

2. Put the chopped white chocolate in a small double boiler set over low heat and stir until melted and smooth. Do not heat above 110° to 115°F (about 45°C), or it may get lumpy (see page 47). Test the heat with an instant-read thermometer or remove pan from heat just as soon as the chocolate starts to melt, then stir it until completely smooth.

3. Put the chopped dark chocolate into the workbowl of a food processor fitted with the steel blade. Process for about 60 seconds, until reduced to a fine, even powder. Turn off the machine.

4. In a small pan (preferably with a spout), combine the water, coffee powder if using, and sugar. Stir, bring just to a boil, and stir to dissolve the sugar. With the processor running, slowly pour the boiling syrup through the feed tube onto the chocolate. Process about 10 seconds, or until the chocolate is melted. Scrape down the workbowl and process for another few seconds to be sure the chocolate is absolutely smooth. Leave the machine running and add small pieces of butter, one at a time, through the feed tube. Process 1 or 2 minutes. Scrape down the bowl and check to see that all the butter has melted into the chocolate.

With the machine still running, pour the eggs through the feed tube over the chocolate. Process just 2 or 3 seconds, to blend. If you have not added coffee to the sugar syrup, add other flavoring now and pulse to blend.

5. Pour the batter into the prepared pan. Smooth the top.

If using a springform pan, set it in the middle of the foil; press the foil against the pan sides to make a leak-proof jacket for baking in the waterbath.

6. Check the melted white chocolate; it should be creamy and smooth; if it has begun to thicken, stir it over a pan of hot water for a few seconds. When smooth, put it into the paper decorating cone, fold down the top, and follow the

Baking Time   30 to 35 minutes at 350°F (175°C)

Quantity   One 9-inch cake (serves 10 to 12)

Pan Preparation   Grease bottom and sides of pan with solid shortening. Line the bottom of the cake pan (but not a springform pan) with a round of wax paper or baking parchment cut to fit. Lightly grease the paper if used.

Feathered Chocolate Glaze diagrams (see page 447) to create the topping pattern. Briefly, you draw spiral or parallel lines of white chocolate on the cake top, then pull the blade of a table knife in alternating directions through the lines.

7. Place the baking pan inside a roasting pan big enough to hold it with a little room on all sides. Pour hot water into the larger pan until it reaches about one-quarter of the way up the sides of the cake pan. Carefully set the pans in the lower third of the preheated oven.

Note: To avoid the danger of splashing water onto the cake while lifting the pan into the oven, you can place the pans in the oven before adding the water.

Bake the cake for 30 to 35 minutes, or until the dark chocolate top feels barely firm and slightly rubbery to the touch; it should not stick to your fingertip. The feather design should still look very white. When the pan edge is tapped, the cake center should remain firm, not rippled as if still liquid. Remove pans from the oven, then lift out the cake pan, set it on a wire rack, and cool for 20 to 30 minutes. Remove the foil jacket on a springform pan, if used.

Run a knife blade between the cake and the pan sides. The cake should be warm, rather than hot, at this point.

(*Note:*   If overbaked, the white chocolate will darken to brown, but the cake will still taste fine. You can hide an overbaked design by spreading on a thin coating of melted dark chocolate.)

8. If you have used a springform pan, undo the spring from the cooled cake and remove the sides, leaving the cake on the pan bottom. If using a regular round cake pan, top the cake with a piece of strong plastic wrap, cover it

with a cardboard cake disk, and invert. Lift off the pan and peel off the paper. Top with a second, foil-covered cake disk and invert once again. Remove the top disk, peel off the plastic wrap, and leave the feathered pattern facing up.

Note: Be sure to use plastic wrap, not foil, for this inverting task, because foil will stick and mar the surface design.

Cool cake completely, and—for a solid texture—refrigerate at least 24 hours before serving. Or wrap in plastic and foil and freeze. If you want to decorate the cake sides before serving, press on toasted sliced almonds. If cake is cold, brush on preserves or melted chocolate first so that nuts will stick.

Chocolate Mousse Cake

*W*ith a texture somewhere between pudding and cheesecake and an intense chocolate flavor, this cake makes world-class chocoholics swoon. It is one of the cakes I always mention when asked my favorites from this collection. It stands as a monument to good taste without any adornment at all, but if you wish, you can serve it on a platter napped with Crème Anglaise or Champagne Sabayon Sauce. For a party presentation, pipe rosettes of coffee-flavored whipped cream on top of the cake.

Note: I prefer to serve this cake about 1 hour after it is unmolded from its pan, when the inner core is still slightly warm and soft as pudding. The texture of the cake becomes firm as it chills. Though the cake becomes more dense, it is also excellent made a day or two ahead and refrigerated.

CRUST

1 cup pecans or hazelnuts, toasted (see page 42)
   (5 ounces; 140 g)
1 tablespoon granulated sugar
Pinch of salt
3 tablespoons unsalted butter, melted

CAKE

16 ounces best-quality bittersweet or semisweet
   chocolate, chopped (2½ cups plus 1 tablespoon;
   454 g)
1 cup heavy cream
6 large eggs, at room temperature
1 teaspoon vanilla extract
¼ teaspoon ground cinnamon
⅓ cup sifted all-purpose flour (1½ ounces; 45 g)
¼ cup granulated sugar (1¾ ounces; 50 g)

GARNISHES (OPTIONAL)

Candied coffee beans or miniature chocolate chips
½ cup chilled heavy cream, whipped with 1 teaspoon
   instant coffee powder and 1 tablespoon sugar

SAUCE (OPTIONAL)

Crème Anglaise (page 418) or Champagne Sabayon
   Sauce (page 364)

1. Prepare pan as directed. Position rack in center of
oven. Preheat oven to 325°F (165°C).

2. Coarsely grind the toasted nuts with the tablespoon
of sugar and the salt in a food processor or nut chopper;
you need about 1¼ cups ground nuts. Combine nuts with
melted butter, then press them into an even, fairly thin
layer over the pan bottom and 1½ inches up the sides. Set
the pan aside. In hot weather, refrigerate the nut-lined pan.

3. In the top pan of a double boiler set over hot, not
boiling, water, combine the chopped chocolate with

Advance Preparation The
cake can be made a day or
two in advance, covered, and
refrigerated. Or cool the cake
thoroughly, wrap airtight, and
freeze. Defrost in the refrigerator overnight before serving.

Special Equipment 9-inch
springform pan, small
saucepan, double boiler,
chilled bowl and beater for
whipping cream, nut chopper
or food processor fitted with
metal blade

Baking Time 35 minutes at
325°F (165°C)

Chilling Time If not serving cake warm, chill for at
least 3 hours.

Quantity One 9-inch cake
(serves 12 to 14)

Pan Preparation Gener-
ously spread softened butter
on bottom and sides of pan.

½ cup of the cream. Stir on and off until chocolate is melted. Remove pan from the heat, stir to blend thoroughly, and set the chocolate cream aside to cool.

4. In the large bowl of an electric mixer, beat the eggs, vanilla, and cinnamon. Add the flour and sugar and beat on high speed until pale in color and very foamy. The mixture will increase in volume considerably. With a KitchenAid mixer on speed #8, beat for a full 10 minutes; with other mixers it can take 15 to 18 minutes of beating. Don't cheat, the air beaten in now is essential to the texture of the finished cake.

5. In a chilled bowl with chilled beater, whip remaining ½ cup cream until soft peaks form. Set aside.

6. If the top pan of your double boiler is small, transfer the melted chocolate mixture to a large mixing bowl before beginning this step. Stir about 1 cup of the foamy egg batter into the melted chocolate to lighten it, then fold remaining egg batter into the chocolate in 4 additions. Finally, fold in the whipped cream.

7. Turn the batter into the prepared pan, smooth the top, and bake in the preheated oven for 35 minutes, or until the outer third of the top puffs up somewhat; the center will still be soft and flat. Timing is critical here, so watch for the rising of the outer edge and remove the cake when this is clearly visible.

8. Cool the cake on a wire rack for 20 minutes. Remove the sides of the springform pan but leave the cake on the bottom. Either serve the cake in 1 hour, when the center will still be soft (it will not slice neatly), or chill it for 3 to 4 hours to allow the texture to become firm for neat slicing.

9. Once it is chilled, you can slide the cake from the pan bottom to a flat platter, using a broad spatula. If you wish, decorate the cold cake with piped-on rosettes of coffee-flavored whipped cream and garnish with candied coffee beans or miniature chocolate chips. Serve plain or with a sauce or cream (see headnote).

Seven- or Eight-Layer Chocolate Cake

*T*his recipe is dedicated to my father, Harold Gold, because it was one of his favorite cakes. I remember, as a child, always counting the layers just to check, feeling triumphant when the number varied, as it often did and still does, from the seven we considered traditional to nine or even twelve, depending upon the whim of the chef. Now the choice is yours.

This cake is a composite of several classic recipes: the génoise sponge cake, a deluxe French egg-yolk buttercream, and a dark chocolate glaze. Their general techniques will be outlined below, but for equipment lists and specific instructions, you are referred to each individual recipe.

CAKE

1 recipe vanilla-flavored Génoise Sponge Cake (page 216), baked as a sheet in a 10- × 15-inch jelly-roll pan (see instructions, page 220). When it is cold, trim ⅛-inch crisp edges from the sheet cake, then cut it crosswise into 4 equal sections, each about 9¾ × 3⅜ inches. With a serrated knife, split each section horizontally to make 8 layers, each ¼ inch thick. Stack the layers between sheets of plastic wrap, then wrap the entire stack to keep it fresh until ready to assemble the cake. If you are planning to freeze the cake, do not cut it up until shortly before assembling.

FILLING AND FROSTING

Double recipe (4 cups) Deluxe French Chocolate Buttercream (page 386)

Chocolate Water Glaze (page 414) or Fabulous Chocolate Glaze (page 412)

GARNISH

Chopped pistachio nuts or leftover chocolate buttercream piped in a shell border around bottom edge of cake

Advance Preparation The vanilla génoise sponge cake that forms the layers can be made well in advance and frozen. The Deluxe French Chocolate Buttercream can be made several days in advance, brought back to room temperature, and whipped before using. The filled and frosted cake can be wrapped in plastic and stored in the refrigerator for several days, or it can be frozen. It is best made a day or two before serving. Bring to room temperature to serve.

Equipment For cake, filling and frosting, and glaze, see individual recipes. In addition, you will need plastic wrap, a serrated knife, an icing spatula, and a cardboard cake board 3⅜ × 9¾ inches; you can cut this from the side of a corrugated cardboard box. Cover the cardboard with foil. You will also need a wire rack set over a tray. If you plan to pipe a decorative buttercream border on the finished cake, prepare a 16- to 18-inch decorating bag with a #6 star tip.

Quantity One strip cake, 3⅜ × 9¾ inches (serves 8 to 10)

1. Prepare the cake as directed in the recipe. Set out the split layers, wrapped, until ready to fill. Be sure the buttercream has been whipped and is at room temperature, smooth and spreadable.

2. Set one ¼-inch-thick strip of cake on the foil-covered board. Top with a fairly thin layer (³⁄₁₆ inch) of chocolate buttercream and cover with another cake strip. Repeat. Remember not to make the filling layers too thick, because there are a lot of them. Continue building up filling and cake layers until the seventh or eighth cake layer (your choice) is set on top, cut side down. Frost the sides, then the top, with the same buttercream, smoothing it as evenly as possible by holding the icing spatula against the cardboard base as a guide while you pull it across the cake sides. Set the cake on a plate in the refrigerator to chill until the buttercream is firm.

3. While the cake chills, prepare the chocolate glaze. Set the chilled cake on a wire rack placed over a tray to catch drips, and pour a generous amount of warm chocolate glaze over it. Tilt the cake to make the glaze flow evenly; spread the glaze with the icing spatula. Make the top smooth and let glaze drip down the sides. Sprinkle on chopped pistachio nuts if using them. Set the cake aside for at least 30 minutes, until the glaze hardens. In very hot weather, refrigerate to set the glaze. When the glaze is set, you can pipe a buttercream border if you wish. Or press chopped pistachio nuts around the lower edge of the cake (see page 434).

Jo's Blitz Torte

*A*lso known as Meringue Cake Torte, or Blitz Kuchen, this delectable cake is a combination of meringue and butter cake layers baked right on top of each other. I have not been able to confirm this, but I suspect the title comes from the fact that, as quick as lightning, *Blitz* in German, or in a wink, *Blinz,* you will have baked 2 cakes at one time. If the technique is a surprise, the result is even more so—a wonderful blend of tender, fine-grained cake and crisp meringue that is then filled with vanilla pastry cream and fresh fruit. This is the perfect summer party cake because the unusual texture showcases the fruit so well. I have adapted this recipe from one shared with me by my Vermont friend and expert baker Jo Trogdon Sweatt.

BUTTER CAKE BATTER

1 cup sifted cake flour (3½ ounces; 100 g)

1 teaspoon baking powder

⅛ teaspoon salt

½ cup unsalted butter (1 stick; 110 g), cut up, at
    room temperature

½ cup granulated sugar (3½ ounces; 100 g)

4 large egg yolks, at room temperature

1 teaspoon vanilla extract

⅓ cup milk

MERINGUE CAKE BATTER

4 large egg whites, at room temperature

¼ teaspoon cream of tartar

1 cup sifted superfine sugar (7 ounces; 200 g)

1 tablespoon granulated sugar blended with
    1 teaspoon ground cinnamon

⅓ cup sliced almonds (1 ounce; 30 g) or chopped
    pecans

Advance Preparation The cake can be prepared a day or so in advance and wrapped airtight. It is better not to freeze it, because the meringue tends to soften. Refrigerate the filled and iced cake; for best texture, assemble it no more than 3 or 4 hours in advance of serving. Make the Vanilla Pastry Cream several hours in advance, or the day before, and chill it before adding it to the cake.

Special Equipment Two 8- or 9-inch layer pans 1½ inches deep, small bowl, sifter, rubber spatula, extra bowl and beater for egg whites; for pastry cream, see recipe. In addition, you will need a paring knife, icing spatula, chilled bowl and beater for whipping cream, 8- or 9-inch cardboard cake disk (optional), serving plate.

Baking Time 30 to 35 minutes at 350°F (175°C)

Quantity One 2-layer 8- or 9-inch cake

Pan Preparation Spread solid shortening on the bottom and sides of pans, dust them evenly with flour, and tap out excess flour.

FILLING

½ recipe (1⅓ cups) Vanilla Pastry Cream (page 347), with the following changes: use ¾ cup milk, 3 egg yolks, a scant ½ teaspoon almond extract along with the vanilla, and stir in ¼ cup sour cream at the end. Prepare and chill in advance. (You can substitute ¾ cup heavy cream, whipped with 2 tablespoons of sugar.)

FRUIT

2 to 3 cups fresh berries, picked over, hulled, rinsed, and dried quickly on paper towels, or peeled sliced ripe peaches or nectarines

1. Prepare pans as described. Position rack in center of the oven. Preheat oven to 350°F (175°C).

2. Make Butter Cake batter first: Sift together the flour, baking powder, and salt, and set aside. In a large mixing bowl, cream together the butter and ½ cup granulated sugar until completely blended into a smooth, granular paste. One at a time, beat in the egg yolks, then add the vanilla.

With the mixer on lowest speed, alternately add flour mixture and milk to butter mixture, beating after each addition and beginning and ending with flour.

3. Divide the batter evenly between the prepared pans, smoothing the top with a rubber spatula. Set pans aside.

4. Make the Meringue Cake batter: In a clean bowl with clean beaters, whip the egg whites and cream of tartar until fluffy. Gradually add 1 cup superfine sugar, whipping until the whites are nearly stiff but not dry (page 261).

5. Divide the meringue evenly between the cake pans, spreading it gently over the butter cake batter. Sprinkle half of the cinnamon sugar over each meringue layer, then top each with half of the sliced almonds.

6. Bake the layers in the preheated oven for 30 to 35

minutes, or until the meringue top is a darkened ivory color and crisp to the touch on top; inside it will still be soft. The cake will begin to shrink from the sides of the pan. Cool the layers in their pans on a wire rack. Run the blade of a knife between the cake and pan sides to loosen, then top each layer with a plate or rack and invert. Lift off the pans.

7. To assemble the cake: On a cardboard cake disk or a plate protected by strips of wax paper (see page 429), place 1 cake layer, meringue side *down*. Spread the butter cake surface with the chilled pastry cream and top it with berries or sliced fruit. Add the second cake layer, meringue side *up*. Store the cake in the refrigerator.

Old-Fashioned Country Shortcake

*S*hortcake is an all-American classic with many regional variations. New Englanders, myself included, favor unsweetened baking powder biscuits, while Southerners prefer sweet biscuits made with heavy cream. A plain eggy sponge cake is sometimes served as the base, as is angel-food cake, Scotch shortbread, or even a flaky piecrust. But in my opinion, anything other than a rough, lumpy biscuit is an imposter, a City Shortcake rather than the Real Thing, which has just the right texture to absorb the tart berry juices and balance the rich taste of the sweetened whipped cream.

Note: This recipe is for old-fashioned unsweetened baking powder biscuits; add sugar if you wish. You may bake the cake in 2 thin layers, in which case each layer will have a rather crisp top, or in 1 medium-thick layer, in which case you will split the baked cake, resulting in 2 softer, more porous surfaces upon which to pile the berries and cream. Or you may make 12 individual biscuits, which are split before being filled with berries and cream.

The
shortcake can be baked in advance, wrapped airtight, and
frozen. Or it can be made a
day in advance, wrapped airtight, and stored at room
temperature. To avoid soggy
cake, do not assemble until
just before serving.

Special Equipment   Sifter,
8-inch round cake pan
2 inches deep or two 8-inch
pans 1½ inches deep or a
cookie sheet (for individual
biscuits) chilled bowl and
whisk or beaters for whipping
cream, bowl for berries

Baking Time   12 to 15
minutes at 450°F (232°C)

Quantity   One 2-layer
8-inch cake (serves 8), or 12
individual biscuits

Pan Preparation   Spread
baking pan(s) with solid
shortening or butter.

CAKE

2 cups sifted all-purpose flour (8½ ounces; 240 g)

1 tablespoon baking powder

¾ teaspoon salt

2 tablespoons granulated sugar (optional)

¼ cup unsalted butter (½ stick; 60 g), at room
    temperature, cut up

¾ cup milk or heavy cream

FRUIT

1 quart fresh ripe strawberries, washed, gently patted
    dry or drained on paper towels, and hulled (or
    substitute any other type of berries)

½ to ¾ cup granulated sugar (3½ ounces; 100 g), or
    to taste

TOPPING

Butter (optional)

1 cup heavy cream, chilled

2 tablespoons sifted confectioners' sugar

1 teaspoon vanilla extract

1. Prepare pan(s) as directed. Position rack in center
of oven and preheat oven to 450°F (232°C).

2. Sift flour, baking powder, salt (and sugar if using it)
into a large mixing bowl. Cut in the butter until the mixture resembles coarse meal. Lightly stir in the milk or
cream until dough is just blended and clumps together.

3. To make individual shortcakes, drop 10 to 12 three-
inch rounds of batter from a spoon onto the greased
cookie sheet.

If you are making 2 cake layers, divide the dough
equally between 2 prepared cake pans. Smooth the top
more or less flat with the back of the spoon. Or spoon all
the dough into a slightly deeper cake pan to make a single
cake that will be split horizontally after baking.

4. Bake the cake(s) in the center of the preheated oven for 12 to 15 minutes, or until golden brown; the thicker cake may take a minute or two longer, and is done when a cake tester inserted in the center comes out clean. Cool the pan on a wire rack for a minute or two, then remove the cake(s) and cool on a rack. If splitting the single biscuit cake layer, wait until it is cold, then use a serrated knife to slice it horizontally with a sawing motion. If making individual biscuits, "saw" them into halves while still warm and spread them with butter if you wish.

5. To make the filling, select about 12 perfect whole berries and set them aside. Slice remaining berries and stir them together in a bowl with ½ to ¾ cup sugar. Set the bowl aside.

6. Assemble the shortcakes shortly before serving time to prevent the biscuits from becoming soggy. Gather all the ingredients. Then, in a chilled bowl with chilled beater, whip the cream with the confectioners' sugar and vanilla until soft peaks form.

To assemble the individual shortcakes, set 1 biscuit half, cut side up, on a plate, top with some whipped cream and sliced berries, then add the second half, cut side down. Top with more whipped cream and garnish with a few choice whole berries.

To assemble a single large cake, place 1 shortcake or 1 layer, cut side up, on a serving plate. Top it with about half of the whipped cream and half of the sugared, sliced berries. Cover with the second shortcake or layer, cut side down, and top with remaining sliced berries. Spoon on remaining cream and garnish with the reserved whole berries.

Trifle

*T*rifle is an English classic, as popular today as it was in Queen Victoria's time and probably long before. There are as many recipes for trifle as there are chefs serving it, for it is basically a style, or genre, of "pudding" as the English call it, rather than a specific formula. The idea is to line a deep glass bowl with layers of wine-soaked sponge cake or ladyfingers, fruit preserves, sliced fresh fruit or berries, and vanilla pastry cream. Sometimes macaroon crumbs or toasted almonds are included; the top is always lavishly covered with sweetened whipped cream and a sprinkling of toasted almonds or perhaps grated chocolate.

There is plenty of room in this recipe for creative license: adjust quantities to the size of your guest list; substitute leftover cake or thin-sliced jelly roll; vary the type of wine or use rum, or omit the alcohol and try coffee or fruit puree or fruit juice on the cake; vary the type of jam or fruit preserves; add an additional layer of wine-sprinkled cake in the middle; and select fresh or canned, drained fruit and/or berries in season. You can also prepare individual trifles in goblets or glass bowls.

3 ounces ladyfingers, about 12 (page 332), or sponge cake or one génoise layer (page 216) split into thirds each ¼-inch thick

About ½ cup Marsala, Muscat, or Sauternes wine or cream sherry

¾ cup finest-quality jam or seedless preserves (such as peach, plum, raspberry, or blackberry)

2 cups sliced fresh strawberries or raspberries, picked over, rinsed, dried, and sprinkled with 1 or 2 tablespoons of granulated sugar, or 2 cups sliced and sugared fresh ripe peaches, pears, bananas, pineapple, or other ripe fruit

1 recipe (2½ cups) Vanilla Pastry Cream (page 347), prepared in advance and chilled

¾ cup coarsely crushed crisp macaroons or amaretti (12 cookies)

¾ cup chilled heavy cream, whipped with 1 tablespoon granulated sugar and ½ teaspoon vanilla extract, or 1 tablespoon brandy or wine

2 tablespoons toasted sliced almonds

1. Line a bowl or soufflé dish with the ladyfingers or cake, arranged in a single layer no more than ¼ inch thick. Cut cake pieces to fit side by side, covering the bottom and sides of the bowl. Sprinkle 5 to 8 tablespoons of the wine on the cake.

2. Spread the cake with a coating of jam. Top the jam with about one third of the prepared fruit.

3. Spread on about half of the pastry cream and top this with half of remaining fruit and half of the amaretti or macaroon crumbs.

4. Add remaining pastry cream.

5. Top pastry cream with remaining fruit and amaretti crumbs.

6. Spread all the whipped cream on the top, or put the whipped cream in a pastry bag fitted with a star tip and pipe a decorative pattern on top of the trifle. To garnish, sprinkle on the toasted sliced almonds.

7. Cover the trifle and chill for a minimum of 3 hours before serving.

Advance Preparation   In order for the flavors to blend and mellow, it is best to prepare the trifle a day, or at least several hours in advance; cover and refrigerate until ready to serve.

Note: The Vanilla Pastry Cream must be made in advance and chilled before adding it to the trifle; allow time for this, or prepare pastry cream a day in advance.

Special Equipment   2-quart glass bowl or soufflé dish, chilled bowl and beater for whipping cream, pastry bag fitted with #6 star tip (optional), frying pan for toasting sliced almonds

Chilling Time   See Advance Preparation.

Quantity   Serves 4 to 6 (see introduction if you want to enlarge the recipe)

Bowl Preparation   None

Elegant and Special Cakes • 329

Panforte di Siena

This nougat candy-cake is a traditional Christmas specialty of Siena, Italy. If it is hard to label, the reason is that there is nothing else quite like the dense fruit- and nut-filled layer scented with honey, spices, and cocoa. The cake is so rich that it is served in very small cubes. In Italy panforte is rarely made at home because it is so widely available in stores, packaged in its characteristic flat, round box wrapped with colorfully printed Florentine paper. If you can't get to Siena for Christmas, try this at home; it is surprisingly easy to make.

Advance Preparation The cake can be made ahead, wrapped airtight, and kept about a month. For longer storage, wrap it well and freeze. Thaw at room temperature before serving.

Special Equipment Large saucepan, frying pan, nut chopper or food processor, wax paper, wooden spoon, grater, mixing bowl, baking pan 13½ × 8¾ × 2 inches, sifter, knife, spatula.

Baking Time 45 to 50 minutes at 275°F (135°C), plus 5 minutes longer with topping

Quantity 3 pounds (1.3 kg) panforte

Pan Preparation Spread butter on bottom and 1 inch up the sides of pan.

1 cup honey
1 cup granulated sugar (7 ounces; 200 g)
1 cup unsifted all-purpose flour
    (5 ounces; 140 g)
¼ cup unsweetened cocoa such as Baker's or Droste
    (¾ ounce; 20 g), unsifted
2 teaspoons ground cinnamon
½ teaspoon ground allspice
¼ teaspoon ground mace (optional)
1½ cups unblanched hazelnuts, toasted (see page 42)
    and coarsely chopped (6 ounces; 180 g)
1½ cups toasted and coarsely chopped blanched
    almonds (6 ounces; 180 g)
Grated zest of 1 large orange (2 to 3 tablespoons)
1 pound candied mixed fruits, chopped (454 g)
Confectioners' sugar

1. Prepare pan as described. Position rack in center of oven. Preheat oven to 275°F (135°C).

2. Combine the honey and sugar in a large saucepan and set over medium-low heat. Stir with a wooden spoon for about 10 minutes, or until the sugar melts. Remove pan from heat. Measure the flour, cocoa, cinnamon, allspice, and mace directly into the honey-sugar mixture after it is removed from heat. Immediately stir ingredients together well. Add toasted and chopped nuts, grated orange zest, and chopped candied fruits. Stir hard until mixture is well blended, without any big lumps of fruit.

3. Spoon batter into the buttered pan and spread it evenly. Bake in the preheated oven for 45 to 50 minutes, or until a cake tester inserted in the center comes out clean.

4. Remove pan from the oven and sift a ⅛-inch-thick layer of confectioners' sugar over the cake top. It should be just thick enough to cover the cake completely. Return pan to the oven and bake for another 5 minutes. Remove from oven and cool on a wire rack.

While the cake is still slightly warm, cut it with a sharp paring knife into ¾-inch squares. To store the cake pieces, wrap them in plastic wrap or foil. When cold, the cake will be quite hard.

Ladyfingers

*L*adyfingers are delicate finger-shaped sponge biscuits. When properly made they have a light eggy flavor, a slightly soft interior with a tender, spongy crumb, and a crisp outside crust that results from a dusting of sugar just before they are baked. Homemade ladyfingers bear little resemblance to the soft, cottony product sold in the supermarket under the same name. They are easy to prepare once you know the tricks, and there are a few; when you have mastered the art, you will find it a breeze to whip them up to line a charlotte mold or Baked Alaska, or just to serve plain alongside fresh berries and cream.

In the French pastry repertoire, ladyfingers fall into the family of *petits gâteaux secs* (little dry cakes, literally); they are known as *biscuits à la cuiller,* or "spoon cookies," because until the beginning of the nineteenth century when the pastry bag was invented, they were formed by dropping the batter from a spoon.

The basic technique for this classic recipe is the same as that used for making sponge cakes. Egg yolks and sugar are ribboned together with flavoring, while the egg whites are stiffly beaten in a separate bowl. Finally, some of the whites are folded into the yolks, then remaining whites are alternately folded in along with the sifted flour. This last step is the critical stage; folding must be gentle and light to maintain full volume, and you must stop while there are still powdery streaks of flour visible. If you fold until flour is completely blended in, the batter will be overworked and will deflate when the fingers are shaped. The ladyfingers then spread and flatten in the oven.

Advance Preparation Ladyfingers can be baked ahead, wrapped airtight, and kept at room temperature for a week, or they can be frozen.

Special Equipment 2 or 3 flat cookie sheets, 16- to 18-inch-long pastry tube fitted with ½-inch #6 plain tip, regular-size strainer or sieve and small (2½- or 3-inch diameter) strainer, separate bowl and beater for whipping egg

⅔ cup sifted cake flour (2½ ounces; 70 g)
3 large eggs, separated, at room temperature
½ cup (3½ ounces; 100 g) plus 1 tablespoon sifted superfine sugar
1 teaspoon vanilla extract
Pinch of salt
Confectioners' sugar

1. Prepare pans as described. Put together the pastry tube and tip and set it nearby. Position racks so the oven is divided into thirds. Preheat oven to 300°F (150°C).

2. Sift the flour, then return it to the sifter and put it in a small bowl. The flour will later be sifted directly onto the batter.

3. In the large bowl of an electric mixer, beat the egg yolks with ½ cup of the superfine sugar and the vanilla until the mixture is thick and light-colored, and forms a flat ribbon falling back upon itself when the beater is lifted. This takes 2 to 3 minutes in the KitchenAid mixer on speed #8, or 6 to 7 minutes with other mixers. Once or twice, stop the machine and scrape down the beater and the inside of the bowl.

4. With a clean bowl and beater, whip the egg whites with a pinch of salt until foamy. Add remaining 1 tablespoon superfine sugar and whip until the whites are nearly stiff but not dry. It is important to catch this stage; the whites should look shiny, and you should be able to invert the bowl without causing the mass of whipped whites to slide.

5. Using a rubber spatula, scoop about one quarter of the whites into the yolk mixture and fold them lightly together. Streaks of the whites should remain visible.

Sift about one quarter of the flour over the whipped batter, fold the mixture once or twice, then add another quarter of the whites and fold gently. Repeat, alternately sifting on the flour, adding some of the whites, and folding them very lightly into the batter. Use all remaining flour and whipped whites.

To fold correctly, see page 71. Leave some powdery flour streaks showing. Do not blend thoroughly. Do not mix or stir.

6. Set out a 4-cup measure or bowl as a holder for the pastry bag while you fill it. Fold down a generous 4- or 5-inch cuff, then press the side of the narrow end of the bag into the base of the metal tip (diagram a) so the batter does not run out when the bag is filled.

whites, rubber spatula, 4-cup Pyrex liquid measuring cup or jar of similar size.

Baking Time   About 15 minutes at 300°F (150°C)

Quantity   24 to 30 ladyfingers, 1½ × 4 inches; enough to line a 2-quart French charlotte mold, or any mold of equivalent size.

Double the recipe to line the top and bottom of the mold with disks made of ladyfinger batter, and also to line sides with regular ladyfingers.

Pan Preparation   Spread pans with butter, not solid shortening, then dust with flour; tap out excess flour. Alternatively, you can dab a little butter in the corners of the pans, then line them with baking parchment. Spread butter on the parchment, then dust with flour; tap out excess. The butter "glues" the paper onto the sheets.

a

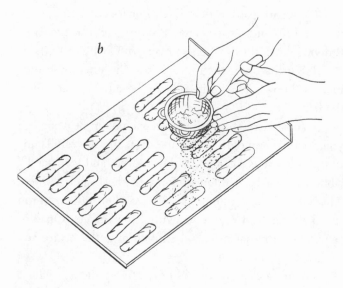

b

Add about one third of the batter. Lift up the bag cuff, twist it closed just above the batter, and pipe out neat single-line fingers 3 to 3½ inches long and 1 inch apart on the prepared sheets. The batter should not spread and flatten but rather should stay in place and remain slightly rounded after piping. If it flattens and runs, you have overfolded and deflated the whites; you can still bake the fingers but their shape will be flatter and wider than otherwise.

7. Put a couple of tablespoons of confectioners' sugar into the smallest sifter and sift an even dusting of sugar over the top of each ladyfinger on the cookie sheet (diagram b).

Then hold the cookie sheet on a slant, or invert it over the sink, and give it a tap to shake off excess sugar. The batter will not run if it has the correct consistency.

8. Set the ladyfingers in the preheated oven and bake for about 15 minutes, or until they are a pale golden color around the edges; the tops will have a slightly crackled

appearance, dotted with some of the sugar. Let the lady-fingers cool for 2 or 3 minutes, not longer or they start to stick, then lift them with a spatula and cool them on a wire rack. If baking them on parchment, you can cool the ladyfingers on the sheets, then peel off the parchment backing.

Fillings, Frostings, Icings and Glazes, Sauces and Syrups

ABOUT WHIPPING CREAM

THERE IS A wide variety of creams on the market, each with specific characteristics that must be understood by the baker. Read about Cream, page 22.

"Heavy" or "heavy whipping" cream is what you want to use, as both have the essential 36 to 40 percent butterfat content, whether stated on the carton or not. A well-prepared whipped cream should be smooth, light, and able to hold its shape; it should not be lumpy, yellowish, or buttery, all indications of overbeating and separation of cream into butter and water. If the whipped cream is too soft, it was not whipped enough, or was too fresh, too warm, or too low in butterfat.

Sweeteners for Whipped Cream

Superfine, granulated, or sifted confectioners' sugar can be used in whipped cream, but should be added after the cream is partially whipped. If added too early, the sugar can impede whipping. Confectioners' sugar contains about 3 percent cornstarch, which acts as a mild stabilizer; use this sugar if you will hold the cream before serving it. Honey can be substituted for sugar in whipped cream if the honey is liquefied and strained. Stir the honey gently into the cream after it is whipped stiff.

How to Whip Cream

To whip cream properly, be sure the cream, bowl, and beater are chilled. In hot weather, whip the cream over a pan of ice water. To whip cream by hand, use a large balloon whisk or rotary beater and a large bowl, preferably metal. You can do the job more quickly and easily with an electric mixer, its largest balloon beater and its metal bowl well chilled. Put the bowl and beaters in the freezer for a few minutes before use. The colder the cream and utensils, the firmer the butterfat in the cream and the stiffer the whipped results.

Stages of Whipped Cream

CHANTILLY CREAM • This is when soft peaks appear, before the cream is really firm. Chantilly cream is best for adding to mousses and Bavarian creams. This is also the point at which flavoring and/or sugar should be added to cream that will be whipped more.

CREAM BEATEN STIFF • The best idea is to hand-whisk your cream from the Chantilly stage to stiff, even if you started the job with an electric mixer, to prevent overbeating by controlling and observing the exact moment when the cream stiffens.

At the stiff stage, swirl lines from the beaters are clearly visible in the cream; they do not melt away. Firm peaks hold on the beater. Be careful about this stage; it occurs quickly; the time differs, depending on what type of mixer or hand utensil you use, and the beating should be halted at once. If you beat too long, you will have butter. To rescue slightly overwhipped cream, gently whisk in 2 tablespoons cold milk or unwhipped cream; it sometimes works.

How to Hold Cream Whipped in Advance

To hold regular (unstabilized, see below) whipped cream, be sure to sweeten it with confectioners' sugar so as to benefit from the stabilizing power of its cornstarch content. To hold this cream for several hours, put it into a cheesecloth-lined strainer set in a bowl and refrigerate. Discard liquid.

To Stabilize Whipped Cream

Professional bakers add gelatin or cornstarch to their whipped cream to guarantee that it will remain stiff for approximately 24 hours. This stabilized cream can also be guaranteed to hold its shape when piped through a pastry bag in fancy shapes.

GELATIN STABILIZER • For every 1 cup of chilled heavy cream to be whipped, dissolve 1 teaspoon unflavored gelatin in 2 tablespoons cold water or cream. Heat the gelatin until melted, then cool it but keep it liquid. Whip the cream until soft peaks form (Chantilly stage), then slowly add the gelatin while hand-whisking until stiff.

CORNSTARCH STABILIZER • For every 1 cup of chilled heavy cream to be whipped, add 2 tablespoons confectioners' sugar and 1 teaspoon cornstarch. Combine the sugar and cornstarch in a small saucepan and gradually stir in ¼ cup of heavy cream. Bring it to a boil, stirring constantly, and simmer for a few seconds until thickened. Remove from the heat and cool to room temperature. Whip remaining cream until it begins to thicken, just when the beater marks begin to show. Hand-whisk in the thickened cream mixture and whisk until stiff peaks form.

Handy Measurement Notes for Whipping Cream

• Cream approximately doubles in volume when it is whipped; 1 cup chilled heavy cream = 2 cups whipped.
• To frost the top of an 8- or 9-inch cake, you will need 1 cup whipped cream; to fill 2 layers this size, you will need 1 cup whipped cream; to frost the sides of a 2-layer 8- or 9-inch cake, you will need about 1 cup whipped cream. Therefore, you will need a total of 3 cups whipped cream to fill and frost a 2-layer cake.
• To fill and frost a 3-layer cake, you will need 4 cups whipped cream.
• For every 1 cup cream to be whipped, allow 2 tablespoons sifted confectioners' sugar and 2 tablespoons flavoring liqueur, or to taste.

Flavored Whipped Cream Filling and Topping for Cakes

*U*nless otherwise noted in the recipes below, whip the chilled cream just to Chantilly stage, or soft peaks, add the flavoring extract or liqueur and sugar, then whip or hand-whisk to stiff peaks. Chill, or use the cream immediately.

Quantity   All recipes make 3 cups whipped cream, to fill and frost a 2-layer 8- or 9-inch cake; use 2 cups chilled heavy cream to make 4 cups, whipped, for a 3-layer cake.

Rum Cream

1½ cups chilled heavy cream
3 tablespoons rum, or 1 teaspoon rum extract, or to taste
3 to 4 tablespoons sifted confectioners' sugar

Amaretto or Almond Cream

1½ cups chilled heavy cream
3 tablespoons Amaretto liqueur plus ½ teaspoon almond extract
3 to 4 tablespoons sifted confectioners' sugar

Cassis Cream

1½ cups chilled heavy cream
4 tablespoons double crème de cassis liqueur (black-currant flavor, tints cream pink)
3 tablespoons sifted confectioners' sugar

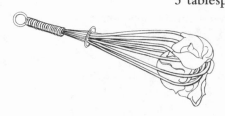

Hazelnut (Filbert) Cream

1½ cups chilled heavy cream
3 tablespoons hazelnut liqueur (Frangelico)
3 tablespoons sifted confectioners' sugar, or to taste
¾ cup toasted (see page 42) and ground hazelnuts
    (3 ounces; 90 g)

Note: Praline Powder made with hazelnuts (see page 450) can be substituted for the toasted and ground nuts; if using praline, omit sugar.

Mint Cream

1½ cups chilled heavy cream
3 tablespoons white crème de menthe liqueur (green
    type will tint cream green) plus scant
      ½ teaspoon peppermint extract
4 to 5 tablespoons sifted confectioners' sugar, or to taste

Orange Cream

1½ cups chilled heavy cream
Grated zest of 1 orange
3 tablespoons orange-flavored liqueur
Generous ½ teaspoon orange extract
3 tablespoons sifted confectioners' sugar

Apricot Cream

1½ cups chilled heavy cream
3 tablespoons apricot liqueur, or to taste
4 tablespoons sifted confectioners' sugar

Peach Cream

1½ cups chilled heavy cream
3 tablespoons peach liqueur, or to taste
½ teaspoon orange extract
3 or 4 tablespoons sifted confectioners' sugar

Ginger Cream

1½ cups chilled heavy cream
3 tablespoons confectioners' sugar sifted together
    with generous ½ teaspoon ground ginger
1 to 2 tablespoons crystallized ginger, finely minced,
    or to taste

Note: Whip the cream to soft peaks, add the sifted
ginger and sugar. Whip stiff, then fold in the minced crystallized ginger.

Coffee Cream

4 teaspoons instant espresso coffee powder dissolved
    in 1½ cups chilled heavy cream
4 to 5 tablespoons sifted confectioners' sugar, or to
    taste

Cocoa Cream

1½ cups chilled heavy cream
¼ cup confectioners' sugar sifted with
    1½ tablespoons unsweetened cocoa and a pinch
    of ground cinnamon

Chocolate Cream

1½ cups chilled heavy cream
4 ounces bittersweet chocolate, chopped fine

Note: Put cream in a saucepan and bring just to a boil. Remove from the heat and stir in the chopped chocolate until it is completely melted. Chill until very cold, then whip. Sifted confectioners' sugar may be added to taste if you wish.

Mocha Cream

Prepare Cocoa or Chocolate Cream (preceding recipes), but add 2 teaspoons instant coffee powder dissolved in the chilled cream before whipping.

Orange-Chocolate Cream

Prepare Cocoa or Chocolate Cream (preceding recipes). Add 3 tablespoons orange-flavored liqueur and grated zest of 1 orange. If desired, add ½ teaspoon orange extract to enhance orange flavor.

Praline Cream

1½ cups chilled heavy cream
½ to ¾ cup Praline Powder (page 450)
½ teaspoon almond extract (optional)

Whip cream, then fold in powder and extract.

Butterscotch Cream

1½ cups chilled heavy cream
1 cup firmly packed dark brown sugar (9 ounces;
   255 g)
1 teaspoon vanilla extract

Combine all ingredients in a bowl. Stir well to soften and partially dissolve the sugar. Whip stiff.

Maple Cream

1½ cups chilled heavy cream
½ cup pure maple syrup

Whip the cream to soft peaks. Fold in the syrup. Hand-whisk to stiff peaks.

Vanilla Pastry Cream (Crème Pâtissière)

*V*anilla Pastry Cream is a classic thickened custard used as a filling in cakes and pastries. You can vary the quantity of eggs from the traditional 6 yolks to 2 cups of milk to 4 yolks (my preference), or just use 2 whole eggs; remember, the more yolks, the richer the sauce.

By changing the flavoring, you can create endless variations; see 12 suggestions following the master recipe. For a lighter, fluffier texture, you can also fold in some whipped cream.

⅔ cup granulated sugar (4½ ounces; 130 g)
2 tablespoons cornstarch
2 tablespoons all-purpose flour
Scant pinch of salt
4 large egg yolks, or 2 to 3 yolks,
    or 2 whole eggs
2 cups milk
1 vanilla bean, slit lengthwise, or
    2 teaspoons vanilla extract
2 tablespoons unsalted butter

Advance Preparation Pastry cream can be made ahead and refrigerated, covered, for a week.

Special Equipment 2½-quart heavy-bottomed non-reactive pan, whisk, sieve, mixing bowl, plastic wrap or wax paper

Quantity About 2⅓ cups

1. On a piece of plastic wrap, combine the sugar, cornstarch, flour, and salt. In a saucepan, combine and whisk together the egg yolks or whole eggs and the milk. Gather the corners of the plastic wrap containing the starch mixture; pour it on top of the eggs and milk and whisk well to be sure all the cornstarch and flour are dissolved. Add the vanilla bean (if using vanilla extract, add it at the end of the recipe).

2. Set the pan over moderate heat and cook the custard for about 12 minutes, until thickened and brought to a boil. To do this, stir on and off for the first 5 minutes, then stir constantly for about 7 minutes longer, until the cream really thickens and reaches a boil, when you will see fat heavy bubbles work their way to the surface and burst between stirs. Occasionally, use a whisk instead of a spoon, to break up any lumps. Boil for 1 full minute while stirring constantly, covering the entire bottom of the pan with the spoon. Remove pan from the heat. The cream is cooked when smooth and thick enough to leave a clearly defined line when you draw your finger through the cream coating the back of the spoon.

3. Remove the vanilla bean, rinse it, and set it aside to reuse. If you have not used the bean, stir in the vanilla extract at this point. Add the butter and whisk until melted and blended in. Pour the cream through a sieve into a bowl. Stir in additional flavoring if using it. To prevent a skin from forming on top of the cream, press a piece of plastic wrap into the surface or dab the cream with butter or sift on a light coating of confectioners' sugar. Cool. Cover and refrigerate.

VARIATIONS

Liqueur-Flavored Pastry Cream Prepare Vanilla Pastry Cream. Add 2 tablespoons dark rum, kirsch, or other liqueur of your choice, stirred into the cream along with the vanilla extract.

Praline Pastry Cream Prepare Vanilla Pastry Cream. Fold into the finished, warm cream ½ cup Praline Powder (page 450).

Hazelnut Pastry Cream Prepare Vanilla Pastry Cream. Fold into the finished, warm cream ½ cup Praline Powder (page 450) made with hazelnuts. Add 1 or 2 tablespoons hazelnut liqueur.

Almond Pastry Cream Prepare Vanilla Pastry Cream. Fold into the finished, warm cream ½ cup Praline Powder (page 450) made with almonds, or add 1 teaspoon almond extract. Or, instead of praline powder, you can use ½ cup ground blanched almonds to make this into Frangipane Cream.

Orange Pastry Cream Prepare Vanilla Pastry Cream. Add 1 tablespoon grated orange zest to the milk-yolk mixture before cooking. Stir 2 to 3 tablespoons orange-flavored liqueur into the finished, warm cream. Do not strain the cream or the orange zest will be lost.

Coffee Pastry Cream Prepare Vanilla Pastry Cream but dissolve 1½ tablespoons powdered instant coffee into the milk before whisking it into the egg yolks.

Chocolate Pastry Cream Prepare Vanilla Pastry Cream. Melt 3 or 4 ounces finest-quality chopped semisweet or bittersweet chocolate in the top pan of a double boiler, then stir it into the finished, warm cream.

Mocha Pastry Cream Prepare Vanilla Pastry Cream. Melt 3 ounces chopped semisweet chocolate in the top pan of a double boiler. In a small bowl, dissolve 4 teaspoons powdered instant coffee in 1 tablespoon hot water. Stir into this 1 cup of the finished, warm cream. Add to the entire cream mixture and whisk in the melted chocolate.

Butterscotch Pastry Cream Prepare Vanilla Pastry Cream. Substitute ½ cup dark brown sugar for all the granulated sugar.

Diplomat Cream Prepare Vanilla Pastry Cream; chill. Stir or whisk the cold pastry cream until soft and smooth. Whip ½ cup chilled heavy cream to soft peak stage with 2 tablespoons confectioners' sugar and ½ teaspoon vanilla extract. Fold whipped cream into chilled pastry cream. Use immediately.

Instant Pastry Cream For desperate moments when time is precious, prepare 1 small package "instant-type" French vanilla pudding using 1 cup milk. Whip ½ cup heavy cream to soft peaks and fold it into the pudding along with 1 teaspoon vanilla and/or almond extract. Or, for an even better (though packaged) flavor, use "cooked-style" pudding prepared as directed on the box. Fold in the whipped cream and extract.

White Chocolate Mousse

*T*his recipe was adapted by my friend and Boston pastry chef Kristin Eychleshymer, from a recipe given to me by Vicky Zeph, a talented New York chef. Kristin has transformed the flavor base and added a boiled sugar syrup to give the mousse a rich satiny texture. Don't be put off by making the syrup—it doesn't have to reach any specific temperature, it just needs to boil a minute to melt the sugar. The flavors are well balanced: the touch of rum cuts the sweetness of the chocolate without asserting its identity. For orange flavor, substitute up to 3 tablespoons of orange liqueur and add the grated zest of ½ orange. The texture is light and velvety, perfect for filling and icing a Chocolate Sponge Roll (page 237), or for serving alone in stemmed goblets topped with fresh berries or grated bittersweet chocolate or chocolate curls (page 456). The mousse freezes well (it never gets totally hard-frozen), for do-ahead entertaining.

Note: Select the finest quality white chocolate; it should have a high cocoa butter content (first item on ingredients label) so that it will melt smoothly. Brands I like include Ghirardelli Classic White Confection, Baker's Premium White Chocolate Baking Squares, Guittard Vanilla Milk Chips, Lindt, Tobler, and Callebaut White.

4 tablespoons unsalted butter (2 ounces; 60 g),
    softened but not melted
1½ cups heavy cream, chilled
½ teaspoon vanilla extract
2 teaspoons dark rum, or 2 teaspoons rum extract
6 ounces best-quality white chocolate, chopped fine
    (1 cup; 170 g)
¼ cup granulated sugar (2 ounces; 50 g)
¼ cup water
4 large egg yolks

1. In a bowl, beat the butter with a wooden spoon or electric mixer until creamy; at this stage it will incorporate well into the chocolate. Set butter aside; do not refrigerate.

In a chilled bowl with chilled beater, whip the cream until soft peaks form. Fold in flavoring extracts and/or rum, whip a few more strokes, and refrigerate.

2. Place the chopped chocolate in the top of a double boiler set over, not touching, hot water, and stir until chocolate melts. Don't let chocolate get too hot; above 115°F (45°C) it may clump and turn grainy. To be safe, when chocolate begins to melt, simply remove the pan from the heat and stir until smooth and creamy. Set chocolate aside.

3. In a small saucepan, bring sugar and water to a boil and boil for 1 full minute, to melt the sugar. In a mixing bowl using the electric mixer, beat the yolks until very light and pale in color. With mixer on medium speed, pour the sugar syrup slowly alongside the beater in the mixing bowl, blending syrup with the yolk foam. Add melted chocolate and beat on medium-low speed until cool. Beat in softened butter 1 tablespoon at a time.

4. After the mixture is completely smooth and at room temperature (not hotter), check temperature of the whipped cream. If it has softened on standing, whisk it briskly back to soft peak stage. Then whisk about ½ cup of this cream into the chocolate mixture to lighten it. Finally, fold in remaining whipped cream. Cover and refrigerate mousse at least 3 to 4 hours, until it reaches spreading consistency, or freeze.

Advance Preparation
Mousse should be made several hours or a day in advance so it can chill and thicken to spreading consistency. It can be kept covered in the refrigerator up to 1 week, or frozen. As it does not harden completely when frozen, it can be served directly from the freezer.

Special Equipment   Double boiler, instant-read spot thermometer, rubber spatula, chilled bowl and beater for whipping cream, electric mixer

Quantity   4 cups, to fill and frost two sponge rolls or fill one 3-layer 9-inch cake; makes eight ½-cup servings of mousse alone

Chocolate Mousse

One of life's greatest pleasures, chocolate mousse comes in many variations. Use the best-quality chocolate you have for this treat (see Chocolate, page 46), as it will determine the flavor of the finished product. Always rich and wonderful, chocolate mousse can be dark and intense, or dark, intense, and creamy, or all of the above *and* made with cooked egg yolks (thereby avoiding the uncooked eggs in traditional recipes that might possibly present a health hazard). Chocolate mousse should always be kept refrigerated; leftovers can be frozen.

This chocolate mousse is a classic recipe containing uncooked eggs, and has an intensely chocolate flavor. The use of coffee powder enhances the taste but is optional. You can make it with or without the whipped cream, which, naturally, makes it even richer as well as smoother and a little softer, and increases volume to a total of 8 cups. If you need less volume, cut the cream to ½ cup, for a total of 7 cups. With or without cream, this recipe can be served in goblets as a dessert all by itself, or used to fill and frost cakes.

Chocolate Mousse Cake Filling, a variation, follows the same preparation technique. I created it to fill the layers of a hazelnut dacquoise cake; it spreads easily and stays smooth and creamy when chilled a long time. Compared to the first recipe, this is still chocolaty, but it is a little lighter because it contains less chocolate and a lot less butter; nevertheless, with 1½ cups heavy cream, it is seriously rich.

New-Style Chocolate Mousse, following, is also rich and chocolaty, but is made with eggs cooked in a little cream, to remove any possible danger of bacteria from raw eggs. Use that recipe if you are uncomfortable eating raw eggs.

CHOCOLATE MOUSSE

12 ounces best-quality semisweet or bittersweet
   (not unsweetened) chocolate, chopped
   (2 cups; 340 g)
¾ cup unsalted butter (1½ sticks; 170 g), cut up
5 large egg yolks (if making half the recipe, use 3 yolks)
1 teaspoon instant espresso coffee powder, dissolved
   in 2 teaspoons hot water (optional)
2 tablespoons dark rum, brandy, Amaretto, Grand
   Marnier, or Frangelico (hazelnut liqueur) (optional)
8 large egg whites, at room temperature
Pinch of salt
¼ cup superfine sugar (1¾ ounces; 50 g)
1 cup heavy cream, chilled (optional)

1. Melt chocolate and butter together in top of a double boiler set over, not touching, gently simmering water.
Stir to melt completely. When smooth, remove from the
heat, set aside to cool until chocolate is comfortable to
touch, then add yolks, beating after each addition. Beat in
coffee if used, and other flavoring.

2. In the large bowl of an electric mixer, beat the
whites and salt until fluffy, add sugar gradually, and beat
until stiff but not dry.

Test the temperature of the chocolate—it should be
75° to 80°F (25°C), slightly cooler than body temperature, so it will blend smoothly with the egg whites. If
chocolate is too warm, refrigerate it for a few minutes; if
too cold, stir over a bowl of warm water. Stir about one
quarter of the whites into the chocolate to lighten it, then
use the rubber spatula to fold the remaining chocolate
into the whites in several additions.

3. If using the cream, whip it in a chilled bowl with a
chilled beater (with vanilla if making Chocolate Mousse
Cake Filling); beat until soft peaks form. Fold the
whipped cream into the mousse right after folding in the
whipped egg whites.

Advance Preparation   The
mousse can be made in ad-
vance and refrigerated a day
or two. When prepared for
cake filling, it may need to be
refrigerated to thicken to
spreading consistency.

Special Equipment   Electric
mixer; chilled bowl and
beater for whipping cream if
used, rubber spatula

Quantity   6 cups (without
1 cup cream, whipped), to fill
and frost a 3- or 4-layer
9-inch cake; makes nine
⅓-cup servings of mousse
alone; when 1 cup whipped
cream is added, makes 8 cups
total.

The mousse should be evenly colored, with no white streaks. Refrigerate to bring to spreading consistency.

Note: Mousse will become dry on the surface after about an hour at room temperature; if you plan to garnish the cake with nuts or chocolate curls, add them to the mousse as soon as the cake is frosted, while the surface is still soft.

VARIATIONS

. . . .

CHOCOLATE MOUSSE CAKE FILLING

Note: Use ingredients below, but follow procedure above, steps 1, 2, and 3, for regular Chocolate Mousse.

Quantity 7 cups, to fill and frost 3 or 4 meringue or dacquoise or buttercake layers; makes fourteen ½-cup servings of mousse alone

10 ounces bittersweet (not unsweetened) chocolate (280 g), chopped
½ cup unsalted butter (1 stick; 110 g), cut up
4 large eggs, separated, at room temperature
1 teaspoon vanilla extract
Pinch of salt
3 tablespoons superfine sugar
1½ cups heavy cream, chilled

CHOCOLATE MOUSSE, NEW-STYLE

This quick but flavorful mousse contains egg yolks precooked in some cream to remove any possible danger of bacteria from uncooked eggs. The yolk mixture is whisked with melted chocolate, then folded into whipped heavy cream. To speed the process, I have eliminated the egg white meringue. The result is a little less unctuous than a classic mousse but still creamy on the tongue. It is soft enough to serve as a dessert by itself as soon as it is made (it is creamiest at room temperature) and firms slightly as it chills. To make New-Style Mocha Mousse, stir 1 to 2 teaspoons instant coffee powder into the cream just before whipping.

6 ounces semisweet or bittersweet (not unsweetened) chocolate, chopped (1 cup morsels; 170 g), or combine half semisweet and half bittersweet chocolate

2 tablespoons light corn syrup

3 large egg yolks

½ cup heavy cream, at room temperature, plus 1 cup, well chilled

1. Melt chocolate in top of double boiler set over, not touching, hot water; stir, remove from heat, stir until smooth, and set aside to cool.

2. In small, heavy-bottomed pan set over medium-low heat, whisk together corn syrup, yolks, and ½ cup room-temperature cream. Whisk and stir continuously for 5 to 7 minutes, or until mixture is thick, covers a spoon, and reaches 150°F (66°C) for 2 minutes, or 160°F (71°C) for a moment on an instant-read thermometer.

3. Strain the yolk mixture into the cooling chocolate and immediately whisk hard, making the chocolate shiny and satin-smooth. Cool until warm, not hot, to the touch.

4. Using a chilled bowl and beater, whip remaining 1 cup of chilled cream to soft peaks. Check temperature of chocolate—it should feel warm but comfortable to the touch. Fold chocolate into cream, cover, and refrigerate until ready to serve. Bring to room temperature before spreading on cake or serving alone as a dessert.

Advance Preparation
Mousse can be prepared, covered, and refrigerated up to 2 days in advance. It can also be frozen; bring to room temperature before spreading or serving.

Special Equipment   Double boiler, small heavy-bottomed saucepan, instant-read thermometer, strainer, chilled bowl and beater for whipping cream

Quantity   3 cups to fill and frost a 2-layer 8- or 9-inch cake; makes eight ⅓-cup servings of mousse alone as a dessert

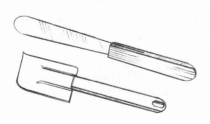

Strawberry or Raspberry Mousse or Cake Filling

*J*n the summer, make this mousse with whatever berries are delectably ripe—strawberries, raspberries, even blackberries or blueberries, to name just a few. Or, you can substitute the puree of any other fruit—passion fruit, mango, cherries, or cranberries; see the variations that follow this recipe. Serve the mousse garnished with the fresh berries it contains.

Advance Preparation   The mousse can be made 1 or 2 days ahead, covered, and refrigerated.

Special Equipment   1½ to 2-quart heavy-bottomed saucepan, wire whisk, medium-size metal mixing bowl, large bowl of ice water, double boiler, strainer, small saucepan, rubber spatula, chilled bowl and beater for whipping cream

Quantity   About 4 cups, to fill a 3- or 4-layer cake; makes six to eight ½-cup servings of mousse alone

3 teaspoons unflavored gelatin
¼ cup cold plus ½ cup boiling water or
    fruit juice
1½ tablespoons freshly squeezed lemon juice
2 to 4 tablespoons granulated sugar, or to taste
Pinch of salt
1 cup fresh strawberry or raspberry puree, strained
    to remove most (but not all) seeds, or one 12-
    ounce bag frozen whole unsweetened berries,
    thawed and pressed through a strainer (use fruit
    plus juice to make 1 cup)
3 tablespoons fruit-flavored liqueur (optional); for
    strawberries or raspberries, use framboise
    (raspberry eau de vie), or Chambord (raspberry
    liqueur), or crème de cassis (black currant
    liqueur), or Grand Marnier
¾ cup heavy cream, chilled

1. Sprinkle the gelatin over the cold water or juice in a 1½- to 2-quart saucepan and set it aside for 2 or 3 minutes to soften. Stir in ½ cup boiling water or juice and stir until gelatin is completely dissolved. Stir in lemon juice, 2 tablespoons sugar, the salt, and berry puree. Taste and add more sugar if needed. Set pan on low heat and stir well until sugar is dissolved. Add liqueur, if used. Transfer fruit to a metal bowl.

2. To thicken the mousse, you can refrigerate it 45 to 60 minutes, stirring every now and then, until thick as a pudding. To speed the process, you can set the metal fruit bowl into a bowl of ice water and stir on and off for 10 to 15 minutes, until the mixture feels thick, mounds on the spoon, and looks like a soft pudding. Remove the bowl from the ice water before the mousse sets hard; if it gets too stiff, stir it over a pan of very warm water until soft and smooth.

3. Using a chilled bowl and beater, whip the cream until soft peaks form, then fold it into the chilled and thickened fruit. Spoon the mousse into a bowl, or individual dessert dishes, and refrigerate at least 3 hours, or overnight, to set before serving plain or spreading between cake layers. Chill filled cake before serving, and refrigerate leftovers.

VARIATIONS

. . . .

Passion Fruit or Mango Mousse   Prepare Strawberry Mousse, above, substituting 1½ cups thawed frozen passion fruit concentrate or fresh or canned mango puree for the berry puree.

Passion fruit or mango concentrate, frozen or canned, can be obtained at some gourmet shops or from some of the mail-order sources (page 477) in this book. Fresh mangoes are seasonally available from May through September, but are imported year-round. Use only fully ripe mangoes that yield gently to the pressure of your finger; 2 large ripe mangoes, peeled, sliced, and pureed, should yield about 1¾ cups puree.

Tangerine Mousse   Prepare Strawberry Mousse, above, but instead of the berry puree, substitute 1 can (6 ounces) frozen tangerine juice concentrate mixed with just ¾ cup water or orange juice. Use ⅓ cup sugar, and add the grated zest of 2 tangerines or 1 orange.

Eggless Custard Buttercream

*I*f you want the satiny texture of a custard buttercream without the extra richness of egg yolks, make this cornstarch-thickened custard icing. Be sure to boil the cornstarch-milk mixture to eliminate the taste of uncooked starch.

Advance Preparation The buttercream can be prepared up to a week in advance and refrigerated, or it can be frozen. Bring to room temperature and whip before spreading on a cake.

Special Equipment
Medium-size mixing bowl, cup, 2-quart saucepan, large bowl of ice water

Quantity 3 cups, to fill and frost an 8-inch 2- or 3-layer cake

1 cup plus 2 tablespoons unsalted butter (2¼ sticks; 260 g), softened but not melted
4 tablespoons cornstarch
1¼ cups milk
⅔ cup granulated sugar (4½ ounces; 130 g)

FLAVORING
2 teaspoons vanilla extract or 1 tablespoon instant coffee powder dissolved in the milk, or 3 or 4 ounces semisweet chocolate, melted and cooled

1. In a bowl, beat the butter with a wooden spoon until soft and smooth; at this stage it will be easily incorporated into the custard.

2. In a small bowl, dissolve the cornstarch in ¼ cup of the measured milk. Combine remaining milk with the sugar (and coffee if using it) in a 2-quart saucepan set over moderate heat. Bring the mixture to the boiling point, stirring on and off to dissolve all the sugar.

3. Stir the cornstarch mixture to be sure it has not settled. Whisk some of the hot milk into the cornstarch mixture to warm it, then pour the cornstarch mixture into the saucepan and whisk the ingredients over moderate heat for about 4 minutes while it comes to a full boil. Boil, stirring, for 30 full seconds. The custard should be thick and smooth like a pudding. Remove pan from the heat and whisk hard until custard is smooth and glossy. Add the vanilla extract if using, or the melted and cooled chocolate if using.

4. Transfer custard to a clean metal bowl and stir it over ice water for a couple of minutes, until completely cool to the touch throughout. If too warm, it will melt the butter. With an electric mixer, beat the custard for a few seconds. With the mixer running, beat in the smooth butter, 1 tablespoon at a time, beating on high speed after each addition. After all the butter is incorporated, whip the mixture on high speed for a full 30 seconds. Use the buttercream at once or cover and refrigerate.

Viennese Custard Buttercream

*B*utter is beaten into vanilla custard to make this rich and creamy blend used for filling and icing classic Viennese tortes and layer cakes. For Chocolate and Coffee Custard Buttercreams, see the variations following the master recipe.

1 cup unsalted butter (2 sticks; 230 g), softened but
    not melted
1½ vanilla beans, slit lengthwise, or 1½ teaspoons
    vanilla extract
1 cup milk
3 large egg yolks
½ cup granulated sugar (3½ ounces; 100 g)
1 tablespoon cornstarch

Advance Preparation The buttercream can be made up to a week in advance and stored, covered, in the refrigerator. Bring it to room temperature and whip to soften before using.

Quantity 2½ cups, to fill and frost an 8- or 9-inch 2-layer cake

    1. Beat the butter with a wooden spoon until soft and creamy so it will be easily incorporated into the custard. Set the butter aside; do not chill it.

    2. In a 2-quart saucepan, combine the vanilla beans and ¾ cup of the milk and set over moderate heat. Scald the milk until small bubbles appear around the edges. Remove the milk from the heat and set it aside for the vanilla beans to infuse for about 5 minutes, then remove the beans. Or add vanilla extract at the end of the recipe.

    While the milk heats, whisk together in a medium-size bowl the remaining ¼ cup milk, the egg yolks, sugar, and cornstarch.

3. Whisk the hot milk into the yolk mixture, then return the yolk-milk mixture to the saucepan and whisk it constantly over moderate heat until it just reaches the boiling point; this will take about 7 minutes. Don't stop whisking or the custard will cook on the bottom. When done, it will be as thick as a pudding and generously coat the whisk.

At once, remove pan from the heat and whisk the custard hard until it looks smooth, satiny, and not at all separated. If you have not used vanilla beans, whisk in vanilla extract now. Chill the custard in the refrigerator, or speed the process by stirring it over a pan of ice water until it is completely cool to the touch throughout. If too warm, it will melt the butter.

4. With an electric mixer, beat the custard for a few seconds; leave the mixer running and begin to add the softened butter, 1 tablespoon at a time. Beat on high speed after each addition, then go back to medium-high speed and add more butter. Scrape down the sides of the bowl and the beaters several times during this process. When the butter is added slowly enough and beaten sufficiently, you will have a perfect emulsion, like a mayonnaise, and it will not separate. If, however, separation starts, just beat on high speed with a little more softened butter until smoothed out. After incorporating all the butter, whip the buttercream on high speed for 1 full minute. Use immediately or store in a covered container in the refrigerator.

VARIATIONS

. . . .

Chocolate Custard Buttercream Prepare Viennese Custard Buttercream, but add 2 or 3 ounces of melted and cooled semisweet chocolate to the cooled custard *before* adding the butter.

Coffee Custard Buttercream (2½ cups) Follow the basic procedure for Viennese Custard Buttercream using these ingredients:

1 cup unsalted butter (2 sticks; 230 g), softened but
    not melted
⅓ cup granulated sugar (2¼ ounces; 65 g)
2 tablespoons cornstarch
Pinch of salt
2 tablespoons instant coffee powder or
    1 tablespoon instant espresso coffee powder
¾ cup warm water
3 large egg yolks

1. Beat the butter until creamy. Put the sugar, corn-starch, and salt in a heavy 2-quart saucepan. In a small bowl, dissolve coffee powder in the warm water, then whisk in the yolks. Whisk the coffee-yolk mixture into the dry ingredients in the pan. Set over heat and whisk constantly while bringing just to the boiling point, when the custard will be as thick as a pudding.

2. Remove custard from the heat, whisk hard, then stir it over a pan of ice water until completely cool to the touch. With an electric mixer, beat the custard, then beat in the soft butter, 1 tablespoon at a time. Scrape down bowl and beaters. Beat the finished mixture on high speed for 1 full minute. Buttercream should be perfectly smooth.

Zabaglione Sauce

*Z*abaglione *(zabaione)* is an easily prepared wine custard made by whipping egg yolks, sugar, and Marsala or other wine in a double boiler. Traditionally served in wine goblets as a dessert in itself, zabaglione can also be served with sliced ripe peaches or berries and a piece of sponge or chiffon cake. When a little gelatin is added to the recipe, it will hold its shape when used as a cake or jelly-roll filling (see variation following).

Zabaglione may be served warm as soon as it is made, or it can be chilled and served cold, or even frozen. Note that chilling, or adding gelatin, reduces the volume, and the recipe should be doubled for the cold method. For a fluffier consistency, the chilled sauce can also be folded into whipped heavy cream.

Zabaglione was invented by the Italians, who taught it to the French. In France they call it *sabayon,* and replace the Marsala with dry white wine or Champagne to make Champagne Sabayon Sauce. Germans and Austrians make a similar sauce, called *Weinschaum* or *Weinschaumsaucen.*

Note: The classic zabaglione is made with the ratio of 1 egg yolk to 1 tablespoon sugar and half a large eggshell of Marsala or other wine.

Special Equipment Double boiler, large bowl of ice and water

Quantity Warm method, about 2 cups; four ½-cup servings as a dessert, 6 servings as a sauce over sliced cake or fruit. Cold method, about 1½ cups, 3 servings.

4 large egg yolks
4 tablespoons granulated sugar
8 tablespoons Marsala wine

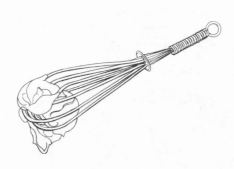

TRADITIONAL WARM METHOD (MAKES ABOUT 2 CUPS) • Off the heat, in the top pan of a double boiler, stir together the egg yolks and sugar. Then set the pan over, not touching, gently boiling water. Whisk constantly, gradually adding the wine. Whisk until the mixture foams, doubles in volume, and thickens, 4 to 5 minutes. During the later stage of whisking, lower the heat so the water just simmers. The sauce is done when it generously coats a spoon and falls from it in thick, heavy drops. "Cook until the spoon cries only one tear," explains Italian cooking authority Giuliano Bugialli. Serve the sauce immediately, while still warm.

COLD METHOD (MAKES ABOUT 1½ CUPS) • Double the recipe for more than 3 servings, as chilling reduces the volume.

The advantage of this method is that the zabaglione can be made up to 6 or 8 hours in advance. Prepare a large bowl of ice cubes and cold water; set it aside. Proceed as for warm method, whisking the yolk-sugar-wine mixture in the top pan of a double boiler for 4 to 5 minutes, until increased in volume and thick enough to coat a spoon generously. At once, remove the top pan of the double boiler from the heat and set it into the pan of ice water. Whisk the zabaglione over ice water until the sauce is completely cold. At this stage, you can fold in whipped cream or other flavoring if you wish. Pour the cold zabaglione into a bowl or serving goblets and refrigerate until needed. Or cover with plastic wrap and freeze. Serve cold or frozen (the texture never completely solidifies even when frozen).

Add to the basic recipe:

• 1 cup whipped heavy cream, folded into cold zabaglione

• 1 teaspoon vanilla extract, stirred in after cooking is complete

• **Southern Italian Style:** Replace the Marsala with dry white wine and add the grated zest of 1 orange or tangerine.

• **French Sabayon Sauce:** Replace Marsala with dry Champagne (Champagne Sabayon Sauce) or use a dry white wine or cream sherry; or flavor a white wine zabaglione with Grand Marnier or other liqueur.

• Fold ⅓ to ½ cup drained puree of fresh strawberries or raspberries and 1 cup whipped cream into the finished and cooled sauce just before serving.

• **Creole Sabayon:** Prepare cold method zabaglione with dry white wine and 2 teaspoons grated orange zest. Into the finished sauce fold 1 cup whipped heavy cream and 1½ teaspoons instant coffee powder dissolved in 3 tablespoons dark rum. Top with a little grated bittersweet chocolate.

Zabaglione Cake Filling

*T*his filling is made by adding a little gelatin and whipped cream to the basic Zabaglione Sauce above. Prepare the filled cake in advance and refrigerate it about three hours for the filling to set; be sure to bring it to room temperature before serving. It is soft and delectable, yet holds its shape when sliced.

1. Prepare Zabaglione Sauce, cold method, with 4 egg yolks. Add 1½ teaspoons unflavored gelatin plus ½ cup chilled heavy cream, whipped, following this procedure:

First set out a large bowl containing ice cubes and cold water. In a small saucepan, sprinkle 1½ teaspoons gelatin over ¼ cup of cold water. Let this sit for about 3 minutes to soften the gelatin, then stir the mixture over low heat until the gelatin is dissolved completely. Do not boil. Remove pan from the heat and set it aside.

2. Follow the basic procedure to whisk yolks, sugar, and Marsala in the top pan of a double boiler until increased in volume and thick enough to coat a spoon generously and fall from it in a thick, heavy ribbon. At this stage, whisk in the dissolved gelatin.

3. Remove the top pan from the double boiler and set it into the ice water. Whisk the custard in the ice-water bath on and off for about 10 minutes, until custard is cold and beginning to thicken. When ready, it will mound on the spoon like a soft creamy pudding; it will hold its shape softly on the spoon and be neither runny nor hard and rubbery.

Note: If the custard sets too hard and jells, just put the bowl over a pan of hot water and whisk for a few seconds until the custard softens and smooths out. Then proceed.

4. While the custard is chilling, whip the ½ cup heavy cream. As soon as the custard is at the pudding stage, fold in the whipped cream. Spread the custard on a jelly roll or between cake layers. Refrigerate the cake at least 3 hours, or until about 30 minutes before serving; serve at room temperature.

Quantity   2 cups, to fill a 3-layer 8- or 9-inch cake; 1½ cups will generously fill 1 jelly roll.

Lemon Curd

*T*raditionally rich, this version of lemon curd is made with 5 egg yolks, and it is worth every one of them. The result is absolutely smooth and deliciously tart—perfect for filling a sponge cake or angel-food roll. It is equally good as filling for a vanilla- or citrus-flavored layer cake.

Note: Most classic versions of Lemon Curd are thickened exclusively with the egg yolks in the recipe; however, for cake filling, I find the addition of cornstarch gives a better texture.

Special Equipment   Double boiler

Quantity   Scant 2 cups, enough to fill two jelly rolls or 3-layer 8- or 9-inch cake

½ cup unsalted butter (1 stick; 110 g), cut up
1 cup granulated sugar
Grated zest of 2 lemons, about
    5 teaspoons
⅓ cup freshly squeezed lemon juice
1 whole large egg plus 5 egg yolks
1 tablespoon cornstarch, dissolved in
    2 tablespoons cold water

1. Place the butter in the top pan of a double boiler set over simmering water. When the butter has melted, stir in the sugar, lemon zest, and juice. Whisk on and off until the sugar is melted, about 5 minutes.

2. Combine the whole egg and egg yolks in a small bowl and whisk them together until well blended. Whisk in the cornstarch and water mixture.

Pour about one quarter of the hot lemon mixture into the yolks while whisking hard so the yolks become warm but do not poach. Pour the warmed yolks into the rest of the hot lemon mixture in the top pan of the double boiler, again whisking the mixture hard to avoid poaching the eggs.

3. Cook the custard over simmering water, whisking continually, for a good 5 minutes, until it is thick enough to coat the back of a spoon generously. A line drawn down the back of the spoon with your finger should not

close up readily. Remove pan from the heat, pour the lemon curd into a clean bowl, and top it with a piece of plastic wrap to prevent formation of a skin. If you have time, set it aside until cool, then refrigerate. It will thicken more as it cools.

To speed the cooling, you can set the metal top of the double boiler right into a large bowl of ice water and stir the lemon curd until it is cool. Then you can refrigerate it until thick enough to spread; do not put it on a cake until completely cold.

Lemon Cake Filling

*T*his old New England recipe for a tart cornstarch custard is used for filling jelly rolls or layer cakes. It is extremely flavorful, but contains much less fat than the Lemon Curd (preceding recipe), a consideration for cholesterol watchers.

¾ cup granulated sugar (5¼ ounces; 150 g)
3 tablespoons cornstarch
2 teaspoons all-purpose flour
Pinch of salt
1¼ cups water
2 large egg yolks
Grated zest of 1 lemon, about 2 teaspoons
¼ cup freshly squeezed lemon juice
1 tablespoon unsalted butter or stick margarine, cut up

1. In a 2-quart saucepan off the heat, combine the sugar, cornstarch, flour, and salt. Slowly stir in the water, blending with a spoon or whisk until no lumps remain. Set the pan over high heat and stir constantly until the mixture comes to a full rolling boil. Boil for 1 full minute while stirring constantly. The mixture should be very thick and smooth.

Advance Preparation   The filling may be made a day or two in advance and stored, covered, in the refrigerator.

Special Equipment   2-quart saucepan, grater, rubber spatula, 1½-quart bowl, plastic wrap

Quantity   2 cups, to fill 2 jelly rolls or to fill one 3-layer 8-inch or 9-inch cake

2. In a 1½-quart bowl, whisk the egg yolks with the lemon zest and juice, then whisk vigorously while adding about half of the hot thickened cornstarch mixture. Return the warmed yolk mixture to remaining hot mixture in the pan and whisk over low heat for 3 minutes.

3. Remove pan from the heat, add the butter, and stir until it is melted. Cool the custard, top with plastic wrap to prevent a skin from forming, and refrigerate until needed. The custard thickens more as it cools.

Orange Cake Filling

Advance Preparation   The filling may be made a day or two in advance and stored, covered, in the refrigerator.

Special Equipment   2-quart saucepan, grater, rubber spatula, 1½-quart bowl, plastic wrap

Quantity   2 cups, to fill 2 jelly rolls or to fill one 3-layer 8-inch or 9-inch cake

½ cup plus 2 tablespoons granulated sugar
(4¼ ounces; 120 g)
3 tablespoons cornstarch
2 teaspoons all-purpose flour
Pinch of salt
Grated zest of 1 orange
1½ cups orange juice
2 large egg yolks
1 tablespoon unsalted butter or stick margarine,
cut up

1. In a 2-quart saucepan, combine the sugar, cornstarch, flour, and salt. Slowly stir in 1¼ cups of the orange juice, stirring until no lumps remain. Use a whisk if necessary. Bring the mixture to a full boil, stirring constantly. Boil for 1 full minute.

2. In a small bowl, whisk the egg yolks with remaining ¼ cup orange juice and the orange zest. Whisk in half of the hot mixture, pour the warmed yolk mixture into the pan, and stir over low heat for 3 minutes. Stir in butter. Cool.

Light Orange Curd Cake Filling

*T*his easy-to-prepare egg-free cake filling is thickened with cornstarch instead of the classic, and extra-rich, complement of egg yolks and butter. It is not too sweet (add 2 extra tablespoons of sugar if you prefer it sweeter) and has a fine orange flavor and the consistency of a smooth pudding. Use it to fill a jelly roll or layer cake.

⅓ cup granulated sugar (2¼ ounces; 65 g)
1½ tablespoons cornstarch
1 teaspoon all-purpose flour
Pinch of salt
Grated zest of half an orange (about 1½ tablespoons)
¾ cup fresh orange juice
1 teaspoon fresh lemon juice
1 teaspoon orange extract
3 tablespoons heavy cream
1 teaspoon orange-flavored liqueur (optional)
1 tablespoon unsalted butter, softened (optional)

Advance Preparation The curd can be prepared in advance and refrigerated for 1 or 2 days.

Special Equipment Heavy-bottomed nonreactive saucepan

Quantity 1 cup, enough to cover one jelly roll or one cake layer; recipe can be doubled.

1. In a heavy-bottomed nonreactive saucepan, whisk together the sugar, cornstarch, flour, and salt. Add the grated zest, juices, and extract. Whisk to dissolve the cornstarch.

2. Place the pan over medium heat and whisk and stir constantly until the mixture comes to a full bubbling boil. Allow to boil 1 full minute, until the curd is no longer cloudy and is thick enough to generously coat the back of a spoon. Remove pan from heat.

3. Stir in the cream, liqueur, and softened butter if used, blending them well. Cool the curd, then refrigerate. It thickens as it cools; if stirred occasionally, the curd will be ready to use in 35 to 45 minutes.

Lane Cake Filling

*L*aden with chopped nuts and fruit, this bourbon-scented custard is used to fill the Alabama specialty known as Lane Cake (page 90).

Special Equipment Double boiler

Quantity 2 generous cups, to fill one 3-layer 8- or 9-inch cake

8 large egg yolks
1 cup sugar (7 ounces; 100 g)
⅓ cup lightly salted butter
      (5⅓ tablespoons; 80 g)
½ cup chopped Maraschino cherries, or
      3 tablespoons apricot preserves
1 cup pecans, finely chopped (4 ounces; 110 g)
¼ cup dried pitted dates, chopped (1¾ ounces; 50 g)
½ cup seedless raisins (preferably half golden, half black), finely chopped (2½ ounces; 70 g)
½ cup sweetened shredded coconut (1½ ounces; 45 g)
3 tablespoons bourbon
Grated zest of 1 orange
¼ teaspoon ground nutmeg

1. In the top pan of a double boiler over moderate heat, combine the egg yolks, sugar, and butter. Whisk constantly while cooking for about 20 minutes, or until all the sugar is dissolved and the custard thickens enough to coat a spoon.

2. Remove pan from the heat and stir in all remaining ingredients. Cool completely. When it is cold, divide the filling into halves and spread between the layers of the 3-layer Lane Cake. Frost the cake with Boiled Icing (page 402).

Note: This filling can be made a day ahead and refrigerated. Bring to room temperature and stir until smooth enough to spread.

Toffee Cream Filling

This is one of the easiest and best-tasting cake fillings I know, made from crushed candy folded into whipped cream. Making it is child's play (put the candy in a plastic bag, seal, and pound with a rolling pin), but the flavor depends upon using a fine-quality toffee. I like to use Heath or Skor bars, available in any supermarket.

2 cups heavy cream, chilled

5 tablespoons sifted superfine or confectioners' sugar

¼ cup (2 ounces) hazelnut liqueur (Frangelico) or ¾ teaspoon almond extract

1 teaspoon vanilla extract

1 cup chopped chocolate-coated toffee candy, in ⅛- to ¼-inch bits (4¾ ounces; 135 g), made from 4 crushed Skor bars (1.4 ounces each), or 4 crushed Heath Bars (1⅜6 ounces each)

1. Using a chilled bowl and beater, whip the cream for a few seconds, then sprinkle on the sugar while continuing to whip until cream forms soft peaks. Add liqueur or almond extract and vanilla extract and whip until almost stiff. Don't overbeat because folding in the candy continues to work the cream, and you do not want it to turn into butter.

2. If you plan to frost the cake, remove about 1¾ cups of the whipped cream and reserve it in the refrigerator. Fold the chopped toffee into the remaining whipped cream.

3. Fill cake layers with toffee cream, then frost cake sides and top with reserved, sweetened whipped cream. Refrigerate.

Advance Preparation Toffee Cream should be prepared just before using. Filled cake should be refrigerated, or frozen. If used with meringue or dacquoise layers, cake can be filled about 4 hours before serving, and refrigerated.

Special Equipment Self-sealing plastic bag and rolling pin or hammer; chilled bowl and beater for whipping cream

Quantity About 4 cups, to fill and frost a 3-layer 9-inch cake; to fill and frost a sponge roll, make half the recipe.

Vanilla Bavarian Cream Filling

 his classic, rich Vanilla Bavarian Cream may be used to fill layers of ladyfingers or sliced chocolate sponge cake, or served in goblets alone as a dessert topped with a few fresh raspberries or a Chocolate Curl or Chocolate Leaf (pages 456 and 454). It is extra special when accompanied by Fresh Raspberry Sauce (page 420).

Advance Preparation The filling can be made 1 or 2 days ahead, covered, and refrigerated.

Special Equipment 3-quart heavy-bottomed saucepan, wire whisk, teacup, large bowl of ice water, double boiler, sieve or strainer set over 1½-quart bowl, small saucepan, rubber spatula, chilled bowl and beater for whipping cream

Quantity 4 cups, to fill a 3- or 4-layer cake; makes eight ½-cup servings as a dessert alone

3 teaspoons unflavored gelatin
¼ cup cold water
2 cups milk
1 vanilla bean, slit lengthwise, or 1½ teaspoons
    vanilla extract
1 teaspoon cornstarch
6 large egg yolks
⅔ cup granulated sugar (4½ ounces; 130 g)
½ cup heavy cream, chilled

1. Sprinkle the gelatin over the cold water in a small saucepan and set it aside for 2 or 3 minutes to soften. Stir over low heat just until gelatin is completely dissolved; do not boil. Rub a drop between your fingers to test for smoothness.

2. Combine the milk and vanilla bean in a 3-quart saucepan. Transfer about 1 tablespoon of the milk into a teacup and stir with the cornstarch until dissolved; set it aside. Heat the milk until scalding, when small bubbles appear around pan sides; do not boil. Remove from heat and let cool about 5 minutes. Lift out the vanilla bean (if you are using vanilla extract instead, do not add yet), scrape seeds out into milk, then discard bean or add to canister of granulated sugar for flavor.

3. While milk is heating, combine the yolks and sugar in a large bowl and beat with an electric mixer until the mixture is light, thick, and forms a flat ribbon falling back on itself when the beater is lifted. Stir the cornstarch in

the teacup with about 1 tablespoon of the warm milk to liquefy, then whip it into yolks. Remove bowl from the mixer stand if used.

4. Pour about a cup of the milk into the yolk foam while hand-whisking it vigorously so the yolks do not cook. Return all the warm yolk mixture to the milk in the saucepan and whisk over moderate heat 7 to 8 minutes, or until the custard is thick enough to generously coat the back of a spoon; you should be able to draw a line through the coating with your fingertip and leave a mark that does not close up.

Strain the custard into a bowl. Check the gelatin; if it has begun to thicken, stir over low heat a few seconds until liquefied and smooth. Whisk the gelatin into the strained custard along with the vanilla extract if used instead of a bean.

5. To thicken the filling at this point, you can refrigerate it for about 30 minutes, stirring every now and then, until it is like a pudding. To speed the process, you can set the metal (not glass) custard pan into a bowl of ice water and stir on and off for about 14 minutes, until the custard begins to thicken, mound on the spoon, and look like a soft pudding. Remove pan from ice water before custard sets hard. If it sets too hard, stir it over a pan of very warm water just until soft and smooth.

6. Using a chilled bowl and chilled beater, whip the heavy cream until soft peaks form, then fold it into the chilled and thickened custard. Pour the custard into a bowl (or individual dessert dishes) and refrigerate at least 3 hours, or overnight, to set before serving plain or spreading between cake layers. Chill filled cake before serving, and refrigerate leftovers.

Chocolate Mint Bavarian Cream Filling

This delightful chocolate cream is scented with mint to cut the richness. Use it to fill layers of sponge cake or ladyfingers or serve in goblets alone as a dessert topped by a sprig of mint and a thin, crisp cookie.

Note: You can use this filling to make a charlotte: Lightly oil one 1½-quart cylindrical mold or charlotte pan and line the bottom with wax paper. Cover pan bottom and sides with about 24 single Ladyfingers (page 332), then fill with cream, top with plastic wrap, and chill 4 hours to set; unmold and serve with whipped cream.

Advance Preparation The filling can be made 1 or 2 days ahead, covered, and refrigerated.

Special Equipment 2 small saucepans, scissors, double boiler, strainer or sieve set over 1-quart bowl, whisk, rubber spatula, chilled bowl and beater for whipping cream

Quantity 3½ cups, to fill a 4-layer cake; makes seven ½-cup servings as a dessert alone

6 ounces semisweet chocolate, chopped (1 cup; 170 g)
1 vanilla bean, slit lengthwise, or 1 teaspoon vanilla extract
2 cups milk
2 teaspoons unflavored gelatin
¼ cup cold water
5 large egg yolks
¼ cup granulated sugar (1¾ ounces; 50 g)
2 tablespoons crème de menthe
¼ teaspoon peppermint extract or peppermint oil
½ cup heavy cream, chilled

1. Melt the chopped chocolate in the top of a double boiler set over simmering (not boiling) water. While the chocolate melts, prepare a custard sauce:

Add the vanilla bean to the milk in a saucepan. (If you do not have a bean, add extract to the finished custard.) Heat the milk just until scalding, when small bubbles appear around pan sides; do not boil. Lift out the vanilla bean if used, scrape seeds back into the milk, and discard bean or add to granulated sugar canister.

2. Sprinkle the gelatin over the cold water in a small saucepan and set it aside for 2 or 3 minutes to soften. Stir

over low heat just until gelatin is completely dissolved; do not boil. Rub a drop between your fingers to test for smoothness.

3. In a mixing bowl, whisk together the egg yolks and sugar until thick and light. Whisk about half the hot milk into the yolks, beating constantly so the yolks do not cook, then pour the warmed yolks back into the remaining hot milk, whisking hard. Heat the milk-yolk mixture over low heat, stirring constantly until the custard thickens enough to coat the back of a spoon; you should be able to draw a line through the coating with your fingertip and leave a mark that does not close up. Do not boil the custard or it will curdle.

Check the gelatin; if thickened, stir gently over low heat just until liquefied. Strain the custard into a bowl, then whisk in the dissolved gelatin and vanilla extract if used instead of a bean.

4. Little by little, whisk the melted chocolate into the warm custard, blending completely. Whisk in the crème de menthe and extract.

To thicken the filling at this point, you can refrigerate it for about 1 hour, stirring every now and then, until it begins to feel thick, mound on the spoon, and look like a soft pudding. To speed the process, you can set the bowl of chocolate custard into a larger bowl of ice water and stir on and off for about 25 minutes, until it looks like a pudding. If the custard sets too hard, stir it over a pan of very warm water just until soft and smooth.

5. Using a chilled bowl and beater, whip the heavy cream until soft peaks form, then fold it into the chilled and thickened chocolate filling. Pour the mixture into a bowl or individual dessert goblets and refrigerate at least 4 hours before serving plain or spreading between cake layers. Chill filled cake before serving, and refrigerate leftovers.

$\mathcal{T}$OPPINGS

Toasted Coconut Topping

$\mathcal{U}$se this to garnish the top and/or sides of a "tropical" cake.

Quantity   1 cup, to top one 8- or 9-inch cake or one 8 × 12 sheet cake

1 cup sweetened shredded or flaked coconut, or grated fresh coconut

Spread coconut on a sheet of foil with the edges turned up and bake in a preheated 375°F (190°C) oven for 6 to 8 minutes, tossing the coconut occasionally to color it evenly until golden brown. Cool and add to cake as a garnish.

Streusel Nut Topping

*U*se this crunchy nut-crumb topping on fruit crisps, coffee cakes, or fruit-nut cakes; it adds texture and is not as sweet as regular icing.

⅔ cup firmly packed light or dark brown sugar
  (4½ ounces; 130 g)
7 tablespoons butter (100 g), at room temperature,
  cut up
½ cup plus 2 tablespoons all-purpose flour
  (3½ ounces; 100 g)
1 cup finely chopped walnuts (4 ounces; 110 g), or
  use pecans or almonds
½ teaspoon each of ground cinnamon and nutmeg

Combine all ingredients in a mixing bowl. Crumble and pinch them together with your fingertips, making pea-size crumbs. Spread the mixture evenly over the cake before baking as directed in recipe.

Note: If the butter is too warm, the mixture will cling together and refuse to crumble; chill if necessary.

Advance Preparation
Streusel topping can be made ahead and frozen or stored in a covered jar in the refrigerator for several days before using. Leftover streusel can be frozen.

Quantity About 2½ cups. Use 1½ cups to top a 9-inch cake, 1¾ cups to top a cake 11¾ × 7½ inches, the full recipe (2½ cups) to top a cake 13 × 9 inches, and 1½ times the recipe (3¾ cups) to top a cake 15 × 10½ inches.

Meringue Crumb Topping

*C*rumbs of crisp flavorful meringue make a delicious topping when sprinkled over a cake frosted with whipped cream, buttercream, or mousse. The scraps may be left over from trimming meringue or dacquoise cake layers into neat rounds, or you can make the meringue specifically for decorative purposes, following the recipe for cake disks or plain meringue (page 263). Use a decorating bag fitted with a ¼-inch plain tip to pipe the meringue into long ropes or fingers. Flavor the meringue after it is whipped with some unsweetened cocoa powder (3 tablespoons for 4 egg whites) to make chocolate meringue topping. Once the meringue ropes or fingers are baked crisp, break or cut them into short lengths and press them gently onto a frosted cake.

All-Purpose Frosting

*T*his quick-and-easy recipe is a so-called American-style frosting; it is less rich than a buttercream.

Quantity About 2½ cups, to fill and frost an 8- or 9-inch 2-layer cake

¼ cup unsalted butter or stick margarine, or solid white vegetable shortening (½ stick; 60 g)

Pinch of salt

1 teaspoon pure flavoring extract (vanilla, almond, lemon, or orange)

4 to 4½ cups sifted confectioners' sugar (16 ounces; 454 g)

5 tablespoons milk, or as needed

In an electric mixer, cream the butter or margarine until soft. Beat in the salt and flavoring extract. With the mixer on lowest speed, gradually beat in the sugar and milk. Scrape down the sides of the bowl and the beater. Beat on high speed until creamy. Add more milk if needed to reach spreading consistency. This can be made in advance and stored, covered, in the refrigerator for up to 1 week. Bring to room temperature and whip smooth before using.

Royal Icing

Royal icing becomes very hard when air-dried and is used for specialty cake decorations and trimming. Traditional recipes, such as Royal Icing I below, are made with uncooked egg whites. If you are not comfortable using uncooked whites, prepare Royal Icing II, made with either pasteurized powdered egg whites or bakers' meringue powder sold in gourmet shops and by mail order (see Sources, page 477).

To prevent royal icing from drying out as you work, cover the bowl with a damp towel or plastic wrap. To save a decorating bag filled with leftover icing, store it in a sealed plastic bag; it will stay soft for several hours.

ROYAL ICING I

2 large egg whites, at room temperature
⅛ teaspoon cream of tartar
Pinch of salt
3½ cups sifted confectioners' sugar (12¼ ounces; 350 g), or as needed
2 tablespoons lemon juice, or as needed

Special Equipment Sifter, electric mixer, plastic wrap

Quantity Royal Icing I: 2 cups, enough to add decorations to one 3-layer 9-inch cake; Royal Icing II made with powdered egg whites, about 2½ cups; made with meringue powder, about 3 cups

Combine whites, cream of tartar, and salt in a mixing bowl and beat to blend. With mixer on lowest speed, add the sugar slowly, beating smooth after each addition. Add only enough lemon juice to bring icing to a spreading consistency. Scrape down bowl and beaters often. Sift in more sugar, or add juice, to adjust texture.

ROYAL ICING II

2 tablespoons plus 2 teaspoons powdered egg whites
   or meringue powder
½ cup very warm water
5½ to 6 cups sifted confectioners' sugar (21 ounces;
   600 g), or as needed

Whisk together powdered egg whites or meringue powder and water in a large bowl, then let stand 3 to 5 minutes to soften the powder so it will blend smoothly. Press out any dry lumps with the back of a spoon. Whisk well. Add about 1 cup of sifted sugar and beat with the electric mixer. Be sure icing is smooth before adding more sugar, a cup at a time; whip until stiff peaks form. Adjust consistency by adding more sugar or a few drops of warm water as needed. Keep icing covered at all times to avoid drying out.

Confectioners' Frosting

*T*his creamy icing is the one to use for forming roses and leaves because the solid shortening gives it body and holds up, especially in warm weather. You can also use this for frosting any type of cake, but it will be less rich and flavorful than a classic buttercream. For flavoring ideas, see Basic Quick Buttercream on the following page.

½ cup unsalted butter or stick margarine (1 stick; 110 g), at room temperature
½ cup solid white vegetable shortening (3 ounces; 85 g)
1 teaspoon pure flavoring extract (vanilla, almond, lemon, or orange)
4½ cups sifted confectioners' sugar (16 ounces; 454 g), or as needed
2 tablespoons milk, or as needed

Quantity About 3 cups, to fill and frost an 8- or 9-inch 2-layer cake

In an electric mixer, cream the butter and shortening until smooth and well blended. Add the flavoring extract. With the mixer on lowest speed, gradually beat in the sugar. Scrap down the sides of the bowl and the beater. Add the milk and beat on high speed until frosting is light and fluffy. Add 1 or 2 tablespoons more milk if too dry. Cover the icing with plastic wrap or a damp cloth to prevent drying until ready to use. Store it in a covered container in the refrigerator for up to 2 weeks. Whip before using.

VARIATION

. . . .

Chocolate Confectioners' Frosting Prepare the basic recipe, but beat into the finished icing

4 ounces unsweetened chocolate, melted and cooled, plus 2 tablespoons milk.

Basic Quick Buttercream

*T*his all-purpose buttercream is less rich than the classic French buttercream and contains a larger proportion of confectioners' sugar. Note the ten flavor variations following the basic recipe.

Quantity   About 2½ cups, to fill and frost an 8- or 9-inch 2-layer cake

½ cup unsalted butter (1 stick; 110 g), softened but not melted
1 large egg yolk (optional)
Pinch of salt
1 teaspoon vanilla extract
4 to 4½ cups sifted confectioners' sugar (16 ounces; 454 g)
5 or 6 tablespoons heavy cream or milk, or as needed

In an electric mixer or food processor, cream the butter until soft, then beat in the egg yolk if using it, the salt, and the vanilla. With the mixer on low speed or pulsing the processor, add about ¼ cup of the sugar. Beat smooth. Alternately add cream and remaining sugar, blending smooth between additions. Scrape down sides of bowl. Add more cream if too stiff, chill to harden if too soft.

VARIATIONS

· ·

Lemon   Omit the vanilla; use 1 teaspoon grated lemon zest plus 1 or 2 tablespoons fresh lemon juice as part of the liquid.

Orange   Omit the vanilla; use grated zest of ½ orange and substitute orange juice for the cream.

Pineapple   Omit the vanilla; add 1 teaspoon lemon juice and ⅔ cup drained crushed pineapple. Add more sugar if needed.

Sour Cream   Substitute sour cream for the heavy cream. Especially good when used with chocolate flavoring.

Almond   Omit the vanilla; use ¾ teaspoon almond extract, or to taste.

Almond-Praline   Add to finished almond buttercream ½ cup Praline Powder made with almonds (page 450).

Maple-Praline   Add 1 teaspoon maple extract along with the vanilla and stir into the finished buttercream ½ cup Praline Powder made with walnuts (page 450).

Dark or Milk Chocolate   After adding the first ¼ cup of sugar to the mixture, beat in 4 to 6 ounces melted and cooled semisweet or milk chocolate; use only as much cream as necessary to reach spreading consistency.

Coffee   Increase the vanilla to 2 teaspoons; before adding, dissolve in the vanilla 2 teaspoons instant coffee powder.

Creamy Mocha   Contains no egg yolks. Try this for frosting the Bûche de Noël (page 240).

Follow the basic procedure but use the following ingredients:

¾ cup unsalted butter (1½ sticks; 170 g), at room
   temperature
2 ounces semisweet plus 1 ounce unsweetened
   chocolate (total ½ cup; 85 g), chopped and
   melted in a double boiler
1½ teaspoons instant coffee powder dissolved in
   2 teaspoons vanilla extract
Pinch of salt
3 cups sifted confectioners' sugar (10½ ounces;
   300 g)
3 to 6 tablespoons heavy cream, as needed

Classic French Buttercream

*A*lso called Mousseline Buttercream, this is the best there is—rich, silky, and well worth the extra trouble of cooking a sugar syrup to whip into the yolks before adding the butter. For a lighter version, you can add some meringue—see Classic French Buttercream with Meringue, following the master recipe. Other variations include Deluxe French Chocolate Buttercream, Coffee, Orange, Lemon or Lime, and Orange-Chocolate Buttercream.

Advance Preparation This buttercream can be made up to 2 weeks in advance and refrigerated; it can be frozen for up to 2 months. Bring it to room temperature and whip to soften it before using.

Special Equipment Double boiler, 2-quart heavy-bottomed saucepan, wooden spoon, candy thermometer, electric mixer

Quantity 2 cups, to frost top and sides of an 8- or 9-inch 2-layer cake. To double this recipe, use 1 cup granulated sugar (200 g) and 1½ cups butter (3 sticks; 330 g); other ingredients double evenly.

1 cup unsalted butter (2 sticks; 220 g), softened but not melted, cut up

½ cup plus 1 tablespoon granulated sugar (rounded 3½ ounces; 100 g)

⅛ teaspoon cream of tartar

¼ cup water

4 large egg yolks

FLAVORING (OPTIONAL)
2 teaspoons vanilla extract, or 2 tablespoons liqueur (fruit or nut flavor) or rum or brandy. Other variations follow recipe.

1. In a mixing bowl, use a wooden spoon to work the butter until softened and creamy; at this stage it will properly blend into the buttercream. Set butter aside.

2. In a saucepan, combine the sugar, cream of tartar, and water. Stir a few times, then cook over moderate-high heat until the sugar is dissolved and the syrup looks clear. Raise the heat and begin to cook down the syrup. Several times during this period, wash down the pan sides with a pastry brush dipped into cold water to remove any sugar crystals. Bring the syrup to a gentle boil, and boil *without stirring* for 6 or 7 minutes, or until the candy thermometer reads 238°F (114°C).

3. While the sugar boils, put the egg yolks in a heat-proof bowl and beat with an electric mixer for several minutes until pale in color and foamy.

As soon as the syrup reaches the proper temperature, turn the electric mixer to medium-low speed and pour the hot syrup into the yolks in a slow steady stream directed just between the bowl and the beater; if you pour on top of the beater, threads of sugar syrup will harden too quickly. Do not scrape out the syrup bowl, use only the syrup that pours easily; the rest will be hardened. Beat the mixture until the bowl feels cool to the touch, for 8 to 10 minutes; time depends upon weather as well as bowl temperature. To speed the cooling, you can set the bowl into a pan of ice water and use a hand beater. The buttercream will thicken as it is whipped and cooled.

4. Stick your finger into the whipped buttercream; it should feel cool to the touch; if too hot, it will melt the butter.

With the mixer still running, add the butter, 2 teaspoons at a time. If the bowl temperature is correct, the icing should form a smooth mayonnaise-like emulsion. Continue to add butter slowly, beating well after each addition. Then beat for a full 3 minutes longer, or until the mixture is smooth and fluffy.

Note: If making this buttercream in advance to be stored, put it in a covered container unflavored and refrigerate. It is best to add the flavoring just before use.

Note: If the buttercream has been refrigerated or frozen, bring it to room temperature and whip before spreading.

5. To use the buttercream, whip it until smooth, then beat in the flavoring liqueur, or see the suggestions following. If necessary, chill the buttercream to spreading consistency. It may tend to curdle if whipped while too cold; to remedy this, whip it over a pan of very warm water, but do not let the buttercream melt. Or beat in an additional 4 to 8 tablespoons of softened unsalted butter.

Deluxe French Chocolate Buttercream Melt 4 ounces semisweet or bittersweet chocolate in the top pan of a double boiler. Let cool and stir into 1 recipe of finished Classic Buttercream.

Deluxe Orange-Chocolate Buttercream Prepare Deluxe French Chocolate Buttercream and add 2 tablespoons Grand Marnier and the grated zest of 1 orange.

Coffee Buttercream Prepare Classic recipe. For flavoring use 2 tablespoons coffee liqueur plus 2 teaspoons instant espresso powder dissolved in 2 teaspoons hot water.

Orange, Lemon, or Lime Egg-Yolk Buttercream Prepare Classic recipe. For flavoring use 2 tablespoons orange liqueur plus the grated zest of 1 orange or 2 lemons or 2 limes and ¾ teaspoon orange or lemon extract.

Classic French Buttercream with Meringue Prepare ½ recipe All-Purpose Cold Method or Swiss Method Meringue (page 263), using 2 egg whites plus 4 tablespoons sugar. Prepare Classic Buttercream recipe or any variation. After beating in the butter and flavoring, fold in the meringue. This lightens the buttercream and also makes it spread farther. The 2-egg meringue will add 1½ cups volume to the basic buttercream recipe.

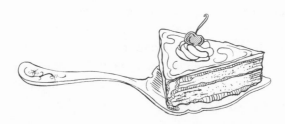

Cream Cheese Frosting

This traditional frosting for Carrot Cake (page 111) is quick, easy to make, and not too sweet. Prepared in the food processor, it can be ready in about 1½ minutes. See variations following for Orange and Chocolate Cream Cheese Frosting.

8 ounces (½ large package; 227 g) regular cream
    cheese, at room temperature
½ cup unsalted butter (1 stick; 110 g), at room
    temperature
Pinch of salt
1½ teaspoons vanilla extract
4 cups sifted confectioners' sugar (14 ounces; 400 g)

Quantity 2½ cups; enough for an 8- or 9-inch layer cake, or 9- or 10-inch tube cake, or a 9- × 13-inch sheet cake

In the workbowl of a food processor fitted with the metal blade, or with an electric mixer or wooden spoon, blend the cream cheese and butter together until very smooth and creamy. Beat in the salt and vanilla. Gradually add the sifted sugar, beating until smooth. The longer you beat, the softer the frosting will become. When soft enough to be spread, frost the cake. Refrigerate in hot weather.

VARIATIONS

Orange Cream Cheese Frosting Prepare Cream Cheese Frosting, but add 1 or 2 tablespoons frozen concentrated orange juice and the grated zest of 1 orange.

Chocolate Cream Cheese Frosting Prepare Cream Cheese Frosting but add 3 to 4 tablespoons sifted unsweetened cocoa, to taste. If the frosting is too stiff, thin it with a few drops of cream or milk.

French Buttercream Ménagère
(Home-Style Buttercream)

*B*ecause this recipe contains only 2 egg yolks, it is less rich than Classic French Buttercream (page 384). It is really a compromise between the classic recipe and Basic Quick Buttercream (page 382), which is made entirely without raw egg yolks but with a great deal more sugar.

You can adapt this recipe to any flavor; note lemon, orange, chestnut, chocolate velvet, hazelnut-chocolate variations following the basic recipe. The buttercream hardens as it is chilled; in very hot weather, refrigerate cakes iced with this buttercream.

Quantity   About 2 cups, to frost top and sides of 8- or 9-inch 2-layer cake

1 cup unsalted butter (2 sticks; 220 g), softened but
    not melted
2 large egg yolks
Pinch of salt
1 teaspoon vanilla extract
1½ to 2 cups sifted confectioners' sugar
    (about 7 ounces; 200 g), as needed

With an electric mixer, cream the butter until smooth, then add the egg yolks, one at a time, beating after each addition. Add the salt and vanilla and a little of the sugar and beat smooth, then gradually beat in additional sugar until the buttercream reaches spreading consistency. If it starts to look curdled, add a little more sugar and beat on high speed. Chill to stiffen if too soft to spread.

VARIATIONS

. . . .

Lemon Buttercream Ménagère   Prepare basic recipe, but add the grated zest and strained juice of 1 lemon. You will need about 2 cups sugar; use a few tablespoons more sugar to smooth out the buttercream if it begins to curdle.

Orange Buttercream Ménagère   Prepare basic recipe, but add the grated zest of ½ an orange, ½ teaspoon orange extract, and about 3 tablespoons orange juice or orange-flavored liqueur, or as needed. You will need about 2 cups sugar; use a few tablespoons more sugar to smooth out the buttercream if necessary.

Chestnut Buttercream Ménagère Prepare basic recipe, but flavor with ⅔ cup chestnut puree, 1 more teaspoon vanilla extract, and 3 tablespoons dark rum or brandy. Use 2 cups sugar, or as needed to reach desired consistency.

Chocolate Velvet Buttercream Chop 4 ounces semisweet chocolate (115 g) plus 2 ounces unsweetened chocolate (55 g) and melt them together in the top pan of a double boiler. Remove chocolate from the heat and set it aside to cool to room temperature, not more than 70°F (21°C). Prepare basic recipe; beat in the cooled melted chocolate before adding the egg yolks. Use about 1½ cups sugar. This makes about 2⅔ cups.

Hazelnut-Chocolate Buttercream To the Chocolate Velvet Buttercream above, add ½ cup finely chopped toasted hazelnuts and 2 to 4 tablespoons (to taste) of hazelnut liqueur (Frangelico).

Quick Coconut Icing

*C*ream cheese cuts the sweetness of this coconut icing, and using the food processor makes it quick work.

Quantity   2 cups, to frost top and sides of an 8-inch 2-layer cake or the top of one 8- × 12-inch sheet cake

8 ounces cream cheese (227 g)
¾ teaspoon coconut extract
6 tablespoons heavy cream or milk
5 tablespoons canned sweetened coconut cream, such as Coco Lopez
2½ to 3 cups sifted confectioners' sugar (8¾ ounces; 250 g), or as needed

GARNISH
1 cup sweetened shredded coconut, toasted (see Index), to sprinkle on the frosted cake

In a bowl, or in the workbowl of a food processor, combine the cream cheese, coconut extract, heavy cream, and coconut cream. Slowly add the sifted sugar, blending until smooth. Add more sugar if the icing is too soft. Spread icing on cake, then sprinkle with toasted coconut.

Penuche Icing

*L*ike a buttery caramel fudge, this icing is wonderful on spice or nut cakes. The process resembles that for making fudge and requires serious stirring to get the correct texture, but the result is worth it.

2 cups firmly packed dark brown sugar (18 ounces; 510 g)
1½ cups granulated sugar (10½ ounces; 300 g)
¼ teaspoon salt
¾ cup milk
6 tablespoons lightly salted butter (3 ounces; 85 g), cut up
2 tablespoons light corn syrup
2 teaspoons vanilla extract

Quantity   3 generous cups, to fill and frost a 2- or 3-layer 8- or 9-inch cake

1. Combine all ingredients except the vanilla in a 2-quart heavy-bottomed saucepan. Stir to blend, then set over moderate-high heat and bring slowly to a boil. This takes about 8 minutes. Cover the pan for 3 minutes at the beginning to allow condensation to melt down any sugar crystals that may form on the pan. Do not stir. Boil the syrup without stirring for 1 full minute.

2. Remove pan from the heat and set it in a large pan of ice water. Stir the penuche now and then for about 10 minutes, until icing is lukewarm to the touch. Stir in the vanilla.

3. At this point beat the penuche like fudge. Use a wooden spoon and hand-beat for 10 to 15 minutes, until it reaches spreading consistency. Spread icing on the cake. The icing will air-dry and lose its stickiness in about 30 minutes, but the inside will remain like fudge.

Brown Sugar Caramel Icing

*L*ike Penuche, this icing has a fudgelike consistency and a strong caramel flavor but is easier to make. Use it for caramel cake or white, yellow, or nut layer cake. For a spice cake, use the variation for Sugar 'n' Spice Icing.

Quantity   1½ cups, to ice the top of a sheet cake 8 × 12 inches or the top and sides of a 2-layer 8-inch cake; double the recipe to both fill and frost a layer cake.

1 cup firmly packed dark brown sugar (9 ounces; 255 g)
6 tablespoons milk or heavy cream
5 tablespoons lightly salted butter (2½ ounces; 70 g)
2 cups sifted confectioners' sugar (7 ounces; 200 g)

In a 2-quart saucepan, combine the sugar, milk or cream, and butter. Bring to a boil over moderate heat, stirring constantly. Boil for 2 full minutes, stirring. Remove from heat and cool until comfortable to touch. Stir in the sifted sugar and beat well until the icing reaches spreading consistency.

VARIATIONS

. . . .

Sugar 'n' Spice Icing   Prepare Brown Sugar Caramel Icing, but substitute light brown sugar. After stirring in confectioners' sugar, add ¾ teaspoon vanilla extract, ¾ teaspoon lemon juice, 1 generous teaspoon ground cinnamon, and ½ teaspoon each of ground ginger, nutmeg, and allspice. If doubling the recipe, do not double the spices; prepare as listed here, then adjust quantities to taste.

Broiled Caramel-Nut Icing

*T*his is one of the few icings you can successfully put on a warm-from-the-oven cake. It is good on spice, white, or yellow cakes.

¼ cup unsalted butter (½ stick; 60 g), melted
½ cup firmly packed dark brown sugar (4½ ounces; 130 g)
¼ cup light cream or milk
½ teaspoon vanilla extract
⅛ teaspoon each of ground cinnamon and nutmeg
⅛ teaspoon salt
1 cup finely chopped pecans (4 ounces; 110 g), or chopped walnuts, and/or shredded sweetened coconut

Quantity 1 generous cup, to top an 8- or 9-inch-square cake. Double the recipe for a larger sheet or a layer cake.

Combine all ingredients and beat them thoroughly in a bowl. Spread the icing over the warm or cold cake and put it 4 to 5 inches beneath the heat source of a preheated broiler. Broil for about 3 minutes, or just until the icing is light brown and bubbly; watch carefully lest it burn. Remove cake from the broiler and cool the icing completely before serving the cake.

Mocha Frosting

Quantity   3 cups, to fill and frost the top and sides of a 2-layer 8- or 9-inch cake. Double recipe to fill and frost a 2- or 3-layer cake generously, or to frost a 4-layer cake.

½ cup unsalted butter (1 stick; 110 g), at room temperature
6 cups sifted confectioners' sugar (21 ounces; 600 g)
⅓ cup sifted unsweetened cocoa (¾ ounce; 20 g)
7 tablespoons strong coffee, or 1 tablespoon instant espresso powder dissolved in 7 tablespoons boiling water
2 teaspoons vanilla extract

In the large bowl of an electric mixer, beat the butter until very soft and creamy. With the mixer on very low speed, beat in about 2 cups of the sugar. Stop the mixer and scrape down bowl and beaters. Add remaining sugar and the cocoa alternately with the coffee, beating until very smooth and creamy. Beat in the vanilla.

Note: For an even richer icing, use ¾ cup butter.

Peanut Butter Icing

Quantity   1⅓ cups, to cover a sheet cake 8 × 12 inches. Halve the recipe to frost the top of an 8- or 9-inch-square cake; double the recipe to fill and frost a 2-layer 8-inch cake.

¼ cup unsalted butter (½ stick; 60 g), at room temperature
½ cup honey
1 cup peanut butter, smooth or chunky
Pinch of salt

In a medium-size bowl combine all ingredients and beat by hand or with an electric mixer until creamy and smooth. Spread on cooled cake. Serve as is or broil.

To broil this icing, set the frosted cake about 2½ inches below the heat source of a preheated broiler for a minute or two, watching constantly lest it burn. The icing should be golden brown and bubbly when done.

Orange Wine Icing

*D*ry sherry or wine cuts the sweetness of this icing and gives it a sophisticated flavor. For a non-alcoholic icing, substitute orange juice or cream. To make Orange Madeira Icing, use Madeira wine instead of sherry. The icing is best used just after beating; it becomes quite firm when refrigerated.

½ cup unsalted butter (1 stick; 110 g), at room
    temperature
2½ cups sifted confectioners' sugar (8¾ ounces;
    250 g)
1 generous teaspoon grated orange zest
3 tablespoons fresh orange juice
1 teaspoon fresh lemon juice
½ teaspoon vanilla extract
½ teaspoon orange extract
1½ tablespoons dry sherry or orange-flavored
    liqueur

Quantity 2 cups, to fill and frost two 7- to 8-inch cake layers or one 9-inch (6-cup) tube cake. Double the recipe to fill and frost 2 or 3 layers or a large sheet cake.

In the large bowl of an electric mixer, cream the butter until soft and smooth. Add 1 cup of the sugar, orange zest, and all the juice, extracts, and liqueur. Beat until creamy; don't worry if it looks curdled. Little by little, add remaining sugar, beating slowly until smooth, then beat on high speed for 1 to 2 minutes, until light and fluffy. Beater marks will show in icing and it will hold shape well. Apply icing to cake (keep icing layer rather thin) at this point for best results. You can adjust the thickness of icing by adding a little more liquid if needed.

Seven-Minute Icing

*S*even-Minute Icing is really a quick and easy version of Boiled Icing (page 402), and the results are similar: a white satin meringue with a texture somewhere between whipped cream and melted marshmallows. Seafoam Icing, Maple, Coconut, Orange, Lemon, and Peppermint Seven-Minute Icing are variations that follow the master recipe. *Note:* Seven-Minute Icing can be used for Lord or Lady Baltimore Cake instead of the classic Boiled Icing.

Quantity 2½ cups, to fill and frost a 2-layer 8- or 9-inch cake

2 large egg whites
1½ cups granulated sugar (10½ ounces; 300 g)
5 tablespoons cold water
2 teaspoons light corn syrup
¼ teaspoon cream of tartar
1 teaspoon vanilla extract

1. Combine all ingredients except the vanilla in the top pan of a double boiler set over boiling water. Immediately begin beating with a whisk or hand-held electric mixer. If using the mixer, start at medium-low speed for 4 minutes, then increase to high for 3 to 6 minutes longer. With a whisk it can take up to 13 or 14 minutes. Whip until the icing is a satiny foam that holds very soft peaks and mounds on the beater.

2. Remove pan from the heat, stir in the vanilla, then beat hard for 1 full minute longer, or until the icing is a little thicker. Spread on the cake at once. After it air-dries, the outer surface will lose its stickiness but the inside will remain soft. Don't ice cakes with this more than 6 hours in advance, because the icing tends to become granular after long standing.

Seafoam Icing   This has a caramel flavor and makes 4 cups. Prepare Seven-Minute Icing, but replace the granulated sugar with 1½ cups firmly packed dark brown sugar (13½ ounces; 385 g). If you wish, add ½ teaspoon almond extract along with the vanilla.

Maple Seven-Minute Icing   Prepare Seven-Minute Icing, but replace the sugar with ¾ cup pure maple syrup. This whips to stiff peaks in about 6 minutes.

   Note: Don't freeze a cake covered with this icing; when it thaws, the icing breaks down and gets runny.

Coconut Seven-Minute Icing   Prepare Seven-Minute Icing, but add ½ teaspoon coconut extract and stir in ½ cup sweetened shredded coconut. Spread more coconut on the frosted cake.

Orange Seven-Minute Icing   Prepare Seven-Minute Icing, but substitute ½ teaspoon orange extract for the vanilla and add 2 teaspoons grated orange zest.

Lemon Seven-Minute Icing   Prepare Seven-Minute Icing, but use only 3 tablespoons water plus 2 tablespoons lemon juice in the pan at the start. Add to the finished icing 1 teaspoon grated lemon zest.

Peppermint Seven-Minute Icing   Prepare Seven-Minute Icing, but add ½ teaspoon oil of peppermint or peppermint extract and 4 tablespoons finely crushed peppermint candy. If you must, tint this icing a very light pink or green with a drop of vegetable food coloring.

Italian Meringue Buttercream

*T*his elegant, light-textured buttercream is not too sweet, holds up well in hot weather, and will take any type of flavoring. The procedure, which sounds more difficult than it is, involves whipping a cooked sugar syrup into beaten egg whites, then adding softened butter. The technique is slightly more exacting than for Swiss Meringue Buttercream, but the result is more stable and long-lived because the sugar syrup is cooked. In extreme heat, Italian Meringue Buttercream is the best choice.

Advance Preparation This buttercream spreads most perfectly and the texture is lightest when freshly made; however, it can be made in advance, covered, and refrigerated up to 1 week, or frozen up to 1 month. Bring buttercream to room temperature and whip smooth before using.

Special Equipment 2-quart heavy-bottomed saucepan, mercury candy thermometer, pastry brush, mixing bowl and wooden spoon, stand-type electric mixer, metal pan of ice water to hold sugar syrup pan

Quantity 4 cups, to fill and frost an 8- or 9-inch 2-layer cake

1½ cups unsalted butter (3 sticks; 330 g), softened but not melted
Pinch of salt
⅓ cup water
1 cup granulated sugar (7 ounces; 200 g)
1 tablespoon white corn syrup, or ⅛ teaspoon cream of tartar
4 large egg whites, at room temperature

FLAVORING (*SELECT ONE*)
1 teaspoon vanilla or other extract
Grated citrus zest
1 tablespoon instant espresso coffee powder dissolved in 1 tablespoon hot water
3 or 4 ounces melted and cooled bittersweet chocolate
4 ounces melted and cooled best-quality white chocolate
3 tablespoons rum, or brandy, or liqueur (fruit- or nut-flavored)
¼ to ⅓ cup Praline Paste (page 450), to taste, softened with a little cream

1. With an electric mixer or wooden spoon, work the butter and salt until soft, smooth, and creamy; at this stage it will properly blend into the meringue. Set butter aside; do not chill.

2. Combine the water, sugar, and corn syrup or cream of tartar in a saucepan and bring to a boil. Set the candy thermometer in the pan. Several times during cooking, wash down the pan sides with a pastry brush dipped into cold water to remove any sugar crystals. Allow syrup to boil without stirring for about 8 minutes, or until the thermometer reaches 238°F (114°C; soft-ball stage). Near the end of the cooking time (about 228°F; 109°C) begin to whip the egg whites while keeping a sharp eye on the syrup thermometer.

Whip the whites until nearly stiff, but not dry. Don't overwhip; when whites are close to being done, put mixer on its lowest setting so you can whip whites while watching the syrup.

3. As soon as the syrup reaches 238°F (114°C; no higher), remove pan from the heat and set it near the mixer in a pan of ice water, which will stop the cooking. Check the egg whites; they should look satiny and hold quite firm peaks but should not be dry.

With the mixer running on medium-high speed, slowly pour the hot syrup over the whites in a thin, steady stream. Continue whipping on high speed after all the syrup has been added; as you beat, the whites will increase in volume, be satin-smooth, and quite stiff. Reduce mixer speed to medium-low and whip for 5 to 10 minutes longer, or until completely cool to the touch throughout. Feel the bowl as well as the meringue.

4. When sure that the meringue is cool enough not to melt the butter, you can begin to add it. Give the butter a few turns just to be sure it is smooth and soft enough. With the mixer on medium speed, add butter to the meringue 1 tablespoon at a time, beating continuously. If the meringue starts to curdle, increase mixer speed to high and blend well, then lower speed and continue adding butter. When completely smooth, beat in flavoring of your choice, a few drops at a time. Use the buttercream immediately if possible, or store covered in the refrigerator or freezer. If chilled, bring to room temperature and whip before spreading on a cake.

Swiss Meringue Buttercream

This light, fluffy icing is buttery and not too sweet. It has a luscious satin texture and white color, and is fine for wedding cakes that must be on display in warm weather. The technique is quick and easy: a Swiss Meringue (page 264) is made by warming egg whites with sugar, whipping them to stiff peaks, then beating in softened sweet butter. The result is similar to Italian Meringue Buttercream (preceding recipe), but the method is quicker.

4 large egg whites (½ cup)
¾ cup granulated sugar (5¼ ounces; 150 g)
1¼ cups unsalted butter (2½ sticks; 285 g), softened but not melted
¼ teaspoon cream of tartar
Pinch of salt

FLAVORING
1 teaspoon vanilla (or other flavor) extract; or
    1 tablespoon grated orange or lemon zest plus
    1 teaspoon orange or lemon extract; or 4 squares
    semisweet chocolate, melted and cooled, then
    whipped into 1 cup of the finished buttercream
    before being blended into the whole mixture

1. Combine the egg whites and sugar in the large metal bowl of an electric mixer and set it over a pan of simmering water on the stove. Put the candy thermometer in the bowl. Stir the whites and sugar frequently as they warm to 120°F (49°C) and the sugar dissolves. As the temperature rises, stir more often.

While the mixture is warming, cream the butter by hand or with an electric mixer, beating until butter is soft and smooth. At this stage it will incorporate easily with the buttercream. Set the butter aside; do not chill it.

2. As soon as the egg white and sugar syrup has reached the correct temperature, remove it from the heat, add the cream of tartar and salt and whip with the electric mixer until stiff but not dry. The whites will be very shiny. With the mixer on medium speed, continue whipping until the whites are cool to the touch throughout; this can take about 10 minutes. Touch the bowl as well as the whites to check the temperature; if too warm, the whites will melt the butter.

3. When egg whites are cool to the touch, continue to whip them while adding the softened butter, 1 small spoonful at a time. Whip after each addition. The buttercream will start to deflate when the first few spoons of butter go in, but by the end it will look thicker and fluffier. When the butter is all in, add the flavoring of your choice and whip for a few seconds to blend. Use at once or refrigerate in a covered container for later use.

Advance Preparation   The texture and spreading quality of this buttercream are best when it is freshly made. However, it may be refrigerated a week in advance or frozen for up to 1 month. Bring to room temperature and whip before using.

Special Equipment   Large metal bowl for electric mixer, pan containing hot water upon which the metal bowl can sit, wooden spoon, separate bowl and beater for softening butter, mercury candy thermometer or spot instant-read thermometer

Quantity   About 3 cups, to fill and frost an 8- or 9-inch 2-layer cake. Recipe can be doubled.

Boiled Icing

*S*hiny, sticky, and luxurious, the peaks of the marshmallow-like boiled icing remind me of childhood birthday cakes. Also known as Divinity or White Mountain Icing, this is in fact a classic Italian Meringue with a slight adjustment in the cooking temperature of the syrup that is poured over the whipped egg whites. Endless variations are possible; recipes follow for Rocky Mountain, Beige Mountain, Lane Cake Icing, Lord and Lady Baltimore, Lemon, Orange, Cocoa, and Coconut.

Special Equipment   2-quart heavy-bottomed saucepan, mercury candy thermometer, pastry brush, electric mixer, metal pan of ice water for cooling sugar syrup (optional)

Quantity   About 3½ cups, to fill and frost an 8- or 9-inch 2-layer cake

¾ cup plus 2 tablespoons granulated sugar
(6¼ ounces; 175 g)
⅓ cup water
1 tablespoon white corn syrup, or ⅛ teaspoon cream of tartar
3 large egg whites
2 tablespoons granulated sugar
1 teaspoon vanilla extract (optional)

Follow the procedure for making Italian Meringue (page 398). To summarize, combine sugar, water, and corn syrup in a saucepan; heat to dissolve the sugar, then bring to a boil. Boil without stirring (wash down pan sides with a pastry brush dipped into water to remove sugar crystals) until the recommended temperature is reached (see below). When almost at the end of the boiling time, begin to whip the egg whites. Whip until fluffy, add remaining 2 tablespoons sugar, and whip until stiff but not dry.

Note carefully: for Boiled Icing, boil syrup for about 7 minutes, until the candy thermometer reads 230°F (110°C). Lift the pan from the heat (the syrup continues to cook from internal heat) and watch thermometer until it reaches 235°F (about 112°C), *not* 238°F (114°C) as required for Italian Meringue. At 235°F the syrup will make a thin thread when dropped from the side of a metal spoon. At this point, not a higher temperature, pour the syrup slowly over the whipped whites with the electric mixer running on medium speed. Continue to whip for 3 to 4 minutes longer to thicken and cool the icing. Whip in the vanilla or other flavoring.

When the icing is cool, stiff, and very glossy, apply it to the cake. Use an icing spatula or the back of a spoon to create characteristic swirls. As the icing cools, the outer surface dries and loses its stickiness, but on the inside it will remain creamy.

VARIATIONS

Rocky Mountain Icing   Use this to fill a 1-2-3-4 Cake (page 83), turning it into Rocky Mountain Cake. Prepare Boiled Icing, adding the vanilla. Reserve 1 cup of the icing and set it aside. Into the rest stir 1 cup sweetened flaked coconut, ½ cup chopped seedless raisins, ½ cup currants, 1 cup chopped blanched almonds, and ¼ teaspoon almond extract. Use the fruited icing to fill the 3 layers of the cake. Spread the reserved plain icing on the cake top (do not ice the sides at all) and sprinkle with ½ cup flaked toasted coconut.

Beige Mountain Icing   Prepare Boiled Icing, but substitute 1½ cups firmly packed brown sugar for the granulated sugar.

Lane Cake Icing and Lady Baltimore Icing   Both are the same as regular Boiled Icing, made with vanilla extract.

Lord Baltimore Icing   Prepare Boiled Icing, adding the vanilla. Reserve a scant 2 cups of icing. Fold into remaining icing 2 teaspoons lemon juice, ½ teaspoon orange extract, ½ cup crushed crisp macaroon cookies (not powdered), ¼ cup toasted sliced almonds, ¼ cup chopped toasted pecans, and 12 glacéed red cherries, chopped. Use the fruited icing to fill the 3 layers of the cake. Spread the reserved plain icing on the top and sides. If you don't have quite enough icing for a generous side coat, spread it thinner around the lower edges and press on toasted sliced almonds.

Lemon Boiled Icing   Prepare Boiled Icing, but substitute 1 tablespoon lemon juice for the vanilla extract and add ½ teaspoon grated lemon zest.

Orange Boiled Icing   Prepare Boiled Icing, but substitute 1 tablespoon frozen orange-juice concentrate, thawed but not diluted, for the vanilla extract. Add 2 teaspoons grated orange zest.

Cocoa Boiled Icing   Prepare Boiled Icing, but sift 4 tablespoons unsweetened cocoa into 1 cup of the finished and cooled icing. Stir this into the entire batch and whip to blend.

Coconut Boiled Icing   Prepare Boiled Icing, but add 1 teaspoon coconut extract. You can stir into the icing 1 cup sweetened flaked coconut if you wish, or (as I prefer) sprinkle the flaked coconut on top of the icing after it is spread on the cake, working quickly before the surface dries.

Tangerine Glaze for Cheesecake

*T*his tangy glaze garnished with tangerine segments is the perfect topping for Tangerine Cheesecake, but it also adds a flourish to plain cheesecake or sponge cake. For variations, substitute regular, mandarin, or blood oranges, and orange juice.

½ cup granulated sugar (3½ ounces; 100 g)
2 tablespoons cornstarch dissolved in ⅓ cup cold water
⅔ cup fresh or frozen tangerine juice
1 or 2 drops each of red and yellow vegetable food coloring (optional)
3 tangerines, peeled, pitted, divided into segments with membranes removed

Quantity   About 1⅛ cups, to top one 9- or 10-inch cake

1. In a saucepan combine the sugar, dissolved cornstarch mixture, and juice. Stir smooth and bring to a boil while stirring constantly. Boil for 1 full minute. If you wish, stir in just enough food coloring for an orange tone. Taste and adjust for sweetness if necessary. Cool the sauce.

2. When the cheesecake is completely cold, stir the glaze to be sure it is at spreading consistency, then spread a generous ½ cup on the cheesecake. Drop peeled tangerine segments or other sliced fruit into remaining glaze and stir gently just to coat. With tongs, lift the fruit to the top of the cake and arrange in a decorative pattern. Pour remaining glaze over the cake top. It takes about 1 hour in the refrigerator for the glaze to set.

Strawberry Glaze

*T*his fruit-filled glaze is perfect on vanilla or citrus-flavored cheesecakes, but it also makes a fine topping for plain sponge cakes. Use any type of fresh berries in season, or substitute frozen berries.

Quantity 1½ cups, to top one 9- or 10-inch cake

1 quart ripe strawberries (20 ounces; 560 g), or other berries, washed and hulled
½ cup granulated sugar (3½ ounces; 100 g), or to taste, depending on sweetness of berries
1½ tablespoons cornstarch dissolved in ¼ cup cold water
2 teaspoons lemon juice
1 tablespoon butter

1. Pick over the berries; crush enough of the least perfect looking ones to make 1 cup pulp. Place the pulp in a 1½-quart saucepan along with the sugar and dissolved cornstarch mixture. Stir well and bring the mixture to a boil over moderate heat. Stir constantly while boiling for 1½ to 2 minutes, until the glaze is thickened and clear. Remove pan from the heat and add the lemon juice and butter, stirring until the butter melts. Cool the glaze to room temperature.

2. When the cake is completely cold, arrange reserved whole berries on top, then spoon on about ⅔ cup of the glaze. Chill the cake; it will take about 1 hour in the refrigerator for the glaze to set. Pass any remaining glaze, to serve as a sauce, in a small bowl at the table.

ABOUT ICING GLAZE

ICING GLAZES BLEND confectioners' sugar and flavoring liquids plus, occasionally, melted butter and cream. Glazes are meant to flow smoothly and drip; they are not thick enough to spread with a knife. Because glazes are made with confectioners' sugar, which contains cornstarch and has a raw taste when uncooked, be sure to use sufficient flavoring.

Icing glazes are used when a rich, thick frosting is undesirable, for example, on certain chiffon, spice, fruit, or nut cakes. Often the glaze is used on a ring-shaped cake, where it covers the top and drips down the sides. On holiday cake rings and loaves, glazes can be decoratively studded with candied fruits and nuts.

Vary the amount of liquid in the recipe to control the fluidity of the glaze, making it softer if you wish it to drip down the cake sides, or stiffer if you prefer a thicker, less transparent look. Vary the flavor of the glaze to match that of your cake; use maple or cinnamon for a spice cake, lemon or orange for a fruit or nut cake, and vanilla if you are not sure which way to go.

Since the glaze is thin, it will not conceal uneven blemishes in the cake's surface. To remedy this, you can sprinkle the glaze, before it hardens on the surface, with finely chopped nuts, toasted coconut, finely crumbled Praline Powder (page 450), nutmeg, cinnamon, or a little grated lemon or orange zest. Be sure to select a garnish that goes with the icing. Or you can apply 2 coats of glaze. To do this, spread one thin coat to seal the crumbs on the cake's surface, then add a second coat that flows easily and drips down the cake sides; even with 2 coats, the total glaze should be quite thin.

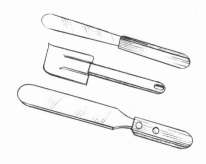

Basic Icing Glaze

Quantity   About ½ cup glaze, to top one 8- or 9-inch-square or tube cake or a sheet cake 8 × 12 inches. Double the recipe to top a sheet cake 9 × 13 or a tube cake 10 × 4 inches.

1⅓ cups sifted confectioners' sugar (4¾ ounces; 135 g)
1 to 3 tablespoons cream, as needed to thin glaze
Flavoring, used with or in place of cream:
  ½ teaspoon lemon or orange extract, or 3 drops maple extract, or 1 tablespoon very strong coffee, or 1 to 2 tablespoons bourbon, or fruit- or nut-flavored liqueur

Combine all ingredients in a small bowl, beat well until smooth, and check flavor and consistency—the glaze should drip from a spatula in a sheet. Add more liquid to thin, more sifted sugar to thicken glaze.

Orange or Lemon Icing Glaze

To turn Orange Icing Glaze into Lemon Icing Glaze, follow the recipe below but substitute grated lemon zest and use all lemon juice.

Quantity   1 scant cup (about 14 tablespoons), to top an 8- or 9-inch tube cake. Double recipe for 10-inch tube cake.

¾ cup sifted confectioners' sugar (2⅔ ounces; 75 g)
1 teaspoon grated orange zest
3 tablespoons fresh orange juice
2 teaspoons fresh lemon juice

Combine all ingredients and blend until smooth. Adjust for consistency and flavor, adding a little more sifted sugar or juice if needed. Glaze should be applied in a thin coating.

Ganache: Icing Glaze or Chocolate Filling

A blend of melted chocolate, heavy cream, and flavoring, ganache is a versatile mixture. Its flavor is intensely chocolate, less sweet than a buttercream, and its texture is silky smooth. When warm, ganache flows like cream and can be poured over cake as an icing glaze; it will set with a dark color and high gloss but remain like fudge under the surface. At room temperature, it can be whipped until fluffy and light-colored (ganache soufflé), then spread as a filling and icing on cakes. It can also be piped through a pastry bag to make decorations.

Note: Two methods for preparation are given here—the conventional method in which the chocolate is melted in the double boiler with the cream, and the quicker food-processor method in which the hot cream is poured through the feed tube onto the machine-ground chocolate.

The ganache can be prepared ahead and refrigerated, covered, until needed. Bring to room temperature, or warm in a double boiler, before applying as a glaze; whip before using as a filling.

8 ounces best-quality semisweet or bittersweet chocolate, such as Lindt Excellence or Tobler Tradition, chopped fine (or use some milk chocolate if you want a sweeter ganache)

1 cup heavy cream

2 or 3 tablespoons liqueur (coffee, fruit, or nut flavor, or rum or brandy), or 1 teaspoon vanilla or other extract

Note: For Mocha Ganache, use 2 teaspoons instant coffee powder dissolved in 1 tablespoon hot water or 3 tablespoons coffee liqueur; for Raspberry Ganache, use 3 tablespoons Chambord liqueur.

1½ tablespoons white corn syrup (optional), used only in ganache icing glaze, to ensure smoothness

Special Equipment (depends upon method used and whether the ganache is used as a glaze or a whipped filling): Double boiler, hand-held electric mixer or food processor, saucepan, large bowl containing ice and ice water

Quantity About 2⅓ cups before whipping. As a glaze, makes enough for two 9-inch 2-layer cakes. When whipped, makes enough to fill three 9-inch layers or to fill and frost a 2-layer 8-inch cake. Make half of the recipe if using ganache only to fill between 2 layers.

CONVENTIONAL METHOD (ABOUT 2⅓ CUPS) • Combine the chocolate and cream in top pan of double boiler set over, not in, hot water. Heat until the chocolate melts. Remove from heat and stir to blend well. Stir in the liqueur and corn syrup if using it.

To use the ganache as a dark chocolate glaze, let it cool until just barely lukewarm, then pour generously over a cake set on a rack over a tray. Tilt the cake to help the glaze flow.

Note: For the smoothest finish, first give the cake an undercoating of Apricot Glaze (see page 415) or buttercream. Chill the coated cake before pouring on the glaze.

To use the ganache as a spreadable filling or icing, set the bowl of melted chocolate in a larger bowl of ice water.

Note: If the bowl is tippy, set it on a ring made from a draped tea towel. With a hand-held mixer, beat the chocolate mixture for about 5 minutes, or until ganache is cool, lighter in color, nearly double in volume, and has become thick and creamy. At this stage, it should be of spreading consistency. If necessary, adjust the consistency by adding more cream to soften it, or chilling to harden.

When you first apply whipped ganache, you will see lots of air bubbles. As you work the ganache with the icing spatula as it is applied, the texture smooths out perfectly and the bubbles disappear.

FOOD PROCESSOR METHOD (ABOUT 2 CUPS) • Break the chocolate into chunks, put it in a processor fitted with the metal blade, and process to a fine powder. Place the cream in a pan over moderate heat and bring just to the boiling point. Do *not* boil. With the machine running, pour the hot cream slowly through the feed tube onto the chocolate. Blend until completely smooth. Twice, stop machine and stir down the sides. Add liqueur or other flavoring and corn syrup if using it. Pulse to blend.

To use this as a glaze, pour the warm, fluid ganache on the cake, spreading gently with a spatula as needed. To use as an icing and/or filling, cool without stirring (for darker color), or stir it over ice water until cool (for a lighter tone), then whip to spreading consistency.

Note: For a more intense chocolate flavor, you can increase the quantity of chocolate to 12 ounces, but leave the other ingredients unchanged.

. . . .

Franni's Ganache Glaze (1 cup) This recipe comes from Franni's Café-Pâtisserie in Montreal. It is a wonderful all-purpose glaze for any type of cake.

6 ounces semisweet or bittersweet chocolate (1 cup; 170 g), broken up, or 1 cup chocolate morsels
¼ cup unsalted butter (½ stick; 60 g)
½ cup heavy cream
½ teaspoon vanilla extract
½ teaspoon rum or brandy
2 tablespoons sifted confectioners' sugar

Use the food processor method: Grind the chocolate into powder in the processor, scald the butter and cream in a saucepan, then pour the hot mixture over the chocolate with the machine running. Scrape down the bowl, add flavorings and sugar, and process until smooth. Spread over cake while still warm.

Note: Half of this recipe (½ cup) is sufficient to cover one 9½-inch cheesecake.

Fabulous Chocolate Glaze

*T*his superb and foolproof chocolate glaze sets with a firm surface and high gloss, though inside it retains the texture of a creamy fudge. It gives cakes and tortes a professional bakery look and taste. Be sure to use the finest chocolate you can find, for the glaze takes its flavor from the chocolate, even if liqueurs or extracts are added. Note that this is not a sweet glaze; it will be exactly as sweet as the chocolate you use, as no sugar is added.

The chocolate glaze is applied to the cake when warm, and flows on, spreading easily. After about 30 minutes, it sets. Use it for Sachertorte (page 289) or any other fine chocolate or nut cake or torte. To achieve a perfectly smooth surface on the cake, apply 1 thin coat of glaze, let it harden for 30 minutes, then apply a second coat.

Note: Fingerprints will mark the glaze, so be careful. Lift the finished cake from underneath, using a broad spatula or cake cardboard.

Quantity 1½ cups glaze, enough to coat a 2- or 3-layer 9-inch cake

½ cup plus 1 tablespoon unsalted butter (4½ ounces; 130 g), at room temperature, cut up
9 ounces best-quality semisweet or bittersweet chocolate, such as Lindt or Tobler, cut into small pieces (1½ cups; 270g)
1½ tablespoons corn syrup

FLAVORING (*SELECT ONE*)
Mocha: 1 teaspoon instant espresso coffee powder dissolved in 1 tablespoon boiling water
Orange: 2 tablespoons Cointreau or other orange liqueur plus 1 teaspoon orange extract
Hazelnut: 2 or 3 tablespoons hazelnut liqueur (Frangelico)
Brandy: 2 or 3 tablespoons any brandy
Non-alcoholic flavoring: 1½ teaspoons any pure extract such as vanilla, almond, or orange

1. Combine the butter, chocolate, and corn syrup in the top pan of a double boiler set over, not in, hot water. When melted remove from heat and stir until very smooth and glossy. Stir in the flavoring.

2. Place the cake on a wire rack over a tray. While the glaze is warm, pour 1 thin layer, about ½ cup for an 8-inch cake, on top of the cake and allow it to flow. With an icing spatula, spread the glaze evenly so it drips down onto the sides. Spread more glaze around the sides. Set the cake aside for about 30 minutes, until the glaze no longer feels tacky to the touch (test a side, not the top, or the fingerprint will show). In hot weather, refrigerate to set.

While the first coat hardens, press a piece of plastic wrap or wax paper directly onto the top of remaining glaze to prevent it from forming a skin. If this glaze has cooled and stiffened at all during the wait, set it back over hot water for a few minutes and stir until warm and smooth. Then pour a second coat of glaze over the cake. Use the spatula with a *very* light touch to smooth the warm glaze across the top. Allow the glaze to set for at least 30 minutes without touching it. It will harden and become very glossy.

Chocolate Water Glaze

*T*his is my adaptation of a glaze developed by Albert Kumin when he was pastry chef at the famed Four Seasons Restaurant in New York. In this recipe, water replaces cream used in a traditional glaze; this one tastes equally delicious, sets with a fine gloss that retains a fudgelike consistency underneath, and holds up well in hot weather.

The recipe is easy to follow if you remember to whisk in enough water at the beginning to prevent the chocolate from seizing. Cakes coated with this glaze can be frozen.

Quantity About 1½ cups, more than enough to glaze one 9-inch 2- or 3-layer cake

12 ounces best-quality semisweet or bittersweet chocolate, chopped (2 cups; 350 g)
6 tablespoons very hot water, or more if needed

1. Melt the chocolate in the top pan of a double boiler set over hot, not boiling, water. Stir until smooth. Whisk the hot water into the chocolate all at once (*not* slowly or the chocolate may seize) until the chocolate is satiny smooth. It will have the consistency of softly whipped cream. If you wish the glaze more liquid, whisk in 1 or more tablespoons hot water.

2. Set the cake on a rack over a tray and pour a generous amount of glaze in the center. Tilt the cake to help the glaze flow; spread it with an icing spatula. Set aside, or refrigerate in hot weather, to set the glaze. The gloss disappears when refrigerated but returns at room temperature. Beware of fingerprints on the glaze; they show.

Cocoa Icing Glaze

½ cup sifted unsweetened cocoa, preferably Dutch-
process (1⅓ ounces; 38 g)
½ cup granulated sugar (3½ ounces; 100 g)
½ cup heavy cream
¼ cup unsalted butter (½ stick; 60 g), cut up

Quantity 1⅓ cups, to glaze the top and sides of an 8- or 9-inch 2-layer cake or torte

Combine all the ingredients in the top pan of a double boiler set over hot, not boiling, water and stir until the mixture is shiny and smooth, about 5 minutes. Remove pan from the heat and set it aside to cool for about 5 minutes. Pour the glaze over the top of the cake, and use an icing spatula to spread it evenly over the top and around the cake sides. Refrigerate the cake to harden the glaze.

Apricot Glaze

*T*his is an all-purpose glaze used to undercoat cakes before icing, or to top fruit-cakes.

1 cup best-quality apricot preserves

Quantity 1 cup, to coat a 2-layer 8- or 9-inch cake

Stir preserves in a small saucepan over medium heat until melted. Stir and cook about 2 minutes longer, bringing preserves to a boil. Cook until thick enough to coat a spoon. Strain preserves through a sieve. Cool slightly and use pastry brush to coat the cake with lukewarm glaze as directed in recipe. Chill cake to set the glaze.

Firm Apricot Glaze

*T*his recipe is preferred when a glazed cake top must be held several hours before serving. The addition of gelatin keeps the glaze from melting.

Quantity ½ cup, to top an 8- or 9-inch cake

½ cup best-quality apricot preserves
1½ teaspoons unflavored gelatin
2 tablespoons kirsch, or other fruit-flavored liqueur or fruit juice

Stir preserves over medium heat in a small saucepan until melted. Strain preserves through sieve. Remove solids, then return strained preserves to saucepan. Add gelatin and liqueur. Stir over medium heat until gelatin completely dissolves. Bring to a boil for barely 30 seconds, then cool slightly. Apply lukewarm glaze to cake. Chill cake to set glaze.

Crème Fraîche

While there is no exact American duplicate of the classic French *crème fraîche*, the following recipe will give you a satisfying approximation. Serve *crème fraîche* over fresh sliced fruit or warm fruit cobbler, or alongside a slice of rich dark chocolate cake.

1 cup heavy cream (8 ounces)
½ cup sour cream (4 ounces; 110 g)

Quantity   About 1 cup

In a mixing bowl, whisk the creams together. Cover with plastic wrap, and let sit at room temperature for about 8 hours, until thickened. Line a strainer with a double thickness of paper towels or a coffee filter and set it over a bowl. Turn the cream into the lined strainer and let it drain overnight, or up to 24 hours, in the refrigerator, covered with plastic wrap. Discard the thin liquid and store the thicker cream left in the strainer in a covered glass jar in the refrigerator; it will keep for about a week.

Vanilla Custard Sauce (Crème Anglaise)

A rich soft custard sauce primarily thickened with egg yolks, this is pure heaven served with Chocolate Mousse Cake (page 318) or Feather-Topped Truffle Cake (page 315). The addition of a little cornstarch in this recipe is insurance for smooth thickening.

Advance Preparation The sauce may be made early in the day, or up to 2 days ahead, and stored, covered, in the refrigerator. To serve warm, reheat it in a double boiler, stirring over warm, not hot, water.

Special Equipment 2-quart heavy-bottomed, nonreactive saucepan, whisk or electric mixer, 2 bowls, wooden spoon, double boiler, strainer, mercury candy thermometer (optional)

Quantity 2 cups

1 vanilla bean, or 2 teaspoons vanilla extract
1¾ cups milk
4 large egg yolks
1½ teaspoons cornstarch
4 tablespoons granulated sugar

ADDITIONAL FLAVORING (OPTIONAL)

1 tablespoon orange-flavored liqueur or dark rum

1. If using a vanilla bean, slit it lengthwise, place it in a saucepan with the milk, and bring slowly to a boil. During this time, beat together in a bowl the egg yolks, cornstarch, and sugar until the mixture is thick, light-colored, and forms a flat ribbon falling back on itself when the beater is lifted.

2. When the milk just boils, remove it from the heat. Pour about half of the hot milk onto the yolk mixture in a slow stream while whisking constantly. Then pour the warm yolk mixture into the saucepan with remaining milk. To be safe, you can now set the pan in the bottom of a double boiler. Or set directly on low heat and watch it very closely. Stir the sauce constantly with a wooden spoon until thick enough to leave a clearly defined line when you draw your finger through the cream on the back of the spoon (170°F; about 77°C).

3. Remove custard from the heat and strain it into a bowl. Do not overcook, or it will tend to curdle, though the cornstarch helps prevent this. At this point, stir in the vanilla extract and any other flavoring if using it. Cool the sauce completely, then cover and chill.

Warm Berry Sauce

*T*his quick and easy-to-make sauce is delightful served warm over slices of sponge cake for a family dinner or an elegant Sunday brunch. I also like it on vanilla ice cream and waffles. Use fresh or frozen raspberries, blueberries, strawberries, or whatever is in season.

2 cups fresh berries, rinsed, hulled, and sliced, or an equivalent amount of frozen berries

⅓ to ½ cup granulated sugar (amount depends upon type and sweetness of fruit; 2¼ to 3½ ounces; 65 to 100 g)

1½ to 2 tablespoons freshly squeezed lemon juice, to taste

Grated zest of ½ lemon, about 1½ teaspoons

½ cup water

1 teaspoon cornstarch dissolved in 2 tablespoons cold water

Quantity 3 cups

Combine all ingredients in a saucepan set over moderate heat. Stir gently and bring to a gentle boil. Stir until the sauce is clear and thickened. Remove from the heat. Reheat sauce just before serving.

Fresh Raspberry Sauce

*T*his ruby-colored sauce can be made with fresh or frozen berries. Serve it with any sponge cake, Chocolate Mousse Cake (page 318), Feather-Topped Truffle Cake (page 315), or Vanilla Bavarian Cream (page 372).

Advance Preparation   The sauce can be made 2 or 3 days ahead, covered, and re-frigerated.

Special Equipment
Medium-size nonreactive saucepan, strainer set over a bowl

Quantity   About 1⅛ cups if completely strained; 1½ cups with some seeds

3 cups fresh raspberries, picked over, hulled, rinsed, and gently dried on paper towels, or one 12-ounce bag frozen whole unsweetened berries
3 tablespoons granulated sugar, or to taste
3 tablespoons water or orange juice
1 tablespoon cornstarch
3 tablespoons raspberry liqueur (Chambord), or eau de vie (framboise), or crème de cassis (optional)

1. In a medium-size nonreactive saucepan, combine the berries, sugar, and 2 tablespoons water or juice. Set over medium heat and cook, stirring and mashing the berries with the back of a large spoon, for about 3 minutes, until the berries release their juice and the sugar dissolves.

2. To remove the seeds, transfer the cooked berries to a strainer set over a small bowl. Stir and press on the berries with a spoon, then scrape any puree from the underside of the strainer into the bowl. Return the puree to the saucepan, and discard all or some of the seeds.

3. In a cup, dissolve the cornstarch in the remaining 1 tablespoon of water or juice. Add it to the puree and set the pan over high heat. Bring to a boil, stirring constantly. Boil 45 to 60 seconds, until thickened and no longer cloudy. Remove from the heat and stir in the liqueur if using. Taste and adjust sugar if necessary. Cool sauce before serving.

Hot Lemon Sauce

*T*his old-fashioned New England specialty is served warm over gingerbread fresh from the oven. The sauce can be made in advance and refrigerated, but it should be warmed before serving.

1 cup granulated sugar (7 ounces; 200 g)
½ cup lightly salted butter (1 stick; 110 g)
¼ cup water
1 egg, lightly beaten
1 teaspoon grated lemon zest
3 tablespoons freshly squeezed lemon juice

Quantity   About 1⅓ cups

Whisk together all ingredients in a 1½-quart heavy-bottomed saucepan set over moderate heat. Bring to a boil, whisking constantly. Boil for 1 full minute. Remove from heat. Serve warm.

Butterscotch Sauce

A rich buttery sauce with a thick, creamy consistency. Serve this warm over unfrosted vanilla, spice, or sponge cake and/or ice cream.

Quantity 1 cup

¼ cup unsalted butter (½ stick; 60 g)
½ cup firmly packed light brown sugar (3½ ounces; 100 g)
½ cup heavy cream
Pinch of salt
1 teaspoon vanilla extract

Melt the butter in a medium-size, heavy-bottomed saucepan. Add the sugar, cream, and salt and stir until well blended. Bring to a very gentle boil and cook for about 5 minutes, stirring occasionally. Remove from the heat and stir in the vanilla. Serve warm or cold; the sauce thickens as it cools. Store refrigerated in a covered jar.

Rich Chocolate Sauce

T his is the ultimate sauce to top cake and ice cream. For the most intense chocolate flavor, use 4 ounces semisweet and 4 ounces unsweetened or bittersweet chocolate; if you prefer a sweeter mixture, use all semisweet. This sauce is quite thick.

Advance Preparation Can be made up to a week ahead and stored in a covered jar in the refrigerator. Warm over low heat before serving.

Special Equipment Double boiler, whisk, rubber spatula

Quantity About 1¼ cups

8 ounces semisweet chocolate, or substitute 4 ounces bittersweet or unsweetened chocolate for half the semisweet
½ cup heavy cream

FLAVORING (OPTIONAL)
1 teaspoon vanilla extract; or pinch of ground cinnamon; or 1 or 2 tablespoons rum, or orange, raspberry, or almond-flavored liqueur, or to taste

Melt the chocolate with the cream in the top pan of a double boiler set over simmering water. Remove pan from the heat just before all the chocolate is melted. Whisk until completely smooth. Whisk in the flavoring liquid. Serve warm. Thin with more cream if desired.

Note: You can also make this in the food processor by chopping the chocolate, then processing it until powdered. Heat the cream to the boiling point and slowly pour it through the feed tube onto the chocolate with the motor running. Process until completely smooth and melted. Add flavoring and pulse.

Cake Soaking Syrup

This flavored syrup is brushed or sprinkled on split layers of génoise or sponge cake to add flavor and moisture before filling. Beware of adding too much alcohol to the syrup, it may overpower the flavor of your cake.

Add the syrup to the cake layers in an allover pattern, taking care to reach the outer edges as well as the center. Do not saturate the cake or it will fall apart when the layer is lifted.

As a general guide, use:

2½ to 3 tablespoons flavored syrup brushed on each ¼-inch-thick sponge cake layer;

3 to 4 tablespoons flavored syrup brushed on each ½-inch-thick layer; for a moist ½-inch layer you can use up to ⅓ cup of syrup.

1 cup granulated sugar (7 ounces; 200 g)
1 cup water

Quantity 1½ cups, enough for two or three 8-inch cakes

FLAVORING
3 tablespoons fruit- or nut-flavored liqueur or rum or brandy; or 1 teaspoon extract (vanilla, maple, rum, etc.); or 3 or 4 tablespoons strained fruit puree

Combine the sugar and water in a heavy-bottomed saucepan; boil, stirring, to dissolve all the sugar. Remove pan from the heat, cool, and store the syrup. Add flavoring just before filling a cake. The syrup can be refrigerated in a covered jar for about 6 weeks.

VARIATIONS

. . . .

Orange or Grand Marnier Syrup
3 tablespoons Grand Marnier or other orange liqueur

Almond Syrup
1 teaspoon vanilla extract, 2 tablespoons Amaretto
    liqueur, ¼ teaspoon almond extract

Rum Syrup
3 tablespoons dark rum plus 1½ teaspoons vanilla
    extract

Coffee Syrup
2 teaspoons instant coffee powder dissolved in
    1 tablespoon hot water

Note: Warmed pure maple syrup, unadulterated, or the syrup from poached fruit or fruit packed in cans, may also be used as soaking syrup; taste first and adjust the flavor if necessary.

Decorating

CAKES

TO PREPARE CAKES FOR FILLING
AND DECORATING

. . . .

BEFORE BAKED CAKE layers can be filled or frosted, they are prepared by one of the following methods:

1. Often a sponge cake, génoise, or torte will be cut horizontally into thin layers before filling. To do this, first set the cake on a cardboard disk, a turntable or lazy Susan, or a piece of foil. Place one hand flat on the cake top and with the other, hold a serrated knife blade against the side of the cake. Turn the cake away from the blade as you make a gentle sawing motion, cutting a shallow groove into the cake all the way around the edge (diagram a, page 428). This marks the layer. Then go around again, sawing deeper, but not quite through; finally, cut clean through. Slide a cardboard cake disk, a sheet of foil, or an edgeless cookie sheet between the layers for support and lift off the top layer. Never lift the layer without supporting it, or it may crack.

Another method for splitting a sponge cake is to cut a groove in the cake with a serrated knife as described, then wrap a length of strong button thread or dental floss around the groove. Cross the thread ends, and keep pulling with even pressure until you sever the layer (diagram b, page 428). Support and remove the layer as described.

When cutting layers, you may wish to make a very shallow vertical groove in the side of the cake before you begin the layers. This notch will be a guide when reassembling the cake, so the layers line up properly (diagram c, page 428).

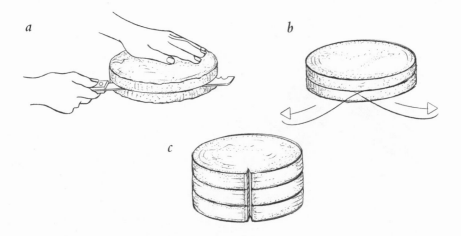

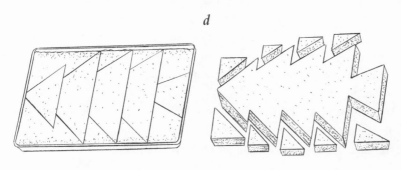

2. If the baked shape is to be altered, it should be cut now. (Review Shaped Cakes, page 448.) Cut a pattern or template out of paper, set it on the cake, and mark around the edge with a toothpick or a knife tip. Remove the template and cut around the marked line with a serrated knife (diagram d). For intricate shapes, a grapefruit knife can be helpful. For pound cake or butter cake, a paring knife works more easily than a serrated blade. (Freeze cake scraps for snacks or crumbs or shortcake.)

3. If the top of any layer of the cake is domed, level it off with a long-bladed serrated knife so your filled cake will be flat when the layers are stacked (diagram e).

4. When ready to frost the cake, brush all the surface crumbs off the sides and top with your hand or a pastry brush.

5. Put a dab of jam or icing in the center of a cake cardboard or flat plate or turntable. This icing is just to hold the cake in place.

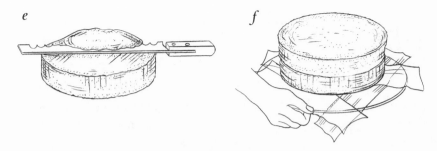

e   *f*

6. To protect the serving plate while icing the cake, cut 4 or more narrow strips of wax paper or parchment and set them around the bottom of the cake, sliding them slightly underneath. This paper covers the plate edges, and will be pulled out once the decorations are complete (diagram f).

7. Apply flavored syrup or filling between the layers and assemble them.

8. If a smooth icing surface is important, paint on a layer of warm Apricot Glaze (page 415). Use a jam that complements the flavor of your cake and its icing.

First set your cake on its cardboard on a wire rack set over a jelly-roll pan (to catch drips). Use an icing spatula to spread the glaze over the top first, then down and around the sides. Remember that a glaze is not an icing and should not be as thick. Glazes are meant to be thin, unless used in a heavy coat for a cake topping. Some glazes, particularly chocolate glazes, are poured onto the cake, then spread across the top and around the sides with an icing spatula (diagram g). If necessary, scrape up the dripped glaze, warm it if thickened, and reapply it to the cake.

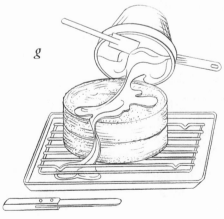

g

ABOUT CAKE FROSTING AND DECORATIONS

WITH A FEW tools and some basic techniques, one can easily achieve very elegant results in cake decorating. Less is more; cakes actually look more appetizing and appealing when their decorations are understated rather than overdone.

QUANTITY TABLE FOR FILLING AND FROSTING CAKES

Cake Shape and Size	Cups of Icing Needed
8- or 9-inch round layer, to cover top only, for filling or frosting	½ to 1
10- to 12-inch round layer, top only	1⅓
14-inch round layer, top only	1½
2-layer 8- or 9-inch round cake, top and sides plus filling	2½ to 3½
2-layer 8- or 9-inch round cake, top and sides only, no filling	1½ to 2½
2-layer 8- or 9-inch round cake, sides only, no filling, no icing on top	1 to 1½
3-layer 8- or 9-inch round cake, top and sides plus filling	4
8-inch-square cake, top only	¾ to 1
8- × 2-inch round cake, top and sides	1½ to 1¾
8- × 12-inch sheet cake, or 9- × 13-inch sheet cake, top only	1½ to 2
10½- × 15½-inch sheet cake, top only	2
9- × 5- × 3-inch loaf, top only	½ to ¾
9- × 5- × 3-inch loaf, top and sides	1½
9- to 9½- × 3¾-inch tube, top and sides	2½ to 3
10- × 4-inch tube, top and sides	3 to 4
2- to 3-inch diameter cupcake	2 tablespoons
12 cupcakes	1 to 1½ cups

Cake Shape and Size	Cups of Icing Needed
To glaze one 9-inch round cake	1 cup glaze
To cover with meringue the top and sides of one 8- or 9-inch cake	3½ to 4 cups meringue made with 4 egg whites
To fill one 10-inch jelly roll (made from 10- × 15-inch sheet cake)	1 to 1½ (up to 2 cups for whipped cream)

About Quantities Needed for Filling and Frosting Cakes

The amount needed for each cake will vary with the type of icing, the thickness it is spread, and the quantity used between the layers, if any. You may prefer to fill the cake with preserves, fruit slices and whipped cream, or another type of icing. Changing the filling adds variety to the cake and also allows more icing for decorating the outside. In the preceding table, the icing quantities are given only as a general guide. Fluffy or boiled icing requires about ⅓ more than a buttercream. Icing glaze is applied when soft and runny and will be much thinner than an icing that is spread on the cake. Specific icing yields are given with each recipe. If you are planning to decorate the cake after frosting it, make at least ½ recipe more icing.

Icing for Decorations

The consistency of the icing is very important: use a fairly soft icing to spread all over the cake. Use a medium-stiff icing to pipe borders that must hold their shape. Use a fairly soft icing for writing that must flow evenly yet hold its shape without drooping. Use a stiff icing containing a high ratio of solid white shortening (page 381) to make flowers with three-dimensional petals.

Coloring Decorative Icing

U.S. Certified food colors are those that meet FDA purity guidelines and are considered edible. In the small amounts that these colors are added to cake icing, they are probably perfectly safe to use and ingest. However, the safety of some of the approved colors has been questioned, and many home cooks prefer to avoid them altogether. If you want a substitute, look for natural substances with coloring properties: undiluted frozen orange-juice concentrate or egg yolks will tint icing a yellow color, as will saffron and turmeric (though the latter leaves a curry flavor). Beet juice, cranberry juice, and many types of strained berry preserves produce shades of pink and rose; coffee tints icing beige, and chocolate can be blended in varying amounts for a wide range of beige-to-brown tones. You should be aware of the properties of the coloring used: liquid vegetable food colors are water-based and may not blend well with some types of buttercream; if added to melted white chocolate, they may cause it to seize and harden into an unusable mass. It is usually preferable to use professional bakers' paste or powder colors, which are available in many gourmet and cookware shops, department stores, and baking and candy supply houses (see Sources, page 477).

HOW TO FROST A CAKE

. . . .

FIRST PREPARE THE cake for icing following the guidelines on page 427; to do this, use a serrated knife to level the layers. Brush off the crumbs. Split the cake into thinner layers if you wish, making a vertical notch to help realign the layers later.

Set out a cardboard cake disk cut to fit the layers. Dab a little icing on the disk to anchor the cake in place. Set the first layer on the disk (diagram a). Add filling on top of this layer, then add the next layer. Repeat, adding and filling all layers. Check to see that the layers are lined up evenly.

If you are concerned that the filling may bleed out and discolor the icing (strawberry preserves and white boiled icing for example), first pipe a ring of icing around the edge of the layer to be filled; then spread the filling inside the ring. This icing ring acts as a dam to prevent the filling from reaching the outside of the cake (diagram b).

If you have a decorating turntable, place the cake on it. You may want to

anchor the cake to the turntable with a dab of icing. To prevent crumbs from getting into the icing, brush the cake off. If you wish, you can spread warm Apricot Glaze (page 415) over the cake top and sides to guarantee crumb-free icing. Chill the glazed cake to set the glaze before adding the icing.

Spread a generous amount of icing around the cake sides, then on the top (diagram c). Finally, smooth the sides and top, removing excess icing. It is better to start with extra icing, building up a good layer, than it is to press against the sides and lift crumbs in an attempt to spread a skimpy amount of icing. If using a turntable, hold your spatula upright against the side of the cake in a fixed position while rotating the turntable away from the blade (diagram d). This smooths the sides. To even the top of a very large cake, you can use a metal ruler wider than the cake's diameter, drawing the ruler across the top in a single motion (diagram e), making a flat surface. This can also be done in several motions with a long spatula. Finally, smooth the top edges by sweeping the spatula from the rim of the cake toward the center. If you have trouble getting the top perfectly smooth, dip the blade of your longest spatula in hot water, shake it off, and draw across the cake top, smoothing the surface.

How to Decorate Cake Sides with Nuts or Crumbs

Use toasted and ground or chopped nuts, or toasted and sliced almonds, or crushed cake, cookie, or meringue crumbs. Put ¾ to 1 cup nuts or crumbs in a bowl (the exact amount depends upon the cake size and the density of nuts you wish on the cake). For ease in applying the nuts, it helps to have the cake fastened with icing to a cardboard cake disk. Pick up the cake with one hand and with the other scoop up some nuts or crumbs into the palm of your hand. Press the nuts or crumbs up against the cake sides with your hand, allowing the excess to fall back into the bowl or onto wax paper (diagram f). You can also achieve this effect by frosting only the cake sides, not the top, then holding the cake by its top and bottom and rolling the frosted sides in nuts or crumbs (see below, f).

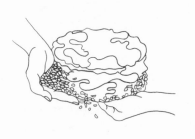
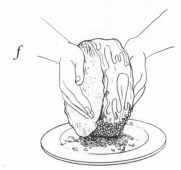

PASTRY BAGS AND TIPS

FOR PIPING ICING, meringue, or whipped cream into decorative patterns on cakes, a decorating tube or pastry bag fitted with a fancy tip is the answer. Pastry bags are the easiest to use because they are flexible, fit into your hand well, and release their contents with slight finger pressure. Metal syringe-type tubes are handy for writing icing messages. Small paper or parchment cones are easy to make for piping soft icing or melted chocolate into decorative patterns.

Pastry bags lined with plastic or made of nylon are the best type to use because they are flexible and do not absorb fat. Bags are available in sizes from 7 inches to nearly 24 inches long; select one larger than you think you need.

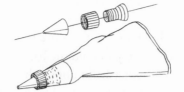

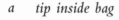

a   tip inside bag   *b   coupler assembly*   *syringe-type*
decorating tube

Use the smallest bags for delicate designs, the largest for piping stiff batters or foams. For general all-purpose decorations, I use a 16-inch nylon bag. Wash the bags in hot water and air-dry them after use. The decorating tip can be dropped inside the bag so it sticks out of the hole (diagram a), or you can use a coupler assembly, usually sold with the tips. This is most convenient because the coupler allows you to change tips simply by removing an outer ring (see diagram b). If you attach the tip by dropping it inside the bag, you must re-move the icing to insert another tip into the bag, a rather messy procedure. Alternatively, you can just hold a new tip over the outside of the old one, changing the configuration of the icing design as you continue to squeeze the bag. This usually works, but occasionally icing oozes out between the tips.

How to Fill a Pastry or Decorating Bag

To fill the bag, fold back a 4- or 5-inch cuff. It may help you to stand the bag tip down inside a measuring cup. Use a broad spatula to add icing, filling the bag no more than half full. With your fingers, squeeze the icing down into the tip and twist the bag closed. The icing is forced into the tip; press out a little icing to be sure there is no air trapped in the tip (diagram c).

c

How to Use the Bag

To use the bag, hold the twist-closure between the thumb and fingers of one hand; with this gesture you hold the bag closed and apply pressure to squeeze out the icing. The other hand guides the bag (diagram c) and helps support its weight. For most designs, the bag is held at either a 90-degree or 45-degree angle to the cake top.

How to Make Paper Cones

To make a paper cone, cut a wax paper or parchment triangle about 12 by 15 inches. Pull the long side of the paper around its midpoint, making a cone. Hold the cone tight while wrapping the second point around; tuck in all the ends (diagrams a through f). Cut a tiny bit off the cone tip to make a round tip or cut a triangle-shaped hole to make icing leaves or petals. Or, you can simply drop a metal decorating tip into a paper cone (the best way to guarantee an even line). Fill the paper cone, then fold down the top. This cone can be held and used with one hand. After use, the paper cone is discarded, but save the metal tip if using it. Baking parchment triangles 15 × 15 × 21 inches, 100 to a pack, are sold in some gourmet and cookware shops; this is a convenient way to have readily available decorating cones. The paper cones

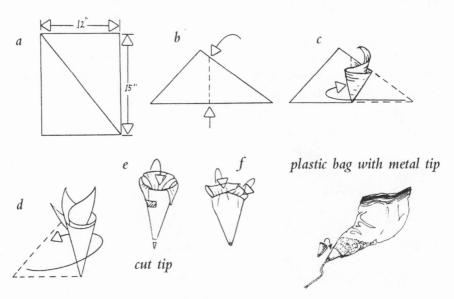

are used almost exclusively by professional chefs for doing fancy work and piping melted chocolate. In an emergency, you can also use a small plastic bag. Fill the bag, twist it closed, and cut a pin-size hole in one corner, or drop in a metal decorating tip, see diagram below.

About Decorating Tips

Decorating tips come in hundreds of sizes and shapes. Be sure that the tips you select fit the size of your decorating bag; small tips will fall out of the end of the large bags. For our purposes, we recommend the use of a star tip, preferably #6, ½ inch, for use with the 16-inch pastry bag. You should have an open star and a partially closed star, a plain round tip for writing, a leaf tip, and a rose petal tip for making roses and other flower petals and ribbons. A basket-weave tip is essential for achieving the correct basket texture.

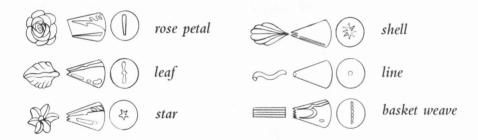

The most common border designs used in this book are shells and rosettes. To make shells, use the #6, ½-inch, slightly closed star tip, or #18, 22, 25, 26, 27, 28, or 30. Hold the star tip at a 45-degree angle to the cake top. Press out the icing, lift the tip slightly as the shape bulges out, then press down gently onto the cake while releasing pressure and pulling sharply away, forming a tail. To make a shell border, repeat, beginning the next shell on the tail of the last. As you proceed with the border you will feel a rocking motion with your hand. You can also curve the shells to alternate sides, like a series of opposing commas. A single shell with a long tail is called a claw; a series of side-by-side claws makes another decorative border.

To make rosettes, use the slightly closed star tip, #14, 16, 18, 21, or 22, for example, or the #6, ½-inch, star tip. Hold the tip perpendicular to the cake top. Press out icing, then pull up sharply while giving a circular twist to

the bag. To make a more twisted rosette, move the bag in a small circle as you press out the icing. To make stars or small flowers use the open star tip #4 and repeat the above motion without the twist at the end. If you make the small stars side by side, you have an attractive border.

The plain round tip, #2, 3, 4, 5, and 7, for example, can be used for writing, dots, beads, strings or ropes, flower stems, or scroll work. Draw a design, or trace one, onto a piece of paper, then top it with baking parchment, which is transparent. "Draw" the icing lines directly over the drawing. If you do this with royal icing or melted chocolate, let the design harden, then peel off the parchment.

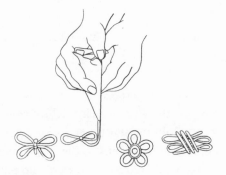

To make a simple basket-weave design, you will need both the plain round tip and the basket-weave tip #47. First pipe 2 vertical lines an even distance apart using the round #3 or #4 tip. Second, with the basket-weave tip, pipe 3 horizontal lines crossing the first 2 at the top, middle, and bottom. Now draw one new vertical line in the middle that extends from the top to the bottom of the 3 basket-weave lines. Again using the basket-weave tip, pipe 2 horizontal lines filling in the weave between the original 2 verticals (diagrams a, b, c, page 439). Repeat.

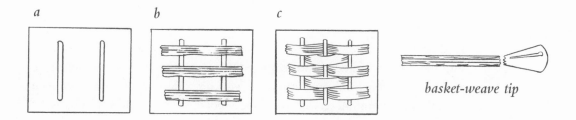

a   *b*   *c*

basket-weave tip

Hints for Successful Decorating with Tips

The amount of pressure on the pastry bag, the size of the tip, and the consistency of the icing will determine the amount of icing flowing out. By increasing the pressure and moving the bag slowly, you can increase the size of the line being piped. Practice on wax paper on the table before making designs on the cake. Be sure to sift confectioners' sugar through a fine sieve before making icing that will be piped through a small round tube; the smallest lump in the icing can block the tip. If this happens, use a toothpick poked into the tip to release the blockage. After use, soak decorating tips in hot water until clean; use a toothpick to free icing stuck in small openings.

CAKE DECORATING IDEAS AND TECHNIQUES

THE FOLLOWING SUGGESTIONS include a wide variety of cake decorating ideas. Most are quick and easy for a fast effect with minimum skill and effort; some are more complex. Use this section for reference and as a starting place for your own ideas; often just looking at the illustrations will get your creativity going. If inspiration fails you, fall back on a simple border of piped icing shells or rosettes; they always look elegant and give a fine finish to a cake without much extra work. Or, where appropriate, top a simple whipped-cream icing with a border of fresh whole berries garnished with mint leaves. When in doubt, remember: Keep the decorations simple.

Fresh Flowers

Fresh flowers provide instant decorations for a cake. However, you must be sure the flowers are edible varieties, even though they are not meant to be edible decorations, only trimmings. If you have doubts, consult your state agricultural extension service or a local botanist. Since flowers might be touching the cake, be sure they are grown without pesticides, rinsed with water, and gently patted dry. Keep flowers in water until ready to use. Safe flowers include blossoms of wild strawberries, nasturtiums, mint, pear, and apple blossoms, citrus blossoms and leaves, scented geraniums, and roses. Do *not* use lilies of the valley or mistletoe.

I like to decorate a cake top with a mini-bouquet of flowers. To do this, set the bouquet into a small bottle or baby food jar containing a little water or moist florists' clay and position it in a hole cut into the top of the cake. Or, you can put one or two perfect blossoms into a plastic stoppered tube sold by florists for holding long-stemmed roses. Poke the tube directly into the cake. Remove flower containers before cutting the cake.

Sugared flower petals are easy to prepare and make sparkling decorations. Use fresh, clean rose petals, for example. Brush them with egg whites, then sprinkle with granulated sugar and air-dry on wax paper for at least one hour before positioning petals on a cake.

Note: Small bunches of regular or champagne grapes or tiny pears or lady apples may be coated and sugared in the same manner.

Stencil Designs

Paper doilies make excellent stencils for cake tops, and plastic doilies are sold in some cookware shops for this purpose. Stencils make instant decorations on plain or frosted cake tops.

To use, simply set the stencil (doily) flat on the cake top. Sift on confectioners' sugar for a white design or unsweetened cocoa or cinnamon for a dark design on a white cake. Very carefully lift up the stencil, leaving the design below (diagram a, page 441).

Comb Designs

Decorating combs are flat metal triangles with teeth of different sizes on each edge. These are sold in cookware shops; a clean new hair comb or a serrated knife blade makes a fine substitute. To use a comb, first frost the cake with a buttercream or sugar icing. Smooth the surface flat, then put the comb against the surface and draw it across in a wavy pattern (diagram b, below). You can hold the comb against the sides and repeat the design, or press sliced toasted nuts onto the cake sides.

Paper Strip Designs

This is a variation on the stencil. Use this technique on an uncoated cake or on a cake topped with any icing, glaze, or even with chocolate curls or shavings. Simply cut 3 or 4 strips of paper longer than the width of the cake. Set the paper strips at evenly spaced intervals across the cake (diagram c, below). Sift confectioners' sugar, unsweetened cocoa or ground cinnamon, depending upon the color desired, over the cake top. Carefully lift off the paper strips, leaving stripes on the cake (diagram d, below). A plaid effect is created by repeating the design in the opposite direction.

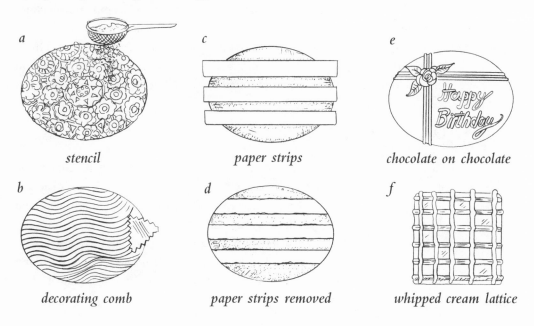

a

stencil

c

paper strips

e

chocolate on chocolate

b

decorating comb

d

paper strips removed

f

whipped cream lattice

Chocolate on Chocolate Designs

Frost the cake with any chocolate icing or glaze. Chill the cake to set the icing or glaze. Melt about ⅓ cup semisweet chocolate morsels (60 g) with 1 tablespoon butter in the top pan of a double boiler. Stir the mixture until perfectly smooth. Put the melted chocolate into a paper decorating cone (page 436) with a small round hole in the tip; or use a #2 round metal tip. Pipe the chocolate into the pattern shown (diagram e, page 441): It is simply 2 sets of intersecting straight lines set off to one side of the cake. Write a message in the large open space. To get fancy, put a real rose (or a chocolate rose, see page 461) at the point where the lines intersect. The color contrast on this cake comes from using different shades of chocolate for the icing. Unsweetened or bittersweet chocolate on a milk chocolate glaze (medium-brown) gives good contrast. Use this same design with white chocolate lines on a dark chocolate cake; omit the butter when melting white chocolate.

Whipped Cream Lattice

Flavored Whipped Cream (page 342), including chocolate or coffee whipped cream, can be piped through a pastry bag fitted with a star tip. In addition to the obvious rosettes and border designs, you can pipe overlapping parallel lines to create a lattice pattern (diagram f, page 441). Or, make one row around the edge of the top and another row around the bottom edge as borders. This is particularly attractive on a rectangular cake. If the whipped cream must be held for several hours before serving, use stabilized whipped cream (see page 341).

Drizzled Lines

This is a variation on the chocolate decoration above, but much easier. Simply melt the unsweetened chocolate with butter as directed but omit the paper cone. Prepare a previously frosted cake. Dip a fork into the slightly cooled chocolate, then drizzle parallel lines across the cake top in one direction, then in the other, creating a crosshatched pattern. The melted dark chocolate will stand out even on a milk chocolate icing but can be used on any other icing as well. Instead of dark chocolate, try white chocolate lines drizzled on dark chocolate icing (diagram g, page 443).

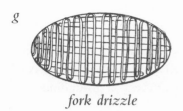

g

fork drizzle

h

chocolate-dipped nuts

Chocolate-Dipped Nuts

Melt 1 or 2 ounces of semisweet or bittersweet chocolate in the top pan of a double boiler or in the microwave. Stir smooth. Hold blanched almonds with a pair of tweezers or your fingertips and dip them up to their center in the melted chocolate. Set them on foil and refrigerate to set the chocolate. Arrange the half-dipped nuts in 1 or 2 concentric rings on the cake top (diagram h, above).

Chocolate Curls

White or dark chocolate curls are quick and easy to make. Coat your cake with a buttercream icing. Make the Chocolate Curls (see page 456) and arrange them in a random jumble covering the top (diagram i, below). To highlight dark chocolate curls, you can sift a tiny bit of confectioners' sugar over them.

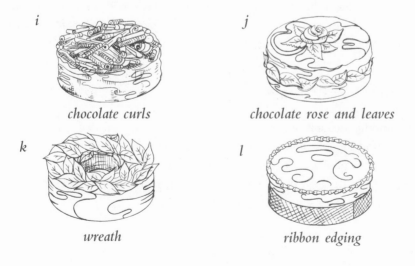

i

chocolate curls

j

chocolate rose and leaves

k

wreath

l

ribbon edging

Chocolate Shavings

Bittersweet or semisweet chocolate can be shaved across a grater (page 457), with the shavings falling directly onto a frosted cake. Cover the top completely. Press more shavings onto the cake sides or press on ground nuts.

Feathered Chocolate Glaze, Cut-Out Chocolate Shapes, and Chocolate Ruffles

See pages 445 and 464.

Chocolate Roses

See page 461.

Use the dark or white chocolate plastic roses or apricot roses in combination with Chocolate Leaves (diagram j, page 443).

Chocolate Leaves or Wreath

See page 454.

Make a border design around a cake top by setting chocolate leaves end to end or overlapping them slightly. You can alternate white and dark chocolate leaves for added drama. To make a wreath cake, cover the top of a tube cake with overlapping rows of chocolate leaves (diagram k, page 443). For a Christmas wreath, add a frosting or satin fabric bow.

Ribbon Decoration

For a stunning decoration, simply wrap a wide piece of satin or metallic ribbon around the cake and fasten it with a little frosting "glue." For a "country" look, use gingham or floral ribbon. If the ribbon is too stiff for the frosting to hold it, use a straight pin but be sure to remove it when removing the ribbon before serving (diagram l, page 443).

Portrait Cake

This is fun for adults as well as children. If you feel artistic, look at a photograph and try for a likeness; otherwise, make it a caricature, picking up obvious characteristics (red hair, blue eyes, freckles) (diagram m).

Measles or Chicken Pox Cake

This is for children, to brighten an otherwise uncomfortable time. Draw the face and hair with colored buttercream. Apply "measles" all over the face with tiny cinnamon hots or other round red candies. For a "thermometer" in the mouth, use the stem of a candy cane or a striped candy stick (diagram n).

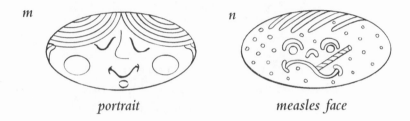

m   *n*

portrait   *measles face*

Feathered Chocolate Glaze

This technique looks so professional that it is intimidating to many inexperienced bakers. Actually, it is one of the easiest and quickest designs to make. It always works and always gets rave reviews for its elegant appearance. Don't be afraid to try it, just look at the diagrams first; it takes longer to describe than to do it.

The idea is to frost the cake or torte with any fondant or glaze, then pipe fine lines of a contrasting color icing across the top. Both icings must be soft enough to flow slightly; this does not work well with buttercream. When a knife blade is pulled through the lines in alternating directions, a classic wave pattern is produced. This is the design commonly used on Napoleon pastries.

Note: You can vary the technique by using white lines on a dark cake or dark lines on a light cake.

Special Equipment paper cone (see page 436), wire rack set over jelly-roll pan, icing spatula, thin-bladed knife and damp cloth, small plastic bag

CAKE

Any layer cake or torte. To give the glaze a smooth surface to adhere to, the cake may be previously undercoated with Apricot Glaze (page 415) or any buttercream, and chilled in the refrigerator until the undercoating is set.

ICING

Chocolate glaze such as Ganache Icing Glaze (page 409), Fabulous Chocolate Glaze (page 412), or Chocolate Water Glaze (page 414).

DECORATIVE LINE ICING

Melted white chocolate (page 49); or Basic Icing Glaze, sifted confectioners' sugar and water (page 408) for white lines. For dark lines on a white glaze, melt 2 ounces semisweet chocolate with a teaspoon of stick margarine or solid shortening. Put the line icing into a paper cone with a small round hole in the tip; fold over the cone ends to seal, then set the filled cone in a plastic bag to prevent icing from drying out before use.

a

b

1. Place the prepared cake on a wire rack set over a tray. Warm and stir the base coat glaze until it reaches pouring consistency. Pour a generous amount of glaze onto the center of the cake, then tilt the rack to help the glaze flow evenly (diagram a). Guide the glaze with an icing spatula; it should coat the top and sides evenly but be fairly thin (diagram b). Work quite quickly, as the glaze thickens as it cools.

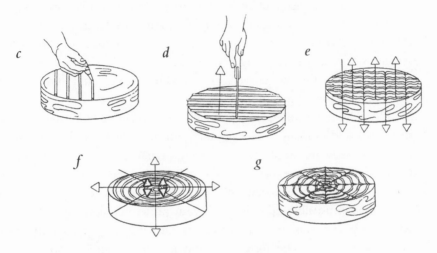

2. While the base coat glaze is still soft on top, squeeze a little line of icing out of the paper cone to test the flow, then draw parallel vertical lines about 1 inch apart across the top of the cake (diagram c). Turn the cake 180 degrees so these lines are now horizontal. Draw a thin knife blade through the lines at 1½-inch intervals (diagram d). Begin in the center of the cake and work toward the edges to keep the spacing even. Now turn the cake entirely around and again draw the knife through the lines, going between your previous lines (diagram e) and pulling in the opposite direction to make a series of connected brackets. Remember not to cut with the knife, just pull it lightly through the surface. This technique can also be used to make a spiral pattern (diagram f). To do this, first pipe a spiral on the cake top, then draw the knife from the center to the rim at even intervals in alternating directions (diagram g).

SHAPED CAKES

· ·

FOR SPECIAL OCCASIONS such as birthdays, anniversaries, and holidays you may wish to make a cake in the shape of a number, letter, train, clown, or other figure. These can be done in a variety of ways with a variety of baking pans, and the subject is material for a book in itself. However, here I want to give just a few ideas and general tips to guide the creative process.

First, select a cake batter with a firm grain; any layer, pound, or butter cake is fine. Avoid cakes containing chunks of nuts or raisins or chocolate bits, which will obstruct neat edges when the cake is cut into shape, or will weaken the structure when the cake is used to form a "built" figure made of several pieces joined together.

Consider the baking pan(s) you will use. Specialty pans formed into fancy shapes are sold in many cookware and gourmet shops as well as in hardware and department stores; always select the heaviest quality pan available. Santa Claus, Christmas Tree, Snoopy, and a host of other shapes are common. These pans are not necessary, however. With a little ingenuity and imagination, you can usually improvise with your present equipment and come out with satisfying results. With a rectangular pan, you can cut a variety of modular blocks that can be moved around in endless combinations to create baking areas of the desired shape; the little blocks can also be used to make cube-shaped cupcakes—a good way to use up extra batter or form modular building blocks for cake constructions.

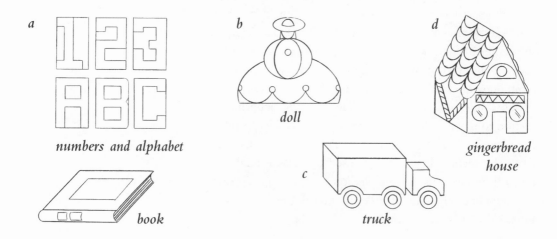

a

numbers and alphabet

book

b

doll

c

truck

d

gingerbread house

Consider the size of the finished cake: the easiest and most common shapes are made from sheet cakes baked in a large rectangular roasting pan approximately 11 or 12 × 17 inches. This rectangular flat shape is excellent for cutting into all the letters of the alphabet, and all the numbers. The flat rectangle is also used to create an opened or closed book-shaped cake. For these cakes, see diagram a.

To make a hemisphere-shaped skirt for a doll cake, you can bake the cake in a rounded bowl. Cut a hole in the center of the inverted cake and insert a small doll, leaving her torso sticking up. Decorate the skirt with icing, and add a hat of fresh flowers or ribbon and lace. For the dress bodice, use a piece of lace, or icing piped directly onto the doll; an inexpensive plastic doll from the five- and ten-cent store in the best for this purpose (diagram b).

Trucks and trains can be fashioned from cakes baked in loaf pans or 8-inch-square pans. For wheels, use Oreo cookies or other round cookies or candies (diagram c).

A gingerbread house can be made from a solid rectangle of cake as well as from the traditional gingerbread cookie dough. To make a solid gingerbread cake house, use loaf-shaped cakes or 8-inch cake pans as basic building blocks and follow a pattern and decorative ideas from a traditional gingerbread house (diagram d).

As a general guide, it is important to make a sketch of the finished shape before going to the trouble of baking a cake, only to find it is not a practical shape. Avoid thin shapes, which will be fragile; stick to sturdy forms and simple ideas; a bold statement is most effective. Use decorative icing piped through a bag or fresh flowers or candies and cookies for decorative trimmings. If you need more ideas, look at the cake shapes on page 448 or see illustrations in children's books. For very elaborate sculptured cakes (a portrait head, a piano), first model the shape from clay to simplify the form and determine the most efficient cake pan to use. Use buttercream icing as glue to fasten all pieces as well as to decorate the finished shape.

Use a serrated knife to cut shapes from cake. Keep the cut edges neat. Brush crumbs from cut surfaces. For small curved cuts, use a serrated grapefruit knife.

Assemble the cake on a sturdy base. Try covering a cookie sheet or flat tray with foil, or use a foil-covered jelly-roll pan. A mirror makes an attractive base; bind the edges, which may be sharp, with masking tape or colored cloth Mystic tape.

Special Effects, Flavorings and Decorative Techniques

Praline Powder and Praline Paste

*N*ut brittle is called praline, *pralin* in French. To make it, sugar is caramelized with toasted almonds and/or hazelnuts, then poured onto a slab and allowed to harden. When this brittle candy is powdered it makes "praline" or praline powder, an extremely flavorful preparation that is added to buttercreams, mousses, Bavarian cream, or whipped cream, or used to decorate cakes or other desserts. The classic proportions for making praline require an equal weight of nuts and sugar. The water in this recipe is added to smooth the melting of the sugar; it quickly evaporates.

To vary the flavor, praline powder can be made with pecans, walnuts, or other nuts, instead of the classic almonds and hazelnuts. Skins may be left on the almonds to add flavor, although they are always removed from the hazelnuts.

Note: Many recipes require the nuts to be toasted (see page 42) before they are added to the syrup at the amber stage; this is fine for hazelnuts, because they have to be toasted anyway so that their skins may be rubbed off before use. However, with almonds and other nuts, you can save time and achieve the same result simply by putting the untoasted nuts directly into the syrup as soon as the sugar has melted. In this manner, the nuts are cooked along with the sugar syrup, and the flavor of the finished product is enhanced.

When praline powder is worked in the food processor for about 6 minutes, it becomes a paste, like a nut butter. This is called Praline Paste, and it can also be used to flavor icings or creams.

1 cup granulated sugar (7 ounces; 200 g)

6 tablespoons water

1 cup whole blanched almonds (5 ounces; 140 g); or use half hazelnuts, toasted and skinned (page 42), plus half blanched almonds (either toasted in advance or added to the melted sugar syrup)

1. Combine the sugar and water in the saucepan or a copper sugar pot, and set over moderate heat. Swirl the pan, or stir once or twice, until the sugar is dissolved. Bring to a gently bubbling boil for a full 3 minutes, swirling the pan occasionally and washing down the pan sides with a pastry brush dipped into cold water to dissolve any sugar crystals that may have formed.

2. Add the nuts (if *not* previously toasted); swirl the pan gently to coat nuts with melted sugar syrup, then return the syrup to a boil. Without stirring, cook over medium-high heat for 12 to 15 minutes after reaching the boiling point. Occasionally wash down the pan sides with a brush dipped into cold water.

3. At this point, the syrup should have reached the hard-crack stage (295°F [146°C] to 310°F) and become light amber in color. If using *toasted* nuts, stir them in now. Cook until the syrup just begins to darken slightly, at about 335°F (168°C). Then pour out the nuts and syrup onto the oiled pan. Spread the nuts in a single layer with the back of a spoon and set them aside to cool.

4. When the nut brittle is cold, break it up into small pieces. In several batches, process it to fine crumbs or powder in a food processor or blender, or with a mortar and pestle.

Note: As the nut brittle cools, it may appear slightly cloudy. Don't worry; this is caused by the oil and moisture content of the nuts, which varies. Store the praline powder in an airtight container.

Advance Preparation   Praline powder can be made well in advance and refrigerated in an airtight container for several months or stored at room temperature for about 2 weeks.

Special Equipment   1½-quart heavy-bottomed saucepan, rough-textured towel (for skinning hazelnuts), mercury candy thermometer (nice but not essential), marble slab or jelly-roll pan or cookie sheet lightly coated with flavorless vegetable oil or butter, blender or food processor, airtight storage container, pastry brush.

Quantity   About 1½ cups

Praline Paste

Quantity About 1 cup

Prepare Praline Powder. Leave it in the food processor or blender and work it for 6 to 10 minutes longer, until the nut oils are released and the mixture resembles a slightly dry nut butter. Processing time and texture vary with the oil content of the nuts. Store the paste in an airtight container in the refrigerator. Use the paste to flavor cake fillings, creams, and buttercream icing.

Candied Citrus Peel

*C*andied citrus peel is one of my favorite treats and, fortunately, it is not hard to prepare. There are three points to note carefully: the thickness of the peel, the blanching needed to remove natural bitterness, and the syrup temperature (230°F; 110°C), which controls the texture. *Note:* Before starting, scrub whole fruit with a vegetable brush to remove any chemical residue.

FRUIT
About 2 cups (loosely packed) peel cut from 4
    oranges or 2 grapefruits or 6 lemons or limes
    (see step 1)

SYRUP
1 cup granulated sugar (7 ounces; 200 g)
½ cup water
2 tablespoons light corn syrup, or
    ¼ teaspoon cream of tartar

COATING
1 cup granulated sugar (7 ounces; 200 g) plus extra
    for layering peel if it is to be stored

1. With a sharp paring knife, quarter the oranges or grapefruit, then remove the quarter-segments of peel. With lemons and limes, slice off the peel, cutting right down to the beginning of the fruit. Cut wide strips of peel and leave on the white pith. Ideally, orange peel should be about ⅛ inch thick, though if more it does not matter. Do not cut off the peel with a vegetable peeler; the zest alone is too thin to give the correct texture.

2. Put the peels into a saucepan, cover with cold water, and bring to a boil. Lower the heat and boil gently for 15 minutes. Turn off the heat and let the peel stand in the hot water for 15 minutes. Drain in a colander and rinse with cold water. The peel will be soft. Grapefruit peel is more bitter than the others and is best blanched in 3 changes of cold water, each brought to a boil, then simmered for 10 minutes.

3. With a teaspoon, carefully scrape off and discard the soft white pith inside each segment of peel. It is easily removed. Slice the peel in ¼-inch-wide strips.

4. Combine in the saucepan the sugar, ½ cup water, and corn syrup or cream of tartar. Stir, then bring to a boil, swirling the pan several times to dissolve the sugar. Wash down the pan sides with a pastry brush dipped in cold water. When the syrup boils and looks clear, add the peels. The syrup should cover them. Put the candy thermometer in the pan. Boil the peel gently over moderate heat for about 30 minutes, or longer, until the syrup reaches 230°F (110°C; thread stage, just before soft-ball stage) and most of the syrup has been absorbed. With a slotted spoon, transfer the peel to a bowl or pan of sugar and toss. Then set the pieces on the paper-covered tray or rack to dry. After drying for several hours or overnight, the peel should be crisp outside but flexible and chewy inside. If too flabby, it was not cooked long enough at a high enough temperature; if it cracks when bent, it was cooked at too high a temperature. Store in layers of sugar in an airtight container.

Advance Preparation   Candied peel will last at least a year if packed in layers of granulated sugar in an airtight container and kept in a cool, dry location or the refrigerator.

Special Equipment   Paring knife, cutting board, 1½-quart heavy-bottomed, nonreactive saucepan, strainer or colander, mercury candy thermometer or instant spot thermometer, pastry brush and glass of cold water; tongs, soup bowl or pan with sides, wax-paper-covered tray or cookie sheet with sides or wire rack set over wax paper

Quantity   About 2 cups

5. To use the candied peel as a garnish, it can be diced or left in thin strips. To make a delectable candy even more so, dip all or half the length of each strip into melted semisweet or white chocolate; use this to garnish the tops of cakes. Set candy-dipped strips on wax paper and refrigerate to set the chocolate. Chocolate-covered peel can be made well in advance and stored in a cool place.

Chocolate Leaves

Chocolate leaves are made by coating real leaves with melted chocolate. When the chocolate is hard, the real leaf is peeled away, leaving an edible garnish for cakes. Both white and dark chocolate are used for making leaves; the procedure is the same, though solid shortening is not used with the white chocolate. Read about Chocolate (page 46).

Advance Preparation
Chocolate leaves can be prepared well in advance and stored in a protective airtight container in the refrigerator for a week or two; leaves can also be frozen for several months.

Special Equipment Double boiler, leaves (see Note following), wax paper, tray, pastry brush or small spatula for applying chocolate (though I prefer to use my finger)

Quantity As a rough guideline, 1 ounce of melted chocolate will coat about 6 leaves, depending upon their size; 8 ounces will make roughly 50

8 ounces semisweet chocolate, milk chocolate, or
    white chocolate (230 g), chopped
2 teaspoons solid white shortening (used only with
    dark chocolate)

1. Melt the chocolate, and shortening if using it, in the top pan of a double boiler over hot (125°F; about 50°C) water. If using white chocolate, be careful not to let the water get too hot or the white chocolate will become grainy and lumpy; use a spot thermometer to be sure the white chocolate gets no hotter than 115°F (about 45°C); ideally, keep the temperature between 100° and 110°F (about 40°C) and the water beneath it about 125°F (about 50°C). Stir the chocolate to blend it smooth. Set it aside to cool until comfortable to the touch.
2. Set clean, dry leaves, vein-patterned sides up, on a wax-paper-covered tray. (Note that the most pronounced vein pattern is generally on the underside of the leaf.) With a pastry brush, small spatula, or your fingertip,

spread a generous ⅛-inch layer of chocolate on the leaves, one at a time (diagram a). Brush the chocolate out to the edges, but not over them. Try to avoid thinning the edges too much. Set the coated leaves, chocolate side up, on a wax-paper-covered tray and place the tray in the refrigerator or freezer for a few minutes, until the chocolate is hard-set.

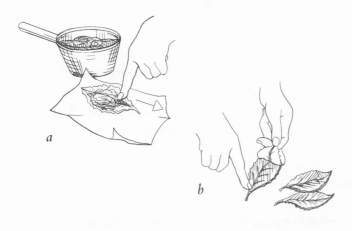

3. To make curled leaves, allow the chocolate leaves to cool partially, then set them onto the curved surface of a French-bread pan or a tube-shaped cake pan and chill to set. If curved too soon, the melted chocolate will all run to the middle of the leaf.

4. When the chocolate is completely set, remove the firm leaves from the refrigerator or freezer. Allow the leaves to stand at room temperature for 30 to 60 seconds. Carefully break off any uneven chocolate edges that wrap over onto the front of the real leaves. Then, starting at the stem end, peel the real leaves away from the chocolate (diagram b). Handle the chocolate leaf as little as possible. Set the chocolate leaves back on the tray or in a protective container and refrigerate or freeze until needed. Reuse the real leaves, coating them with more chocolate as long as they hold their shape.

leaves. Five to 6 leaves are enough to top a 9-inch cake, but you should always make extras in case some break. Excess melted chocolate can be poured into a paper muffin cup and chilled, to be stored and reused for another purpose.

A Note About Leaves For the prettiest effect, use gracefully shaped leaves with a waxy surface and a pronounced pattern of veins on one side. Lemon, magnolia, camellia, gardenia, ivy, and rose leaves work well. However, be aware that certain types of leaves can be poisonous! If you are uncertain, check with a nursery or a botanist or the state agricultural extension service. I use lemon or camellia leaves from a local florist, who also supplies them to neighboring restaurants. Be sure to wash and dry the leaves before using them to remove any chemical sprays. If you have a misshapen or extra-large leaf, simply cut it to size with scissors before coating it with chocolate; or cut it to the desired shape; for example, a rounded leaf can be turned into a maple or holly leaf before being coated with chocolate.

Note: If this is your first time, it is best to make a few test leaves at the start to determine the quality of the chocolate coating. Chocolate leaves should have a delicate appearance; ease up if you made the chocolate too thick. If, on the other hand, the chocolate shatters when the leaf is peeled away, apply more chocolate the next time and warm the leaf a little longer before peeling it off.

Chocolate Curls

Professional pastry chefs make chocolate curls, or long fat chocolate cigarettes, by spreading a coating of melted chocolate over a marble slab. When the chocolate (usually a coating chocolate) is nearly set, they draw a wide-bladed sharp knife across the surface, causing a thin sheet of chocolate to roll up on itself in a long curl. It takes practice, but this is the classic technique.

Curls can be made with either white or dark chocolate; white curls are dramatic on a dark chocolate icing and dark chocolate curls can be highlighted with a faint sifting of confectioners' sugar.

An easy method to produce small but acceptable chocolate curls is to draw a swivel-type vegetable peeler across the surface of a thick candy bar or piece of block chocolate. Be sure you work over a sheet of wax paper and lift the completed curls with toothpicks poked into their sides. The trick is to have the chocolate at the correct temperature. If it is too cold and hard, the curls will crumble or shave; if too soft, they will collapse. The easiest thing to do is set the chocolate in a barely heated oven for 10 to 15 minutes. Some ovens are warmed sufficiently by their pilot lights. In warm weather, use the sun. Often just the heat of your hand holding the chocolate will warm it; work on one side of the chocolate bar, then turn it around so the warmer side (previously resting on the palm of your hand) is facing up. If the chocolate feels too soft, chill it slightly; experiment until it works. Chocolate curls can be stored in a protective airtight box in the refrigerator or freezer.

Grated Chocolate

To grate or shave chocolate for a decorative topping or to press onto iced cake sides, simply take a piece of block chocolate, a chocolate bar, or a 1-ounce square of chocolate and pass it across the medium-size holes of a box grater. This can be done over a piece of wax paper or directly over the cake top. Unused grated chocolate can be stored in the refrigerator or freezer in an airtight container; it requires no thawing before use.

Chocolate Bark

Melt chocolate in the top pan of a double boiler. Spread it in a ⅛-inch-thick layer on wax paper or foil. Set the paper on a tray and refrigerate it for about 5 minutes, until chocolate is hard. Remove the paper from the refrigerator. Hold the paper in your hands and bang it back and forth, splintering the chocolate into long slivers. Press the slivers onto the surface of a frosted cake to create a bark-like effect. This is most commonly used for the Bûche de Noël or Yule Log Cake (page 240).

Plastic Chocolate Ribbons and Roses

*F*or years I avoided making this marvelous material for two reasons: First, I feared it was too complex and second, most recipes called for ingredients I don't have around on a regular basis: gum tragacanth and cocoa butter. Recently, a friend in Canada taught me the following simple formula, and now nothing can stop me. Try it, if you like shaping things with your hands; it couldn't be easier or more fun.

When melted white or dark chocolate is blended with light corn syrup it becomes a very pliable substance perfect for shaping into cake decorations. This so-called plastic chocolate is like clay, more flexible than plain chocolate, and perfect for making chocolate leaves or curls, modeling into lifelike roses, rolling flat into ribbons, or cutting out with cookie or canapé cutter shapes for flat or interlocked 3-dimensional shapes.

Advance Preparation   Plastic chocolate can be stored refrigerated for up to 12 months.

Special Equipment   Double boiler, instant-read-out spot thermometer (optional), plastic wrap, rolling pin, dough scraper or spatula, 6-inch icing spatula, hand-cranking pasta machine (optional)

Quantity   ¾ to 1 cup plastic chocolate. White chocolate makes 8½ ounces, 245 grams. Dark chocolate makes 9 ounces, 255 grams. One batch makes 5 or 6 roses or a complete "skin" to cover a 9-inch 3-layer cake.

7 ounces semisweet chocolate or white chocolate (200 grams), chopped fine
¼ cup (2 ounces) light corn syrup
Confectioners' sugar (for white chocolate), or unsweetened cocoa (for dark chocolate)

Note: White chocolate can be delicately tinted with confectioners' paste or powdered (not liquid) colors.

1. The procedure is the same for dark or white chocolate. Place the chopped chocolate in the top pan of a double boiler set over 125°F (about 50°C) water. At this temperature the white chocolate, especially, will remain perfectly creamy and smooth. When melted at too high a temperature, the protein in white chocolate can stiffen and the mixture become lumpy or granular. Stir the chocolate until melted and completely smooth; it should be 100° to 110°F (about 40°C), not higher.

Remove pan from the heat and use a rubber spatula to scrape the melted chocolate into a clean bowl. Set the chocolate aside for about 5 minutes, until lukewarm.

2. Pour on the corn syrup *all at once* and stir with a wooden spoon for about 10 seconds, until the chocolate

thickens and looks dull. It is important not to add the syrup slowly.

Note: If you overbeat the white chocolate, the syrup may start to separate out. Ignore it, and carry on.

3. Place the lump of chocolate on a square of plastic wrap, press it into a flattish package, and wrap well. Set the wrapped chocolate in a cool place (on a marble counter or in a cool pantry) for 45 to 60 minutes. This period of chilling and firming is important. In the heat of midsummer, I have had to refrigerate my chocolate to firm it, and this has done it no harm other than to make it more difficult to soften for shaping.

4. After firming, the chocolate must be rolled out and folded several times. Working the chocolate develops its plasticity. If the chocolate is too hard, first bring it to room temperature, or at least to a flexible stage. Working and kneading the chocolate with warm hands may do this, but if it has been refrigerated and is really hard, you can speed the warming—very carefully—by placing the unwrapped chocolate on a piece of paper in the microwave. For white chocolate, use Defrost for 3 to 6 seconds; for semisweet chocolate go to 10 seconds and test for softness. If still hard, try 2 seconds more and retest. When partially soft, knead the chocolate with your hands.

If you are working with both white and dark chocolate on the same day, always work white chocolate first, so the dark does not discolor the white. This is especially important when kneading on the countertop or when rolling the chocolate in a pasta machine.

a

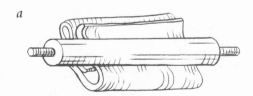

5. Before rolling out white chocolate, sprinkle some confectioners' sugar on a cool counter and on a rolling pin; for dark chocolate, use unsweetened cocoa. Roll the chocolate into a strip about 4 inches wide and 15 inches long. Fold the strip into thirds like a letter and roll again (diagram a, page 459). Repeat 3 or 4 more times. This process resembles working with puff pastry, giving the dough 4 turns. After rolling, the chocolate should be smooth, flexible, and easy to handle. Wrap the chocolate in plastic wrap and set it aside until ready to mold. Or refrigerate for later use.

VARIATIONS

. . . .

Chocolate Ribbons

BY HAND • Bring the chocolate to flexible consistency. Roll it with the rolling pin to the desired thickness, usually 1/16 inch, bearing in mind that it should look delicate but still be strong enough to handle. Cut the rolled chocolate ribbon into strips and set them on your cake. You can make a bow (diagram b) or a 2-toned ribbon by combining a wide ribbon of one color with a narrow ribbon of another color set on top of it and rolling them both together (diagram c).

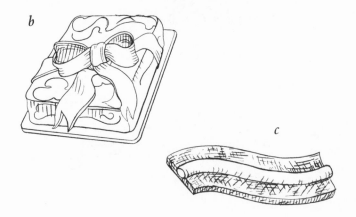

WITH THE PASTA MACHINE • To make ribbons, break off about one third of the total plastic chocolate and shape it into a flattish rectangle. Dust it lightly with either confectioners' sugar or cocoa (remember to do white chocolate first). Pass the chocolate through the widest setting of the machine, then fold it, re-shape it, and pass it through once more. Repeat, but reduce the setting one notch. Repeat until desired thickness is reached. To make striped ribbons, you can add a white strip on top of a chocolate strip or vice versa, and roll them both together; however, in my experience this usually results in wavy or crooked lines.

Chocolate Roses   There are two basic ways to fashion chocolate roses: by hand, shaping the petals with an icing spatula, and by rolling the chocolate thin with a rolling pin or pasta machine and then cutting out petals with a knife or scissors. Whichever method you use, the assembly technique is the same. The icing spatula technique is adapted from one I learned from Chef Albert Kumin.

To shape the petals with an icing spatula, form the chocolate into a cylinder roughly 1¼ inches in diameter and set it on the counter. Hold one hand on the roll, and with the other hand, use a small icing spatula to spread or smear some chocolate from the end of the roll onto the counter. Make a rough petal shape about 1½ inches square. Fan out the chocolate until the rounded outer edges are so thin they trail away; the petal will be thicker where it joins the roll (diagram a, page 462). Cut the petal loose from the roll (diagram b, page 462), then slide the spatula beneath it and scrape it off the counter (diagram c, page 462). Repeat, making between 7 and 12 petals for a full-size rose.

To make petals from plastic chocolate that has been rolled out flat, simply cut out 1½-inch squares, then round them into petal forms.

To give dark or white chocolate plastic a sheen, and to remove the cut-edge look, set the petals flat on the counter and lightly polish them by rubbing with the "pinky" side of your fist, moving your hand lightly and rapidly in a circular motion on top of the petal.

To fashion a budlike core for the rose, or to make a bud that stands alone, form a lump of chocolate into a cone about 1½ inches tall and about ¾ inch wide at the base. Be sure the tip is very pointed (diagram d).

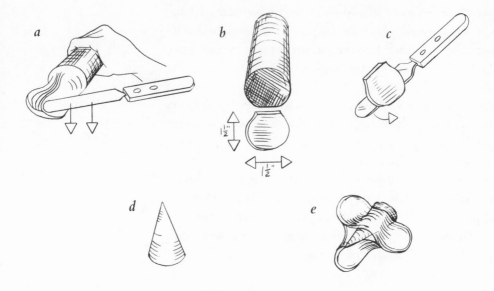

To add petals for the bud, place 3 petals against the cone so each petal faces the others and joins them at the sides. The point of the cone barely peeks out from the center. If you look straight down on the bud at this stage, it should look like a 3-bladed propeller (diagram e). Pull each petal around in the same direction, turning the petals slightly downward as they go (arrow, diagram f). Pinch the top edges of each petal, making them thin and delicate. Roll back the edges of each petal for a lifelike appearance. To complete a bud, pinch the cone in at the bottom, rounding the bud form as shown (diagram g). Cut off excess base.

To complete the single bud, you can cut out 3 small narrow leaves, press the back of a knife into the chocolate to make veins, and press the leaves around the base of the bud.

To make a full-size rose, omit the leaves and keep adding petals to the bud. As you add petals, overlap each one about ⅓ before adding the next. After the 3 petals that form the bud, add 4 petals in one round, then 5 in the next round. Pinch the base of each petal to the bottom of the bud to fasten it. When the rose is the correct size, again pinch the base to round it. Cut away excess base, making a flat bottom. With a delicate touch, roll back the top edges of each petal, then open the petals up slightly, giving the rose a lifelike appearance (diagram h). Stand the rose on a dish until the chocolate hardens, then set it on your cake.

The roses can be made weeks in advance and kept at cool room temperature or refrigerated in protective covered plastic boxes.

To make Chocolate Leaves to accompany the buds or full-sized roses, use rolled white or dark plastic chocolate cut to leaf shapes, pressing the back of the knife into the leaf to make veins (diagram i). Or use melted chocolate spread on real leaves (page 454).

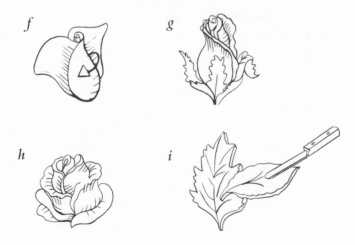

f

g

h

i

Cut-Out Plastic Chocolate Shapes

*T*hese are the easiest of all the shapes to make. Follow the directions for rolling out plastic chocolate. Use cookie or canapé cutters, or a paring knife drawn around a homemade cardboard template, cutting or stamping out the pieces. If the shapes are to be set flat on the top or sides of a frosted cake, the chocolate can be about 1/16 inch thick to go around the sides of a cake: Cut rectangles (diagram a) and press them into the buttercream or whipped-cream icing in an overlapping pattern all around.

To make interlocking, free-standing shapes, cut 2 shapes (a tree, for example), then make a slot in the center from the top to the middle of one shape and from the middle to the bottom of the other. Set one shape into the other, crossing them so the shape stands by itself (diagram b).

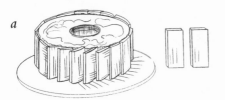  

Chocolate Ruffles

*T*his oft-copied decoration was perfected in Paris by pâtissier Gaston Lenôtre, whose pastry shops all offer the glamorous Meringue d'Automne. It is basically 3 crisp meringue layers filled with a chocolate mousse, but the exciting thing about it is its icing. The entire cake is cloaked in a skin of leathery chocolate (rather than a glaze or icing), and the top is a mass of stiff chocolate ruffles. A light dusting of confectioners' sugar before serving adds just the right highlight. The effect is dramatic, to say the least, but it is not at all hard to copy once you know the tricks.

The biggest secret is the use of plastic chocolate (page 458). Professional bakers make the wrapping layer with plain melted couverture chocolate, spread flat, partially stiffened, then picked up and draped around the cake. The chocolate must be at exactly the right temperature but often becomes brittle, cracking apart. This is definitely not for beginners. However, with plastic chocolate, it is a piece of cake. In fact, 1 recipe (7 ounces chocolate plus 2 ounces corn syrup) makes exactly the amount needed to cover on 9-inch 3-layer round cake.

To do this, sprinkle a little cocoa on the counter and the rolling pin, then roll out the flexible chocolate into a strip 5 × 30 inches. If the counter is well coated, the strip will not stick. Pick up the strip and drape it around the cake, setting the bottom edge of the strip even with the bottom of the cake and draping the excess over onto the cake top. It should reach nearly to the center, but not cover the top completely. The chocolate ruffle will fill in the center. Overlap the ends of the strip, and use your hands to mold the chocolate gently to the cake. Gather and pleat the top so it is fairly flat (diagram a, below). To make ruffles for the top, you have two choices. The quickest and easiest is not actually the prettiest, but it may be close enough. For this, you need a second batch of plastic chocolate; roll the

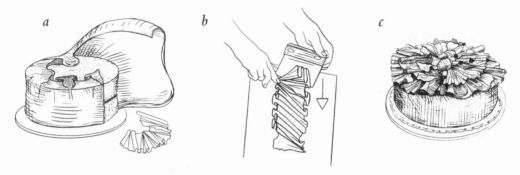

chocolate very thin, cut it into strips about 2 inches wide, and gather one long edge, making a ruffle. Set sections of ruffle in concentric circles on the cake top, adding a small curl in the center. Sift a tiny bit of sugar on top.

To make more authentic, lacier ruffles, melt about 8 ounces semisweet chocolate in the top pan of a double boiler. Spread the melted chocolate onto the back of a jelly-roll pan 10 × 15 inches to a thickness of about 1/16 inch. Set the chocolate aside in a cool room, or refrigerate, just until "leather hard," when an edge can be picked up and bent without cracking; do not chill hard.

With a 3-inch-wide putty knife or dough scraper, make the ruffles by scraping the chocolate toward yourself in strips. The trick to getting it to gather is to hold one finger at the side of the strip as it is formed, causing the chocolate to gather up by your finger and fan out on the other side (diagram b). Set sections of ruffled chocolate around the cake top, making concentric circles and adding a small curl in the center (c). Sift a tiny bit of confectioners' sugar on top.

Apricot Roses

*T*o decorate an apricot-flavored cake, nothing is as elegant as an apricot rose. It is a cinch to make if you cut the petals out of a sheet of pure dried apricot "leather" (also called fruit roll), sold in health-food stores, delicatessens, and supermarkets. If you don't have the fruit roll, you can substitute sheets of rolled dried apricots.

Note: Fruit leather and fruit roll are made in many fruit flavors; you can select the color and flavor that best complement your cake (cherry, raspberry, strawberry, orange, etc.) instead of apricot, if you wish. These roses can be prepared up to 2 weeks in advance and refrigerated.

Equipment Scissors or kitchen shears, wax paper, rolling pin for apricot halves, toothpicks, tray

Quantity One average "fruit leather" roll (the type sold in health-food stores or delis, not the boxed super-market variety) usually weighs 1 ounce and comes rolled in a 7-inch-diameter disk. It will make 1 rose with 12 petals. The boxed supermarket Fruit Roll-Ups, such as those made by General Mills, weigh ½ ounce each and come in 4½-inch squares. You will need 2 roll-ups to make 1 rose. If using dried apricot halves, you will need about 15 large moist halves to make 2 roses.

TO MAKE ROSES WITH APRICOT LEATHER • Cut the fruit leather with its paper backing in place. Peel off the backing before using the cut shapes to form the rose. Shape the roses following the directions and diagrams for plastic chocolate roses on pages 461–463. Briefly, start with the central bud, cutting a rectangle about 3 × 1½ inches, then rolling it up into a cone. Around this add the petals. Cut the petals about 1½ inches square, then round the top edges, shaping the roses as directed. To make the petals adhere, simply press the pieces together; the warmth of your fingers will make them stick. If you have scraps left over, overlap them and pinch them together to make larger pieces for more rose petals. After adding enough petals, pinch the base firmly, then roll back the top edge of each petal with your fingertip to open out the rose and make it look lifelike. Use the scissors to cut away excess base.

TO MAKE ROSES WITH DRIED APRICOT HALVES • Place several moist apricot halves, sticky side down, on a piece of wax paper. Cover with another paper and roll out apricots until very thin. Repeat, rolling out all the pieces. To see how the rose bud and full rose will look, see the diagrams on page 463.

To form the central bud, roll 1 apricot half, sticky side in, onto itself, forming a tight cone. Press it together to make it firm. To add a petal, press the base of 1 rolled apricot half, sticky side in, onto the central bud. Pinch it at the base to make it stick. Add another petal overlapping half of the first. Add 2 or 3 more petals, depending upon the size of the apricot halves and the desired rose size. If you need to hold the base together, push a toothpick through the bottom of all the petals. With knife or shears, trim off the excess base below the petals, making a flat stand.

To give a lifelike look to the petals, use your fingertip to roll or curl the petal tops outward, opening up the rose.

Set the roses on their flat stands on a plate or tray and refrigerate or freeze (to speed up setting) until firm.

Meringue Mushrooms

*M*eringue mushrooms are traditionally used to garnish the Bûche de Noël or Yule Log Cake (page 240). They also make attractive decorations or dessert treats in their own right. Maida Heatter, the acknowledged master of this confection (as well as many others), tells me the meringues that she keeps in her southern Florida home have lasted for over a year; moreover, she says she has no trouble producing them in a tropical kitchen, though she prefers air conditioning and avoids humid days. These lifelike mushrooms are less temperamental and easier to make than one would think, and the fact that they keep so well means they can be prepared well in advance.

Advance Preparation

Meringue mushrooms should be stored at room temperature in a loosely covered container, not airtight. They should remain crisp for months, even up to a year. Do not freeze them.

Special Equipment   16- to 18-inch pastry bag fitted with ½- to ¾-inch round tip, 2 cookie sheets, aluminum foil, small strainer, 4-cup Pyrex measure (as a stand for filling the pastry bag), rubber spatula, flat tray, double boiler, teaspoon, 2 empty egg cartons for supporting cooling mushrooms (if you don't have any empty egg cartons remove the eggs temporarily), paring knife

Baking Time   1 hour at 225°F (107°C)

Cooling Time in Oven with Heat Turned Off   30 to 45 minutes

Quantity   About 3 dozen mushrooms; quantity depends upon size

Pan Preparation   Cover cookie sheets with foil

MERINGUE

1 recipe All-Purpose Meringue (page 263), cold or Swiss method, made with 4 large egg whites, pinch of salt, ¼ teaspoon cream of tartar, 1 cup superfine sugar (note increase over master recipe, which calls for ½ cup sugar) and 1 teaspoon vanilla extract

GARNISH

2 tablespoons unsweetened cocoa
2 ounces semisweet chocolate

1. Prepare the pans as directed. Set a small strainer in a cup or small bowl and add a couple of tablespoons of cocoa. Do not sift, just leave it until needed. Position the oven shelves to divide the oven in thirds. Preheat oven to 225°F (107°C).

2. Prepare the meringue as directed in the recipe, beating whites, salt, and cream of tartar until fluffy, then gradually whipping in the sugar, 2 tablespoons at a time. After all the sugar has been added, whip the whites for an additional 7 to 8 full minutes, to be sure they are stiff and satiny and contain no grains of undissolved sugar. Pinch the meringue between your fingers; you should not feel any sugar granules. Total beating time from start to finish is between 15 and 18 minutes.

3. Spread a dab of meringue under each corner of the foil on each cookie sheet to hold it in place. To prepare the pastry bag, set it tip down in a 4-cup measure and fold back a 4- or 5-inch cuff (see illustrations, page 435). With a rubber spatula, transfer all or most of the meringue to the pastry bag. Lift up the bag cuff and twist the ends closed.

4. Pipe the mushroom stems first. Hold the bag at right angles to 1 foil-covered cookie sheet. With the tip pointing straight down, squeeze gently on the bag while

lifting it slowly up. The idea is to pipe a small stem 1 to
1½ inches tall, slightly fatter at the base, sticking straight
up off the sheet. Leave about 1 inch of space and repeat.
Make many stems in rows. Don't worry if some are irregular or fall over. Sift a little cocoa on the stems, then
put them right into the oven, on the top shelf.

To pipe the mushroom caps, hold the pastry bag at
right angles to the foil and form even rounds of meringue
1 to 1½ inches wide and ¾ inch thick. These should vary
in size somewhat, just as real mushrooms do (diagram a).
Space the caps about ½ inch apart on the sheet. Use your
fingertip to smooth any peaks on top of the meringue
caps. Sift a little cocoa over the caps, then set them in the
oven. Continue making stems and caps to use up remaining meringue. Be sure you have extras, as some always
break. Save scraps to garnish cakes.

5. Bake the stems and caps in the preheated oven for
about 1 hour. Then turn off the oven heat and prop the
door open but leave the meringues in the oven to continue drying out for another 30 to 45 minutes. The
meringues are done when they are crisp, dry through, and
stiff enough to be lifted off the foil. They become crisp as
they cool. Break 1 piece into halves to test it. Bake them
longer if needed; they must be hard.

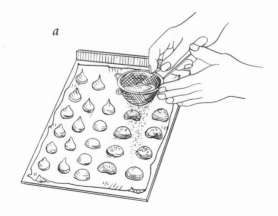

a

Remove meringues from the oven and carefully peel off the foil. Set the shapes on a clean flat tray, or on more foil.

6. Melt the chocolate in the top pan of a double boiler set over hot, not boiling, water.

7. To assemble the mushrooms, the caps must be prepared. Cradle each cap in the palm of your hand while using the tip of a paring knife to "drill" a hole gently in the flat underside for the stem to fit in. Don't press on the cap.

8. Dip the tip of each stem in melted chocolate, then gently poke the tip into the prepared depression in the underside of the cap (diagram b). Set the mushrooms upside down in an egg carton until the chocolate is hard. Refrigerate the mushrooms to speed the setting if the weather is hot.

9. Store the mushrooms in a loosely covered container at room temperature.

Appendices

RECIPES FOR SPECIAL NEEDS

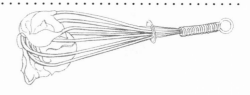

High Altitude Baking

WHEN I BAKE at altitudes 3,000 feet above sea level, I always wonder whether my New England cakes will rise properly. The answer is that sometimes they do; many more times, my recipes need adjustment. Sugar/flour ratios need altering, slightly more liquid may be added, baking powder is usually shaved a tad, and baking times and temperatures can change. Unfortunately, there are few all-purpose rules. It is best to try your favorite cake recipes at your altitude once exactly as written to see how they behave before tinkering. The higher the altitude, the more adjustments will be needed.

In any case, the baker should be aware of the general conditions caused by high altitude and their theoretical remedies. At 3,000 feet above sea level, there is less humidity in the atmosphere and a decrease in air pressure. Low humidity makes a dry climate that causes flour to be drier, so it will absorb more liquid. A recipe may need a little more liquid to maintain proper consistency. Decreasing atmospheric pressure causes gases to expand more easily. In cake-baking, decreased atmospheric pressure can have a dramatic effect: baking powder and soda, with their leavening power, are infused with such enthusiasm they can cause a cake to rise until it literally bursts and then collapses. To prevent this, decrease the amount of leavening slightly. Angel and sponge cakes depend for leavening upon whipped air, which, like leavening, tends to go too far too fast. The remedy: whip whites to medium-soft peaks instead of stiff peaks. You may also add strength with a bit more flour and a bit less sugar. If you also increase the baking temperature 15° to 25°F, the batter may be able to set before the air bubbles or leavening gases become too expansive.

As altitude increases, both air pressure and the boiling point of water decrease. At sea level, water boils at 212°F (100°C); at 3,000 feet above sea level, at 207°F; at 5,000 feet, at 203°F (95°C). The result is that more water evaporates during the baking process, and baked goods tend to dry out. In a cake, this can mean little moisture and too much sugar, which can weaken cell structure; in extreme cases, this alone can cause a cake to fall. Cutting back sugar and/or adding a little liquid usually helps. Rich cakes containing a high ratio of fat may have similar problems, because fat can weaken cell structure; try cutting 1 to 2 tablespoons of fat from your recipe.

For specific recommendations for your altitude, consult the Agricultural Extension Service of a nearby university. Your local library, bookstore, or cookware shop probably stocks hometown cookbooks and will be a resource for finding cooks and bakers willing to share practical advice.

General tips to guide you in adapting sea level baking recipes to altitudes above 3,000 feet:

- Reduce sugar in your recipe 1 to 3 tablespoons per cup of sugar used
- Increase the liquid by 1 to 4 tablespoons
- Reduce fat in very rich cakes by about 2 tablespoons
- Reduce each teaspoon of baking powder by ⅛ to ¼ teaspoon
- Increase oven temperature about 25°F

Sources and Suppliers for Special Ingredients and Equipment

Bridge Kitchenware
214 East 52nd Street
New York, NY 10022
(800) 274-3435; Fax (212) 758-5387
www.bridgekitchenware.com
Catalogue
Domestic and imported baking pans, tools, utensils

The Broadway Panhandler
477 Broome Street
New York, NY 10013
(212) 966-3434 or 1-866-COOKWARE
www.broadwaypanhandler.com (to view stock; no e-commerce)
Complete line of cake-baking and decorating equipment

Cooks InOvation
8919 Summit Avenue
Cincinnati, OH 45242
(513) 984-5212; Fax (513) 984-5212
Unique "*Culinique* Filled Cake" pans; broad metal cake-lifting spatula; ball-bearing turntable for cake decorating

Dean and DeLuca
560 Broadway
New York, NY 10012
(800) 999-0306 or (212) 226-6800
www.dean-deluca.com
Catalogue: (800) 221-7714
Wide variety of baking equipment; ingredients, including extracts, chocolate and cocoa, flour, dried fruits and berries, frozen fruit concentrates and purees, including mango, passion fruit, and strawberry

Dean and DeLuca
3276 M Street, NW
Washington, DC 20007
(202) 342-2500
(800) 925-7854

King Arthur Flour Baker's Catalogue
P. O. Box 876
Norwich, VT 05055–0876
(800) 827-6836; Fax (800) 343-3002
www.kingarthurflour.com
Catalogue
Complete line of cake-baking and decorating ingredients and equipment, including nonstick pan liners, chocolate, cocoa, flour, extracts, powdered egg whites, meringue powder, dried buttermilk powder

New York Cake and Baking Distributors
56 West 22nd Street
New York, NY 10010
(800) 942-2539 or (212) 675-2253
www.nycakesupplies.com
Catalogue
Complete line of chocolates, pastry, cake-baking and decorating supplies; also online "superstore" for all cake-baking supplies

Penzeys Spices
P. O. Box 933
W19362 Apollo Drive
Muskego, WI 53150
(800) 741-7787; Fax (262) 679-7878
www.penzeys.com
Flavorful spices and pure extracts; especially good cinnamon and ginger
also located at
151 Westport Avenue, Norwalk, CT (203) 849-9085 *and*
3028 Hennepin Avenue, Minneapolis, MN (612) 824-9777

Simpson and Vail
P. O. Box 765
3 Quarry Road
Brookfield, CT 06804
(800) 282-8327; Fax (203) 775-0462
www.svtea.com
Catalogue
Tahitian vanilla beans and extract, flavored citrus oils, specialty chocolates,
honey, unrefined sugar

Sweet Celebrations Inc.
P. O. Box 39426
Edina, MN 55439-0426
(800) 328-6722
www.sweetc.com
Catalogue
Complete line of cake-baking and decorating equipment; cake-decorating
ingredients, including powdered egg whites, meringue powder, praline paste

Williams-Sonoma, Inc.
Mail Order Department
7720 NW 85th Terrace
Oklahoma City, OK 73132
(800) 541-2233
www.williams-sonoma.com
Catalogue
Wide variety of cake-baking equipment and many baking ingredients

Wilton Industries
2240 West 75th Street
Woodridge, IL 60517
(630) 963-1818; Fax (888) 824-9520
www.wilton.com
Wilton Yearbook and supply catalogue
Full line of cake-decorating supplies; wide variety of equipment; decorating ingredients, including Wilton meringue powder

Vanns Spices Ltd.
6105 Oakleaf Avenue
Baltimore, MD 21215
(410) 358-3007; Fax (410) 358-1780
www.vannsspices.com
Catalogue
Exceptional spices (especially many types of cinnamon), seasonings, wide variety of baking extracts

$\mathcal{I}$NDEX